D1452505

IMAGINING A GREATER GERMANY

IMAGINING A GREATER GERMANY

Republican Nationalism and
the Idea of Anschluss

Erin R. Hochman

CORNELL UNIVERSITY PRESS   **ITHACA AND LONDON**

Cornell University Press gratefully acknowledges receipt of a subvention from the William P. Clements Department of History at Southern Methodist University, which aided in the publication of this book.

First published 2016 by Cornell University Press
Printed in the United States of America

Library of Congress Cataloging-in-Publication Data

Names: Hochman, Erin R., 1981– author.
Title: Imagining a greater Germany : republican nationalism and the idea of
    Anschluss / Erin R. Hochman.
Description: Ithaca : Cornell University Press, 2016. | Includes bibliographical
    references and index.
Identifiers: LCCN 2016012386 | ISBN 9781501704444 (cloth : alk. paper)
Subjects: LCSH: Anschluss movement, 1918–1938. | Austria—Politics and
    government—1918–1938. | Germany—Politics and government—1918–1933. |
    Nationalism—Austria—History—20th century. | Nationalism—Germany—
    History—20th century.
Classification: LCC DB97 .H55 2016 | DDC 320.540943/0943609042—dc23
LC record available at http://lccn.loc.gov/2016012386

Cornell University Press strives to use environmentally responsible suppliers and materials to the fullest extent possible in the publishing of its books. Such materials include vegetable-based, low-VOC inks and acid-free papers that are recycled, totally chlorine-free, or partly composed of nonwood fibers. For further information, visit our website at www.cornellpress.cornell.edu.

Cloth printing   10   9   8   7   6   5   4   3   2   1

For my parents

Contents

Acknowledgments

The writing of this book would not have been possible without support from numerous individuals and institutions. My time at the University of Toronto significantly shaped my approach to this project. Jennifer Jenkins deserves much appreciation for playing a formative role in my intellectual development. Doris Bergen, Derek Penslar, and James Retallack also offered numerous thought-provoking suggestions on my work, which challenged me to think in more complex ways about nationalism and German politics. As the project developed, advice from Pieter Judson helped me to sharpen my thinking about Austrian history. At Southern Methodist University, I have been lucky to have exceptionally supportive colleagues in the Clements Department of History. In particular, Kathleen Wellman and Andrew Graybill have served as wonderful mentors. Additionally, I am grateful to the history department, as well as the Center for Presidential History and the Clements Center for Southwest Studies, for organizing a workshop that provided me with feedback on an earlier draft of the book. Belinda Davis and Annemarie Sammartino not only came to Dallas to attend the workshop, but also offered me detailed and constructive criticism that aided me in strengthening my arguments. I am very appreciative that Thomas Adam, Edward Countryman, Ruth Ann Elmore, Jeffrey Engel, Andrew Graybill, James Hopkins, John Mears, Brandon Miller, Donald Niewyk, Daniel Orlovsky, Rachel St. John, Kathleen Wellman, and Laurence Winnie took the time to participate in the workshop and offer additional suggestions. I also thank the anonymous reviewers for their incisive comments. Roger Haydon, Emily Powers, Sara Ferguson, and other staff at Cornell University Press deserve recognition for helping me to bring this book to fruition. An early version of chapter 1 appeared as "*Ein Volk, ein Reich, eine Republik*: *Großdeutsch* Nationalism and Democratic Politics in the Weimar and First Austrian Republics," *German History* 32, no. 1: 29–52, which was published by Oxford University Press on behalf of the German History Society.

This book is primarily based on archival research. I am therefore indebted to the archivists and librarians at the Archiv der Sozialdemokratie of the Friedrich-Ebert-Stiftung in Bonn, the Bundesarchiv Berlin, the Politisches Archiv des Auswärtigen Amts in Berlin, the Staatsbibliothek zu Berlin, the Österreichisches Staatsarchiv in Vienna, the Österreichische Nationalbibliothek, the Archiv der Stadt Salzburg, the Salzburger Landesarchiv, the Steiermärkisches

Landesarchiv in Graz, the Steiermärkisches Landesbibliothek, the Verein für die Geschichte der Arbeiterbewegung in Vienna, the Archiv des Karl von Vogelsang-Instituts in Vienna, the Wienbibliothek, and the Wiener Stadt- und Landesarchiv for their assistance along the way. Special thanks go to Mag. Susanne Fröhlich at the Österreichisches Staatsarchiv and Heidrun Louda at the Archiv der Sozialdemokratie for taking the time to help me find relevant files within their holdings. The staff at the Interlibrary Loan Offices at the University of Toronto and Southern Methodist University aided me as well. Generous financial support from the German Academic Exchange Service, the Joint Initiative for German and European Studies and other centers at the University of Toronto, the Ontario government, Southern Methodist University, the Sam Taylor Fellowship Fund, and the American Historical Association enabled me to make research trips to Germany and Austria and to write up my findings. Furthermore, the German Historical Institute in Washington, D.C., offered me the opportunities to learn about paleography and archival research at the 2005 Summer Seminar in Germany and to gain worthwhile feedback on my work at the 2010 Transatlantic Doctoral Seminar.

I owe a great deal to a wonderfully supportive network of friends and family. In Toronto, Auri Berg, Katie Edwards, Liz Hamm, Michelle Hoffman, Stacy Hushion, Mark László-Herbert, Peter Mersereau, and Andrew Tracy were always willing to provide a sympathetic ear and to read my work. During my travels to Germany and Austria, Deborah Barton, Brian Feltman, Marlies Schacherl, Janek Wasserman, Chris Wiley, and Charlotte Wilson not only shared in my excitement over good archival finds, but were also great company in exploring Berlin and Vienna. At SMU, Sabri Ates, Jon Brunstedt, Jill Kelly, Ada Kuskowski, and Brandon Miller have been both wonderful colleagues and friends. In Dallas, I am also extremely fortunate to have met Cole Jackson, whose thoughtfulness and encouragement were vital in helping me to finish this book. Above all, I would like to thank my family. I wish my grandmother, Shirley Bell, could have seen the completion of this work. My deepest gratitude goes to my parents, Cindi and Henry Hochman, who have been a constant source of love and support over the years. It is to them that I dedicate this book.

Abbreviations

AA	Auswärtige Angelegenheiten
AdR	Archiv der Republik
AdsD	Archiv der sozialen Demokratie der Friedrich-Ebert-Stiftung, Bonn
AVA	Allgemeines Verwaltungsarchiv
AZ	*Arbeiter-Zeitung*
BAB	Bundesarchiv Berlin
BBZ	*Berliner Börsen-Zeitung*
BKA	Bundeskanzleramt
BMfHW	Bundesministerium für Heereswesen
BT	*Berliner Tageblatt*
BVP	Bayerische Volkspartei (Bavarian People's Party)
CSP	Christlichsoziale Partei (Christian Social Party)
DDP	Deutsche Demokratische Partei (German Democratic Party)
DNVP	Deutschnationale Volkspartei (German National People's Party)
DöTZ	*Deutschösterreichische Tages-Zeitung*
DR	*Das Reichsbanner* (journal)
DVP	Deutsche Volkspartei (German People's Party)
GDVP	Großdeutsche Volkspartei (Greater German People's Party)
HiR	*Heim ins Reich* (journal)
MRP	Ministerratsprotokolle
NFP	*Neue Freie Presse*
NL	Nachlass
NPA	Neues Politisches Archiv
NSDAP	Nationalsozialistische Deutsche Arbeiterpartei (National Socialist German Workers' Party)
NWT	*Neues Wiener Tagblatt*
OeD	*Oesterreich-Deutschland* (journal)
ÖStA	Österreichisches Staatsarchiv
PAAA	Politisches Archiv des Auswärtigen Amts, Berlin
Präs.	Präsidium
PrK	Präsidentschaftskanzlei
RP	*Reichspost*

SDAP	Sozialdemokratische Arbeiterpartei Österreichs (Social Democratic Workers' Party of Austria)
SLA	Salzburger Landesarchiv
SPD	Sozialdemokratische Partei Deutschlands (Social Democratic Party of Germany)
StLA	Steiermärkisches Landesarchiv
TA	Tagblattarchiv
U.Allg.	Unterricht Allgemein
VDA	Verein für das Deutschtum im Ausland (Association for Germandom Abroad)
VGA	Verein für die Geschichte der Arbeiterbewegung, Vienna
VZ	*Vossische Zeitung*
WB	Wienbibliothek im Rathaus
WNN	*Wiener Neueste Nachrichten*
ZGS	Zeitgeschichtliche Sammlung

IMAGINING A GREATER GERMANY

Introduction

The weekend celebrations began with a torchlight parade by paramilitary groups that culminated in the symbolic burning of the boundary posts between Germany and Austria.[1] As the posts landed on the pyre, a roar of approval emanated from the twelve thousand torchbearers.[2] Two days later, following a parade of over one hundred thousand Reich Germans and Austrians, prominent politicians assembled in a theater to highlight the meaning of the festivities.[3] To the cheers of the audience, three Reich German speakers expressed their firm desire for an *Anschluss*, or a political union between Germany and Austria. The final speaker at the ceremony hailed from Austria. "For us Germans in Austria, a powerful impulse prevails to return once again to the Reich [*wieder heimzukommen zum Reiche*]," he announced to thundering applause.[4]

At first glance, the reader might associate such symbolism and proclamations with Nazi propaganda. After all, the Nazis are known for their orchestration of mass rallies and their relentless determination to expand Germany's boundaries. In particular, the celebrations described above conjure up images of the Anschluss in 1938, when Adolf Hitler annexed his native country to the Third Reich. On that occasion, Austrians joyously greeted the arrival of the German army and

---

1. "Das Reichsbannerfest in Magdeburg," *Arbeiter-Zeitung* (*AZ*), 22 February 1925, 1.
2. "Echo aus Oesterreich," *Das Reichsbanner* (*DR*) (Beilage), 15 April 1925, o.S.
3. "Die 100000 in Magdeburg," *Vossische Zeitung* (*VZ*) (Abendausgabe), 23 February 1925, 1–2.
4. "Die Wünsche für den Anschluß Oesterreichs an Deutschland," *Neue Freie Presse* (*NFP*) (Morgenblatt), 24 February 1925, 3–4. All translations are my own unless otherwise noted.

Nazi leaders, while unleashing a vicious wave of anti-Semitic violence against their Jewish neighbors. The torchlight parade and ceremony of the paramilitary groups appear to embody the type of aggressive and racist nationalism associated with the Nazis, and Germany more generally.

Such assumptions overlook the complexities surrounding German national-ism and the struggle for political legitimacy in interwar Central Europe. The festivities described above, for example, included not a single Nazi. They took place in 1925 in Magdeburg, Germany, on the occasion of the one-year anni-versary of the Reichsbanner Schwarz-Rot-Gold (Reichsbanner Black-Red-Gold), the veterans' association dedicated to the protection of the Weimar Republic. The three Reich German speakers calling for an Anschluss represented each of the parties involved in the Reichsbanner: Reichstag president Paul Löbe, a member of the Social Democratic Party of Germany (SPD); former chancellor Joseph Wirth, a member of the Catholic Center Party; and Reichstag delegate Ludwig Haas, a member of the left liberal German Democratic Party (DDP) and a lead-ing figure in the Central Association of German Citizens of Jewish Faith. Joining the Reichsbanner in this demonstration for a republican form of government and Austro-German unity was a small contingent of Austrians from the Repub-likanischer Schutzbund (Republican Protection League), the paramilitary arm of the Social Democratic Party of Austria (SDAP). The head of this organization was the Austrian orator, Julius Deutsch, who was also a target of anti-Semitic attacks because he had been born in Hungary to a Jewish family. Although there were differences within and among these parties, together they constituted the most consistent defenders of the republican form of government and can there-fore be grouped under the label of republicans, a term they used to describe themselves and their common cause.[5] These republicans envisioned a different outcome to an Austro-German political union from that imagined by the Nazis. An Anschluss would create, as Deutsch proclaimed, "a single, unified German

---

5. On divisions within the parties see Ellen Lovell Evans, *The German Center Party: A Study in Political Catholicism, 1870–1933* (Carbondale: Southern Illinois University Press, 1981), chaps. 12–19; Thomas Knapp, "The German Center Party and the Reichsbanner: A Case Study in Political and Social Consensus in the Weimar Republic," *International Review of Social History* 14, no. 2 (1969): 159–179; Donna Harsch, *German Social Democracy and the Rise of Nazism* (Chapel Hill: University of North Carolina Press, 1993); Larry Eugene Jones, *German Liberalism and the Dissolution of the Weimar Party System, 1918–1933* (Chapel Hill: University of North Carolina Press, 1988); Anson Rabinbach, *The Crisis of Austrian Socialism: From Red Vienna to Civil War, 1927–1934* (Chicago: University of Chicago Press, 1983). Although all four parties contained competing factions, the Center Party was most divided in its attitude toward democracy. Only the left wing of the Center Party is included under the republican heading because of the right wing's criticism of the Weimar Republic, hostility to working with the SPD and DDP, and growing authoritarianism. On divisions among the four parties see chapter 4.

Volk in a German republic from Neusiedler Lake to the North Sea, from the Kara-
wanks to the Baltic Sea."[6] Not only did the political basis and territorial scope
of a republican *Großdeutschland* (a Greater Germany including Austria) greatly
contrast with Nazi notions about race and space, but so too did their definitions of the *Volk*, a word that can be translated as both *nation* and *people*. As the
backgrounds of the participants in the celebration suggest, republicans embraced
socialists and Jews—groups whose national credentials were contested by the
political right—as members of a German nation.

This book explores how republicans in both states sought to popularize democracy in the wake of a disastrous war and bitter defeat. Through an examination of political rallies, commemorations, and debates about official symbols,
I argue that the support for an Anschluss and belief in the *großdeutsch* idea (the
historical notion that Germany should include Austria) were central to republicans' imaginative and persistent attempts to legitimize the Weimar and First Austrian Republics. Both republics weathered constant attacks by a diverse group of
conservatives and right-wing radicals, who mobilized anti-Semitic, anti-Marxist,
and antidemocratic forms of German nationalism to denounce the republican
form of government. For the political right, the democratic republics and their
proponents were un-German. Republicans countered these claims, insisting that
various German nationalisms existed. They aimed at nothing less than fashion-
ing their own version of German nationalism, one that stood in direct opposition
to the exclusionary and violent nationalisms of the political right.

To create their own form of nationalism, republicans contrasted their *großdeutsch* (greater German) nationalism with the *alldeutsch* (pan-German) nationalism and conservative nationalism of their opponents. For republicans, it was
"self-evident" that "the *großdeutsch* idea has nothing in common with the *alldeutsch* fantasies" that sought "the oppression and subjugation of foreign people,"
as Wilhelm Nowack, a Reichsbanner leader affiliated with the DDP, declared.[7]
Alldeutsch nationalism, in the eyes of republicans, was based on militarism and
imperialism, while conservative nationalism was focused on loyalty to the very
monarchies—the Habsburgs of Austria and the Hohenzollerns of Prussia—that
had prevented national unity in the nineteenth century. In contrast, *großdeutsch*
nationalism was rooted in the very movement that first sought to create a united
Germany. Looking back to the revolution of 1848, when representatives at the
Frankfurt Parliament desired to create a Greater Germany with a parliamentary
government, interwar republicans argued that a democratic tradition did indeed

---

6. "Die Wünsche für den Anschluß Oesterreichs an Deutschland," *NFP* (Morgenblatt), 24 February 1925, 3–4.

7. W. Nowack, "Kein Preußen und kein Oesterreich," *DR*, 15 December 1924, o.S.

exist in German history. As further proof of their national credentials, republicans loudly voiced their support for an Anschluss. Despite calling for a revision of Germany's boundaries, republicans were quick to point out that they did not wish to overturn the entire postwar order. As members of internationalist causes ranging from socialism to the pan-European movement, they stressed that they would seek an Anschluss only through peaceful means and would await the approval of the Council of the League of Nations. An Anschluss, in their eyes, would even strengthen the prospects of peace by serving as an important step in the creation of a united states of Europe. Moreover, although they clearly believed that the Volk extended beyond state boundaries, and consequently beyond purely civic definitions of nationhood, they did not subscribe to a restrictive understanding of a German national community. Republicans were not entirely immune from chauvinism, but their inclusion of Jews and immigrants in a *großdeutsch* nation shows that they promoted a tolerant form of nationalism.

Given the distinctive roots and aims of their nationalism, republicans could assert that "the *Großdeutschland* of the Nazis will never ever be our *Großdeutschland*. We will wage the fiercest fight against whoever wants a Germany that should prove to be dangerous to world peace; however, we welcome fighters who want to create a *großdeutsch*, free, and social republic with us."[8] This statement by Walter Kolb, a cofounder of the Reichsbanner and the head of the Republican Student Cartel, at a 1926 republican rally in Vienna serves as an eloquent reminder that there were multiple understandings of Germanness during the Weimar era. The triumph of Nazi ideas about politics and nationalism was far from inevitable after 1918.

The Shifting Boundaries of Germanness

The fierce contests that emerged between republicans and their opponents over the nature of German nationalism and politics had their roots in both the nineteenth century and the immediate postwar situation. Such debates first arose when no state by the name of Germany existed and German speakers lived scattered throughout principalities, kingdoms, duchies, empires, and free cities in East Central Europe. Beginning in the early nineteenth century, in response to the French Revolutionary and Napoleonic Wars, contemporaries spoke of the existence of a "German Question" that needed to be resolved. The German Question historically encompassed a multitude of issues related to geography, politics, and population: Where should the boundaries of a German nation-state be

---

8. "Eine Anschlußkundgebung der republikanischen Studentenschaft," *AZ*, 11 July 1926, 13.

drawn? What form of government would be best suited to a German nation-state? Who could be considered members of a German nation? The delegates of the Frankfurt Parliament in 1848–1849 took up these questions as they tried to form the first German nation-state. Although they agreed to grant rights to Jews and linguistic minorities, the precise boundaries of the state and especially its constitutional arrangement were heavily debated. Should the new Germany be *kleindeutsch* (excluding the Austrian Empire), *großdeutsch* (including the federal lands of the Habsburg monarchy), or the "Reich of seventy million" (including all the Habsburg lands)? The delegates could not find a satisfactory answer to this question because of their inability to reach an agreement on the relationship between the new German state and the Habsburg Empire.[9] Ultimately, this dispute within the confines of the Frankfurt Parliament became irrelevant when the Austrian and Prussian monarchies crushed the revolution.

The failure of the Frankfurt Parliament did not put an end to the question of German unity, as the two major Central European powers—the Habsburgs and the Hohenzollerns—jockeyed for power in the region. With Prussia's victory in the Austro-Prussian War of 1866 and Otto von Bismarck's creation of Germany in 1871, the questions of boundaries appeared to be solved: Austria was to be left out of a future German state. However, the Prussian-led solution failed to provide a conclusive answer to all aspects of the German Question prior to the First World War. Within the *Kaiserreich*, the biggest remaining question revolved around acceptance into the national community. With the increasing prominence of racial pseudoscience in the late nineteenth century, many on the political right argued that Jews and linguistic minorities could never be German because of an immutable ethnic or racial difference. To a lesser degree, Catholics, a minority in Protestant-dominated Imperial Germany, and socialists faced questions about their loyalty to the new state. Worried about Catholics' devotion to the pope and socialists' allegiance to an international working class, Bismarck labeled both groups "enemies of the Reich."[10] Additionally, the

---

9. Brian Vick, *Defining Germany: The 1848 Frankfurt Parliamentarians and National Identity* (Cambridge, MA: Harvard University Press, 2002).

10. It should be noted that unlike for Jews and linguistic minorities, membership in a German national community was not entirely foreclosed to Catholics and socialists. Catholics garnered more acceptance after Bismarck's failed Kulturkampf. The political right doggedly labeled socialists as "*vaterlandslos*," unpatriotic, but the political right was willing to accept them as Germans if they gave up their political views. Geoff Eley, *From Unification to Nazism: Reinterpreting the German Past* (Boston: George Allen & Unwin, 1986), chap. 3; Peter Pulzer, *Jews and the German State: The Political History of a Minority, 1848–1933* (Detroit: Wayne State University Press, 2003), chap. 1; Helmut Walser Smith, *German Nationalism and Religious Conflict: Culture, Ideology, Politics, 1870–1914* (Princeton, NJ: Princeton University Press, 1995); Helmut Walser Smith, ed., *Protestants, Catholics and Jews in Germany, 1800–1914* (Oxford: Berg, 2001).

purported "unification" of Germany in reality led to the exclusion of German speakers living in Austria who had historically been (and remained) connected to larger German-speaking cultural, economic, and political realms.[11] A German *Kulturnation*—the idea of a nation united by culture and language that extended beyond legal state boundaries—continued to exist despite the creation of a *Kleindeutschland* (a Smaller Germany excluding Austria). The German Question took on a different dimension in the multinational Habsburg monarchy, where nationalist activists were increasingly seeking to turn "nationally indifferent" populations "into Czechs and Germans" in an effort to claim greater state resources and political power.[12] Despite these unresolved aspects of the German Question, the idea that the *kleindeutsch* solution should or could be overturned was held by just a fringe minority in the German and Austro-Hungarian Empires.[13]

The Great War and its consequences, however, reopened the very aspects of the German Question that Bismarck had appeared to resolve and galvanized the ongoing debates about national belonging. Military defeat, the collapse of the Hohenzollern and Habsburg Empires, the creation of democratic republics, and the redrawing of the boundaries of Central Europe both compelled and allowed Germans and Austrians to rethink the relationships among nation, state, and politics. The years 1918 and 1919 represented moments of both trauma and possibility.[14] In terms of politics, the revolution of 1918 and the collapse of both the German and Austrian monarchies elicited myriad responses. On the one hand,

---

11. For the view that "unification" amounted to a "division" see John Breuilly, *Austria, Prussia and Germany, 1806–1871* (London: Longman, 2002), and Abigail Green, *Fatherlands: State-Building and Nationhood in Nineteenth-Century Germany* (Cambridge: Cambridge University Press, 2001).

12. Jeremy King, *Budweisers into Czechs and Germans: A Local History of Bohemian Politics, 1848–1948* (Princeton, NJ: Princeton University Press, 2002); Pieter Judson, *Guardians of the Nation: Activists on the Language Frontiers of Imperial Austria* (Cambridge, MA: Harvard University Press, 2006); Gary Cohen, *The Politics of Ethnic Survival: Germans in Prague, 1861–1914*, 2nd ed. (West Lafayette, IN: Purdue University Press, 2006); Nancy Wingfield, *Flag Wars and Stone Saints: How the Bohemian Lands Became Czech* (Cambridge, MA: Harvard University Press, 2007); Tara Zahra, *Kidnapped Souls: National Indifference and the Battle for Children in the Bohemian Lands, 1900–1948* (Ithaca, NY: Cornell University Press, 2008).

13. Roger Chickering, *We Men Who Feel Most German: A Cultural Study of the Pan-German League, 1886–1914* (Boston: George Allen & Unwin, 1984); Andrew Whiteside, *The Socialism of Fools: Georg Ritter von Schönerer and Austrian Pan-Germanism* (Berkeley: University of California Press, 1975).

14. Moritz Föllmer, Rüdiger Graf, and Per Leo, "Einleitung: Die Kultur der Krise in der Weimarer Republik," in *Die 'Krise' der Weimarer Republik: Zur Kritik eines Deutungsmusters* (Frankfurt am Main: Campus Verlag, 2005), 9–41; Rüdiger Graf, *Die Zukunft der Weimarer Republik: Krisen und Zukunftsaneignungen in Deutschland, 1918–1933* (Munich: R. Oldenbourg Verlag, 2008). As these authors point out, the idea of crisis was understood by citizens of the Weimar Republic both pessimistically as a force destroying the old order and optimistically as a force enabling renewal.

there were those, such as the German National People's Party (DNVP) in Germany, who mourned the passing of the royal families and rejected the new government. Yet others embraced the declaration of democratic republics on November 9 in the Reich and November 12 in the rump state of Austria. For the reformist parties of the imperial period—the very parties that would form the basis of the cross-border republican partnership after 1918—the creation of these republics helped to realize their long-standing demands for the democratization of the political order. Radical groups on the right and left of the political spectrum, while despising the creation of republics based on parliamentary democracy, also saw an opportunity to create an entirely new type of political system. Communists hoped to implement radical social and economic changes like those achieved by the Bolsheviks in Russia, and right-wing groups such as the Nazis wanted to create a state based on the ideas of a strong leader and a homogeneous national community. And there were still others—including the German People's Party (DVP) in the Reich, a liberal party that leaned to the right, and the Christian Social Party (CSP), the main Catholic party in Austria, and the Greater German People's Party (GDVP), the radical German nationalists in Austria—who were ambivalent about the new form of government and would variously work for and against its stabilization.

With regard to the boundaries of the nation and state, there was widespread anger over the terms of the Treaty of Versailles, signed by Germany in June 1919, and the Treaty of Saint-Germain, signed by Austria in September 1919. Irrespective of their political viewpoints, Germans and Austrians protested their inability to negotiate the terms of the peace settlement and the territorial losses cemented by the treaties. They decried the uneven application of the right to national self-determination, an idea that had captured the global imagination during and after the war.[15] For Reich Germans, the occupation of the Rhineland for fifteen years, the creation of the Polish Corridor, the loss of Danzig, the League of Nations' mandate over the Saarland, and the later occupation of the Ruhr generated profound dissatisfaction. Adding to their frustration was the Allied prohibition on an Anschluss, which citizens of the Weimar Republic viewed as one way to overcome the bitterness associated with the loss of both the war and territory. Whereas an Anschluss was just one demand that Reich Germans made to ameliorate their postwar disappointment, most Austrians viewed unification with Germany as a matter of life and death. Significantly reduced in size, the rump state was cut off from resources and markets in the other Habsburg successor

---

15. Erez Manela, *The Wilsonian Moment: Self-Determination and the International Origins of Anticolonial Nationalism* (Oxford: Oxford University Press, 2007).

states. "Without the Anschluss with the Reich, German-Austria's economic and national downfall would be guaranteed," asserted a 1919 resolution signed by the members of the SDAP, the CSP, the Styrian Farmers' Party, the German Democratic Party (a forerunner of the GDVP), and the National Socialist Workers' Party (the Austrian Nazis) in Judenburg, Austria.[16] The local representatives of these parties expressed an opinion held by the overwhelming majority of their countrymen: the new state was economically unviable, and the only way that Austrians could survive was by uniting with their fellow Germans in the Reich. It was for these reasons that at the declaration of the Austrian republic, its founders simultaneously called for its dissolution. "German-Austria is a democratic republic," the leaders of the Social Democrats, Christian Socials, and German Nationalists announced on November 12, 1918. In the very next breath, they stated, "German-Austria is a constitutive part of the German republic."[17]

Even amid this resentment and "crisis of sovereignty,"[18] various groups saw the shifting borders as a chance to remake the state and national community. For the extreme right, the collapse of the monarchies offered the tantalizing possibilities of creating a new Germany that could unite all ethnic Germans spread across Central and Eastern Europe and of rolling back the emancipation of Jews, whom right-wing radicals and conservatives alike denounced as un-German. The radical right was not alone, however, in reimagining the boundaries of the state. Republicans, too, perceived the postwar situation as a way to create a Germany that broke with the imperial past. In the Anschluss idea, republicans saw the opportunity to connect the new state system to the historical *großdeutsch* tradition and to realize a form of German unity even greater than Bismarck had achieved. Indeed, although support for an Anschluss appeared across the political spectrum, republicans were, between 1918 and 1933, at the forefront of the movement to achieve it.[19] While central for republicans, an Anschluss was only one piece of the radical right's wish to unify all ethnic Germans. The adherents of the old empires, such as the DNVP, the DVP, and the right wing of the CSP, placed their emphasis on re-creating the German Empire or the Austrian Empire

16. Entschliessung, Z-3997/pn 21.V.1919, in Österreichisches Staatsarchiv (ÖStA), Archiv der Republik (AdR), Bundeskanzleramt (BKA), Auswärtige Angelegenheiten (AA), Neues Politisches Archiv (NPA), Karton (Kt.) 83, Liasse Deutschland I/1, Bl. 166.

17. "Nr. 5/1918, Gesetz vom 12. November 1918 über die Staats- und Regierungsform von Deutsch-Österreich," in *Staatsgesetzblatt für den Staat Deutschösterreich*, Jahrgang 1918 (Vienna: Deutschösterreichischen Staatsdruckerei, 1918), 4.

18. Annemarie Sammartino, *The Impossible Border: Germany and the East, 1914–1922* (Ithaca, NY: Cornell University Press, 2010).

19. Stanley Suval, *The Anschluss Question in the Weimar Era: A Study of Nationalism in Germany and Austria, 1918–1932* (Baltimore: Johns Hopkins University Press, 1974).

(in the form of a Danubian confederation). Moreover, both governments pursued foreign policies that were ambivalent about an Anschluss, with only a few exceptions. Excluding the attempt to form an Austro-German customs union in 1931, the various coalition governments in the Reich prioritized the "lost territories" and the occupation of the Rhineland and Ruhr over the Austrian issue. And, aside from an initial push by the socialist foreign ministers Otto Bauer and Karl Renner to unify the two states immediately after the war and the unrealized 1931 customs union, the Austrian government under the leadership of the Christian Socials shied away from an Anschluss in exchange for much-needed loans from Western powers. Thus, after the First World War, German speakers throughout Central Europe advanced numerous answers to the so-called German Question. The issue of who, what, and where could be considered German was still very much up for debate.

Rethinking German History, German Nationalism, and German Democracy

This book offers a fresh approach to understanding the shifting boundaries of Germanness in the early twentieth century by investigating the entangled histories of Germany and Austria, a topic long neglected by scholars. During the late nineteenth and much of the twentieth centuries, scholars of German history followed the lead of Heinrich von Treitschke, a historian and observer of the "Wars of Unification," who viewed the subject as the story of Prussia's inevitable march to lead a German nation-state. In the last few decades, historians have broken out of this nation-state-centered narrative, thereby enriching our understanding of what encompasses German history.[20] They have investigated regional and confessional cleavages within the Reich to understand how the subjects of Imperial Germany came to identify with the new nation-state.[21] And, with the

---

20. Pivotal to this new approach was James Sheehan's 1981 suggestion to conceive of a German "history of cultural richness and regional diversity, of economic activities and social institutions without national configuration, of relationships which stretch across legally-defined frontiers." James Sheehan, "What Is German History? Reflections on the Role of the Nation in German History and Historiography," *Journal of Modern History* 53, no. 1 (1981): 22. See also Konrad Jarausch and Michael Geyer, *Shattered Past: Reconstructing German Histories* (Princeton, NJ: Princeton University Press, 2003).

21. Celia Applegate, *A Nation of Provincials: The German Idea of Heimat* (Berkeley: University of California Press, 1990); Alon Confino, *The Nation as a Local Metaphor: Württemberg, Imperial Germany, and National Memory, 1871–1918* (Chapel Hill: University of North Carolina Press, 1997); Jennifer Jenkins, *Provincial Modernity: Local Culture and Liberal Politics in Fin-de-Siècle Hamburg* (Ithaca, NY: Cornell University Press, 2003); Smith, *German Nationalism*.

transnational turn, scholars of Germany have elucidated the important connections among globalization, imperialism, migration, and national sentiment in the early twentieth century.[22] Historians of the Habsburg Empire and its successor states have investigated both the successes and failures that national activists encountered in their attempts to nationalize populations in linguistically mixed areas, illuminating the invention and fluidity of nationhood and ethnicity in the region.[23]

Despite these contributions, scholars have continued to overlook the connections between Germany and Austria. Although researchers working on both countries have called for an investigation of the linkages between the two countries,[24] German history and Austrian history continue to constitute two different fields of study. Historians of Germany have seemingly taken Prussia's victory over Austria in 1866 and the subsequent exclusion of Austria from a German nation-state as a reason to exclude Austria from German history. Whereas scholars of Germany have largely neglected Austria, Austrianists have debated the inclusion of Austria in German history.[25] The greater interest in the topic by historians of Austria has to do with the attempt after 1945 to create the idea of an Austrian nation. In the postwar period, a central feature of Austrian national identity was the myth that Austria was Hitler's first victim during his European conquest. Such a claim

---

22. Krista O'Donnell, Renate Bridenthal, and Nancy Reagin, eds., *The Heimat Abroad: The Boundaries of Germanness* (Ann Arbor: University of Michigan Press, 2005); Sebastian Conrad, *Globalization and the Nation in Imperial Germany*, trans. Sorcha O'Hagan (Cambridge: Cambridge University Press, 2010); Caitlin Murdock, *Changing Places: Society, Culture, and Territory in the Saxon-Bohemian Borderlands, 1870–1946* (Ann Arbor: University of Michigan Press, 2010); Sammartino, *Impossible Border*.

23. Cohen, *Politics of Ethnic Survival*; King, *Budweisers*; Judson, *Guardians of the Nation*; Zahra, *Kidnapped Souls*; Murdock, *Changing Places*; Pieter Judson and Marsha Rozenblit, eds., *Constructing Nationalities in East Central Europe* (New York: Berghahn Books, 2005).

24. Sheehan, "What Is German History?"; David Luft, "Austria as a Region of German Culture: 1900–1938," *Austrian History Yearbook* 23 (1992): 135–148; Thomas Brechenmacher, "'Österreich steht außer Deutschland, aber es gehört zu Deutschland': Aspekte der Bewertung des Faktors Österreich in der deutschen Historiographie," in *Ungleiche Partner? Österreich und Deutschland in ihrer gegenseitigen Wahrnehmung: Historische Analysen und Vergleiche aus dem 19. und 20. Jahrhundert*, ed. Michael Gehler et al. (Stuttgart: Franz Steiner Verlag, 1996), 31–53; Philipp Ther, "Beyond the Nation: The Relational Basis of a Comparative History of Germany and Europe," *Central European History* 36, no. 1 (2003): 45–73; Robert Evans et al., "Forum: Habsburg History," *German History* 31, no. 2 (2013): 225–238; Stiftung Haus der Geschichte der Bundesrepublik, ed., *Verfreundete Nachbarn. Deutschland-Österreich: Begleitbuch zur Ausstellung im Haus der Geschichte der Bundesrepublik Deutschland, Bonn, im Zeitgeschichtlichen Forum Leipzig, in Wien* (Bielefeld: Kerber Verlag, 2005). Interestingly, the exhibition and its catalog barely mentioned the years from 1918 to 1938.

25. Fritz Fellner, "Die Historiographie zur österreichisch-deutschen Problematik als Spiegel der nationalpolitischen Diskussion," in *Österreich und die deutsche Frage im 19. und 20. Jahrhundert: Probleme der politisch-staatlichen und soziokulturellen Differenzierung im deutschen Mitteleuropa*, ed. Heinrich Lutz and Helmut Rumpler (Munich: R. Oldenbourg Verlag, 1982), 33–59.

was predicated on the idea that the German and Austrian nations had always been separate, as had their histories. Historians in the Second Austrian Republic therefore played a role in seeking to define a separate Austrian nation.[26] Yet during the interwar period a "national" Austrian identity did not exist, except among a select few.[27] Rather, Austrians, including those seeking to redefine and strengthen a sense of Austrianness, possessed dual identities; they felt themselves to be both German and Austrian.[28] Although numerous historians of Austria have come around to this viewpoint, they still largely avoid writing histories that cut across the Austro-German boundary.

The few subjects that have received cross-border treatment from scholars in both fields are diplomatic relations, the Nazi movement, and the Anschluss of 1938.[29] These works have enriched our understanding of these subjects; yet, as

26. An "Austrian *Historikerstreit*" emerged after Karl Dietrich Erdmann's 1989 publication of *Die Spur Österreichs in der deutschen Geschichte*, which argued that West Germany, East Germany, and the Second Austrian Republic were three states, two nations, and one Volk. Karl Dietrich Erdmann, *Die Spur Österreichs in der deutschen Geschichte: Drei Staaten, zwei Nationen, ein Volk?* (Zurich: Manesse Verlag, 1989). For more on this debate and the creation of an Austrian national identity after 1945 see Peter Thaler, *The Ambivalence of Identity: The Austrian Experience of Nation-Building in a Modern Society* (West Lafayette, IN: Purdue University Press, 2001), chap. 3; Fritz Fellner, "The Problem of the Austrian Nation after 1945," *Journal of Modern History* 60, no. 2 (1988): 264–289; John Boyer, "Some Reflections on the Problem of Austria, Germany, and Mitteleuropa," *Central European History* 22, no. 3/4 (1989): 301–315; Harry Ritter, "Austria and the Struggle for German Identity," *German Studies Review* 15 (Winter 1992): 111–129; Margarete Grandner, Gernot Heiss, and Oliver Rathkolb, "Österreich und seine deutsche Identität. Bemerkungen zu Harry Ritters Aufsatz 'Austria and the Struggle for German Identity,'" and Harry Ritter, "On Austria's German Identity: A Reply to Margarete Grandner, Gernot Heiss, and Oliver Rathkolb," *German Studies Review* 16, no. 3 (1993): 515–523.

27. For claims of Austrian national identity at the time see Suval, *Anschluss Question*, chap. 12; Michael Steinberg, *Austria as Theater and Ideology: The Meaning of the Salzburg Festival* (Ithaca, NY: Cornell University Press, 2000).

28. The list of literature is too long to enumerate. For examples see Ernst Bruckmüller, "Die Entwicklung des Österreichbewusstseins," in *Österreichische Nationalgeschichte nach 1945: Die Spiegel der Erinnerung: Die Sicht von innen*, vol. 1, ed. Robert Kriechbaumer (Vienna: Böhlau, 1998), 369–396; Hanns Haas, "Staats- und Landesbewußtsein in der Ersten Republik," in *Handbuch des politischen Systems Österreichs: Erste Republik, 1918–1933*, ed. Emmerich Tálos et al. (Vienna: Manz Verlag, 1995), 472–487; Luft, "Austria as a Region of German Culture"; Julie Thorpe, *Pan-Germanism and the Austrofascist State, 1933–1938* (Manchester: Manchester University Press, 2011).

29. Bruce Pauley, *Hitler and the Forgotten Nazis: A History of Austrian National Socialism* (Chapel Hill: University of North Carolina Press, 1981); Evan Burr Bukey, *Hitler's Austria: Popular Sentiment in the Nazi Era, 1938–1945* (Chapel Hill: University of North Carolina Press, 2002); Peter Katzenstein, *Disjoined Partners: Austria and Germany since 1815* (Berkeley: University of California Press, 1976); Alfred Low, *The Anschluss Movement and the Paris Peace Conference, 1918–1919* (Philadelphia: American Philosophical Society, 1974); Alfred Low, *The Anschluss Movement, 1931–1938, and the Great Powers* (Boulder, CO: East European Monographs, 1985); Radomír Luža, *Austro-German Relations in the Anschluss Era* (Princeton, NJ: Princeton University Press, 1975); Robert Kann and Friedrich Prinz, eds., *Deutschland und Österreich: Ein bilaterales Geschichtsbuch* (Vienna: Jugend und Volk Verlagsgesellschaft, 1980). The one exception for the interwar period is Stanley Suval's 1974 book, *The Anschluss Question in the Weimar Era*, which does significantly put republicans at the forefront

this book highlights, the history of Austro-German relations extends beyond the fact that Hitler, a native Austrian, went on to rule Germany, that the Nazi Party spanned both sides of the Austro-German border, or that an Anschluss ultimately resulted in the expansion of Nazi power. In exploring the exchange of people and ideas across the Austro-German boundary, this study revises our understanding of German nationalism and democracy during the interwar period.

The experience of Nazism has long colored the lens through which scholars view German nationalism. During and after the Second World War, scholars, seeking to explain how Nazi atrocities could occur, argued that the roots of the murderous regime could be located in the birth of German nationalism. While the fight against the Third Reich was occurring, historian Hans Kohn developed his now famous theory that there were two types of nationalism: "good" civic nationalism found in places like Britain and France and "bad" ethnic national-ism found in places like Germany.[30] Numerous academics embraced this model, and it has continued to exert an influence on the study of German nationalism. According to this viewpoint, German nationalism was illiberal and *völkisch*—a label that describes an exclusionary, racist, and anti-Semitic understanding of nationhood—from the start.[31]

Through an examination of republican *großdeutsch* nationalism, this book challenges this interpretation of German nationalism. It contributes to an emer-gent body of literature that shows there was no singular form of German nation-alism before 1933. In particular, a growing number of scholars has importantly uncovered the existence of a democratic and republican nationalism in the Wei-mar Republic by investigating phenomena such as the national views of a par-ticular party or republican war commemorations. Although these works show that various republicans in Germany attempted to speak in the name of the Volk to popularize the republic, they have mentioned republicans' appeals to

---

of the *Anschluss* movement at the time. It was published before constructivist views of nationalism emerged, however, and he could not fully explore the contours of republican nationalism. Moreover, like the works on diplomatic relations, Suval's book was concerned with political elites. A recent work on World War I does explore the popular experiences of suffering in both countries but is not focused on the entangled histories of Germany and Austria. See Alexander Watson, *Ring of Steel: Germany and Austria-Hungary in World War I* (New York: Basic Books, 2014).

30. Hans Kohn, *The Idea of Nationalism: A Study in Its Origins and Background* (1944; reprint New Brunswick, NJ: Transaction, 2005).

31. Liah Greenfeld, *Nationalism: Five Roads to Modernity* (Cambridge, MA: Harvard University Press, 1992); Rogers Brubaker, *Citizenship and Nationhood in France and Germany* (Cambridge, MA: Harvard University Press, 1992); George Mosse, *The Nationalization of the Masses: Political Symbol-ism and Mass Movements in Germany from the Napoleonic Wars through the Third Reich* (New York: Howard Fertig, 2001 [1975]); Fritz Stern, *The Politics of Cultural Despair: A Study in the Rise of the Germanic Ideology* (Berkeley: University of California Press, 1961).

großdeutsch ideas only in passing or have dismissed republicans' desire for an Anschluss as naïve.[32] However, as I demonstrate, republican appeals to a transborder German national community must be taken seriously in order to grasp the complicated blend of republican, ethnic, cultural, and internationalist ideas that lay at the heart of their nationalism. Republicans, while desiring to create a loyal citizenry, did not believe that the nation ended at the state's boundaries. These expressions of transborder nationalism, however, were not simply a manifestation of pan-Germanism or a harbinger of Nazi empire, as some scholars have suggested.[33] Republicans qualified their vision of a Greater Germany, limiting its expansiveness while opening the national community to those committed to the German cause. Their nationalism thus defies easy categorization.

In acknowledging the various republican definitions of nationhood, this book moves beyond the binary classifications of "good" civic and "bad" ethnic nationalisms, which place German nationalism in the latter category. Reversing his earlier support for this theory of nationalism, sociologist Rogers Brubaker has argued that the distinction between supposedly inclusive, civic nationalism and exclusionary, ethnic nationalism is meaningless, since all forms of nationalism entail inclusion and exclusion.[34] Yet works that recognize that the Nazis were

---

32. Jürgen Heß, *"Das ganze Deutschland soll es sein": Demokratischer Nationalismus in der Weimarer Republik am Beispiel der Deutschen Demokratischen Partei* (Stuttgart: Klett-Cotta, 1978); Karl Rohe, *Das Reichsbanner Schwarz Rot Gold: Ein Beitrag zur Geschichte und Struktur der politischen Kampfverbände zur Zeit der Weimarer Republik*, ed. Kommission für Geschichte des Parlamentarismus und der politischen Parteien (Düsseldorf: Droste Verlag, 1966); Bernd Buchner, *Um nationale und republikanische Identität: Die deutsche Sozialdemokratie und der Kampf um die politischen Symbole in der Weimarer Republik* (Bonn: Verlag J. H. W. Dietz Nachf., 2001); Manuela Achilles, "Reforming the Reich: Symbolics of the Republican Nation in Weimar Germany" (PhD diss., University of Michigan, 2005); Robert Gerwarth, "The Past in Weimar History," *Contemporary European History* 15, no. 1 (2006): 1–22; Eric Bryden, "In Search of Founding Fathers: Republican Historical Narratives in Weimar Germany, 1918–1933" (PhD diss., University of California–Davis, 2008); Nadine Rossol, *Performing the Nation in Interwar Germany: Sport, Spectacle and Political Symbolism, 1926–1936* (Basingstoke: Palgrave Macmillan, 2010); the special issue, "Culture of Politics—Politics of Culture: New Perspectives on the Weimar Republic," *Central European History* 43, no. 4 (2010); Benjamin Ziemann, *Contested Commemorations: Republican War Veterans and Weimar Political Culture* (Cambridge: Cambridge University Press, 2013).

33. Thorpe, *Pan-Germanism and the Austrofascist State*, chap. 1; Mark Mazower, *Hitler's Empire: How the Nazis Ruled Europe* (New York: Penguin, 2008), chap. 1. For a refutation of this type of argument see Winson Chu, Jesse Kauffman, and Michael Meng, "A *Sonderweg* through Eastern Europe? The Varieties of German Rule in Poland during the Two World Wars," *German History* 31, no. 3 (2013): 318–344.

34. Rogers Brubaker, *Ethnicity without Groups* (Cambridge, MA: Harvard University Press, 2004), chap. 6. For other works that challenge the civic-ethnic dichotomy in the German case see Dieter Gosewinkel, *Einbürgern und Ausschließen: Die Nationalisierung der Staatsangehörigkeit vom Deutschen Bund bis zur Bundesrepublik Deutschland* (Göttingen: Vandenhoeck & Ruprecht, 2001); Vick, *Defining Germany*; Geoff Eley and Jan Palmowski, eds., *Citizenship and National Identity in Twentieth-Century Germany* (Stanford, CA: Stanford University Press, 2008); Manuela Achilles,

not the sole national activists in German-speaking Central Europe still fall into the trap of differentiating between "good" civic and "bad" ethnic nationalisms within Germany itself. They presume that any reference to ethnic ideas, such as the concepts of *Stamm* (tribe, which implies descent) or blood, automatically makes these understandings of nationhood *völkisch*.[35] Such assumptions ignore the flexibility of these terms, which were not yet predicated on Nazi ideals of *Blut und Boden* (blood and soil).[36] As we will see, Jews and ardent opponents of anti-Semitism used these very concepts to explain their connections to their "German brothers" on the other side of the border. Not only did republicans use ethnic concepts in an inclusive way, but they also did so in an effort to inculcate democratic values. This book therefore uncovers an alternative vision of German nationhood, one that had an emotional resonance for the large number of republicans—both prominent politicians and ordinary individuals—who attended *großdeutsch* republican rallies, traversed the Austro-German border, and used a *großdeutsch* justification for republican symbols in the fierce debates over new state flags and anthems.

Although republicans were ultimately unable to realize their vision of a republican Greater Germany, their energetic endeavors to do so demonstrate that the Weimar and First Austrian Republics were not "republics without republicans." As historians of the Weimar Republic have shown, there were indeed enthusiastic republicans and not just "republicans of reason"—individuals who resigned themselves to the new government but did not fervently support it.[37] These

---

"With a Passion for Reason: Celebrating the Constitution in Weimar Germany," *Central European History* 43, no. 4 (2010): 666–689.

35. Eric Kurlander, *The Price of Exclusion: Ethnicity, National Identity, and the Decline of German Liberalism, 1898–1933* (New York: Berghahn Books, 2006); Sammartino, *Impossible Border*, esp. chaps. 4 and 7; Stefan Vogt, "Strange Encounters: Social Democracy and Radical Nationalism in Weimar Germany," *Journal of Contemporary History* 45, no. 2 (2010): 253–281; Adelheid von Saldern, "Volk and Heimat Culture in Radio Broadcasting during the Period of Transition from Weimar to Nazi Germany," *Journal of Modern History* 76, no. 2 (2004): 312–346.

36. On this point see Till van Rahden, "Germans of the Jewish *Stamm*: Visions of Community between Nationalism and Particularism, 1850 to 1933," in *German History from the Margins*, ed. Neil Gregor, Nils Roemer, and Mark Roseman (Bloomington: Indiana University Press, 2006), 27–48; Gosewinkel, *Einbürgern*, 325–326. Also see Winson Chu's argument that *völkisch* thinking was not as prevalent during the Weimar era as scholars once thought: Chu, *The German Minority in Interwar Poland* (Cambridge: Cambridge University Press, 2012). Historians of Nazi Germany have even shown that in practice Nazi racial concepts were far from fixed. See Doris Bergen, "The Nazi Concept of 'Volksdeutsche' and the Exacerbation of Anti-Semitism in Eastern Europe, 1939–45," *Journal of Contemporary History* 29, no. 4 (1994): 569–582; Eric Steinhart, "Policing the Boundaries of 'Germandom' in the East: SS Ethnic German Policy and Odessa's 'Volksdeutsche,' 1941–1944," *Central European History* 43, no. 1 (2010): 85–116.

37. Buchner, *Um nationale und republikanische Identität*; Achilles, "Re-forming the Reich"; Bryden, "In Search of Founding Fathers"; Achilles, "With a Passion for Reason"; Rossol, *Performing*

findings should not, however, just be limited to Germany. This book puts the efforts to defend democracy in transnational perspective. It highlights how republicans in Germany and Austria exchanged ideas and people across the state boundary in order to ward off attacks on the new form of government.[38] In bringing the histories of the German and Austrian republics together, this book also reveals an additional challenge faced by Austrians in trying to grapple with the political changes wrought by the Great War. Unlike in Germany, where no one questioned the existence of the state, there was the widespread belief among Austrians that their country was not viable and consequently should be joined to some larger unit, whether that be to Germany or a Danubian confederation of Habsburg successor states. Those loyal to the republican form of government in Austria (and later even the Austrofascist government) thus had to attempt to create a loyal citizenry in a place where the legitimacy of the state itself was questioned. Regardless of this added difficulty, this book provides another piece of evidence for the argument that neither the First Austrian Republic nor the Weimar Republic was doomed to fail.[39]

To further restore a sense of contingency to the two republics, I also investigate the ways in which citizens engaged with the new form of government and participated in the debates over nationhood. The First World War fundamentally altered the relationship between state and society and expanded the possibilities for

---

the Nation; Ziemann, Contested Commemorations. For a prime example of the "rational republican" argument see Peter Gay, Weimar Culture: The Outsider as Insider (New York: Harper Torchbooks, 1968).

38. Recent work on interwar Austria has made the case for understanding conservative and right-wing politics in the rump state using a transnational perspective. This study adds a new dimension to this development by focusing on republican politics. See Thorpe, Pan-Germanism and the Austrofascist State; Janek Wasserman, Black Vienna: The Radical Right in the Red City, 1918–1938 (Ithaca, NY: Cornell University Press, 2014).

39. For works using the question of failure as their starting point see Norbert Leser, "Austria between the Wars: An Essay," Austrian History Yearbook 17 (1981): 127–142; Ian Kershaw, ed., Weimar: Why Did German Democracy Fail? (New York: St. Martin's Press, 1990); and Richard Bessel, Germany after the First World War (Oxford: Clarendon, 1993). For works that challenge the failure paradigm see Ernst Hanisch, Der lange Schatten des Staates: Österreichische Gesellschaftsgeschichte im 20. Jahrhundert, Österreichische Geschichte, ed. Herwig Wolfram (Vienna: Verlag Carl Ueberreuter, 1994), 263–309; Detlev Peukert, The Weimar Republic: The Crisis of Classical Modernity, trans. Richard Deveson (New York: Hill & Wang, 1989); Peter Fritzsche, "Did Weimar Fail?," Journal of Modern History 68, no. 3 (1996): 629–656; Thomas Mergel, Parlamentarische Kultur in der Weimarer Republik: Politische Kommunikation, symbolische Politik und Öffentlichkeit im Reichstag (Düsseldorf: Droste Verlag, 2002); Achilles, "Re-forming the Reich"; Eric Weitz, Weimar Germany: Promise and Tragedy (Princeton, NJ: Princeton University Press, 2007); Bryden, "In Search of Founding Fathers"; Graf, Die Zukunft der Weimarer Republik; Kathleen Canning, Kerstin Barndt, and Kristin McGuire, eds., Weimar Publics / Weimar Subjects: Rethinking the Political Culture of Germany in the 1920s (New York: Berghahn Books, 2010); Ziemann, Contested Commemorations; Anthony McElligott, Rethinking the Weimar Republic: Authority and Authoritarianism, 1916–1936 (London: Bloomsbury, 2014).

political participation and agency, which had been growing since the rise of mass politics in the late nineteenth century.[40] With the establishment of democratic state systems after the war, citizens took advantage of increased democratic practices to both the benefit and detriment of the parliamentary republics.[41] Availing themselves of a language of rights and responsibilities, citizens asked their government to listen to their opinions and believed that their ideas would be taken seriously by officials. Thus, the fate of the republics was far from decided. Postwar Europe was "a laboratory atop a vast graveyard," to use the evocative metaphor of Tomáš Masaryk, the president of the new neighboring Czechoslovak state.[42] Against the political and economic turmoil caused by the war, citizens of both countries experimented with parliamentary democracy, as well as communism and fascism.[43] The outcome of such experiments was not predetermined. We should therefore not simply view the German-speaking republics as precursors to the Nazi and Austrofascist dictatorships.

Outline of the Book

To elucidate the cross-border connections between the Weimar and First Austrian Republics, this book uses a thematic organization. Chapter 1 examines republicans' rhetorical defense of the republics. Countering claims by the political right that the new republics were un-German, republicans argued that parliamentary

---

40. On the rise of mass politics see Margaret Lavinia Anderson, *Practicing Democracy: Elections and Political Culture in Imperial Germany* (Princeton, NJ: Princeton University Press, 2000); Carl Schorske, *Fin-de-Siècle Vienna: Politics and Culture* (1961; New York: Vintage, 1981), chap. 3. On the importance of the war see Peter Fritzsche, *Germans into Nazis* (Cambridge, MA: Harvard University Press, 1998); Belinda Davis, *Home Fires Burning: Food, Politics, and Everyday Life in World War I Berlin* (Chapel Hill: University of North Carolina Press, 2000); Maureen Healy, *Vienna and the Fall of the Habsburg Empire: Total War and Everyday Life in World War I* (Cambridge: Cambridge University Press, 2004). Also see the body of literature that moves beyond a purely legal understanding of citizenship and rather regards citizenship as a subjective experience and set of practices: Eley and Palmowski, *Citizenship and National Identity*; Kathleen Canning, "Class vs. Citizenship: Keywords in German History," *Central European History* 37, no. 2 (2004): 225–244; Geoff Eley, "Making a Place in the Nation: Meanings of 'Citizenship' in Wilhelmine Germany," in *Wilhelminism and Its Legacies: German Modernities, Imperialism, and the Meanings of Reform, 1890–1930*, ed. Geoff Eley and James Retallack (New York: Berghahn Books, 2003), 16–33; Canning, Barndt, and McGuire, *Weimar Publics*, esp. pts. 2 and 3; Maureen Healy, "Becoming Austrian: Women, the State, and Citizenship in World War I," *Central European History* 35, no. 1 (2002): 1–35; Gary Cohen, "Reinventing Austrian and Central European History," *German Studies Association Newsletter* 33, no. 2 (2008–2009): 28–38.

41. On the latter see Fritzsche, *Germans into Nazis*.

42. Quoted in Mark Mazower, *Dark Continent: Europe's Twentieth Century* (London: Penguin, 1998), x.

43. Peukert, *Weimar Republic*; Fritzsche, "Did Weimar Fail?"

democracy and German nationalism were not at odds. To prove their point, they cited the revolution of 1848 and their support for an Anschluss. In doing so, republicans attempted to create their own form of nationalism by contrasting their *großdeutsch* nationalism with right-wing *alldeutsch* (pan-German) nationalism and conservative nationalism. Even though republicans at times harbored prejudices, they used *großdeutsch* nationalism to support democratic rights and practices, to reconcile national and international allegiances, and to create a national community that cut across religious, political, and social divisions.

Whereas the first chapter is an analysis of the writings of political elites, the following chapters explore popular involvement in republican nationalism by investigating debates about state symbols, commemorations, and political rallies. As scholars have pointed out, symbols and commemorations are central to attempts both to legitimize and protest a particular form of government. Commemorative practices can showcase both unity and divisions within communities. The examination of commemorations, symbols, and rallies is therefore a particularly effective means of exploring the multiple ways in which not only political leaders but also ordinary citizens grappled with the profound changes occurring after World War I.[44] Moreover, these activities show that republicans were not simply paying lip service to the *großdeutsch* idea in order to combat their political opponents. Rather, their desire to unite Germany and Austria was a powerful incentive to action, as the subsequent chapters draw out.

Chapter 2 addresses the clash over state symbols that emerged alongside the intensive debates about the new form of government. It highlights the importance of *großdeutsch* nationalism in republican attempts to defend democracy and its symbolic manifestations. In the Weimar Republic, the decision by the National Assembly to replace the black-white-red imperial standard with a black-red-gold tricolor was hotly contested by those on the political right. Republicans in Germany tried to fend off these attacks by pointing to the use of black-red-gold by *großdeutsch* patriots in the nineteenth century. For Austrians,

---

44. Eric Hobsbawm and Terence Ranger, eds., *The Invention of Tradition* (Cambridge: Cambridge University Press, 1983); David Kertzer, *Ritual, Politics, and Power* (New Haven, CT: Yale University Press, 1988); John Gillis, ed., *Commemorations: The Politics of National Identity* (Princeton, NJ: Princeton University Press, 1994); Maria Bucur and Nancy Wingfield, eds., *Staging the Past: The Politics of Commemoration in Habsburg Central Europe, 1848 to the Present* (West Lafayette, IN: Purdue University Press, 2001); Wingfield, *Flag Wars and Stone Saints*; Emil Brix and Hannes Stekl, eds., *Der Kampf um das Gedächtnis: Öffentliche Gedenktage in Mitteleuropa* (Vienna: Böhlau Verlag, 1997); Karin Friedrich, ed., *Festive Culture in Germany and Europe from the Sixteenth to the Twentieth Century* (Lewiston, NY: Edwin Mellen, 2000); Sabine Behrenbeck and Alexander Nützenadel, eds., *Inszenierungen des Nationalstaats: Politische Feiern in Italien und Deutschland seit 1860/71* (Cologne: SH-Verlag, 2000); Margarete Myers Feinstein, *State Symbols: The Quest for Legitimacy in the Federal Republic of Germany and the German Democratic Republic, 1949–1959* (Boston: Brill Academic, 2001).

the debate over state symbols focused on the national anthem. Political conservatives lamented the replacement of the "Kaiserhymne," written by the beloved Austrian composer Joseph Haydn, with a new song penned by a socialist. In 1929–30, the Catholic-led government discarded the postwar anthem and returned to the Haydn tune with a text by a right-wing priest. To protest the actions of their opponents, the Austrian socialists, drawing on their *großdeutsch* nationalism, suggested another set of lyrics should be sung to the same Haydn tune: "Deutschland, Deutschland über alles"—the national anthem of the Weimar Republic. This chapter also moves beyond simply viewing these debates as symptoms of political fragmentation in the two countries. Through an investigation of letters and petitions sent by individuals and associations to the governments, it explores how contemporaries began self-consciously to practice what they saw as the rights and responsibilities of citizens living in democratic republics.

While this book focuses on the transborder relationship between German and Austrian republicans, it also investigates the particular challenges and opportunities republicans were facing in their respective countries. After all, before republicans could realize their ultimate goal of a *großdeutsch* republic, they had to legitimate the republican and democratic state system at home. Chapter 3 therefore examines the efforts to create a republican holiday in each state. Although republicans in Germany were never able to declare an official state holiday, they managed to stage a de facto republican celebration that included Germans from different political, social, and religious backgrounds. In Austria, the situation regarding a holiday presented the opposite scenario. The Austrian National Assembly easily passed a law creating a holiday to commemorate the founding of the republic, but the yearly commemoration only served to reinforce the divisions between the socialist and Catholic parties in Austria. These different political contexts also explain why the Austro-German republican partnership included socialists, left liberals, and Catholics in Germany and only socialists in Austria.

With the ultimate goal of creating a Greater Germany, republicans did not simply stage such political celebrations within the confines of their state boundaries. Focusing again on the entangled histories of the two republics, chapter 4 investigates the use of cross-border visits and motifs in political commemorations and rallies. In particular, it looks at the relationship between the Reichsbanner Schwarz-Rot-Gold and the Republikanischer Schutzbund. Highlighting the ability of republican *großdeutsch* nationalism to mobilize popular support, thousands of members of the two associations traveled across the border to attend pro-republican festivities, where they received an enthusiastic reception from local populations. Yet this cross-border relationship was not without problems. As explained in the previous chapter, republicans were dealing with vastly different domestic situations. Whereas the Catholics, socialists, and left liberals in Germany collaborated with one another, the Austrian socialists were the lone party in the rump state that was fully committed to the democratic republic. The Austrian socialists' revolutionary rhetoric and attacks on their Catholic political opponents at home therefore stirred tensions between the two republican organizations. These disagreements, however, did not simply originate within the republican coalition. Conservatives and the radical right in both states endeavored to break up the republican alliance. The political right's effort to do so was a sign of the importance of the cross-border republican partnership to the defense of democracy.

While the previous chapters address political commemorations, chapter 5 looks at cultural commemorations for the anniversaries of the deaths of Ludwig van Beethoven in 1927, Franz Schubert in 1928, Walther von der Vogelweide in 1930, and Johann Wolfgang von Goethe in 1932. This chapter explores how Germans and Austrians used these festivals to stage a transborder German community in the interwar period. They hoped that a focus on culture, rather than politics, would help them overcome the sociopolitical fragmentation of the interwar years. At first glance, these cultural celebrations appeared to bridge the numerous divisions running through both societies, as people from various social and political backgrounds wanted to honor these German cultural heroes. Nonetheless, political fights broke out among participants as they interpreted the lives and impact of these cultural figures according to their own divergent worldviews. By investigating these disagreements, this chapter underscores the numerous understandings of Germanness in the Weimar era.

The final chapter explores the culmination of these debates about the nature of German nationalism by examining the politics of the most prominent Anschluss organization of the era, the Österreichisch-Deutscher Volksbund (Austro-German People's League). Marketing itself as a "nonpartisan" association, the Volksbund included the supporters and opponents of democracy, Jews and anti-Semites, Catholics and Protestants, blue-collar workers and the middle classes. Focusing on the association's activities, this chapter investigates how these disparate groups could collaborate even as they were riven by political battles that emerged both within and about the association. Although the Volksbund's members had the shared goal of an Anschluss, clashes arose because of their fundamentally different beliefs about what a future Greater Germany should look like. Indeed, republicans used the association as another platform to promote their version of nationalism, leading a number of conservatives and right-wing radicals to reject it. By looking at both these points of agreement and conflict, this chapter demonstrates the depth of republicans' commitment to the *großdeutsch* idea and brings into sharper relief the divergent views of nationhood held by the political left and right. I also explore the radical changes that affected the association after the 1933 Nazi seizure of power, thereby highlighting the fact that there was no straight line between 1918 and 1938. Only by examining the conflicting attempts to speak in the name of a German Volk can we see the energetic efforts made by republicans in both the Reich and Austria to create and defend a German form of democracy after the Great War. Furthermore, in recognizing the importance of cross-border interactions between Reich German and Austrian republicans, we can appreciate that the attempt to fashion a trans-border German national community was not simply the work of the extreme political right.

1

THE NATIONALIZATION OF DEMOCRACY IN THE WEIMAR AND FIRST AUSTRIAN REPUBLICS

"Are we not national?" The question was intended as a challenge to the litany of abuses hurled at republicans by the political right. For conservatives and right-wing radicals, republicans were antinational, un-German, "a protection force of the French." Angered by these denunciations, Richart Mischler, a native of Bohemia living in Berlin who was the chairman of the Potsdam branch of the Reichsbanner, business director of the Österreichisch-Deutscher Volksbund, and a member of the SPD, posed the question in order to dispute such claims. Republicans, he explained in his answer, did not lack nationalism, as the political right insisted. Rather, "our nationalism is of a completely different type from that of our opponents." He proceeded to dismiss "conservative nationalism," which he labeled as the "spiritual heritage of the *Kleindeutschen*." Republicans were better Germans than the conservatives, he contended, because republican *groß-deutsch* nationalism was "older"—dating back to the Frankfurt Parliament—and more all-embracing than "conservative nationalism." Whereas "conservative nationalism" had excluded "10 million Germans" in Austria from the German nation-state, "our nationalism," Mischler explained, "feels the heartbeat of the entire German Volk, not only Prussia's."[1]

---

1. Richart Mischler, "Das Reichsbanner und Potsdam," in *Das Reichsbanner und Potsdam*, ed. Ortsgruppe Potsdam des Reichsbanners Schwarz-Rot-Gold (Dr. Mischler) (Berlin, o.D.), 15–18, in Archiv der sozialen Demokratie der Friedrich-Ebert-Stiftung Bonn (AdsD), Bestand Reichsbanner Schwarz-Rot-Gold, Exponate 30.

Mischler, however, did not just see a difference between republican *großdeutsch* nationalism and conservative nationalism. He also contrasted a right-wing nationalism based on "*Alldeutschtum*" (pan-Germanness) with a republican nationalism based on "*Großdeutschtum*" (greater-Germanness). As he explained, these two ideas were "not only not identical, but opposites."[2] So what were the differences between the often conflated terms, and why were they significant? *Alldeutschtum*, according to Mischler, was based on militarism and imperialism. It was "that nationalism which through German capital conquers the world from the Flemish coast all the way to the Ganges and which wanted to see it controlled by German weapons."[3] In contrast, *Großdeutschtum* was "outwardly peaceful" and based on "the philosophy of justice, of the right to national self-determination."[4] For Mischler, republicans were thus entirely committed to the German national cause, but in a way that was qualitatively different from that of the political right.

Following a brief overview of conservative and right-wing attacks on the new state systems, this chapter focuses on the rhetorical strategies deployed by republicans to defend and popularize the democratic republics. As Mischler's statements suggest, the *großdeutsch* idea would be crucial to this republican endeavor. In order to prove that democracy was not antithetical to the national good, republicans turned both to nineteenth-century history and the present-day violation of Austrian self-determination. To discredit the monarchies, they pointed to the events of 1848 to prove the existence of a national, democratic tradition in German-speaking Central Europe. Furthermore, they argued that the new form of government was superior to the Habsburg and Hohenzollern monarchies, which had privileged dynastic interests over national ones and caused Austria to be excluded from a German nation-state in 1866.

In addition to citing these historical events, German and Austrian supporters of democracy used their postwar support for an Anschluss in the hopes of not only bolstering democracy in Germany and Austria, but also proving their national credentials. As the leaders of the Anschluss movement in the Weimar era,[5] they sought to refute the political right's claim that they lacked national feeling. By supporting a *großdeutsch* national community linked to democratic values, they argued that they were in fact exhibiting a different type of nationalism from those on the right of the political spectrum. Republicans emphasized

---

2. Mischler, "Das Reichsbanner und Grossdeutschland," in *Festschrift zur Verfassungsfeier 1925, Berlin, 8. und 9. August,* ed. W. Nowack (Berlin: Warenvertrieb des Reichsbanners Schwarz-Rot-Gold, 1925), 18–19, in AdsD, Nachlass (NL) Willy Müller, Abteilung V, box 8, Fasz., 249.

3. Mischler, "Das Reichsbanner und Potsdam," 16–17.

4. Mischler, "Das Reichsbanner und Grossdeutschland," 19.

5. Suval, *Anschluss Question.*

that they wished an Anschluss to be achieved peacefully, in contrast to right-wing foreign policy goals. Moreover, they contended that an Anschluss would lead to the strengthening of peace in postwar Europe and provide an essential step in creating a united continent. For republicans, there was no conflict between having international and national loyalties, just as there was no conflict between being a Jew and a German. Even though republicans were capable of displaying chauvinistic ways of thinking, their version of nationalism looked vastly different from right-wing and conservative nationalisms. This chapter shows that the attempt to reimagine the boundaries of Germanness in more expansive ways was not simply a right-wing endeavor. Consequently, it points to the necessity of recognizing the multiplicity of German nationalisms during the Weimar era.

Debating Democracy and *Deutschtum*

As the idea of the nation became the organizing principle for the new international order after the First World War—demonstrated by the popularity of the notion of the right to national self-determination, the creation of supposed nation-states and national minorities at the Paris Peace Conference, and the formation of an international organization titled the League of Nations—it also became an increasingly important source of identification for many Europeans. In an effort to win popular support and power in their new republics, politicians competed to speak for a German national community.[6] The political right in both Germany and Austria mobilized nationalism in an attempt to discredit the new republics. According to conservative and right-wing parties and associations, the republics were an unsatisfactory answer to the political aspects of the German Question. Mixing a sinister brew of antidemocratic, anti-Semitic, and anti-Marxist ideas, they viewed the new state system and its supporters as adversaries of the national good. Those on the political right attacked especially the socialists in both countries, thereby continuing to advance the prewar idea that the Social Democratic parties were unpatriotic because of their internationalist outlook and connections. Their critiques of the Social Democrats took on a new urgency in light of the Bolsheviks' success in the Russian Revolution, leading

---

6. Rogers Brubaker's idea that "nationhood is not an ethnodemographic or ethnocultural fact" but "a political claim" is useful in this regard. Nationhood "is used . . . to change the world, to change the way people see themselves, to mobilize loyalties, kindle energies, and articulate demands." Brubaker, "In the Name of the Nation: Reflections on Nationalism and Patriotism," *Citizenship Studies* 8, no. 2 (2004): 116. On national mobilization in the Weimar Republic specifically, see Fritzsche, "Did Weimar Fail?"; Fritzsche, *Germans into Nazis*; Moritz Föllmer, "The Problem of National Solidarity in Interwar Germany," *German History* 23, no. 2 (2005): 202–231.

conservatives and the radical right to stir the fears of the middle classes and elites by wrongly equating the socialists with the Bolsheviks.

Over the course of the Weimar Republic, the German political right comprised a diverse set of political parties, patriotic associations, and paramilitary groups: the Freikorps, the German National People's Party, the Stahlhelm, the National Socialist German Workers' Party (NSDAP), the Bavarian People's Party (BVP), the Pan-German League, and others. Although there was internecine struggle among these groups,[7] they agreed that democracy was foreign to Germany.[8] In their eyes, democracy had come to Germany through Allied intervention and, according to the "stab in the back" myth (which falsely claimed that the German army had not lost the war on the battlefield but was stabbed in the back by traitors at home), through the alleged betrayal of socialists and Jews during the First World War. For these groups the Reichstag was the "gravedigger of the German nation and the German Reich,"[9] the Weimar Constitution was really "the constitution from Versailles,"[10] the Social Democrats were "the source of every catastrophe and German suffering,"[11] and Jews were leading to the "corruption of the German people."[12] They railed against the terms of the Treaty of Versailles, or the "Diktat," as they preferred to call it, decrying the "war-guilt clause," reparations, and territorial adjustments. The main concern for the more conservative of these organizations was for "the German territories that were ripped away," the loss of overseas colonies, and the occupation of the Rhineland, Ruhr, and Saar.[13] Radicals, such as the Nazis, did not merely want to return to the prewar boundaries, which for Hitler "were neither complete in the sense of embracing the people of German nationality, nor sensible with regard to geo-military expediency."[14] Rather, he advocated German expansion to the east in order "to secure for the German people the land and soil to which they are entitled on this earth."[15]

Then there was the German People's Party, a liberal party on the right of the political spectrum, which wavered between support of and opposition to

---

7. Larry Eugene Jones, "Nationalists, Nazis, and the Assault against Weimar: Revisiting the Harzburg Rally of October 1931," *German Studies Review* 29, no. 3 (2006): 483–494; Föllmer, "Problem of National Solidarity."

8. Gerwarth, "Past in Weimar History," 7–10.

9. Adolf Hitler, *Mein Kampf*, trans. Ralph Manheim (Boston: Houghton Mifflin, 1971), 271.

10. Alfred Rosenberg, "Die Verfassung von Versailles: Bemerkungen zum Zwangs-Verfassungstag," *Völkischer Beobachter*, 11 August 1928, 1.

11. The phrase is from a 1924 election advertisement created by the United Patriotic Associations of Germany. Quoted in Rohe, *Das Reichsbanner*, 194.

12. Quoted in Weitz, *Weimar Germany*, 98.

13. Quote is from the DNVP's 1920 statement of principles. Quoted in Weitz, *Weimar Germany*, 94.

14. Hitler, *Mein Kampf*, 649.

15. Ibid., 652.

the republic.[16] Under the leadership of Gustav Stresemann, who as foreign minister from 1923 to 1929 did much to restore Germany's position on the world stage, the party reluctantly worked within the boundaries of the republic. This period reflected Stresemann's shift from an avowed monarchist to a supporter of the republic in the years from 1920 to 1922. However, at both the beginning and end phases of the Weimar Republic, the party opposed the new democratic order. Therefore, in 1919 it voted against the Weimar Constitution, proclaimed its loyalty to "the empire" as the "most appropriate form of state,"[17] and vowed to fight "against every destructive effort that seeks to replace the devotion to the national-state and the German people with cosmopolitanism."[18] As the party swung to the right following Stresemann's death in 1929, it denounced Marxism for "breeding a sickly international and pacifist romanticism in the place of a resolute will devoted to the fatherland" and demanded that "everything in constitutional life that is un-German and alien to our nature, everything that places the rule of the masses in the place of the rule of achievement, must be overcome." With regard to the latter point, the party was essentially calling for the dissolution of the democratic republic, insisting on an end to the "exaggeration of parliamentarism" and calling for "the strengthening of the power of the president of the Reich."[19]

In Austria, the attitudes of the radical right and conservatives to the questions regarding democracy and nationalism were more complicated. The actors on the right of the Austrian political spectrum were also a diverse group: the Austrian Nazis, the Austrofascist Heimwehr, the Christian Social Party, the Greater German People's Party, and the Landbund. As in Germany, there were outright opponents of parliamentary rule and equal rights. Beset by rivalries, the Austrian Nazis shared a hatred of democracy, socialists, and Jews. With the Nazi electoral success in Germany in the early 1930s and Hitler's appointment to chancellor in January 1933, the group became emboldened to achieve their principal goal of an Anschluss with Germany in order to create and then join the Third Reich. They tried to destabilize and even overthrow the Austrian government through violent means, the most infamous incident being their assassination of Engelbert Dollfuss, the Austrofascist dictator, in the summer of 1934.[20]

---

16. Jones, *German Liberalism*; Dieter Langewiesche, *Liberalism in Germany*, trans. Christiane Banerji (London: Macmillan, 2000), chap. 5; Weitz, *Weimar Germany*, 92, 94, 104–105.

17. Quoted in Langewiesche, *Liberalism in Germany*, 277.

18. Quoted in Weitz, *Weimar Germany*, 92.

19. German People's Party (DVP), "Program," 1931, in *The Weimar Republic Sourcebook*, ed. Anton Kaes, Martin Jay, and Edward Dimendberg (Berkeley: University of California Press, 1994), 115–116.

20. Bruce Pauley, *Hitler and the Forgotten Nazis*.

Also seeking to use force to topple the republic was the Heimwehr. Although divided by regional factionalism, this paramilitary group aimed at the destruction of the Social Democrats and democracy—a goal it finally achieved in the brief civil war of February 1934—with the financial support of the Italian Fascist dictator Benito Mussolini, the authoritarian regent of Hungary Miklós Horthy, Austrian industrialists, and the right wing of the Christian Social Party.[21] In its Korneuburg oath of 1931, the Heimwehr declared, "We fight against the disintegration . . . of our people by the Marxist class struggle and the liberal economic order." It also "reject[ed] Western democratic parliamentarism and the party state." In place of the current system it sought "a new German conception of state" based on "faith in God, [every comrade's] own hard will, and the command of his leaders!"[22] Although in many respects the Heimwehr made pronouncements similar to those of the Nazis, these statements point to a number of key differences. The two groups were by and large competitors on the radical right. Although a few local groups among the Heimwehr favored an Anschluss, others wanted to maintain an independent Austria. For these Heimwehr members, a political union with Germany would threaten their desire to create a fascist regime rooted in Catholicism.[23] Those favoring Austrian sovereignty still believed that they were part of the German Volk, as the oath makes clear; yet they emphasized Austrian specificities and a particular mission for the rump state as a defender of Christianity.

A number of the leaders of the Christian Social Party, a key architect of the republic alongside the Social Democrats and the German nationalists, would come to back the Heimwehr beginning in the mid-1920s. Indeed, there was a marked shift among many members of the CSP from support, or at least toleration, of the republic to demands for a more authoritarian regime. The epicenter of this changing attitude toward democracy was Prelate Ignaz Seipel, who served as the leader of the CSP and chancellor for much of the republic's existence. By the late 1920s, he was espousing the idea of "true democracy," which amounted to authoritarianism, corporatism, and collaboration with the Heimwehr.[24] In

21. C. Earl Edmondson, *The Heimwehr and Austrian Politics, 1918–1936* (Athens: University of Georgia Press, 1978), esp. chap. 2; Bruce Pauley, "A Case Study in Fascism: The Styrian Heimatschutz and Austrian National Socialism," *Austrian History Yearbook* 12/13 (1976–1977): 257; R. John Rath, "The Deterioration of Democracy in Austria, 1927–1932," *Austrian History Yearbook* 27 (1996): 213–259.

22. Quoted in Edmondson, *Heimwehr and Austrian Politics,* 98–99.

23. As Bruce Pauley notes, "The Austrian Heimwehr had the unique distinction of being the only anti-Nazi fascist organization in Europe." Pauley, "Case Study in Fascism," 251.

24. Ignaz Seipel, "Demokratie und Kritik der Demokratie," *Reichspost (RP)*, 18 July 1929, 3–4. For more on Seipel's ideas see Alfred Diamant, *Austrian Catholics and the First Republic: Democracy, Capitalism, and the Social Order, 1918–1934* (Princeton, NJ: Princeton University Press, 1960),

conjunction with this turn to an antidemocratic position, Seipel and his circle embarked on a process to create a stronger Austrian identity based on imperial and Catholic traditions in an effort to strengthen their hand within the state. Like the Heimwehr, they did not reject membership in a German nation but wished to maintain an independent Austrian state.[25] "For us, the nation [*Nation*], independent of citizenship, is the great cultural community [*Kulturgemeinschaft*]; it stands higher for us Germans than the state," remarked Seipel in a 1926 anti-Anschluss speech.[26] Yet the CSP had an extremely diverse base, and not all members agreed with Seipel's course.[27] The Christian Social Workers' Association, for example, opposed Seipel's alliance with the Heimwehr and wished to see democracy maintained. Many Christian Socials in the provinces also disputed Seipel's position on a political union with Germany and openly supported an Anschluss (even Seipel did not fully close off the possibility of an Anschluss in a 1928 private correspondence on the matter).[28] Although divided on the issues of democracy and an Anschluss, the party was united in its espousal of anti-Marxist and anti-Semitic sentiments, seeing both the socialists and Jews as dangers to Austria.

As with the CSP, the eventual members of the Greater German People's Party, the GDVP, which was founded in 1920, initially supported democracy. Even though the Greater Germans joined the Christian Socials in a coalition for much of the republic, the GDVP did not see eye to eye with its partners on issues of religion and nationalism. As the heir to the defunct liberal movement in Austria, the GDVP was anticlerical. It was also, as its name suggests, a supporter of an Anschluss and an opponent of the CSP's Austrian identity project. Despite these

esp. 106–116; Alfred Diamant, "Austrian Catholics and the First Republic, 1918–1934: A Study in Anti-Democratic Thought," *Western Political Quarterly* 10, no. 3 (1957): 603–633; Guenther Steiner, *Wahre Demokratie? Transformation und Demokratieverständnis in der Ersten Republik Österreich und im Ständestaat Österreich, 1918–1938* (Frankfurt am Main: Peter Lang, 2004); Klemens von Klemperer, *Ignaz Seipel: Christian Statesman in a Time of Crisis* (Princeton, NJ: Princeton University Press, 1972), esp. chaps. 4–7; John Boyer, *Karl Lueger (1844–1910): Christlichsoziale Politik als Beruf* (Wien: Böhlau Verlag, 2010), 413–435; John Deak, "Ignaz Seipel (1876–1932): Founding Father of the Austrian Republic," in *Austrian Lives*, ed. Günter Bischof, Fritz Plasser, and Eva Maltschnig (New Orleans: University of New Orleans Press, 2012), 32–55.

25. Early on Seipel and others around him desired to form a Danubian confederation based on the old Habsburg Empire; however, the opposition of the other successor states prevented this.

26. Quoted in "Vortrag Dr. Seipels über das Anschlußproblem," *NFP*, 13 February 1926, in Politisches Archiv des Auswärtigen Amts, Berlin (PAAA), R73296, IIOe283.

27. For more on the differences between the more moderate and cooperative stance of the CSP in the provinces and the hardline politics of Seipel's circle, see Evan Burr Bukey, *Hitler's Hometown, Linz, Austria 1908–1945* (Bloomington, IN: Indiana University Press, 1986), chaps. 2–4.

28. Paul Sweet, "Seipel's Views on Anschluss in 1928: An Unpublished Exchange of Letters," *Journal of Modern History* 19, no. 4 (1947): 320–323.

significant points of disagreement, the GDVP worked with the CSP because of their shared anti-Marxism and anti-Semitism. The party, which never garnered more than 10 percent of the vote in federal elections, began to lose a steady stream of its members to the Heimwehr and the Nazis. Eventually, in the spring of 1933, the party joined the Nazis to form the Kampfgemeinschaft.[29] Hence, although the parties on the right in both Austria and Germany were a heterogeneous group, they came to see socialists, Jews, and parliamentary democracy as alien influences threatening the German Volk.

Welcoming the establishment of democracy in Germany and Austria, republicans in both countries went to great lengths to counter claims that the republics were a foreign imposition. To do so, they created historical narratives that would demonstrate the links between the German national movement from its early nineteenth-century beginnings and demands for greater political freedom. They highlighted how a pantheon of national heroes had fought for the twin goals of national unity and liberal political reform. Among the patriots mentioned were Ernst Moritz Arndt, Johann Gottlieb Fichte, Carl Schurz, August Heinrich Hoffmann von Fallersleben, Ferdinand Freiligrath, the Lützower Freikorps, the Vormärz *Burschenschaften*, Jacob Grimm, and Ludwig Uhland. Additionally, they cited such seminal events as the Wars of Liberation against Napoleon, the Wartburg festival of 1817, the Hambach festival of 1832, and the Schiller festival of 1859, placing special emphasis on the revolutions of 1848–1849, particularly the Frankfurt Parliament.[30] Republicans underlined that the parliamentary gathering in Frankfurt not only included Austrian representatives, but also sought to create a German nation-state with a parliamentary system. They desired to show that democratic ideas were at the heart of historic efforts to achieve German national unity.[31] As Otto Hörsing, head of the Reichsbanner and a member of

---

29. Isabella Ackerl, "Thesen zu Demokratieverständnis, parlamentarischer Haltung und nationaler Frage bei der Großdeutschen Volkspartei," in *Das Parteienwesen Österreichs und Ungarns in der Zwischenkriegszeit*, ed. Anna Drabek, Richard Plaschka, and Helmut Rumpler (Vienna: Verlag der Österreichischen Akadamie der Wissenschaften, 1990), 147–156; Martin Kitchen, *The Coming of Austrian Fascism* (Montreal: McGill–Queen's University Press, 1980), 45–50.

30. While republicans emphasized shared themes about the Frankfurt Parliament, they disagreed about the meanings of the *Märzgefallenen*. Daniel Bussenius, "Eine ungeliebte Tradition: Die Weimarer Linke und die 48er Revolution 1918–1925," in *Der Griff nach der Deutungsmacht: Zur Geschichte der Geschichtspolitik in Deutschland*, ed. Heinrich August Winkler (Göttingen: Wallstein, 2004), 90–114; Claudia Klemm, *Erinnert—umstritten—gefeiert: Die Revolution von 1848/49 in der deutschen Gedenkkultur* (Göttingen: V&R unipress, 2007), chap. 4; Buchner, *Um nationale und republikanische Identität*, chap. 2; Eric Bryden, "Heroes and Martyrs of the Republic: Reichsbanner *Geschichtspolitik* in Weimar Germany," *Central European History* 43, no. 4 (2010): 639–665. On the more general historical narratives of the Weimar republicans, also see Bryden, "In Search of Founding Fathers."

31. Although traditional interpretations of the Frankfurt Parliament argue that the revolutionaries promoted nationalism over liberal political reform, Brian Vick has skillfully shown that such

the SPD, stated, "In the Frankfurt National Assembly the *großdeutsch* idea was alive, the feeling that the German *Volksstaat* [people's state] must include all Germans. An adverse fate has excluded our Austrian sisters and brothers from their fatherland. However, we stand by them. We will neither stop nor rest until the obstacles, which still today oppose their return home, are cleared away. Thus, we want to create what the men from the St. Paul's Church already had in mind: *the social and democratic* großdeutsch Volksstaat, *the state of the Germans*."[32] By drawing a direct connection between the Frankfurt parliamentarians and themselves, the Weimar republicans hoped to provide the republic and its defenders with national legitimacy. Indeed, Hörsing's use of the word *Volksstaat* attests to the proximity between nationalism and democracy in the eyes of republicans: Volk was understood in both a civic sense (the people as the source of the state's power) and a national sense.

Republicans in the Reich were not alone in attempting to use the democratic and *großdeutsch* legacy of 1848 to legitimize the new form of government. Just like their German sister organization, many Austrian socialists viewed the legacy of the Frankfurt Parliament in national and democratic terms. In an article chastising the allegedly nationalist student associations for their absence from the Austrian republic's one-year anniversary celebrations, the *Arbeiter-Zeitung*, the main socialist paper in the country, pointed out, "Since 1848 the republican idea is already linked with that of German unity."[33] Even the most doctrinaire of the Austro-Marxists interpreted the revolution of 1918 as not simply a social one but also a national one. The leader of the left wing of the Austrian Social Democrats, Otto Bauer, explained, "If the revolution of 1848 has given birth to the idea of German unity, the revolution of 1918 has reawakened it." He then proceeded to demand another revolution to wipe out the Italian and French reactionary forces opposing an Anschluss.[34] Thus, republicans in both countries tried to make a

---

readings are inaccurate. For the delegates, the liberal ideas of liberty and rights were an integral part of national unity and honor. Likewise, interwar republicans saw nationalism and democracy as intertwined and did not privilege one over the other. In this regard, it makes sense that the republicans endeavored to position themselves as heirs to this historical legacy. Vick, *Defining Germany*. For additional information on the interwar republican narrative see Rohe, *Das Reichsbanner*, 227–245; Gerwarth, "Past in Weimar History," 13–16; Bryden, "Heroes." For an opposing view see Bussenius, "Eine ungeliebte Tradition."

32. Otto Hörsing, "1848–1928," *Bundesverfassusungsfeier des Reichsbanners Schwarz-Rot-Gold, vom 11. bis 13. August 1928, Frankfurt am Main, 1848–1928, 80 Jahre*, 17, in AdsD, NL Franz Osterroth, box 53, Fasz. 140. Emphasis in original.

33. "Das Bürgertum und die Republik," *AZ*, 14 November 1919, in Wienbibliothek im Rathaus (WB), Tagblattarchiv (TA), Nationalfeiertag.

34. Otto Bauer, "Drei Gruppen im Anschlußlager," *AZ*, 7 July 1927, in Archiv des Vogelsanginstituts, Kt. 55, Anschluß, Zeitungsausschnitte, 1927. Although Bauer spoke of the need for revolution, the SDAP pursued a reformist agenda. Peter Loewenberg, "Otto Bauer as an Ambivalent Party

connection between their present-day republics and the historic struggle for German national unity.

The ultimate failure of the 1848 attempt to create a greater German nation-state did not weaken republicans' argument regarding the links between nationalism and democracy. In fact, the failure enabled them to declare that a democratic republic was the form of government most compatible with realizing national unity. Republicans in both countries contended that the numerous royal houses within German-speaking Central Europe, especially the Hohenzollerns and Habsburgs, had destroyed not only the Frankfurt Parliament, but also the attempt to achieve German unity.[35] As Karl Renner, the leader of the pragmatic branch of the Austrian Social Democrats, stated at a 1925 Reichsbanner rally in Frankfurt, "The principalities have been our national misfortune."[36] Only a republican and democratic state form, republicans insisted, could pave the way for a *Großdeutschland*, because representative government placed national interests above particularistic ones.

Not all republicans were willing to eschew a connection with the imperial German past. According to the historian Eric Bryden, Weimar republicans were split into two groups over the legacy of the *Kaiserreich*: moderates, who found

---

Leader," in *The Austrian Socialist Experiment: Social Democracy and Austromarxism, 1918–1934*, ed. Anson Rabinbach (Boulder, CO: Westview Press, 1985), 71–79; Ernst Hanisch, *Der Grosse Illusionist: Otto Bauer, 1881–1938* (Vienna: Böhlau Verlag, 2011).

35. Although republicans ignored the *kleindeutsch-großdeutsch* division of the Frankfurt delegates, the republican reading of the Austrian question in 1848 was not entirely untrue. Brian Vick has argued that the schism has been exaggerated. According to Vick, most delegates desired at the very least the inclusion of the Austrian federal lands (and if not during the present moment, at a later date). He also contends that the issue of territorial borders was not the primary reason for the delegates' failure to achieve national unity. Constitutional arrangements, for instance, were a more contentious issue. Vick, *Defining Germany*, 161–171. Additionally, before the delegates ultimately resolved to implement the *kleindeutsch* solution and offer a hereditary crown to the Prussian ruler in March 1849, they had actually voted in favor of a *großdeutsch* solution in October 1848. During this earlier phase of the revolution, representatives approved articles 2 and 3 for a constitution that would provide for the admission of Austria's "German" lands. This arrangement would have required a political reorganization of the Habsburg Empire: only territories deemed to be German could join a united Germany, leaving rulers with non-German territories to maintain their control over them through a "personal union." However, conservatives regained the upper hand in Austria the following month and refused to consider such an arrangement. The possibility of a *großdeutsch* solution was finally closed off with the Habsburg monarchy's institution of a new constitution in March 1849 that maintained the unity of the empire. James Sheehan, *German History, 1770–1866* (Oxford: Oxford University Press, 1989), 688–691; David Blackbourn, *History of Germany, 1780–1918: The Long Nineteenth Century*, 2nd ed. (Oxford: Blackwell, 2003), 120–122.

36. Karl Renner, untitled, in *Großdeutscher republikanischer Volkstag für Südwestdeutschland in Frankfurt a.M., Samstag, den 8., Sonntag, den 9. u. Dienstag (Verfassungstag), den 11. August 1925, Programm und Liedertexte*, 12, in AdsD, Reichsbanner Schwarz-Rot-Gold, Nummer 145. For similar arguments made by Weimar republicans see Bryden, "In Search of Founding Fathers," chap. 5, and "Heroes."

a place for the imperial past in their narratives, and militants, who completely rejected it.[37] Consequently, not all republicans decried Bismarck or saw the "Wars of Unification" as cementing the division of Germany. Moderate republicans saw Bismarck's accomplishments as important stepping stones to the achievement of German national unity and even democracy. Wilhelm Marx of the Center Party thus praised Bismarck's creation of the Reich as "the most valuable inheritance" from the prewar period and lauded Bismarck's decision to introduce universal male suffrage. Yet, even in this favorable reading of imperial German history, a *großdeutsch* understanding of the Germans' past and future took precedence. Marx stressed that the Bismarckian Reich was a "torso"; the "ideal solution" to the so-called German Question—one that was *großdeutsch*, democratic, and peaceful—still had to be achieved.[38] Although republicans differed on the appraisal of the imperial German past, they were united in viewing a *großdeutsch* and democratic state as the highest goal.

One of the most striking examples of the republican attempt to reevaluate the imperial past occurred in commemorations for the fiftieth anniversary of the founding of the Reich on January 18, 1871. Although Austrians had been excluded from the Germany formed that historic day, Reich President Friedrich Ebert of the SPD and Chancellor Constantin Fehrenbach of the Center Party addressed the plight of Austria in an announcement on the anniversary of the *Reichsgründung*. They mentioned their sorrow not only for the territories lost at the Paris Peace Conference, but also for "especially heavily suffering Austria, which with its heart strives toward us as we strive toward it." They concluded, "It must be all of our firm will to continue to hold on to and to strengthen our inner state unity. If political and economic views divide us more than they should, in one thing we are all united: borders shall not divide us. The unity of our German Fatherland is for all of us a part of our beliefs, our love, and our hope."[39] The inclusion of Austria in an official, republican message concerning the formation of a state from which German speakers living in the Habsburg Empire had been specifically excluded demonstrates how, after the war, republicans reinterpreted the past from a *großdeutsch* standpoint.[40]

Residents of the Reich were not alone in finding a place for Austria in this celebration of Bismarck's *Kleindeutschland*. Not only did the GDVP and Pan-German

---

37. Bryden, "In Search of Founding Fathers."

38. "Die Reden im Sportpalast," *Germania*, 18 April 1925, in PAAA, R73293.

39. Ebert and Fehrenbach, draft of newspaper announcement, 18 January 1921, in Bundesarchiv Berlin (BAB), R43I/566, Bl. 79.

40. On interwar professional historians' rewriting of German history see Suval, *Anschluss Question*, chap. 4.

League organize festivities, but both chambers of the Austrian parliament also recognized the anniversary as a way to express the bonds between Germany and Austria.[41] In the Bundesrat, for example, Jakob Reumann, the president of the council and the first Social Democratic mayor of Vienna, garnered unanimous approval of a statement for the fiftieth anniversary of January 18 and sent it to Reich President Ebert. "With wistful nostalgia and yet with confidence have our tribal brothers [*Stammesbrüder*] in the Reich met the eighteenth of January, and we are one with them in the feeling of pain, as well as in the hope for a happy future of the entire German Volk," part of the statement read.[42] Rather than being a date that represented the final exclusion of Austria from Germany, the fiftieth anniversary of the founding of the Reich became a date for Austrians to proclaim membership in a greater German nation. Even the Austrian socialists, who consigned the Habsburg legacy to the dustbin of history, reluctantly saw the fiftieth anniversary of the *Reichsgründung* as a small (although flawed) step toward a national unity that would be achieved only through an Anschluss on democratic grounds.[43]

By focusing on the *großdeutsch* idea, republicans in both countries sought to differentiate their national sentiments from those of their political opponents. The SDAP actually went so far as to call their enemies—the CSP, the Heimwehr, the Nazis, and German conservatives—"antinational."[44] Austrian socialists argued that their foes were no different from the aristocrats and dynasties that had prevented German unity in 1848. Pointing to the Christian Socials' interest in a Danubian confederation and Habsburg symbols, they contended that their chief political rival was "black-yellow," the colors of the Habsburg monarchy, and thus against a Greater Germany.[45] The SDAP used the same label for the Heimwehr. In the wake of growing Nazi success in Germany during the early

---

41. See relevant documents in PAAA, R73287.

42. [Untitled] enclosed in a letter from the Vorsitzende des Bundesrates der Republik Österreich to the Reichspräsident, Vienna, 1 February 1921, in PAAA, R73287, IIOe492. I am following the lead of Till van Rahden in translating *Stammesbrüder* as "tribal brothers." In doing so, I can best render in English the flexibility of the term for contemporaries. Till van Rahden, "Germans of the Jewish *Stamm*."

43. Although the party had supported the empire until its last days, it rejected anything associated with the Habsburg legacy after the war. Austrian socialists described the Habsburgs as oppressors and blamed the ruling family for preventing German unity. Moreover, whereas some republicans interpreted the Bismarckian Reich as a step toward national unity, the multinational Austro-Hungarian Empire did not offer such possibilities.

44. "Die Reaktion gegen den Anschluß," *AZ*, 17 July 1932, in WB, TA, Anschluss 1932–1938.

45. "Seipel und der Anschluß," *AZ*, 30 June 1928, in PAAA, R73301, IIOe1150. They also pointed to the Christian Socials' foreign policy as proof of national betrayal. They criticized the CSP-led government for signing the Geneva Protocols in 1922, which enabled the economically faltering Austrian state to receive loans from the West in exchange for a guarantee of Austrian independence,

1930s, Austrian socialists cast similar aspersions on the enemies of democracy across the border. "The National Socialist flood," asserted the *Arbeiter-Zeitung*, "has once again brought the old ruling classes, the Prussian Junkers and generals, back to power." Given this re-creation of the old Hohenzollern-Habsburg rivalry, the paper proclaimed, "Democracy unites the German Volk, the reaction tears it apart!"[46]

Republicans in Germany did not advance such bold claims against the political right at home. Nonetheless, they did seek both to question the depth of conservatives' national commitments and to posit a form of nationalism distinct from that of the radical right, as Mischler's statements at the opening of this chapter illustrated. He was not alone among Reich republicans in seeking to redefine what true national sentiments looked like. "Arguably no other words are so abused in postwar Germany as the words 'national,' 'love of the fatherland,' 'patriotic' ['*national*,' '*vaterländisch*,' '*patriotisch*']," an article in the Reichsbanner's eponymous journal insisted. Only those who served the German nation, "the entirety of all culturally aware German people on this side of and beyond the boundary posts," fulfilled the definitions of these words. Adherents of the political right had failed in this regard, the article claimed. In the imperial period, they had privileged the interests of the big landowners over those of the majority of the Volk. After the war, they had committed "an assassination against the German Volk" during both the Kapp Putsch, the 1920 attempt by right-wing soldiers to overthrow the Weimar Republic, and the 1922 right-wing murder of Walther Rathenau, the Jewish industrialist and German patriot who had spearheaded Germany's command economy in World War I and was serving as foreign minister at the time of his death. Republicans, on the other hand, served all Germans and were therefore "more essentially national" than the conservatives and right-wing radicals.[47] Moreover, while conservatives longed for a monarchy that had prevented German unity, the republicans in Germany were responsible for "carry[ing] the *großdeutsch* idea to the masses of the German Volk."[48] For republicans in the Reich, only they were capable of overcoming the narrow economic and political interests that had prevented German unity. The *großdeutsch* idea thus enabled republicans in both countries to mount a defense against conservative and right-wing accusations that the republics and their supporters were un-German.

---

befriending Mussolini, and ignoring the plight of the German minority in South Tyrol. "Reichsbanner und Schutzbund," *AZ*, 10 November 1926, in PAAA, R73298, IIOe1946.

46. "Die Reaktion gegen den Anschluß," *AZ*, 17 July 1932, in WB, TA, Anschluss 1932–1938.
47. "Republikanischer Patriotismus," *DR*, 15 July 1925 (Beilage), o.S.
48. "Der Triumphzug," *DR*, 1 March 1925 (1. Beilage), o.S.

An Anschluss and the Politics of Peace

As the statements above suggest, republicans not only looked to the past to prove their commitment to a German nation, but also turned their attention to the position of German speakers in postwar Europe. Foreign policy methods and goals would be central to republican attempts to advance their own version of German nationalism. Although the precise foreign-policy objectives differed among the republican groups, all agreed that Germans' right to self-determination had been violated by the Treaties of Versailles and Saint-Germain. They challenged the ban on an Austro-German political union, the occupation of the Rhineland, Ruhr, and Saar, the awarding of South Tyrol to Italy, and the partition of Upper Silesia, all areas that they saw as fitting within their democratic, national framework.[49] Additionally, after the majority of republicans gave up their claims to the Sudetenland in late 1919,[50] they continued to defend German minority rights in Czechoslovakia and elsewhere in Eastern Europe. While they lent their support to all these causes, republicans became the leaders of the Anschluss movement. In the immediate aftermath of defeat, republicans had hoped to win democracy supporters by achieving a greater degree of German unity than Bismarck had. Even after the Entente made it clear in 1919 that an Anschluss would not be likely in the foreseeable future, republicans continued energetically to support one throughout the Weimar period in hopes of proving their democratic and peaceful credentials to audiences abroad, as well as demonstrating their national credentials to their domestic opponents.[51]

Whereas the French and Czechoslovak governments saw even the mere mention of Anschluss as an indication of revived German imperialism and a call for war, republicans repeatedly stressed that they aimed to strengthen European peace. To make their point, they drew a clear distinction between themselves and annexationist camps in Germany during and after the First World War. As Wilhelm Heile, a member of the DDP and a leading figure in both the Anschluss and pan-European movements, clarified, "The bearers of the desire for an Anschluss in the German Reich are not the black-white-red militarists and reactionaries, but the black-red-gold democrats, who at the same time are the bearers of the

---

49. They viewed the occupation of the Rhine, Ruhr, and Saar as cases of French imperialism, the abuse of Germans' rights in South Tyrol as a crime of Italian Fascism, and the partition of Upper Silesia as a violation of a popular referendum.

50. I have found only a couple of examples of republicans who continued to demand the incorporation of the Sudetenland into a Greater Germany after the initial postwar period: Heinrich Getzeny, "Großdeutsche Republik oder kleindeutsche Monarchie," *Germania* (Morgenausgabe), 10 August 1924, o.S.; "Die Versammlung in der Volkshalle," *AZ*, 31 August 1925, 1–2.

51. Heß, *"Das ganze Deutschland"*; Rohe, *Das Reichsbanner*, 227–265; Gerwarth, "Past in Weimar History," 13–16; Suval, *Anschluss Question*.

idea of a united states of Europe."[52] Numerous supporters of democracy in both countries emphasized that an Anschluss had nothing to do with "a revival of imperialism or annexationism" and would occur only if Austrians desired it. It was, they argued, simply a matter of Austrian self-determination. Furthermore, they underscored that they would work through the League of Nations to achieve it. After all, the peace treaties provided that a political union could happen with the approval of the Council of the League of Nations.[53] In creating a more peaceful climate and a larger economic and political unit in the heart of the continent, an Anschluss would be an important step in the formation of a Pan-Europe. They therefore sought to reassure foreign governments of their goodwill in hopes of winning support for an Anschluss in the League.[54]

While denying that they had militaristic aims, republicans argued that the same could not be said for the supposedly democratic countries that had created the peace settlement. Republicans identified the Entente powers, especially the French government, as enemies of national self-determination and consequently of democracy. In a speech filled with Marxist denunciations of imperialism and capitalism, Austrian socialist Robert Preußler decried the peace settlement. "So the peace treaties are not the realization of the idea—War against war! War against reaction! Furthering of international peace!—but the opposite," he insisted. "The victors have rearmed, ready any time to set out to rob. France ... has become unfaithful to the postulates of 1789."[55] If the supposedly democratic countries of the West were in reality the opposite, so the republican thinking went, then the German and Austrian republicans were the only genuine democrats, owing to their championing of peace and the democratic idea of self-determination.[56] They thereby hoped that they would be able to persuade the Council of the League of Nations to allow an Anschluss. The denunciation of the Entente also implied that

---

52. Wilhelm Heile, "Der 'Anschluss' und der europäische Friede," *Oesterreich-Deutschland* (OeD), October 1928, 1–5, here 5.

53. Löbe quoted in "Große Kundgebung für den Anschluß an Deutschland," *NFP*, 31 August 1925, in PAAA, R73295, IIOe1356. Also see "Geheimrat Kuenzer über den Anschluß," *NFP* (Morgenblatt), 27 October 1926, 6; Karl Renner, "Rundfunkvortrag: Österreichs vergangene und künftige Sendung," 1926, in PAAA, R73298, IIOe1768.

54. For example, republicans won over Victor Basch, a leader of the League of Human Rights, and Léon Blum, the head of the French socialists. "Anschlußgedanke und Selbstbestimmungsrecht der Völker," *Lokal-Anzeiger*, 19 May 1925, in PAAA, R73310; Léon Blum, "Anschluss?-Warum Nicht?," *OeD*, September 1928, 1–2.

55. Quoted in "Der 12. November," *Salzburger Wacht*, 13 November 1923, 1. While republicans decried French imperialism, they believed in Franco-German reconciliation as a way to achieve an Anschluss. Helmut v. Gerlach, "Grossdeutschland und Frankreich," in *Festschrift zur Verfassungsfeier 1925, Berlin* (Berlin: Warenvertrieb des Reichsbanners Schwarz-Rot-Gold, 1925), 19–20, in AdsD, NL Willy Müller, Abteilung V, box 8, Fasz. 249.

56. Also see Suval, *Anschluss Question*, chap. 5.

democracy could not have been a foreign imposition because the victors in the war were not living up to democratic ideals.

Republicans' foreign policy methods and goals thus contrasted greatly with those of the political right in Germany and the radical right in Austria. They sought a peaceful path to achieve an Anschluss and worked within the postwar international system to revise the peace treaties. Of course, republicans certainly hoped that an Anschluss would increase Germany's influence in Europe. They raised the possibility of Vienna being "the great trade center toward the East."[57] On the one hand, they advanced this argument because of their desire to enhance Germany's economic and cultural reach; on the other, they made this point in an effort to allay the fears of those Reich Germans who looked askance at a union with a devastated Austrian economy. However, such declarations did not mean that their avowals of peace and for a united states of Europe were hollow. Although they did at times display chauvinistic attitudes toward other peoples,[58] they still rejected the creation of a "Naumann-ish 'Mitteleuropa'" and the "colonization" of the East.[59] As the Austrian socialists explained, "We recognize the right to self-determination of the other nations of

---

57. "Große Kundgebung für den Anschluss an Deutschland," *NFP*, 31 August 1925, in PAAA, R73295, IIOe1356.

58. In their objections to the fact that Austria had been denied its right to self-determination while other nations were granted it, republican racism occasionally reared its ugly head. In a speech praising the Weimar Constitution for its contribution to "human development," the Austrian socialist General Theodor Körner nonetheless described the "East" as having "nations with no history." "General Körner (Wien)," *DR*, 15 August 1924, o.S. In a similar fashion, *Germania*, the pro-republican Center Party newspaper, objected to the fact that Austria, "one of the most cultivated nations of the world," was denied self-determination in an age when "the Chinese and Indians, yes even the African Negro cries out with growing irresistibility their claims to national self-determination." "Lehre aus der Wiener Unruhen," *Germania*, 23 July 1927 (Morgenausgabe), o.S.

59. The Naumann reference was made by a close associate of his, Hellmut von Gerlach of the DDP. Quoted in "Die Presse über die Wiener Fahrt," *OeD*, November 1925, 18–20, here 20. Also see Renner, "Rundfunkvortrag"; Ernst Diefenthal, "Neudeutscher Imperialismus," *DR*, 1 June 1927, 87. The Weimar coalition parties took a different attitude toward Germany's lost colonies overseas, which points to their privileging of national over supranational aims at times. The DDP remained divided over the colonial question, with greater support for the idea during the first half of the republic. The Center Party included a clause in its 1922 platform demanding Germany's colonies back, in view of missionary work. Even some majority socialists, who came from a primarily anticolonial party in the imperial period, demanded Germany's colonies back in 1918–1919 in hopes of winning over the army and conservative nationalists. Despite support for colonies and adherence to the myth that Europeans were at a more "advanced" stage of development, the SPD often ridiculed the political right for its adherence to scientific racism in the imperial era. Indeed, the SPD, and even the Center Party and the left liberals, had all opposed a ban on mixed marriages in 1912. Jens-Uwe Guettel, "The Myth of the Pro-Colonialist SPD: German Social Democracy and Imperialism before World War I," *Central European History* 45, no. 3 (2012): 452–484; Gosewinkel, *Einbürgern*, 308; Heß, *"Das ganze Deutschland,"* 241–251; "Richtlinien der Deutschen Zentrumspartei, Berlin, 16.

the Habsburg monarchy" and simply "ask for the same right for the German Volk."[60] Thus, even when republicans put national interests over supranational ones, their revisionism looked wholly different from the demands of their political foes.[61]

The supporters of democracy also advanced a vision of a *Großdeutschland* that diverged from that of their conservative and right-wing opponents. When imagining a future Austro-German union, republicans often cited its democratic political system, whereas the political right purposefully avoided any suggestion that a Greater Germany would have a democratic foundation. By linking an Anschluss to the republics, republicans set out to nationalize democracy. Indeed, they argued that the fate of German national unity was dependent on a democratic government. "The Reich as the German nation-state can only maintain its life in the present and can only hope for its development in the future by reconnecting to the ideals and the national will of the old *großdeutsch* democracy, which, suited to the change of the times, leads to the national republic," asserted Hugo Preuss, the chief architect of the Weimar Constitution and a member of the DDP.[62] The reverse was also true for republicans. They hoped that a future Anschluss would stabilize and strengthen the republican form of government in both countries. As Heinrich Hirtsiefer of the Catholic Center Party explained, "The new [democratic] Germany will only truly be formed when German-Austria is incorporated."[63] Their desire to unite peacefully members of a German nation into a single state based on the Weimar Constitution was central to republicans' attempts to create a form of German nationalism compatible with democratic politics.[64]

Januar 1922," in *Deutsche Parteiprogramme seit 1861*, ed. Wolfgang Treue (Göttingen: Musterschmidt Verlag, 1954), 141.

60. "Seipel und der Anschluß," *AZ*, 30 June 1928, in PAAA, R73301, IIOe1150. Also see Paul Löbe, "Imperialismus oder Selbstbestimmung," *AZ*, 31 May 1925, in WB, L121260, Band (Bd.) 1, Fasz. I, Untermappe II, 6; Werner Stephan, "Republikaner und Grenzdeutschtum," *DR*, 15 September 1927, 147–148.

61. On the DDP see Heß, "*Das ganze Deutschland*," esp. 252–316.

62. Hugo Preuss, *Staat, Recht und Freiheit: Aus 40 Jahren deutscher Politik und Geschichte* (Tübingen: Verlag von J. C. B. Mohr, 1926), 473.

63. Heinrich Hiertsiefer [*sic*], "Die Republikanisierung Deutschlands," *NFP*, 17 September 1926, in a letter from the Deutsche Gesandtschaft Wien to the Auswärtige Amt Berlin, 18 September 1926, in PAAA, R73298. Republicans stood the most to benefit from a political union. The socialists in particular would increase their voting bloc, while the power of the political right would become weaker as it became increasingly divided along confessional, regional, and political lines. On this point see "Wer in Oesterreich für den Anschluß ist," *Der Telegraph*, 18 October 1927, in WB, L121260, Bd. 7, Untermappe I, 185; Löbe, "Imperialismus oder Selbstbestimmung," *AZ*, 31 May 1925, in WB, L121260, Bd. 1, Fasz. I, Untermappe II, 6.

64. Also see Heß, "*Das ganze Deutschland*," esp. 336–357.

Republican Conceptions of *Großdeutsch* Nationhood

Just as the republican project of a Greater Germany differed from that of the political right, so too did their understanding of nationhood. Employing broader and more tolerant criteria for membership in a German nation, republicans often refuted the exclusionary logic of conservative and right-wing nationalisms. While republicans emphasized their desire that "all children of the land have equal rights and the same political freedoms, so that everyone can feel at home in the *Heimat* [homeland],"[65] it is also clear from their demands for an Anschluss that their conception of a German nation did not align with citizenship. Given their belief in a transborder German national community, it is useful to examine the boundaries of inclusion and exclusion in the republicans' conception of a *großdeutsch* nation.[66] To do so, this section briefly considers republican treatment of the three groups most harassed by exclusionary nationalists: socialists, Jews, and national minorities. Whereas those on the right insisted that democracy and Germany, socialism and nationalism, and Jew and German were incompatible, republicans argued that these categories were not mutually exclusive.

Of all the republican parties, the socialists bore the brunt of conservative and right-wing attacks. Seizing upon the prewar idea that socialists were unpatriotic because of their internationalist outlook and connections, conservatives and the radical right continued to argue throughout the postwar period that socialists were nationally suspect. In response, socialists maintained both before and after the war that their dedication to the international community and working class did not undermine dedication to a German nation.[67] To illustrate this point, it is helpful to look at the web of interwar organizations in which Paul Löbe participated. Löbe was the president of the Reichstag for most of the Weimar Republic and a prominent member of the SPD. In addition to these political roles within the Reich, Löbe served in leadership positions in a number of organizations whose reach extended beyond the borders of Germany. He actively participated

---

65. For Philipp Scheidemann of the SPD this was a hallmark of "national sentiment," which he contrasted with the intolerant and militaristic "nationalist sentiment of our opponents." Scheidemann, "Zwei notwendige Aufklärungen," in *Das Reichsbanner Schwarz Rot Gold* (Berlin, o.D.), 8–10, here 8, in AdsD, NL Franz Osterroth, box 53, Fasz. 140.

66. Brubaker, *Ethnicity without Groups*, 141.

67. During both periods, revisionist socialists rejected Marx's dictum that "the proletarian has no fatherland" on the grounds that by the late nineteenth century, workers were increasingly gaining rights and thereby invested in the fate of a nation. Eduard Bernstein, *The Preconditions of Socialism*, trans. Henry Tudor (1899; Cambridge: Cambridge University Press, 1993), 163–164; speech by Carl Severing, reprinted in "Feier der Reichsregierung," *Westfälische Neueste Nachrichten*, 12 August 1929, in AdsD, NL Carl Severing, Mappe 15.

in Count Coudenhove-Kalergi's Pan-Europe movement. At the same time, he served as the chairman of the German branch of the Österreichisch-Deutscher Volksbund (Austro-German People's League), an organization that promoted an Anschluss but not necessarily on socialist or even democratic grounds. It underlined its "nonpartisan" nature and brought together leading personalities of different political persuasions, including members of antidemocratic parties, a topic that will be explored in further detail in chapter 6. As chairman of the Volksbund, Löbe was more than simply a figurehead. He helped to organize pro-Anschluss events and, after the formation of Austrian branches of the Volksbund in 1925, was a frequent speaker at Anschluss rallies in Austria.

For a man like Löbe, international aims could easily be reconciled with national ones.[68] At a 1925 Anschluss rally in Vienna organized by the Volksbund, he announced to the crowd that an Anschluss did not mean a "breach of peace." He went on to explain that "as a party man, I come at present from Marseilles, where workers have expressed their desire for peace, and tomorrow I travel to Paris for a rally for German-French understanding in order explicitly to highlight that this understanding is the basis of European peace."[69] Löbe's involvement in these various organizations shows that dedication to the causes of international socialism and peace did not rule out a commitment to *großdeutsch* nationalism. The ability to reconcile these national and international loyalties—loyalties that the political right regarded as incompatible—was due to the existence of various German nationalisms. In a memoir written after the Second World War, Löbe explained that many proponents of the Anschluss movement had possessed a "healthy national feeling," unlike the "bullish nationalism" of the Nazis.[70]

Not only did socialists claim that nationalism and internationalism were compatible, but they also argued that their commitment to a national cause actually strengthened their commitment to international and pacifist causes. As German Social Democrat Hermann Müller-Franken announced on the occasion of the Austrian socialist Karl Renner's sixtieth birthday, "He is a good internationalist because he is a good German, just as Jaurès has demanded that the French socialists had to be good Frenchmen and thereby good internationalists."[71] Müller's praise of Renner as a "good German" and a "good internationalist" illustrates how Social Democrats thought that *großdeutsch* nationalism and internationalism

68. Buchner, *Um nationale und republikanische Identität*.
69. Quoted in "Große Kundgebung für den Anschluss an Deutschland," *NFP*, 31 August 1925, in PAAA, R73295, IIOe1356.
70. Paul Löbe, *Der Weg war lang: Erinnerungen* (1949; reprint Berlin: arani-Verlag, 1990), 132.
71. Hermann Müller-Franken, typed manuscript of "Die Deutsche Sozialdemokratie grüßt Karl Renner!" [1929/1930], in AdsD, NL Hermann Müller-Franken, box 12, Kass. VII, 9.

were intertwined. Indeed, they insisted that their international proclivities actually stemmed from their love of the nation.

In addition to these justifications of their internationalism, they emphasized German-speaking socialists' long-standing connection to the *großdeutsch* idea. They stressed that the founders of the German socialist movement had continually adhered to the belief in a *großdeutsch* nation. During a 1925 meeting of the Krems city council to draft a pro-Anschluss declaration, for example, the Austrian Nazis, the GDVP, the CSP, and the SDAP submitted proposals expressing their support for an Austro-German political union. In their statement, the socialists explained that "above all the Social Democrats ([August] Bebel) were always *großdeutsch*, and as a result always strove for the unification of all German tribes [*Stämme*] in a Reich."[72] Besides praising Bebel, socialists cited the *großdeutsch* convictions of Karl Marx, Friedrich Engels, Wilhelm Liebknecht, and Ferdinand Lassalle.[73] As in the republican historical narratives, socialists hoped to lend themselves national legitimacy by emphasizing that German socialism from its birth had been connected to the movement to create a Greater Germany. For socialists, there was, as Otto Bauer put it, a historical "connection of the ideal of national unity with the ideal of social emancipation." To prove his point, Bauer quoted an 1872 statement by Wilhelm Liebknecht: "A double ideal has been on my mind since my youth: the free and united Germany and the emancipation of the working people."[74]

Socialist support for an Anschluss grew out of their myriad desires to strengthen the hand of their party, achieve further rights for the working class, support democracy, rescue Austria from its alleged unviability, and express their national sentiments. Depending on their audience (and personal inclinations), socialists emphasized certain motivations for an Anschluss over others. In a book titled *The Way to Socialism*, Bauer wrote, "The Anschluss with Germany thus paves the way for us to socialism."[75] Intended for like-minded readers, the book

---

72. Stadtgemeinde Krems a.d. Donau to the BKA, 5 August 1925, in ÖStA, AdR, BKA, AA, NPA, Kt. 84, Liasse Deutschland I/1, 1925, Bl. 808–812, here Rückseite (Rs.) of 811.

73. "Zum 12. November," *Salzburger Wacht*, 11 November 1919, 1; "Die Abschiedsfeier für Ludo Hartmann," *Berliner Tageblatt* (*BT*), 19 November 1920, in ÖStA, AdR, BKA, AA, NPA, Kt. 84, Liasse Deutschland I/1, Kundgebungen für den Anschluss 1920, Bl. 78; Otto Bauer, "Das Anschlussproblem," *Vorwärts*, 9 July 1927, in PAAA, R73299; Ludwig Brügel, "Eine Anschlußkundgebung vor sechzig Jahren: Wilhelm Liebknecht in Wien," *AZ*, 25 July 1929, in WB, TA, Anschluss 1929–1931. Also see Low, *Anschluss Movement, 1931–1938*, 48–52; Helmut Konrad, "Wurzeln deutschnationalen Denkens in der österreichischen Arbeiterbewegung," in *Sozialdemokratie und "Anschluß": Historische Wurzeln, Anschluß 1918 und 1938, Nachwirkungen*, ed. Helmut Konrad (Vienna: Europaverlag, 1978), 19–30.

74. Otto Bauer, "Das Anschlussproblem," *Vorwärts*, 9 July 1927, in PAAA, R73299.

75. Quoted in Hanns Haas, "Otto Bauer und der Anschluß 1918/1919," in *Sozialdemokratie*, ed. Konrad, 36–44, here 37. Ernst Hanisch has elucidated Bauer's overlapping identifications, arguing

stressed the socialist underpinnings of support for an Anschluss. However, at a rally for the Volksbund, the socialist vice-mayor of Vienna, Georg Emmerling, stressed, "We want it [the Anschluss], but not simply because it would benefit us economically. Above all, we want the Anschluss because we feel ourselves one with you [Reich Germans] in cultural terms."[76] Numerous socialists in both countries thus sincerely believed in German nationalism, but a form of nationalism that differed from that of the political right.

While socialists faced insults from conservatives and the radical right because of their internationalist associations, Jews were targets of the political right because of religious, social, and alleged racial differences. Although anti-Semites viewed Jews as a homogeneous group and a foreign element in the German Volk, Jews from Austria and Germany were divided about whether they constituted a religious, ethnic, or racial community, as well as their relationship to a German nation.[77] Jewish opinions on the matter ranged from Zionists who insisted that Jews were a separate nation that needed its own state to Jews who maintained that they could be members of both a Jewish ethnic or religious community and a German national community. Hence, whereas the Zionist *Wiener Morgenzeitung* criticized the socialists for having "gone over to nationalism, [and] striv[ing] for an Anschluss with a Germany sinking ever deeper into reaction," other Jews or those of Jewish heritage saw themselves as Germans and thus joined the Österreichisch-Deutscher Volksbund (a subject to be covered in more depth in chapter 6). In participating in the Volksbund, men like Ludwig Haas, Hugo Preuss, and Julius Deutsch identified as "Germans who professes the *großdeutsch* idea," the only requirement for membership.[78] Indeed, Haas, in an Anschluss speech at the 1925 Reichsbanner commemoration in Magdeburg, referred to "our German tribal brothers [*Stammesbrüder*] in Austria."[79] Echoing the socialists' defense of themselves, this latter group of Jews claimed that the political right had manufactured a false dichotomy. In their estimation, there was no conflict between being Jewish and being German. Upon the death of Haas in 1930, Georg Bernhard, the chief editor of the *Vossische Zeitung* and fellow Volksbund

---

that he understood himself first as an "international Social Democrat," second as a German in Austria in a national sense, and third as a Jew. Hanisch, *Der Grosse Illusionist*, 56.

76. Quoted in "Große Kundgebung für den Anschluß an Deutschland," *NFP*, 31 August 1925, in PAAA, R73295, IIOe1356.

77. Donald Niewyk, *The Jews in Weimar Germany*, 2nd ed. (New Brunswick, NJ: Transaction, 2001), chaps. 4–8; Michael Brenner and Derek Penslar, eds., *In Search of Jewish Community: Jewish Identities in Germany and Austria, 1918–1933* (Bloomington: Indiana University Press, 1998).

78. There was also an annual membership fee (twelve marks in 1925). Österreichisch-Deutscher Volksbund–Vereinsjahr 1925–Hauptvorstand, in PAAA, R73314.

79. "Die Wünsche für den Anschluß," *NFP* (Morgenblatt), 24 February 1925, 3–4.

member, consequently explained, "Germandom [*Deutschtum*] and simultaneously Jewry [*Judentum*] have lost one of their very best representatives. In barely anyone else was the synthesis of German and Jew so genuine and so complete." This statement on Haas was reprinted in the Austrian-Jewish newspaper *Die Wahrheit*, again pointing to the importance of cross-border connections in defining Germanness in this period.[80]

The ability of Jews to join the Volksbund was likely due to the heavy involvement of other republican politicians in the association. After all, the DDP and both socialist parties included Jews among their members, and the Catholic Center Party attracted Jewish bourgeois voters in the wake of the Great Depression and the collapse of the DDP.[81] A piece in the journal of the republican-dominated Berlin Volksbund even criticized an Anschluss speech by a member of the DVP for not considering Jews as Germans and failing to recognize that "Vienna's greatest national merit was to incorporate foreign-language immigrants into the German *Volkstum* [ethnicity] over many centuries." The DVP speaker "has a national criterion that we cannot adopt," the article clarified.[82] This stance contrasted greatly with the parties of the political right, all of whom preached anti-Semitism. Rather than relying solely on anti-Semitic and racist definitions of a German nation, republican ideas about the German Volk consequently tended to be more inclusive.[83]

This, of course, is not to say that republicans never incorporated unsavory elements in their brand of nationalism. Although they counted Jews among their ranks, they were not immune to voicing anti-Semitic stereotypes or failing to defend Jews against anti-Semitic attacks.[84] Furthermore, the supporters of democracy had absorbed the language of blood and descent into their conceptions

---

80. "Ludwig Haas," *Die Wahrheit*, 15 August 1930, 3–4, here 3. While Marsha Rozenblit has shown that a number of Austrian Jews continued to identify with German culture, but not the German Volk, after the war, this stance was not adopted by all Austrian Jews, as this and other examples below demonstrate. Marsha Rozenblit, "Jewish Ethnicity in a New Nation-State: The Crisis of Identity in the Austrian Republic," in *In Search of Jewish Community: Jewish Identities in Germany and Austria, 1918–1933*, ed. Michael Brenner and Derek Penslar (Bloomington: Indiana University Press, 1998), 134–153.

81. Niewyk, *Jews*, 28–29, 71–72.

82. "Auch ein Anschluß-Redner," *OeD*, December 1925, 11.

83. These examples demonstrate that republicans did not simply include Jews on the basis of loyalty to the republican constitution, as Manuela Achilles has argued. Achilles, "With a Passion for Reason," 670.

84. The parties of the Weimar Coalition generally opposed anti-Semitism. Nonetheless, the DDP and SPD sometimes refused to put Jewish candidates on the ballot for fear of right-wing attacks. The SDAP made attacks on "Jewish capitalism" but did not promote racial anti-Semitism. Niewyk, *Jews*, 68–74; Peter Pulzer, *Jews and the German State*, 214–268; Bruce Pauley, *From Prejudice to Persecution: A History of Austrian Anti-Semitism* (Chapel Hill: University of North Carolina Press, 1992), chap. 10.

of nationhood. Hamburg mayor Carl Petersen and Frankfurt mayor Ludwig Landmann of the DDP, as well as Philipp Scheidemann and Adolf Köster of the SPD, for instance, all listed blood as one of the elements unifying Germans and Austrians.[85] Yet we should not equate their use of terms like blood and *Stamm* (tribe, which implied descent) with the deployment of these terms by groups like the Nazis.[86] After all, Petersen had one Jewish parent, and Landmann had been born into the Jewish community. Furthermore, Scheidemann was an outspoken critic of anti-Semitism.[87]

Although the ideas of ethnicity and race had become pervasive in discourses on nationhood by the early twentieth century, the meanings of these concepts had not yet become fixed. For example, in the following speech given to commemorate the Weimar Constitution, Gustav Radbruch, a member of the SPD and legal theorist, simultaneously rejected and used the concept of ethnicity and even race in defining membership in a German national community:

> But for us, the nation [*Nation*] is not a community of descent and blood [*Gemeinschaft der Abstammung und des Blutes*], which does not exist in a pure form; rather, it is a community of historical destiny and a living culture. We do not want to forgo claiming individuals like Adelbert Chamisso and Theodor Fontane, like Friedrich Julius Stahl, Ferdinand Lassalle, and Walter [*sic*] Rathenau as German national comrades [*Volksgenossen*]. In the spirit of a constitution that emphatically commemorates the reconciliation of the people, and even more so racial reconciliation within the German people, how should we not be agreed upon the firmly established awareness that Germans of different descent [*Abstammung*] are nonetheless Germans of the same national spirit and worth!

He continued by explaining that "the German nation [*Nation*] does not end at the German borders. It includes the German minorities in all areas, which our

---

85. Köster, "Rede zur Begruessung oesterreichischer Sänger," undated, in AdsD, NL Adolf Köster, Mappe 27, Nummer 563; Petersen in "Die Verfassungsfeier im Reichstag," in *Der Fünfte Jahrestag der Deutschen Reichsverfassung: Aufmarsch des Reichsbanners Schwarz-Rot-Gold am Verfassungstage 1924*, in BAB, R43I/570, Rs. of Bl. 277; Landmann in "Die Feststadt Wien und der Anschlußgedanke," *NFP*, 23 July 1928, 6, in ÖStA, AdR, Präsidentschaftskanzlei (PrK) 5149/1928; Scheidemann in "Große Kundgebung in Berlin für den Anschluß Deutsch-Österreichs," *NFP*, 19 May 1919, 3–4.

86. Gosewinkel, *Einbürgern*, 325–326.

87. Pulzer, *Jews and the German State*, 274; Donald Niewyk, *Socialist, Anti-Semite, and Jew: German Social Democracy Confronts the Problem of Anti-Semitism, 1918–1933* (Baton Rouge: Louisiana State University Press, 1971), 37.

historical fate has separated from the territory of the German Reich. It includes above all our tribal brothers [*Stammesbrüder*] in German-Austria."[88] He then went on to call for an Anschluss, but notably, and in line with republican foreign policy goals, he did not call for the annexation of German minorities in Eastern Europe.

Radbruch's references to "descent," "racial reconciliation," and *Stamm* again illustrate that ethnic and even racial language was not always used in a racist manner. He appears to group Chamisso and Fontane together owing to their French heritage and to list Stahl, Lassalle, and Rathenau together because of their Jewish heritage. He therefore implies that he considers individuals whose families hailed from beyond the borders of Germany, as well as Jews, to be full-fledged members of a German national community. Furthermore, after earlier having stated that "the nation is not a community of descent and blood," he then bases Austrians' inclusion in a German nation on the notion that Reich Germans and Austrians are "tribal brothers." Radbruch's musings highlight that the use of ethnic and racial ideas in the 1920s was complicated, even confused, and did not necessarily entail a belief in exclusionary nationalism.

Some republicans went even further than Radbruch and stressed that the only prerequisite for membership in a German nation was individual choice, a claim that had already been made by Otto Bauer and Karl Renner in their prewar writings.[89] Likewise, after the war, Wilhelm Külz, a member of the DDP, answered the question "Who is German?" in the following way: "A German is anyone who feels the German experience to be one's own and feels oneself to be jointly responsible for the fate of the German Volk."[90] Referring specifically to *Auslandsdeutsche* (Germans living outside the boundaries of the Reich), Külz made it clear that his conceptualization of a transborder German national community differed radically from the racist understandings of the radical right or even ethnic understandings advanced by many fellow democrats. These statements underline that the definitions of terms like *Volk*, *Volksgemeinschaft* (national community), and *Stamm* were ambiguous and flexible. As historian Till van Rahden has pointed out, minority groups were likely to employ the concept of *Stamm* as a way to participate in the national community, emphasizing the term's association with democracy. After all, the preamble of the Weimar Constitution stated that the

---

88. Gustav Radbruch, *Republikanische Pflichtenlehre: Eine Rede zur Verfassungsfeier* (Kiel: Gauvorstand Schleswig-Holstein Reichsbanner Schwarz-Rot-Gold, o.D.), 4, in AdsD, NL Franz Osterroth, box 53, Fasz. 140.

89. Ian Reifowitz, "Otto Bauer and Karl Renner on Nationalism, Ethnicity and Jews," *Journal of Jewish Identities* 2, no. 2 (2009): 1–19.

90. Quoted in Wolfgang Madjera, "Wer ist deutsch?," *Volks-Zeitung*, 16 March 1926, in ÖstA, AdR, Parteiarchive, GDVP, Zeitungsausschnitte, Mappe 266, 63.

German Volk was "united in its tribes." Thus, republicans used a term like *Stamm* to stress the inclusiveness and diversity of a German nation because it allowed people to maintain their particularistic identities.[91] We should therefore not assume that the use of these terms is an automatic indicator of *völkisch* sentiments.

Although many republicans saw the boundaries of the national community as permeable, they were fairly silent on the issue of national minorities within the boundaries of their countries. In other words, numerous republicans welcomed Danish, Polish, Slovenian, and Croatian speakers living in Germany and Austria to join the German Volk if they wished; however, they rarely spoke about those who desired to remain Danish, Polish, Slovenian, or Croatian in a national sense. In an exceptional case, Paul Löbe, during an Anschluss rally in Wulkaprodersdorf, an Austrian town with a sizable Croatian population, stressed that "the Croatian minority, when the union . . . with Germany is executed, will, in the great German republic, enjoy all those rights which it can lay claim to as a minority."[92] Since republicans wanted the Weimar Constitution to be the basis of a Greater Germany, one can assume that Löbe was referring to article 113 of the constitution, which protected "the free national development" of "sections of the people of the Reich speaking a foreign language." As with the inclusion of this article in the Weimar Constitution, Löbe's statement most likely stemmed from a wish for a "departure from previous discriminatory and oppressive policies [of Imperial Germany], and legal equality for citizens belonging to ethnic minorities," as well as the desire to use minority rights at home in order to better fight for the rights of German minorities abroad.[93]

The fact that republicans showed a much greater concern for the rights of Germans beyond the boundaries of the Reich than the position of national minorities at home points to the limitations of republican *großdeutsch* nationalism. As a result of their attempts to create a German form of democracy, there was a tension between being a citizen of Germany or Austria and being a member of

---

91. van Rahden, "Germans of the Jewish *Stamm*," 27–48; Gosewinkel, *Einbürgern*, 353–368. For similar work on the idea of *Heimat* see Applegate, *Nation of Provincials*; Confino, *Nation as a Local Metaphor*; Jenkins, *Provincial Modernity*.

92. "Das Burgenland will heim ins Reich!," *Wiener Neueste Nachrichten* (*WNN*), 26 July 1928, and "Anschlußkundgebung in Burgenland," *NFP*, 26 July 1928, both in PAAA, R73302, IIOe1327. According to the articles, large numbers of Croatian speakers attended the rally.

93. Karen Schönwälder, "The Constitutional Protection of Minorities in Germany: Weimar Revisited," *Slavonic and East European Review* 74, no. 1 (1996): 44 and 49 respectively. While the constitution guaranteed individual rights, such as the freedom of expression and religion, it also guaranteed linguistic minorities' collective rights. This stance was due to a national understanding of democracy as opposed to a purely liberal one, a position also seen in interwar Czechoslovakia. Wingfield, *Flag Wars and Stone Saints*, chaps. 5–7; Zahra, *Kidnapped Souls*, chaps. 4–5; Andrea Orzoff, *Battle for the Castle: The Myth of Czechoslovakia in Europe, 1914–1948* (New York: Oxford University Press, 2009).

the German Volk. One could be a citizen of the Reich without laying claim to a German national identity, while German-speaking citizens of Austria, Czechoslovakia, and Poland were understood as fellow members of a German nation. Instead of being based purely on civic terms or the notion of *jus soli*, the nation was variously defined by republicans on the basis of language, culture, history, the shared and burdensome experience of the Great War, ethnicity, and an individual decision to join the German Volk.

Yet even when proponents of democracy gave clear precedence to the situation of German speakers abroad over that of minorities at home,[94] they still showed a willingness to uphold their principles of equal rights, freedom, and international peace. Republicans would welcome into the fold those who desired to claim a German national identity, but they were also willing (begrudgingly) to let national minorities continue their existence when they were not a political threat to democracy.[95] Additionally, republicans often fought within the confines of the League of Nations for the right of German national minorities in Eastern Europe to maintain their German language and culture without necessarily calling for their incorporation into Germany. For example, Richart Mischler, himself a Bohemian, explained, "Austria's Anschluss is possible without war being necessary with other successor states of the former Habsburg monarchy, as would be unavoidable, for example, in the case of the Sudeten Germans."[96] Although republicans often conceptualized a German nation as including all the border Germans or even called for a republic as far as the German language sounded in Central Europe, historian Brian Vick's argument about the Frankfurt Parliamentarians is useful when considering the interwar republicans' desire to redraw

---

94. Republicans were in line with the larger trend of the Weimar period in which "*Volkszugehörigkeit*" (national belonging) became more important than "*Staatszugehörigkeit*" (state belonging) because of the territorial rearrangement of Central Europe following the First World War. Gosewinkel, *Einbürgern*, chap. 7, here 345; Sammartino, *Impossible Border*, esp. chaps. 4 and 7.

95. For instance, Austrian socialists in the newly created Burgenland wanted to "get rid of everything that is still Magyar!" They made such demands not based on ethnic differences, but on the notion that "Hungarians" in Austria were friendly to the authoritarian Hungarian government that was funneling money to the CSP to help quash the SDAP. As the Social Democratic newspaper in the region explained, the boundary between Austria and Hungary was a "demarcation line between the barbarism of the East and Western democracy." Gerhard Baumgartner, "Der nationale Differenzierungsprozess in den ländlichen Gemeinden des südlichen Burgenlandes," in *Vom Ethnos zur Nationalität: Der nationale Differenzierungsprozess am Beispiel ausgewählter Orte in Kärnten und im Burgenland*, ed. Andreas Moritsch (Vienna: Verlag für Geschichte und Politik, 1991), 150–155. First quote is from the provincial socialist leader Ludwig Leser on p. 151. Peter Haslinger, "Building a Regional Identity: The Burgenland, 1921–1938," *Austrian History Yearbook* 32 (2001): 105–123. The second quote is on p. 116.

96. Mischler, "Das Reichsbanner und Grossdeutschland," 18–19. Also see Paul Löbe's remarks in "Von den deutschen Minderheiten," *OeD*, May 1928, 8; Werner Stephan, "Republikaner und Grenzdeutschtum," *DR*, 15 September 1927 (Beilage), 147–148.

state boundaries. According to Vick, "though the Arndtian dream of bringing together the whole of the German linguistic community under one national roof enjoyed a certain vague and sloganistic popularity, it never formed the basis of anyone's serious thinking about German national borders."[97] The same holds true for interwar republicans, who made similar rhetorical flourishes while limiting their actual territorial claims. By restricting their focus to the cause of Austrian self-determination, they thus sought to prove that the republican brand of German nationalism would threaten neither European peace nor the independence of other nationalities. Whatever their shortcomings, republicans' nationalism and revisionism were qualitatively different from conservative and right-wing nationalisms. Their *großdeutsch* nationalism was therefore not simply a manifestation of pan-Germanism. And, as the next chapters will further demonstrate, it was at the heart of their efforts to defend democracy.

---

97. Vick, *Defining Germany*, 45–46.

2

THE SEARCH FOR SYMBOLS
The Debates about the German Flag
and the Austrian Anthem

In his famed novel, *Goodbye to Berlin*, Christopher Isherwood not only immortalized the heady atmosphere of Weimar-era Berlin's nightlife, but he also chronicled the growing political tensions in the republic's last years. During a trip to the island of Rügen in the summer of 1931, the protagonist strolls along the beach, noting, "Each family has its own enormous hooded wicker beach-chair, and each flies a little flag. There are the German city-flags—Hamburg, Hanover, Dresden, Rostock and Berlin, as well as the National, Republican and Nazi colors. Each chair is encircled by a low sand bulwark upon which the occupants have set inscriptions in fir-cones: *Waldesruh. Familie Walter. Stahlhelm. Heil Hitler!* . . . The other morning I saw a child of about five years old, stark naked, marching along all by himself with a swastika flag over his shoulder and singing '*Deutschland über alles.*'"[1]

As Isherwood highlights, symbols, both visual and auditory, served as an important way for the population to express outwardly its attitudes toward the state, the political system, and the nation. Furthermore, the vision of various flags and sand bulwarks points to the divisiveness caused and represented by symbolic forms during the Weimar era. This chapter explores the struggle over the state flag and colors in the Weimar Republic, as well as the conflict over the national anthem in Austria. With the change in political systems came the struggle to find new symbols to represent the republics.

---

1. Christopher Isherwood, *Goodbye to Berlin* (1939; reprint London: Triad/Panther Books, 1977), 91.

In Germany, the decision by the National Assembly to make black-red-gold the official colors of the new state led to the so-called *Flaggenstreit*, a "flag fight" between supporters of the new democratic tricolor and proponents of the black-white-red imperial standard. Even a compromise reached by the assembly, which made the merchant flag black-white-red with a small black-red-gold jack in the corner, failed to conciliate the supporters of the imperial colors. During the ensuing struggle, republicans, both political leaders and ordinary individuals alike, pursued different strategies to limit the exhibition of black-white-red banners, as well as to encourage and protect the display of black-red-gold flags. They crafted historical narratives in order to prove that the new colors were not so new after all and were rooted in a national tradition; they proudly displayed the flag to show that the republic did indeed have support; and they passed legislation and issued decrees to enforce the display of the black-red-gold tricolor.

For Austrians, the debate over state symbols focused on the national anthem. During the course of the First Republic, four songs vied for the designation of being Austria's anthem. In need of an anthem for the republic's army to play on official occasions, the rump state's government rejected keeping the imperial tune by Joseph Haydn and the lyrics of "God Preserve, God Protect Our Emperor, Our Country." An entirely new song, "German-Austria, Thou Magnificent Land," composed by Wilhelm Kienzl with lyrics by the socialist leader Karl Renner, became the de facto national anthem of Austria in 1920. This new anthem, however, failed to become popular, leading to calls for a restoration of the Haydn melody. The Christian Social government discarded the Renner-Kienzl anthem in 1929 and 1930 and decreed that "Be Blessed without End" would be the new official anthem. This move by the cabinet restored the Haydn melody with a text by the right-wing priest and poet Ottokar Kernstock, much to the dismay of the socialists. However, the return to the Haydn tune presented a new struggle over the anthem, as three different sets of lyrics could now be sung to the same Haydn melody: "God Preserve, God Protect Our Emperor, Our Country," "Be Blessed without End," or "Deutschland, Deutschland über alles."

The debates about symbols in both countries were not simply legislated or dictated from above. As Isherwood importantly indicates, ordinary members of society, both as individuals and through associations, actively participated in and shaped the contestation and legitimization of symbols. This chapter therefore moves beyond simply investigating the debates about symbols as a symptom of the fragmentation of German and Austrian political culture.[2] It demonstrates

---

2. For works emphasizing fragmentation see Detlef Lehnert and Klaus Megerle, eds., *Politische Identität und nationale Gedenktage: Zur politischen Kultur in der Weimarer Republik* (Opladen: West-deutscher Verlag, 1989); Detlef Lehnert and Klaus Megerle, "Problems of Identity and Consensus in a

TABLE 1.   The official anthems of Austria and Germany

Final anthem of Habsburg Austria	De facto anthem of the First Austrian Republic, 1920–1929	Anthem of the First Austrian Republic and the Austrofascist state, 1929–1938	Official anthem of the Weimar Republic, 1922–1933
"God Preserve, God Protect Our Emperor, Our Country"	"German-Austria, Thou Magnificent Land"	"Be Blessed without End"	"Deutschlandlied" ("Deutschland, Deutschland über alles")
Melody: Josef Haydn	Melody: Wilhelm Kienzl	Melody: Josef Haydn	Melody: Josef Haydn
Text: J. G. Seidl	Text: Karl Renner	Text: Ottokar Kernstock	Text: A. H. Hoffmann von Fallersleben

that these disputes are useful for exploring how Germans and Austrians conceptualized their political agency now that they were citizens of a democracy, a topic
that scholars are only beginning to analyze.[3]

What Isherwood's observation does not take into account, however, are the
complex relationships between various political viewpoints and nationalism.
As this chapter will show, black-white-red flags should not be labeled the only
form of "national" colors, and the enthusiasm for the "Deutschlandlied" did not
simply belong to the extreme right. To counter skeptics and outright opponents
of the republics, committed republicans drew on symbols linked to their *großdeutsch* nationalism, highlighting once again the importance that it had to the
republican struggle for legitimacy. Republicans in the Reich chose and defended
black-red-gold as the best representation of the nation because of its association
with the early nineteenth-century national movement, especially the revolution
of 1848, which had included Austrians and wanted to create a parliamentary
government. Black-white-red was the symbol of a *kleindeutsch* Germany that

---

Fragmented Society: The Weimar Republic," in *Political Culture in Germany*, ed. Dirk Berg-Schlosser
and Ralf Rytlewski (Houndmills, Basingstoke, UK: Macmillan, 1993), 43–59; Ernst Hanisch, "Politische Symbole und Gedächtnisorte," in *Handbuch des Politischen Systems Österreichs: Erste Republik,
1918–1938*, ed. Emmerich Tálos et. al. (Vienna: Manz Verlag, 1995), 421–30; Gustav Spann, "Fahne,
Staatswappen und Bundeshymne der Republik Österreich," http://www.demokratiezentrum.org/
media/data/staatswappen.pdf. Even Thomas Mergel, who has demonstrated that there was far greater
cooperation among opposing delegates in the Reichstag than has previously been thought, argues
that the debates about the flag and holidays led to the intractable divisions between the parties. Mergel, *Parlamentarische Kultur*, esp. 61–65 and 237–238.

3. Nadine Rossol, "Flaggenkrieg am Badestrand: Lokale Möglichkeiten repräsentativer Mitgestaltung in der Weimarer Republik," *Zeitschrift für Geschichtswissenschaft* 7/8 (2008): 617–637.

excluded Austria; only black-red-gold, a symbol admired by all parties in Austria, could serve as the emblem for a Greater Germany, members of the Weimar Coalition parties argued. Austrian socialists encouraged the singing of "Deutschland, Deutschland über alles," the national anthem of the Weimar Republic, in order both to protest their political opponents and to demonstrate their national sentiments. Furthermore, the uses of black-red-gold and the "Deutschlandlied" in the neighboring country played a significant role in republicans' choice of symbol and their attempt to widen support for it and the republics in general. This chapter therefore emphasizes the importance of looking at both Germany and Austria, and the dynamics between them, when examining the debates about political legitimacy in the Weimar and First Austrian Republics.

An exploration of cross-border connections in these debates also highlights differences between the experiments with democracy in the two countries. As the fight over the national anthem in the First Republic demonstrates, Austrians faced additional difficulties in trying to come to terms with the postwar situation. With the traditional characteristics of Austrianness—the multinational empire and the Habsburg monarchy—no longer available for use after 1918,[4] Austrians needed to redefine what it meant to be Austrian. Hence, while citizens of the Reich argued about which flag was authentically German, Austrians debated whether the anthem should symbolize their new rump state and its inhabitants or their membership in a larger German nation. Consequently, throughout the anthem dispute, government officials, political parties, and individuals lent their support to a particular anthem based not only on their political viewpoint, but also the way in which they negotiated the relationship between their Austrian and German identities. Austrians' attempts to find an anthem that could be reconciled with both their party politics and identity politics highlight another striking distinction between the German and Austrian debates: whereas a working-class and bourgeois coalition worked together in Germany to defend the republic and its symbols, Austrians became increasingly hardened along sociopolitical lines in their opposition to their adversaries' anthem preferences.

---

4. On prewar Austrian identity see Daniel Unowsky, *The Pomp and Politics of Patriotism: Imperial Celebrations in Habsburg Austria, 1848–1916* (West Lafayette, IN: Purdue University Press, 2005); Steven Beller, "Kraus's Firework: State Consciousness Raising in the 1908 Jubilee Parade in Vienna and the Problem of Austrian Identity," and Laurence Cole, "Patriotic Celebrations in Late-Nineteenth- and Early-Twentieth-Century Tirol," in *Staging the Past*, ed. Bucur and Wingfield, 46–71 and 75–111 respectively; Marsha Rozenblit, "Sustaining Austrian 'National' Identity in Crisis: The Dilemma of the Jews in Habsburg Austria, 1914–1919," in *Constructing Nationalities in East Central Europe*, ed. Pieter Judson and Marsha Rozenblit (New York: Berghahn Books, 2005), 178–191; Ernst Bruckmüller, *The Austrian Nation: Cultural Consciousness and Socio-Political Processes*, trans. Lowell A. Bangerter (Riverside, CA: Ariadne, 2003), esp. 275–317; Maureen Healy, *Vienna and the Fall of the Habsburg Empire*, chap. 4.

The Flag Debate in Germany

Throughout the Weimar Republic's existence, the issue of the state's colors aroused the political passions of large parts of the German population. This heated debate was not surprising, as the flag served as both a marker of one's opinion about the imperial past and as a barometer for one's feelings on the current form of government. From the moment the press began reporting that the National Assembly in Weimar was debating a change to Germany's official colors, Germans began to voice their opinions in the pages of the press, in messages sent to the government, and at rallies. Louise Modersohn-Breling, a painter living in the artist colony of Worpswede, was one such (newly enfranchised) citizen who felt compelled to make her views on the flag issue known to the government. Writing in March 1919, while the National Assembly was still drafting the constitution, she began by saying, "Please excuse an altogether unpolitical woman, who dares to write to you in order to also raise her little voice for once." While recognizing that some "heroic deeds" were carried out under the colors black-white-red, she argued that these colors were also reminders of the hardships of the Great War. She therefore supported the move in the National Assembly to make black-red-gold the official colors, for as she wrote, "The new Germany needs new colors!"[5] Although somewhat hesitant in its appropriation of the voice of new citizen activity, Modersohn-Breling's letter exemplified the expanded possibilities for political participation and the new forms of agency brought about by the First World War and its political consequences. The letter, one of many received by the government, shows how larger numbers of Germans now exercised what they saw as the rights and responsibilities of a citizen living in a full-fledged democracy.

Numerous Germans, however, used these rights and the enhanced relationship between the government and its citizenry to call for the maintenance of the imperial tricolor and to challenge the new flag. Using the language and practices associated with "rule by the people, for the people," the bearers of black-white-red pursued a number of different strategies in an effort to impact the government's handling of the issue. During the republic's early years, organizations and individuals attempted to communicate their opinions to officials. The Central Association of the Seamen's Guild, the Association of German Maritime Clubs, Freikorps soldiers, the North German Hansabund, and German communities living abroad were among the organizations that wrote letters of protest.[6] Groups

---

5. Letter from Louise Modersohn-Breling to the Ministerpräsident, Fischerhude bei Bremen, 22 March 1919, in BAB, R1501/116480, Bl. 25.

6. For collections of letters received by the government consult BAB, R1501/116480–116485, and PAAA, R98311–R98326.

also tried to demonstrate their strength by organizing petition campaigns. Members of the German People's Party in Görlitz, for example, collected over four thousand signatures in a petition drive during May 1919 to protest any move to change Germany's flag.[7]

To convince the government of the widespread popular support for black-white-red, proponents of the imperial flag organized public gatherings in an effort to make a literal show of strength. In a telegram sent to the Social Democratic member of parliament Philipp Scheidemann in April 1919, a representative of the DVP reported that a gathering of one thousand people in Zeitz supported keeping the black-white-red colors for "patriotic and economic reasons."[8] Such activity was not simply confined to the early postwar period, when the constitution was still being drafted. A full six years after the National Assembly made black-red-gold the official colors of Germany, the German National Workers' League expended a great deal of effort to organize rallies in Landsberg-Warthe, Blumenhagen, Osterode, Gallnow, Schneidemühl, Guben, Dortmund, and Stettin in order to show that its organization, alongside the German National People's Party and "patriotic associations," would "do everything to ensure that the black-white-red flag, under which Germany experienced the greatest political, economic, social, and cultural upturn, once again becomes the legally recognized flag of the Reich."[9]

Moreover, groups such as the Naval League of German Women, a German maritime shipping association, the German People's League Black-White-Red, and the Reich's League "Black-White-Red" appealed to federal officials for a popular referendum to be held on the matter, an act highlighting the democratization of political culture in postwar Germany.[10] Demonstrating particular political savvy for the new democratic system, the last two organizations joined forces "to reestablish the black-white-red flag as the Reich's flag through legal means according to article 73 of the Reich's constitution." According to article 73 of the Weimar Constitution, the president could call for a plebiscite to alter an existing law. Already having gained the support of 1.2 million people, the two groups called on "all German men and women" to send their votes in order to persuade President Ebert to pursue this course of action. These associations explained to readers of the *Deutsche Zeitung* in the spring of 1923, "It is the duty

7. "Schwarz-Weiß-Rot. In Größe entstanden, in Ehren geführt!," *Berliner Neueste Nachrichten*, 8 May 1919, in BAB, R1501/116480, Bl. 45.

8. Telegram from Dr. Duering to Ministerpraesident Scheidemann, 25 April 1919, in BAB, R1501/116480, Bl. 43.

9. See letters in BAB, R1501/116485, Bl. 160–172; 201–202.

10. See letters in BAB, R1501/116480–116485.

of every German citizen eligible to vote to give his vote to our leagues, so that the black-white-red flag waves over us once again." They concluded their request by assuring readers "that every vote is important—also yours."[11] As this example and further ones below demonstrate, the groups aligned with the black-white-red flag possessed an understanding of how to use democratic conceptions for their own benefit.

Among this diverse group backing the imperial standard, a few central arguments about the historical and contemporary importance of the colors black-white-red emerged as a means to substantiate their appeals to the government. The proponents of the imperial standard pointed to the achievements that their flag had come to symbolize both at home and abroad. A statement put forth by the German People's Party in Guben on the 104th anniversary of Bismarck's birth in 1919 nicely sums up this aspect of the black-white-red supporters' case. "Under the colors black-white-red," it declared, "the new German Reich was founded and has grown into a world power, German trade and the German navy have achieved their international reputation."[12] Over the course of the Weimar Republic, adherents of the political right repeatedly cited this association of Bismarck's unification and Germany's attainment of world-power status with the imperial tricolor as a way to justify their position.

The champions of black-white-red were not simply concerned with the reputation of Germany throughout the world; they also pointed to the meaning these colors had for Germans living abroad. Communities of German citizens residing overseas were vocal proponents of the imperial standard in the flag debate. In a referendum organized by the Association of German Citizens in Mexico, only two people affirmed support for the republic's new flag, while eighteen hundred voted in favor of the imperial flag. Some of those in the majority even threatened not to set foot in the German embassy if it flew the black-red-gold flag.[13] As a number of petitions sent from Germans living abroad stated, "These colors [black-white-red] still symbolize today that which was and has remained our strength: the unification of the German tribes!"[14] For these *Auslandsdeutsche* (Germans abroad), the old tricolor was a visual marker of their continued loyalty and connection to the Reich.

---

11. "Für Schwarz-Weiß-Rot," *Deutsche Zeitung*, May 1923, Nr. 232, in BAB, R1501/116480, Bl. 144.

12. Deutsche Volkspartei, Ortsgruppe Guben, 31 March 1919, in BAB, R1501/116480, Bl. 28.

13. Copy of Report 29 from the Deutsche Gesandtschaft in Mexico to the Auswärtige Amt Berlin, Mexico, 23 January 1922, in BAB, R1501/116483, Bl. 50.

14. "Deutsche Männer! Deutsche Frauen!" appears twice in PAAA, R98311, fiche 3.

Residents in the Reich also stressed the significance of the imperial banner for supporting Germans who inhabited areas beyond the borders of Germany. The attendees of a 1919 rally in Neustadtgödens explained, "Black-white-red alone is the bond that connects all Germans abroad with the homeland [Heimat]."[15] And Admiral Adolf von Trotha, a participant in the Kapp Putsch and Nazi movement, warned, "These Germans in the diaspora will probably never acquire a black-red-gold flag for themselves, and the danger exists that they will lose their Germanness and will again simply become cultural fertilizer for other states."[16] Furthermore, in the eyes of the black-white-red supporters in the Reich, the imperial flag had become important to the struggles over Schleswig and East Prussia, as well as the occupied territories of the Rhine, Ruhr, and Saar.[17] For its supporters, black-white-red served both in the past and the present as a way to unite, strengthen, and guard Germans and their interests around the world. In line with the nationalisms of the political right, which put emphasis on the "lost territories" and German world power, the bearers of the imperial flag stressed that any change to the emblem of Germanness threatened to sever the links between the Auslandsdeutsche and the Reich, thereby further diminishing Germany's stature after the war.

Not only did the imperial banner protect the reputation of Germany abroad, but it had also played a role in defending Germany during the Great War, its supporters insisted. With these colors, the army "has fought victoriously against a world of enemies," as the officers of the First Saxon Foot Artillery Regiment Nr. 12 put in a letter to the Prussian war minister. To disregard this flag would be "an ignominy."[18] For the black-white-red devotees, the old flag was closely connected to the sacrifice of the fallen soldiers during the Great War. To properly honor their courage and memory, the imperial flag should be preserved.[19] Any change in the flag would defame the fallen and give the appearance that

---

15. Telegram from Hoefker to the Reichsregierung in Weimar, 18 June 1919, in BAB, R1501/116480, Bl. 73.

16. Nr. 238, Verfassungsgebende deutsche Nationalversammlung. 8. Ausschuß, communication from von Trotha dated 9 May 1919, in BAB, R1501/116480, Bl. 47–49, here Rs. of 48.

17. Gustav Stresemann, "Flaggenfrage und Volksentscheid," Tägliche Rundschau, 22 January 1921, in BAB, R1501/116480, Bl. 112; "Für Schwarz-Weiß-Rot," Deutsche Zeitung, May 1923, Nr. 232, in BAB, R1501/116480, Bl. 144.

18. Letter from the Oberstleutnant u. Kdr of the 1. Sächs. Fussartl. Regts. Nr. 12 to the Preuss. Kriegsminister, Chemnitz, in BAB, R1501/116480, Rs. of Bl. 80.

19. Dr. Jügler, "Die Schuld am Flaggenkrieg," Berliner Börsen-Zeitung (BBZ), 23 September 1927, in BAB, R72/1316, Bl. 145; Telegram from Hoefker to the Reichsregierung in Weimar, 18 June 1919, in BAB, R1501/116480, Bl. 73; Letter from the Hauptgeschäftsstelle des Flottenbundes Deutscher Frauen E.V. to Reichskanzler Dr. Wirth, Leipzig, 1 August 1921, in BAB, R1501/116485, Bl. 1.

Germany had behaved immorally during the war. It would, according to the black-white-red supporters, validate the Treaty of Versailles and the "war-guilt clause."[20]

Although a number of protest letters to the republican government stated that "black-white-red is neither monarchical nor republican," political loyalties played a role in the defense of the imperial colors.[21] Many of those on the right of the political spectrum used the black-white-red flag as a way to protest the new system and proclaim allegiance to the imperial government. An anonymous card from "a German" linked the dislike of the black-red-gold tricolor with praise for the monarchy. Advancing a pessimistic interpretation of Germany's current state, a verse on the card read, "Against Black-Red-Yellow (Gold): Black is the future; Red is the present; Gold was the past." Contrasting the bleak present and future with the glorious past, it continued, "In spite of everything and nevertheless: With God for King and Fatherland: So we want to live and die!!!"[22] Other bearers of the imperial flag went beyond simply praising the monarchy and sought to destroy the republic. The participants in the Kapp Putsch used these colors as their symbol in their 1920 attempt to overthrow the democratic government, as did the right-wing and conservative paramilitary groups of the Freikorps and the Stahlhelm.[23]

Not all black-white-red proponents desired to use the imperial flag to mount a direct challenge to the republic. For those like Gustav Stresemann and his party, the DVP, the desire to maintain the imperial flag did not necessarily entail a rejection of democracy.[24] While claiming "that not only the politics of blood and iron, but also the connections of the ideas of the Frankfurt Parliament [of 1848] to Bismarck's *Realpolitik*, have enabled the building of the Reich," Stresemann, in a 1921 article, pushed for a referendum to reinstate the black-white-red flag. He stressed that the socialists were overreaching in their interpretation of the imperial flag as a "symbol of reaction and monarchist backlash."[25] Rather,

20. Letter from the Oberstleutnant u. Kdr of the 1. Sächs. Fussartl. Regts. Nr. 12 to the Preuss. Kriegsminister, Chemnitz, in BAB, R1501/116480, Rs. of Bl. 80.

21. "Kundgebung für die Wiedereinführung der schwarz-weiss-roten Reichsflagge," enclosed in a letter from the Deutsches Konsulat in Tegucigalpa to Kanzler Fehrenbach, 30 March 1921, in PAAA, R98311.

22. Handwritten card from "ein Deutscher" with black-white-red ribbon pasted on it, 29 July 1922, in BAB, R1501/116485, Bl. 117.

23. Alois Friedel, *Deutsche Staatssymbole: Herkunft und Bedeutung der politischen Symbolik in Deutschland* (Frankfurt am Main: Anthenäum Verlag, 1968), 34.

24. On Stresemann's views see Stephen Fritz, "The Search for Volksgemeinschaft: Gustav Stresemann and the Baden DVP, 1926–1930," *German Studies Review* 7, no. 2 (1984): 249–280.

25. Gustav Stresemann, "Flaggenfrage und Volksentscheid," *Tägliche Rundschau*, 22 January 1921, in BAB, R1501/116480, Bl. 112.

"black-white-red is our pride in the past and our hope for the future."[26] Even the left liberal German Democratic Party, which became a staunch defender of the republican flag, briefly lent its support to the black-white-red banner as a way to protest the Treaty of Versailles, an incident that the advocates of the imperial tricolor used to substantiate their case.[27]

Despite these differences in attitude toward the Weimar Republic, the black-white-red supporters maintained that only these colors could represent the German nation. Indeed, much of the debate between the two sides of the *Flaggenstreit* revolved around which color scheme truly embodied the Volk. For those opposing the republic's new flag, not only did the black-white-red combination symbolize all the best characteristics of Germans, but black-red-gold was un-German. As a 1924 German National People's Party campaign poster for impending elections exclaimed, "We fight for black-white-red," which entailed a battle for all that was "Christian, *völkisch*, national, social."[28] In contrast, many on the political right viewed the black-red-gold-flag as "essentially foreign and unloved," with "colors that *no one* in the fatherland understands."[29]

Relying on their arguments about the existence of multiple forms of German nationalism, republicans went to great lengths to counter their opponents' claims that the black-red-gold flag was an unsuitable national symbol. The distinctive form of nationalism created by republicans thus played a central role in their defense of the Weimar Republic's colors. As part of their attempt to legitimate the republic's flag, republicans cited anew nineteenth-century history in order to demonstrate that these colors were not foreign to Germany. Just as we saw them do in chapter 1 with regard to the democratic form of government, republicans highlighted the use of black-red-gold in the Wars of Liberation against Napoleon, the Wartburg festival, the Hambach festival, the National Assembly of 1848–1849, and the Schiller festival of 1859 in order to argue that the republican colors were central to the intertwined movements for national unity and political reform. On the occasion of a Republican Day hosted by the Reichsbanner Schwarz-Rot-Gold in 1926, the writer and historian Ricarda Huch pointed to this

---

26. Letter from the Deutsche Volkspartei to the Reichsregierung Berlin, Wilhelmshaven, 20 June 1919, in BAB, R1501/116480, Bl. 82.

27. "10 Jahre Schwarz-Rot-Gold," *BBZ*, 4 July 1929, in BAB, R72/1316, Bl. 43. Also see Achilles, "Re-forming the Reich," 100, 105–106, 116.

28. Deutschnationale Volkspartei, "Gegen den Marxismus und seine Schleppenträger!: Schwarz-weiß-rot gegen schwarz-rot-gelb!" [1924] (received through interlibrary loan from the Universitätsbibliothek Heidelberg).

29. First quote is from a letter from the Hauptgeschäftsstelle des Flottenbundes Deutscher Frauen E.V. to Reichskanzler Dr. Wirth, Leipzig, 1 August 1921, in BAB, R1501/116485, Bl. 1. Second quote is from a letter from the Deutscher See-Verein, Ortsgruppe Berlin-Friedenau to the Deutsche Reichsregierung, 2 September 1921, in BAB, R1501/116485, Bl. 35. Emphasis in original.

connection in her affirmation of the republic's flag. "I love the black-red-gold colors," she stated, "as did the German dueling societies and the first German National Assembly [in 1848–1849], which first voiced a patriotic [*vaterländisch*] attitude, an appreciation of freedom and public life, and compassion for the weak and needy and which knew to suffer and die for these ideas."[30]

Furthermore, in reciting their republican version of German history, black-red-gold supporters once again looked beyond the borders of the Reich in their attempt to popularize the republic and its colors. Used by the nineteenth-century national movement, the black-red-gold tricolor was the "emblem of the unity of the whole of Germany, as far as the German tongue sounds, based on a liberal form of state," argued Wilhelm Erman, the former head librarian at the University of Bonn.[31] In an age when national belonging (*Volkszugehörigkeit*) trumped citizenship (*Staatszugehörigkeit*),[32] republicans did not allow supporters of right-wing and conservative ideals to be the sole voice of a German community that extended past state boundaries.

Although Erman, like other republicans, pointed to a wider German community, it was Austria that garnered the attention of the black-red-gold proponents. "Our most important argument in the flag conflict lies in the *großdeutsch* meaning of the colors black-red-gold," proclaimed Heinrich Hirtsiefer, a member of the Center Party and the Catholic union movement.[33] Such an emphasis, which contrasted with the imperial and *völkisch* concerns of the political right, was a direct outgrowth of republicans' decision to use the *großdeutsch* idea as the basis of a republican form of nationalism. The *großdeutsch* idea consequently became a cornerstone of their contention that the republican banner was an authentic German national symbol. As it had in the historical narratives discussed in chapter 1, the revolution of 1848–1849 figured prominently in the justifications of the republican tricolor. The symbol chosen by the members of the Frankfurt Parliament was the black-red-gold banner. Adorning St. Paul's Church, the meeting location of the representatives, these three colors came to represent a *großdeutsch* and democratic solution to the so-called German Question. In the

---

30. Ricarda Huch, "Ich liebe die demokratische Republik," *Festschrift zum republikanischen Tag am 6. Juni 1926 in Weissenfels A.S.*, ed. Reichsbanner Schwarz-Rot-Gold Ortsgruppe Weissenfels a.S. (Alfred Grünbeyer), 20, in AdsD, Reichsbanner, Exponate 24. Also see Ernst Jäger, *Schwarz-Rot-Gold in der deutschen Geschichte: Kulturhistorischer Beitrag zur Flaggenfrage* (Berlin: Druck- und Verlagsgesellschaft Sawage and Co., [1925]).

31. Wilhelm Erman, "Schwarz-Rot-Gold in der Geschichte," *VZ*, 27 January 1925, in BAB, R1501/116480, Bl. 178.

32. Gosewinkel, *Einbürgern*, chap. 7; Sammartino, *Impossible Border*.

33. Heinrich Hiertsiefer [sic], "Die Republikanisierung Deutschlands," *NFP*, 17 September 1926, in a letter from the Deutsche Gesandtschaft Wien to the Auswärtige Amt Berlin, Vienna, 18 September 1926, in PAAA, R73298.

Weimar period, therefore, republicans pointed to this legacy in order to illustrate that the republic's colors were part of an authentic and historically justified national tradition.[34] Hence, on behalf of the thousands gathered for a 1925 Reichsbanner Constitution Day celebration in Neustadt-Ostholstein, representatives of the republican group sent a telegram to the chancellor voicing their support for the black-red-gold flag because it "is the expression of the historical *großdeutsch* people's state [*Volksstaat*]."[35]

While the nineteenth-century attempt at forming a *großdeutsch* democratic state was central to the defense of the black-red-gold flag, republicans also looked to a *großdeutsch* democratic state of the future. Another telegram, sent on behalf of eight thousand individuals gathered in Flensburg for the 1925 Reichsbanner festivities, urged the government to maintain black-red-gold as the official colors because they were an "expression of the coming *Grossdeutschland*."[36] Given the strong support among republicans for an Anschluss, black-red-gold devotees argued that the imperial flag, the symbol of *Kleindeutschland*, would alienate Austrians when a political union finally happened. In a 1928 speech to Reichsbanner members in Potsdam, Otto Baumgarten, a theologian at the University of Kiel, raised this point in explaining why, after an initial reluctance to see the black-white-red flag replaced, he came to "love" the colors black-red-gold. Claiming that under black-white-red neither political freedom nor unity occurred, he added, "Our German-Austrian brothers, who belong to us, could never find themselves together with us under the colors black-white-red, which are foreign to them, while black-red-gold is dear and familiar to them as the colors of German unity."[37]

Baumgarten's statement touches upon another piece of the larger republican project to demonstrate the connections among democracy, the republican standard, and Germanness. Black-white-red represented the narrow dynastic interests of the Hohenzollerns, whose rivalry with the Habsburgs had led to the exclusion of Austria from a German nation-state in 1866. As an essay in an undated pamphlet of the Reichsbanner stated, "The unification of both brother-republics can

---

34. "Festschmuck in den Straßen Frankfurts," in *Gedenkschrift zur Erinnerung an das erste deutsche Parlament* (Frankfurt am Main: Frankfurt Societäts-Druckerei, [1923]), in BAB, R1501/116869, Rs. of Bl. 51.

35. Telegram from the Reichsbanner Schwarz-Rot-Gold in Neustadt-Ostholstein to the Herrn Reichskanzler, 10 August 1925, in BAB, R1501/116485, Bl. 214.

36. Telegram from the Reichsbanner Schwarz-Rot-Gold und der republikanischen "Kriegsteilnehmer" to the Herrn Reichskanzler, Flensburg, 12 August 1925, in BAB, R1501/116485, Bl. 205. Also see Telegram from versammelte Republikaner to the Reichskanzler, Schleswig, 12 August 1925, in BAB, R1501/116485, Bl. 211.

37. "Die Bedeutung der deutschen Nationalfarben," *BT*, 25 October 1928, in BAB, R72/1316, Bl. 79.

only be accomplished by republicans, only by the black-red-gold movement."[38] National unity, according to this standpoint, could happen only under the colors black-red-gold because they represented a democratic form of government, which put national interests above particularistic ones. Hugo Preuss, father of the Weimar Constitution, member of the German Democratic Party, and a target of anti-Semites because of his Jewish heritage, nicely tied together all these various points of the black-red-gold supporters' arguments in a 1924 speech to commemorate the signing of the Weimar Constitution:

> With the colors black-red-gold connects the heartfelt and firm conviction that in the great, German, free system of government, all German national comrades [*Volksgenossen*] must and will find themselves together. The separation of the German brothers in Austria from the shared fatherland, which was caused by the Habsburg and Hohenzollern dynasties, must and will again be overcome through the collapse of these dynasties. The colors black-red-gold symbolize for entire generations the dream of unity and freedom. And, today . . . it is downright absurd when these colors are ostracized by the so-called national side. The true Reich's banner of national unity is thereby ostracized.[39]

Preuss's statement demonstrates once again that the national value of a particular color scheme was at the center of the *Flaggenstreit*. Significantly, he turned the question of who really represented the national interests of Germany against conservatives and the radical right. The continued refusal by the political right in the Reich to support the *großdeutsch* colors enabled Preuss to challenge the nationalism of his opponents, while highlighting republicans' national convictions.

The importance of Austria to the black-red-gold movement was not simply rhetorical. Cross-border interactions and developments within Austria also factored into arguments in support of the Weimar Republic's tricolor. Indeed, the inclusion of the *großdeutsch* colors in the third draft of the Weimar Constitution

---

38. Senator Gerth, "Schwarz-Rot-Gold und Schwarz-Weiß-Rot," *Das Reichsbanner Schwarz-Rot-Gold* (Berlin: Verlag für Sozialwissenschaft, o.D.), 32, in AdsD, NL Franz Osterroth, box 53, Fasz. 140.

39. "Professor Dr. Hugo Preuß in seiner Rede im deutschen Nationaltheater in Weimar am 11. August 1924," *Großdeutscher republikanischer Volkstag für Südwestdeutschland in Frankfurt a.M., Samstag, den 8., Sonntag, den 9. u. Dienstag (Verfassungstag), den 11. August 1925, Programm und Liedertexte*, 16, in AdsD, Reichsbanner Schwarz-Rot-Gold, Nummer 145. For more on Preuss's views see Detlef Lehnert and Christoph Mueller, "Perspectives and Problems of a Rediscovery of Hugo Preuss" (Hugo-Preuss-Gesellschaft e.V., o.D.), http://www2.hu-berlin.de/Hugo-Preuss-Gesellschaft/intro_e.pdf.

was due to the involvement of Austrian officials, particularly Ludo Moritz Hart-mann. Because an Anschluss was still a possibility until the summer of 1919, two Austrian representatives were present at the negotiations of the States' Commit-tee and later in the National Assembly in Weimar. Hartmann was one of these representatives, as well as the Austrian envoy to Berlin, a member of the SDAP, and the son of Moritz Hartmann, the famed poet and German-Bohemian rep-resentative to the 1848 National Assembly in Frankfurt. In debates about the Reich's official colors, Hartmann stated, "Indeed, I believe that I may in fact say that these colors [black-red-gold] associate themselves with the memory of the ideals, which we in Austria still pursue today. In contrast, the colors black-white-red cannot have the popularity in Austria like they have in Germany because the memory of Prussian hegemony is connected with the colors black-white-red."[40] It was at Hartmann's insistence that Austrians would not accept black-white-red as their colors that Preuss added article 3, which stated that the official colors of the Reich would be black, red, and gold.[41]

In affirming the importance of their color scheme to the German Volk, the supporters of black-red-gold also noted the use of their flag in Austria before and after the collapse of the Austro-Hungarian Empire. The use of this flag in Austria was noteworthy because the Habsburg monarchy's official colors were black-yellow and the rump state's official flag was red-white-red.[42] Citing a press notice that mentioned "in German-Austria, they have maintained the black-red-gold colors as the symbol of the *großdeutsch* idea," the Reich Interior Ministry asked the Foreign Office in 1922 for more information about Austrian attitudes toward the black-red-gold flag in order to understand "the continuing battle about the Reich's colors in the population."[43] The German ambassador in Vienna began his answer to the inquiry by explaining that "ever since the fraternities' colors black-red-gold appeared for the first time as a symbol of German national unity at the Wartburg festival for the celebration of the fatherland's freedom in

---

40. Quoted in Paul Löbe, "Österreichs Recht und die Weimarer Nationalversammlung," in *Deutsche Einheit, Deutsche Freiheit: Gedenkbuch der Reichsregierung zum 10. Verfassungstag, 11. August 1929* (Berlin: Zentralverlag, 1929), 200.

41. Buchner, *Um nationale und republikanische Identität*, 77–78; Rohe, *Das Reichsbanner*, 237, fn. 4; Suval, *Anschluss Question*, 25.

42. Following World War I, Christian Social Wilhelm Miklas suggested making red-white-red the colors of a reduced Austria, a proposition approved by the Staatsrat on 21 October 1918. The colors red and white stemmed from the Babenberg dynasty and were most likely a way to reference Austria's imperial heritage without using Habsburg symbols. Gustav Spann, "Zur Geschichte von Flagge and Wappen der Republik Österreich," in *Österreichs politische Symbole: Historisch, ästhetisch und ideologiekritisch beleuchtet*, ed. Norbert Leser and Manfred Wagner (Vienna: Böhlau Verlag, 1994), 37–64.

43. Letter from the Reichsminister des Innern (Brecht) to the Auswärtige Amt, Berlin, 1 May 1922, in BAB, R1501/116483, Bl. 104.

October 1817, they have for the Germans in Austria acquired historical meaning as the symbol of the *großdeutsch* idea." Hence, while the significance of black-red-gold had diminished for Reich Germans after 1871, "these colors remain alive for all Germans in Austria, who carry the longing for a union in their hearts."[44] Two articles, one in the right-wing *Deutschösterreichische Tages-Zeitung* and the other in a Greater German magazine titled *Deutsches Vaterland*, included with his letter affirmed the role that these colors played for German speakers in the Habsburg monarchy.

As the Reich German observers of the situation in Austria noted, the bearers of the black-red-gold banner there occupied a wide range on the political spectrum. On one end of the spectrum were Austrian socialists, who joined the republicans in the Reich to support the black-red-gold flag on both a political and national basis. Echoing the claim by Preuss that republicans were better Germans than their opponents, Otto Bauer, the leader of the SDAP, penned a piece for the main socialist paper in the Reich in which he argued that the champions of black-white-red and black-yellow wanted to go back to the imperial era when the Second Reich "had expelled the German-Austrians" and the Habsburgs had "kept the German-Austrians away from Germany in order to shackle them to an empire that was two-thirds Slav." Whereas the imperial colors were a symbol of this divisive past, black-red-gold represented a promising national future. The republican colors do "not return to the dynasties, whose fight for dominance ripped apart the German Volk; rather, [black-red-gold looks] forward to the one great German republic that alone can unite all the German tribes [*Stämme*] in its fold."[45] Given the shared *großdeutsch* nationalism between the Austrian Social Democrats and the Weimar Coalition parties, Bauer sought to support his fellow republicans in Germany during the *Flaggenstreit*.

In contrast to the situation in Germany, however, republican forces were not the only proponents of these colors in Austria; the radical right in the rump state also saw them as a national emblem. A note with the ambassador's letter explained that because this flag served "as a battle symbol against the un-German environment" during the Habsburg era, "the curious fact often arises that, while in the German Reich black-red-gold, although the constitutionally established colors, are dismissed by large sectors of the population, derided as 'un-German' and maligned, in the neighboring country, black-red-gold, although not the country's colors, are honored and shown everywhere with pride as the noted symbol

---

44. Letter from Deutsche Gesandtschaft Wien (Dr. Pfeiffer) to the Auswärtige Amt, Vienna, 6 June 1922, in BAB, R1501/116483, Bl. 189, and in PAAA, R98314.

45. The piece originally appeared in *Vorwärts* and was reprinted in Otto Bauer, "Das Schwarz-Rot-Gold der Oesterreicher," *OeD*, December 1924, 11.

of Germanness."[46] Right-wing groups in Austria carried the black-red-gold flag at rallies protesting the peace treaties and even praised the colors.[47] In 1924, for instance, a *völkisch* press in Austria produced a booklet that contained a poem praising the "holy colors black-red-gold" alongside a personal dedication from Erich Ludendorff, one-half of the Third Supreme Command in Germany during World War I and a participant in right-wing politics after 1918.[48] Although the German nationalists in Austria acknowledged that they would support the use of black-white-red should the majority of Germans want this flag,[49] they continued to value and use black-red-gold. In Austria, groups with differing political world-views saw the black-red-gold banner as an authentic German symbol, although one invested with different meanings.

Republicans called attention to this widespread use of their flag in Austria in their defense of the black-red-gold tricolor. Echoing Preuss's and Bauer's challenge to the political right, Richart Mischler stated, "If those Prussian enthusiasts feel all-German [*gesamtdeutsch*], then they must stop sullying black-red-gold, the colors which since 1848 are holy for all Germans, all parties in Austria. Otherwise, they [Austrians], those national comrades [*Volksgenossen*] who at last want to return 'home to the Reich,' would have to have concerns, for they would expect the burden of a new monarchism, of a status as second-class citizens behind Prussia."[50] Transborder connections therefore played a central role in the endeavors of republicans in the Reich to challenge the argument that black-white-red was the only symbol that could represent the German Volk.

For supporters of the two color schemes, the *Flaggenstreit* was not simply limited to this inconclusive rhetorical battle. Beyond the war of words, the two sides also took the fight to the streets. Each group pursued two main strategies: the demonstration of its strength and popularity by widely displaying its flag, and the attempt to limit the opponents' ability to display their colors. During the early years of the republic, the proponents of black-red-gold were at a distinct disadvantage in this regard. Because of economic conditions and material shortages, they had difficulties manufacturing the new flag; even the government itself struggled to provide offices, ships, and consulates with the appropriate flag.[51]

---

46. "Schwarz-rot-gold im heutigen Deutsch-Österreich," in BAB, R1501/116483, Bl. 193.

47. For examples of how right-wing Austrians used the colors see reports on the *völkisch* rallies against the peace treaties, in ÖStA, AdR, NPA, BKA, AA, Kt. 224 alt, Kt. 178–79 neu, Liasse Oesterreich 2/4, Versammlungen und Demonstrationen.

48. "Die Oesterreicher und Schwarz-Rot-Gold," *OeD*, December 1924, 15.

49. Dr. Jaeger, "Beiträge zur Flaggen-Frage," *Kieler Zeitung*, May 15, in BAB, R32/304, Bl. 47.

50. Richart Mischler, "Das Reichsbanner und Potsdam," in *Das Reichsbanner und Potsdam*, 15–18, here 17, in AdsD, Reichsbanner, Exponate 30.

51. Achilles, "Re-forming the Reich," 157–161.

Institutions and ships were consequently allowed to continue flying the old imperial flag until January 1, 1922.

Once the production of flags no longer proved to be such a hurdle, republicans saw the flag as a tool to demonstrate the vigor of the republic and their version of nationalism. Republican politicians consequently put out calls for their supporters to show their colors. Thus, when the city of Bochum prepared to celebrate the Ruhr's liberation from French and Belgian troops, the socialist *Volksblatt* warned that right-wing organizations "would like to prove to the federal and provincial governments that the majority of people in the Ruhr stand behind them; they expect to achieve this moral victory through a garish emphasis of black-white-red colors." Calling on the "wide circles of republicans, socialist and bourgeois" to display doubly as many black-red-gold flags as the bearers of black-white-red, the paper declared that the right-wing associations must not be able to reach their goal. "If on the coming Thursday the republicans stand bravely by their colors," the article continued, "then [President] Hindenburg and [Chancellor Hans] Luther will recognize how little the people of the Ruhr think about supporting barren and idiotic nationalism. The intended demonstration by the right will then subside as so many before it. The moral success must be through the colors of the republic. Therefore: Bring out the flags for the demonstration for black-red-gold!"[52]

Central to this endeavor to popularize and defend the black-red-gold tricolor was the Reichsbanner Schwarz-Rot-Gold, whose name and purpose encapsulated these intertwined tasks. As a member of the organization explained on the occasion of the 1926 Constitution Day, the Reichsbanner's objective was "to protect the symbols of the republic and to make them familiar to the entire Volk." Claiming that the association had achieved its goal, the writer forcefully argued that the growing numbers of black-red-gold flags displayed during Reichsbanner marches and hung from the windows of private residences during Reichsbanner events were a demonstration that the "heart of the republic beats here!"[53] Nor did the Reichsbanner limit its activities to the Reich. With chapters located abroad, the Reichsbanner, alongside other local republican groups, also worked to anchor the republic and its colors among *Auslandsdeutsche*. An editor of the liberal *Argentinisches Tageblatt* remarked on the occasion of the ninth anniversary of the Weimar Constitution, "We proudly and happily let our black-red-gold banner

---

52. "Zum Besuch Hindenburgs," 15 September 1925, in AdsD, NL Carl Severing, Abteilung 1, Mappe 127.

53. Gottfried Rade, "3 Jahre—Reichsbanner!," in *Festschrift des Reichsbanners Schwarz-Rot-Gold Gau Hessen-Cassel zur Feier des Verfassungstages 1926*, ed. Gauleitung Hessen-Cassel des Reichsbanners Schwarz-Rot-Gold, 10–11, here 11, in AdsD, NL Franz Osterroth, box 53, Fasz. 140.

unfurl. We have seen the number of our enemies dwindle and the number of our comrades grow in the last nine years."[54] While remarks by both men had a propagandistic purpose, they were not incorrect in assessing the increasing strength of the Reichsbanner. Although constantly challenged by the political right, the organization achieved a considerable amount of success in generating support for the republic and its symbols. Historian Benjamin Ziemann estimates that the organization had about 900,000 members at its peak, a number far larger than the 350,000 individuals who constituted its main opponent, the Stahlhelm.[55] The participants in the Reichsbanner, as well as the people that partook in their celebrations, helped to spread the black-red-gold tricolor across Germany and beyond.

Of course, republican organizations were not alone in viewing the flag as a visual marker of power and support, or lack thereof. The political right, in addition to encouraging its supporters to display the black-white-red flag, used a variety of strategies to curtail support for the republican colors. During the 1928 Constitution Day, for example, an anonymous writer with clear antirepublican tendencies walked around Eisenach to gauge backing for the republic by counting the numbers of flags residents hung up for the celebration. During his tour of some fifty streets and plazas, he claimed to have seen only seven "small" republican flags. Such a poor showing for the republic's colors, in his eyes, proved that the republic and its symbolic manifestations remained unpopular.[56] While highlighting the alleged lack of support for the black-red-gold tricolor, the political right also endeavored to limit the display of it by verbally and physically assaulting the republican flag and its supporters. In one instance, two students, with the encouragement of two Reichswehr soldiers, cut down a black-red-gold flag displayed in Konstanz on the occasion of a Reichsbanner Republican Day. Offering conflicting accounts, the soldiers claimed that they prompted the students to take action by singing "Proudly Waves the Flag Black-White-Red"; the students asserted that they had acted after a soldier displayed a swastika and said "Come, we're going to rip down the Jew-Flag."[57] Regardless of which explanation was true, the episode represented a chief problem faced by the Weimar Republic: the questionable or absent loyalty among individuals populating key state institutions, such as the army.

---

54. "Schwarzrotgold im Ausland," *DR* (Beilage), 23 September 1928, 262.

55. Ziemann, *Contested Commemorations*, 15.

56. "30 Strassen und 7 Fahnen," *Eisenacher Zeitung*, 14 August 1928, in BAB, R1501/125653, here Rs. of Bl. 133.

57. Abschrift, Meldung des Pol. Wachtmeisters Geigges to the Staatsanwaltschaft, Konstanz, 23 May 1926, in BAB, R1501/125653, Bl. 37–39.

Yet republicans did not stand idly by as the political right launched attacks against the republican flag. Adherents of the republic who occupied public office passed a series of laws and issued various ordinances to try to protect the republic's symbols and restrict the exhibition of the imperial flag. The most important piece of legislation was the Law for the Protection of the Republic, which was in effect from July 1922 to July 1929 and from March 1930 to December 1932. Passed in response to the assassination of Walther Rathenau, the law made it illegal to insult the republic or its flag. Democratic authorities at the federal, provincial, and local levels also promulgated a number of decrees that sought to govern the flying of flags on a wide range of objects, including hotels, sailboats, and Reichswehr members' private homes.[58] Significantly, ordinary members of society helped officials to enforce such measures. When a passerby insulted the republican flag that students carried while on a field trip near the border with Holland in 1927, their teacher wrote the offender a letter asking him to apologize or to expect that his slur would be reported to the authorities. With no apology, the teacher called officials' attention to the violation of the Law for the Protection of the Republic. In explaining his rationale for pursuing such actions, the teacher stated that "he felt himself obligated [*verpflichtet*] to do so as a citizen [*Staatsbürger*] and teacher."[59] Thus, despite the worrisome attacks on the republican colors, it is important to recognize that there were individuals who took it upon themselves, as a citizen's duty, to inform the government and state's attorney that the law had been broken, and that a number of civil servants acted to defend the republic.

These strong actions by republicans only elicited further complaints from the right. For opponents of the republican standard, these actions amounted to a betrayal of the very democratic values lauded by the bearers of black-red-gold. Friedrich Everling, a member of the DNVP and later the Nazi Party, maintained that the allegedly democratic parties were "more absolutist than an absolute king" in implementing the various flag decrees.[60] Such measures, according to the supporters of the imperial flag, violated the rights of citizens granted by the Weimar Constitution.[61] Indeed, the bearers of black-red-gold were not the only ones who interpreted their actions through the language of citizenship.

---

58. Erin Hochman, "Staging the Nation, Staging Democracy: The Politics of Commemoration in Germany and Austria, 1918–1933/34" (PhD diss., University of Toronto, 2010), 104–107.

59. Abschrift, 2 J 316/29 (247) 25, Strafsache gegen den Lehrer Ludwig Sager in Lage bei Neuenhaus wegen Beleidigung, 4 July 1929, in BAB, R1501/125653, Bl. 68.

60. Friedrich Everling, "Die Flaggenfrage," undated and untitled newspaper, in BAB, R72/1316, Rs. of Bl. 5.

61. Also see Achilles, "Re-forming the Reich," 162–163.

A resident of Hamburg sent letters to the chancellor, the Reich minister of the interior, and a municipal senator after being told by police that he could not display a black-white-red flag on the occasion of a protest rally called by the federal government against the French and Belgian occupation of the Ruhr in 1923. "According to the Weimar Constitution, every German has the right to express his opinion in speech, writing, and image. The ordinance of the Hamburg police violates this constitutionally established right, and I heavily protest against it along with thousands of residents of Hamburg," the man wrote. This man was especially upset that the police did not prohibit the flying of the red flag, the symbol of the political left, which contravened the fact that "*before the law all Germans are equal.*"[62] The political right thus appealed to the democratic state system in their efforts to challenge it.

Although mostly cynical in their appeals to the Weimar Constitution, conservatives and right-wing radicals did point to the link between nationalism and democracy in an era when national self-determination was the watchword. Both sides of the debate promoted their symbol as the one that could truly represent the German Volk, understood in both a national and civic sense. Those on the political right protested the republican flag as un-German and saw the black-white-red standard as the only symbol that could represent their imperial and *völkisch* understandings of Germanness. Republicans once again used their *großdeutsch* nationalism as a way to repudiate these attacks and generate support for the black-red-gold tricolor. While this debate stemmed from the fact that the supporters of black-white-red and black-red-gold had distinctive and opposing ideas about which political system, borders, and criteria for membership in the national community best suited Germany, they all embraced the expanded arena for participation afforded by the new political order. The *Flaggenstreit* reveals the emotional and political investment of party leaders and everyday individuals in the struggle to redefine the relationship among nation, state, and politics after World War I. Moreover, while the flag debate remained a point of contention among the various political parties, so much so that it even resulted in the resignation of Chancellor Hans Luther in 1926, it also reveals how republicans in Germany and even Austria could achieve cross-party cooperation in their attempts to popularize the democratic form of government and its symbol. As we will see in the next section, the Austrian socialists had no allies, aside from the republicans in Germany, in the fight to defend the republic and its symbolic manifestations.

---

62. Letter to Reichsminister des Innern, Hamburg, 16 January 1923, in BAB, R1501/116483, Bl. 359–364. Emphasis in the original.

The Anthem Debate in Austria

Like Germany, Austria struggled with finding new symbols following the upheaval wrought by the First World War. However, in Austria, no one protested the change of flags. Rather, the need for a new anthem led to a protracted debate among citizens. Such a situation was perhaps not surprising, given the fact that at a time when the defining feature of Austrianness—the Habsburg monarchy—no longer existed, Austrians could turn to their musical heritage as a point of pride.[63] With its praise for the Kaiser, "God Preserve, God Protect" could no longer represent the newly created republic. In particular, the socialists viewed both the text of the old anthem, as well as the Haydn melody, as tainted and therefore unusable. Yet the collapse of the monarchy did not bring about the total demise of the "Kaiserhymne" (emperor's anthem). One of the ways in which this anthem persisted was its use by a number of political commentators, who viewed the well-known text as a means to publicize their opinions about the immediate past or the present situation. Critics of the old order used the retired anthem to ridicule the very authority it had once praised. The famed satirist Karl Kraus, for example, created his own version of "God Preserve, God Protect" a couple of years after the end of the war. Barely changing the text of Seidl's work, he wrote, "God preserve, God protect / our country from the Kaiser! / Powerful without his support, / confident without his hand!"[64] He dreamt up these new lyrics because he found a "fatherland-consciousness" that was not "mature enough for a new melody." Until Austrians reached this point, he simply suggested "filling the imperial lyrics with a new and contrary meaning."[65]

Those on the political right also employed the old anthem in order to air their misgivings about the postwar period. Mixing both deep-seated anti-Semitism and Catholic religiosity, a submission to Richard von Kralik, a conservative, Catholic, anti-Semitic writer, opened with the following verse: "God, preserve, God, protect / our country from the Jews! / Powerful through the support of faith, / Christians, maintain a strong position! / Let us protect our fathers' legacy / from the most terrible enemy! / So that our Volk does not become corrupted, / remain faithfully united!" Kralik, as a monarchist, explained to readers of the Catholic weekly *Das Neue Reich* that he preferred Seidl's text, and snidely added

---

63. Hochman, "Staging the Nation," 226–236.

64. Karl Kraus, "Volkshymne," *Die Fackel* 554 (November 1920): 59. Also see Eckart Früh, "Gott erhalte? Gott bewahre! Zur Geschichte der österreichischen Hymnen und des Nationalbewußtseins zwischen 1918 und 1938," *Österreich in Geschichte und Literatur mit Geographie* 32, no. 5 (1988): 283.

65. Karl Kraus, "Post festum," *Die Fackel* 554 (November 1920): 58.

that it "may also be more to the liking of the Jews."[66] These lyrics were representative of the fear among many Catholics that the new republic, and particularly Jews, would destroy the esteemed position of the church and traditional ways of life.

Whereas these authors did not seriously seek to write a new official anthem, other individuals sought to fill this musical void by creating a song in accord with the country's current state of affairs. Already in the initial months following the collapse of the Austro-Hungarian Empire, lyrics and compositions began to materialize. These early entries welcomed the return of peace after four long years of war. Carl Michael Ziehrer, a well-known composer of military marches and waltzes, wrote and composed the celebratory "German-Austria's Freedom Song" in late 1918. It viewed the present as a "hopeful time," in which "peace returns to every house, / throws all hate out the window, / because we are all now brothers, / here a band of love embraces us."[67] The following month, another individual tried his or her hand at an anthem titled "German-Austria (republican folk song [Volkslied])." As with the first text, this manuscript contained a pacifist message: "The warrior fury is banned, / Never let the world go up in flames, / 'Never again',—so long as the world turns, / So long as a league of nations exists."[68] That same month, Eduard Kolbe composed a melody for lyrics written by Franz Obermann and passed along their "National Anthem of All Germans" to the president of the Provisional National Assembly at the time. They too rejoiced about the end of the bloodshed: "For us, out of misery and death, peace and the sun's rays grow / Freedom and people's happiness, unity and justice."[69]

These particular attempts to create an anthem did not simply exult in the conclusion of hostilities; they also hailed the new democratic form of government. Ziehrer, for instance, did not appear to mourn the passing of the monarchy that had once appointed him to such prominent positions as Hoffballmusikdirector (musical director of the court balls). A little over a month after the republic was established, he embraced it in his second verse, "So vow in German-Austria, / all people whether poor or rich: / We now want to be a free Volk, / a Volk, governed

---

66. "Die provisorische Volkshymne," *Das Neue Reich*, 30 January 1919, reprinted in Früh, "Gott erhalte? Gott bewahre!," 304.

67. C. M. Ziehrer, "Deutschösterreichisches Freiheitslied," *Wiener Bilder*, 22 December 1918, reprinted in Früh, "Gott erhalte? Gott bewahre!," 303, and Johannes Steinbauer, *Land der Hymnen: Eine Geschichte der Bundeshymnen Österreichs* (Vienna: Sonderzahl, 1997), 186–187.

68. "Deutsch-Oesterreich (republikanisches Volkslied)," Perchtoldsdorf bei Wien, January 1919, in Verein für die Geschichte der Arbeiterbewegung, Vienna (VGA), Sacharchiv, Lade 1, Mappe 42–1.

69. Franz Obermann and Eduard Kolbe, "Nationalhymne aller Deutschen," in ÖStA, AdR, BKA, Ministerratsprotokolle (MRP), Kt. 150, MRP Nr. 603 vom 13. Dezember 1929. Also see Steinbauer, *Land der Hymnen*, 25–26.

by the Volk alone. / So reach out your hand brother, / cheers to German-Austria's fatherland!"[70] The author of "German-Austria (republican folk song)" likewise joyously proclaimed, "'German-Austria,'—You free state, / Which the 'German Volk' has founded, / Remain free and strong for all time, / From the heavy yoke, you are free!"[71] And Kolbe and Obermann repeated the refrain, "A loyal salute to you, republic!" alongside such statements as "We are the Volk, which is enthroned: now free and equal / We are the majesty of German-Austria!"[72]

These early efforts to create an anthem also reflected the impulse of most Austrians to turn to their Germanness and Germany now that the multinational empire was gone. Not only did the "German-Austria (republican folk song)" contain references to the "German Volk," a "German hand," and "German brothers," but its author also stipulated that it could be sung to the tune of "Watch on the Rhine," a German nationalist song that had become popular during the Franco-Prussian War of 1870–1871.[73] And if the title "National Anthem of All Germans" was not revealing enough, its creators, expecting an Anschluss would come to pass, made their lyrics adaptable. In a notation, Kolbe and Obermann stated that in the case of an Austro-German union, the references to "German-Austria" should be changed to "*Großdeutschland*" and "German-united Reich."[74] Another suggestion for an anthem discussed the "German *Heimat* [homeland]," which "freedom [has] given us."[75] Pointing to the importance of Germanness for anthem proposals at this time, the State's Office for Education praised one submission for its "good German convictions."[76] The proposals from this period appear to have avoided the later debate about whether the Austrian anthem should be a national anthem about Austrians' Germanness or whether it should be a state anthem primarily concerning Austria. Perhaps the absence of debate was due to fact that these creations arose before the Entente banned an Anschluss in the

70. Ziehrer, "Deutschösterreichisches Freiheitslied," in Früh, "Gott erhalte," 303, and Steinbauer, *Land der Hymnen*, 186–187.

71. "Deutsch-Oesterreich (republikanisches Volkslied)," Perchtoldsdorf bei Wien, January 1919, in VGA, Sacharchiv, Lade 1, Mappe 42–1.

72. Franz Obermann and Eduard Kolbe, Nationalhymne aller Deutschen, in ÖStA, AdR, BKA, MRP, Kt. 150, MRP Nr. 603 vom 13. Dezember 1929. Also see Steinbauer, *Land der Hymnen*, 25–26.

73. "Deutsch-Oesterreich (republikanisches Volkslied)," Perchtoldsdorf bei Wien, January 1919, in VGA, Sacharchiv, Lade 1, Mappe 42–1.

74. Franz Obermann and Eduard Kolbe, Nationalhymne aller Deutschen, in ÖStA, AdR, BKA, MRP, Kt. 150, MRP Nr. 603 vom 13. Dezember 1929. Also see Steinbauer, *Land der Hymnen*, 25–26.

75. Proposal by Ferdinand Rebay and R. Freiherr von Petz, "Deutschösterreichischer Vaterlandsgesang." Quoted in Andreas Holzer, ed., Katalog und Regestenheft zur Ausstellung "Österreich-Ideologie in der Musik," 17, http://www.musikgeschichte.at/regesten/Regesten-1995-s.pdf. Also see Franz Grasberger, *Die Hymnen Österreichs* (Tutzing: H. Schneider, 1968), 98; Steinbauer, *Land der Hymnen*, 23.

76. Quoted in Steinbauer, *Land der Hymnen*, 24.

summer of 1919. At this point, a political union appeared to be a possibility and the course of action preferred by citizens and major parties of the newly created Austrian state.

Significant for future developments, Ottokar Kernstock wrote his first version of "Be Blessed without End" during these early months of the republic. Signaling the important role that active citizens would play in the course of the anthem debate, the work first came about because a local historical association in Graz asked Kernstock if he would author lyrics for Haydn's melody. This association made the request because it wanted to "save for the future the wonderful melody of our former Kaiser's anthem, with which our essentially German [*urdeutsch*] master Josef Haydn has created the most beautiful 'national anthem' [*Volks-hymne*] in the world."[77] Containing four verses, Kernstock's initial draft did not solely refer to Austria, but also spoke of "German-Austria," which was still the name of the state until the Treaty of Saint-Germain prohibited it. The text also mentioned "German *Heimat*," "German work," and "German love."[78]

Interestingly, the association stressed that Haydn was a German composer, and this version of the lyrics underlined Austria's place in the "German *Heimat*." This emphasis stood in stark contrast to the use of this song in subsequent years by those seeking to create a stronger Austrian identity. In the second half of the 1920s, a number of Catholic conservatives began to claim Haydn, his tune, and Kernstock as representatives of Austrianness. A letter by Kernstock to a newspaper in August 1927 showed the radical reinscription of the meaning of the work. The poem "was suggested after the revolution by fellow countrymen loyal to the *Heimat*, who were of the opinion that the Austrian Josef Haydn's melody, solemnly created for Austria, should live on in an Austrian folk song [*Volkslied*]."[79] This change in emphasis, a topic to be explored in more detail below, reaffirms the widespread tendency of Austrians in the initial years of the republic to underscore the Germanness of their state and its citizens.

Also of note is Kernstock's inclusion of democratic ideas in his lyrics. The second verse stated, "No despotism, no vassals! / An open path for every strength! / Equal duties, equal rights! / Free in the arts and sciences! / Strong in bravery, determined in view, / despite every blow of fate, / go forth on the path of happiness, / God with you, German-Austria!"[80] A verse that was later cut when the Christian Social government implemented the piece as the official anthem also referred to

77. The quote comes from a flyer printed in early 1919 by the association. Steinbauer, *Land der Hymnen*, 59.

78. Ibid., 58.

79. Quoted in Grasberger, *Die Hymnen Österreichs*, 121.

80. Steinbauer, *Land der Hymnen*, 58.

German-Austria as the "land of freedom." Considering that Kernstock was a conservative priest who wrote a poem praising the swastika during his brief interest in Nazism in 1923, the poem was surprisingly compatible with the new republic and its ideals. In later years, the Christian Socials would reinterpret this anthem, viewing it as a way to return to a great imperial tradition and as a symbol of their increasingly reactionary and authoritarian politics.

Yet, in spite of the various proposals put forth by the public, Austria was still without an anthem in 1920. By this point, the country needed an anthem that could be used for official occasions. Karl Renner, a leading socialist and the chancellor at the time, proceeded to pen lyrics and find a composer for a new anthem in response to demand from the army.[81] He enlisted his friend, the composer Wilhelm Kienzl, to create a melody, and the two worked together to revise Renner's poem, with the biggest change being the addition of "German-Austria" to the final version.[82] The inclusion of the name "German-Austria" amounted to another affirmation of Austria's Germanness and to a political statement, since this appellation had been specifically forbidden by the Entente in the peace settlement. With the song finished in May, the army first performed the anthem at a ceremony to swear in troops on July 15, 1920 in Vienna.

Although the Renner-Kienzl composition was used for an official event, the government never issued a decree or passed legislation declaring it to be the anthem of Austria. When the army's administrative post in Graz read about the Viennese ceremony, it asked the State Office of Defense for copies of the lyrics and melody, only to be told that this song did not constitute an official state anthem. The defense department recommended that the army post in Graz write directly to Kienzl if it wished to obtain a copy of the song. The historian Johannes Steinbauer plausibly suggests that the government shied away from taking up the matter of the Renner-Kienzl anthem because of the growing tensions within the governing coalition between the Social Democrats and Christian Socials. According to Steinbauer, worries that the use of "German-Austria" would alarm foreign powers was another possible reason that "German-Austria, Thou Magnificent Land" never became a legal symbol.[83]

Despite its unofficial status, the Renner-Kienzl collaboration became the de facto anthem until late 1929. Government documents referred to it as the "federal anthem" (*Bundeshymne*) or "national anthem" (*Nationalhymne*) interchangeably and used it for official events, such as the military celebrations for the state holiday. Already by the third anniversary of the republic in 1921, the

81. Ibid., 29; Grasberger, *Die Hymnen Österreichs*, 98.
82. Steinbauer, *Land der Hymnen*, 35.
83. Ibid., 37–39.

president's office noted that President Michael Hainisch "would remove his hat at the playing of the national anthem because the national anthem constituted the focus of the entire celebration."[84] And, as a 1927 report on a commemorative performance for Beethoven's death indicated, "The playing of the national anthem upon the arrival of the president . . . has proved itself to be very effective because it was the only means by which to signal the attendees to rise from their seats."[85] The application of the words "federal anthem" and "national anthem" to the Renner-Kienzl creation, as well as the song's use for official functions, meant that "German-Austria, Thou Magnificent Land" had for all practical purposes become a state symbol alongside the officially declared emblems of the flag and the coat of arms.

The use of the Renner-Kienzl collaboration for official occasions did not, however, lead to the popular acceptance of the anthem. None other than Eric Hobsbawm, the famed historian who explored the "invention of tradition," looked back at his adolescence in interwar Vienna and recalled "German-Austria, Thou Magnificent Land" as "a piece of (unsuccessful) political invention."[86] On account of this unpopularity, individuals continued to send the government proposals for a new anthem. In particular, many Austrians viewed a return to Haydn as the best way to develop a meaningful symbol. Not only did most Austrian citizens already know the tune, but the melody also represented a link to Austria's great cultural heritage in a period of instability. Although political conservatives would be the primary supporters of the reinstatement of Haydn, the desire to hear Haydn again was not simply confined to the political right. In a 1923 letter concerning the anthem, a self-proclaimed "republican" wrote to Hainisch questioning why Haydn could not be used to honor the republic. As chairman of the parents' association at a boys' primary school, the writer was in the process of organizing festivities for the fifth anniversary of the republic. He explained that he had, "after a difficult struggle," taught the schoolchildren the Renner-Kienzl anthem. Concluding that the song was seldom heard because it was "too hard" to sing, he recommended a return to Haydn. "I believe," the anonymous author opined, "that an anthem, to which that melody would be added, would soon become the common property of the entire Austrian Volk. In the schools, it would inflame the hearts of our youth, the future of our state, with love for

84. PrK 6254/1921, Amtsveranlassung, betr. eine militärische Feier des dreijährigen Bestandes der Republik, in ÖStA, AdR, PrK 6288/1922.

85. PrK 1922/1927, Amtsveranlassung, Festvorstellung des "Fidelio" am 31. März 1927, 9 April 1927, in ÖStA, AdR, PrK 2357/1927.

86. Eric Hobsbawm, *Nations and Nationalism since 1780: Programme, Myth, Reality* (Cambridge: Cambridge University Press, Canto Edition, 1990), 92.

the republic." To make Haydn suitable for the republic, the writer provided his own set of lyrics praising the republic, as well as the "free citizens of all classes" and "freedom, equality."[87] By creating a set of lyrics that honored the republic, this author attempted to make the old imperial tune compatible with the new political situation.

It was during this period that the idea of reinstituting Haydn with lyrics by Kernstock gained momentum. The popularization of the Kernstock-Haydn combination, first suggested in 1919, was due in large part to the efforts of Louise Pibus, a Viennese schoolteacher. Highlighting once again the importance of civic participation in the course of the Austrian anthem debate, she conducted a five-year campaign to gain both official and popular support for this particular song.[88] As early as the spring of 1922, she wrote to the federal government, requesting it to declare Kernstock-Haydn to be the official anthem. She claimed that both the lyrics and the Austrian public showed enough political maturity to allow for the reinstatement of the old imperial tune. Although officials within the Ministry of the Interior and Education did not view the lyrics as problematic, they rejected Pibus's suggestion because of "political concerns" over the Haydn melody.[89] The government's initial response did not, however, dissuade her from continuing her efforts to have "Be Blessed without End" recognized as Austria's anthem.

Rather than simply lobbying the government as individuals had done, she turned her attention to gathering popular support for the Kernstock-Haydn song. She sent the lyrics to newspapers for publication, created postcards to increase awareness of the need for a new anthem and the suitability of "Be Blessed without End," and urged school boards to include the song as part of their curriculum. In her attempts to popularize the song, she demonstrated a keen understanding of the expanded sphere of political action in a democracy, as she mounted a petition campaign in favor of Kernstock-Haydn. Addressing her "dear national comrades" (*Volksgenossen*) in 1923, Pibus explained that according to article 41 of the constitution, any issue able to garner the signatures of two hundred thousand voters or half of all voters in three provinces would become an item of business before parliament.[90] Although in a 1926 letter to the government she stated that she was giving up on the petition drive because of the authorities'

---

87. Full text of the letter is in Steinbauer, *Land der Hymnen*, 45–47.

88. Ibid., 62–72.

89. Ibid., 62–63.

90. Letter from Louise Pibus to mein liebenswerten Volkgsgenossen, Wieder ein Ruf im Sinne Österreichische Volkshymne (Kernstock-Haydn), May 1923, in ÖStA, Allgemeines Verwaltungsarchiv (AVA), Unterricht Allgemein (U.Allg.) 3258, 12733/1926.

reluctance to act and fear that the song would be weakened through continual promotional work, she still enclosed pages of signatures containing about 350 names because she felt herself "personally obligated for the further representation" of the signatories.[91]

Throughout her various activities, Pibus sounded a number of recurring themes with regard to the anthem situation in Austria. According to her, Austria was still in need of a popular anthem, and "Be Blessed without End" would be the best option to fill this musical void. As one of her postcards proclaimed, "We are lacking a people's anthem [*Volkshymne*]!" The postcard proposed a solution to the problem; it contained Kernstock's poem and stated that it should be set to Haydn. This song would bring "honor to our old, eternally young Austria." Yet Pibus did not simply highlight this particular song as a purely Austrian symbol. Like the original commissioners of the text, she initially pointed to the song as a symbol of Austrians' Germanness. The concluding line on the postcard thus exclaimed, "So let this song, as a monument of German loyalty, strengthen us now!"[92] And, during her petition campaign, she emphasized that every signature would create a "monument of German loyalty."[93] For her, the dual identifications were not in conflict, and she mentioned the German aspect of Kernstock-Haydn until 1925. Nonetheless, "Be Blessed without End" would become a symbol increasingly associated by political conservatives with Austrianness and used to oppose both the socialists and the radical right, which supported symbols associated with Germanness.

Not only did Pibus move easily between the identifications with Austrianness and Germanness, but she also saw the imperial origins of the melody as unproblematic. In suggesting a return to Haydn, Pibus advanced an argument commonly made by Austrians and Germans to legitimize their political pursuits at the time: she stressed that she had no political motivations or affiliations. She frowned upon party politics and saw "Be Blessed without End" as a way to create unity among Austrians.[94] Furthermore, she contended that Kernstock's lyrics and Haydn's melody had gained widespread acceptance. As she noted in a 1925 letter to the federal government, "Numerous enthusiastic letters prove the sympathies of the population,—the new text appears after all to be a masterpiece, which allows the variedness of political feeling to become harmonized in a unified whole.

---

91. Letter from Louise Pibus to the hohe Bundeskanzler-Amt von Österreich, Vienna, 1 May 1926, in ÖStA, AVA, U.Allg. 3258, 12733/1926.

92. Postcard by L. Pibus, "Die neue Volkshymne," in ÖStA, AVA, U.Allg. 3258, 12733/1926.

93. Letter from Louise Pibus to mein liebenswerten Volksgenossen, Wieder ein Ruf im Sinne Österreichische Volkshymne (Kernstock-Haydn), May 1923, in ÖStA, AVA, U.Allg. 3258, 12733/1926.

94. See her statements reprinted in Steinbauer, *Land der Hymnen*, 64–66.

And the old melody,—never legally supplanted by a new one—sounds since then repeatedly in public without any further obstructions."[95]

As they had done in 1922, government officials refused to act upon Pibus's suggestion. Again in 1923, an official in the Ministry of Education rejected the use of Haydn, saying that the melody was "completely filled with the patriarchal spirit of the empire." Moreover, he gave a positive evaluation of the Renner-Kienzl anthem, which "is filled by a modern democratic-republican spirit."[96] He maintained again in 1925 that the circumstances were "not suitable" to institute a new anthem when one was already in place.[97] A year later, however, he reversed his earlier position about the two songs.[98] While observing that the Renner-Kienzl song had failed to catch on with the public, he also no longer viewed Haydn's tune as outdated. "The suggestion to connect the old Haydn melody, a masterpiece of Austrian music, with a text that supports the state's changed political affairs and to declare it once again as the Austrian national anthem," he wrote, "would have a lot going for it and would doubtlessly find strong support from the population, which is familiar with the wonderful Haydn melody." Although he approved of the Kernstock-Haydn combination, he remarked that the decision would be up to the parliament and that the chancellor's office deemed a change in the song for official occasions as unnecessary and unsuitable in a period of divisive politics.[99] That same year, officials turned down, for similar reasons, the first request of Carl

95. Letter from Louise Pibus to the Hohe Regierung der Republik Österreich, Vienna, 1 May 1925, in ÖStA, AVA, U.Allg. 3258, 11096/1925.

96. Quoted in Steinbauer, *Land der Hymnen*, 68.

97. Notes from Kobalt on Bundesministerium für Unterricht, Gegenstand: Bundeskanzleramt, Louise Pibus, offizielle Genehmigung der "Neuen Volkshymne," 11 May 1925, 11096/25-III, in ÖStA, AVA, U.Allg. 3258, 11096/25.

98. As Steinbauer notes, the official (Kobalt) most likely changed his mind after reading a brief on the topic by the former director of the National Library, Dr. Donabaum. Pibus had gone to see Donabaum, pleading for him to intervene on her behalf with the Ministry of Education. Following this meeting, he wrote a letter to Kobalt in which he identified both the advantages and drawbacks of the Kernstock-Haydn song. He noted that in 1923, President Michael Hainisch was enthusiastic about "Be Blessed without End." Kobalt then corresponded with Vice-Chancellor Felix Frank of the GDVP, who stated that his party would most likely be supportive of Kernstock-Haydn since Germany had declared the same Haydn tune as its official anthem in 1922. Kobalt also spoke with one of Seipel's advisers, but worries of a conflict with the socialists prevented any of these parties from acting. Much to his surprise, Kobalt noted that even the socialist Otto Glöckel seemed supportive of the idea of reverting to Haydn with a new text. Yet nothing came of these conversations. By the time Pibus met with him in 1926, Kobalt noted that the CSP was in favor of "Be Blessed without End" but that the socialists were strongly against it. Moreover, he pointed out that the GDVP would prefer "Deutschland, Deutschland über alles" to Kernstock. Steinbauer, *Land der Hymnen*, 70–73. The original letter can be found in Letter from Hofrat Donabaum to Ministerialrat Kobalt, Vienna, 9 March 1926, in ÖStA, AVA, U.Allg. 3258, 12733/1926.

99. Notes from Schwegel (BKA), 9 July 1926, on Bundesministerium für Unterricht, BKA: Louise Pibus, offizielle Genehmigung der "Neue Volkshymne," Geschäftszahl 12733-I, 30 June 1926 in ÖStA, AVA, U.Allg. 3258, 12733/1926.

Vaugoin, the Christian Social vice-chancellor and defense minister, to institute Kernstock-Haydn as the anthem for the army.[100]

Although Pibus's efforts did not meet with immediate success, the movement to replace the Renner-Kienzl anthem with Haydn gained momentum. In the same year that the education official changed his assessment of the two musical pieces, the *Reichspost*, a newspaper representing the views of the right wing of the Christian Social Party, published an article in support of restoring Haydn. Austria had become "the land of songs—without songs," according to the 1926 article. This situation was particularly lamentable because Austria, "which has given more to German music than anyone else, the *Heimat* of countless songs that have made their way around the entire world, thus possesses no national song [*Nationallied*] today." Characterizing Renner's lyrics as "odd" and "naïve," the article explained that only a few specialists related to the de facto anthem. To remedy this problem, the article took its cue from "the completely unpolitical idea held by many sides" and lobbied for a return to the "immortal Haydn anthem."[101]

Three years later, the Christian Social–controlled cabinet began seriously to consider reinstating Haydn with the lyrics by Kernstock as part of its overhaul of the constitution. To win support for the initiative in the autumn of 1929 and to defend the new anthem after its implementation in December of that year, conservative Catholics mounted a two-pronged anthem campaign: on the one hand, they attacked the Renner-Kienzl song, and on the other they elaborated a detailed argument about why Kernstock-Haydn should be the new anthem of Austria. From the moment the cabinet began to consider changing the anthem to Kernstock-Haydn in October 1929, conservatives cheered the idea of replacing the Renner-Kienzl song. Whereas the 1926 *Reichspost* article critiqued Renner's lyrics on aesthetic grounds, criticism of "German-Austria, Thou Magnificent Land" became politically charged in 1929. In his speech at the December cabinet meeting that led to the anthem change, Defense Minister Vaugoin critiqued Renner's poem for having "revolutionary symptoms."[102] The *Wiener Neueste Nachrichten*, a German nationalist paper, similarly supported the anthem switch, proclaiming, "So will Austria finally be freed from the 'revolutionary rubbish,' which more than any other thing oppressed the Austrian soul . . . and disfigured the Austrian countenance."[103]

---

100. Steinbauer, *Land der Hymnen*, 75.

101. "Das Land der Lieder—ohne Lieder," *RP*, 27 June 1926, in WB, TA, Nationalhymne 342.228.

102. Vaugoin (Vizekanzler und Bundesminister für Heereswesen), Beilage K zu Punkt 13 des MRP Nr. 603 von 1929, Bundesministerium für Heereswesen (BMfHW), 59.869-Präsidium (Präs.) von 1929, 10 December 1929, in ÖStA, AdR, BKA, MRP, Kt. 150.

103. "Die Frage der Bundeshymne geregelt," *WNN*, 15 December 1929, in ÖStA, AdR, Parteiarchive, GDVP, Zeitungsausschnitte, Mappe 241, 02/c.

As the reference to the "Austrian soul" demonstrates, many on the political right began increasingly to speak about "Be Blessed without End" as an authentically Austrian symbol. Although the final version of Kernstock's poem chosen by the cabinet still kept mentions of "German work" and "German love," and proponents of this song still spoke of the German character of Austrians, the right wing of the Christian Social Party in particular began to place more emphasis on the specifically Austrian origins and nature of the song. In the eyes of writers at the *Reichspost*, Haydn was "one of the greatest sons of his land and his tribe, [one] of the most Austrian among Austria's composers."[104] By returning to his melody, Austria would have a "*Volkshymne*," which "breathes the peaceable nature and mentality of the Austrian Volk."[105] The reinstatement of Haydn was "proof that Austria had once again found itself after a ten-year odyssey."[106] According to this viewpoint, the Austro-Marxists had led the country astray through their revolutionary tendencies and emphasis on class divisions, and the Christian Socials were now returning Austria to its roots.

The Christian Socials' focus on Haydn, as opposed to Kernstock, was related to their attempts to erase the break between what they saw as a glorious past and an unhappy present. Since Vaugoin's appointment as the republic's defense minister in 1922, he had steadily reintroduced the imperial symbols and military music that his socialist predecessor had abolished. His motion in the cabinet to declare Kernstock-Haydn as Austria's anthem was thus another move to reinforce connections to Austria's imperial past and Catholic heritage. In a speech on the anthem made to a gathering of the Margareten branch of the Christian Social Association in February 1930, he explained to his captivated listeners that he had for years been trying to "reawaken the Austrian tradition in our soldiers" as a way to guard against the destructive tendencies of the Austro-Marxists. "But also in political life and far beyond the army in civilian life, there is no better medicine for a Volk to make progress than tradition," he continued.[107] His statement implied that by honoring and keeping alive Austrian imperial and Catholic traditions, the sociopolitical troubles brought about by war and revolution could be overcome.

These arguments advanced by many Christian Socials supported their broader attempts to create a stronger Austrian identity based on Catholicism and the Habsburg past. Although they believed that Austrians were members of a larger

104. "Sei gesegnet ohne Ende!," *RP*, 17 October 1929, in WB, TA, Nationalhymne 342.228.

105. Vinzenz Goller, "Zur Geschichte der 'Oesterreichischen Bundeshymne,'" *RP*, 25 December 1929, 10.

106. "'Sei gesegnet ohne Ende!," *RP*, 22 December 1929, in WB, TA, Nationalhymne 342.228.

107. "Abrechnung mit dem Demagogentum," *RP*, 5 February 1930, in WB, TA, Nationalhymne 342.228.

German nation, they desired to maintain Austria's sovereignty. The right-wing and Viennese branch of the party opposed an Anschluss because of their fears that their Catholicism and Austrian particularities would be swallowed up by Protestant and Prussian-led Germany.[108] From their vantage point, the reinstatement of an allegedly Austrian symbol would help to strengthen the rump state and their position within it. Related to the increasing emphasis on Austrianness was the turn toward authoritarianism by a number of Christian Social leaders, including Vaugoin and Seipel, in the mid-to-late 1920s. By this point, these men were questioning parliamentarism and lending their support to the Heimwehr, the Austrofascist paramilitary group seeking to crush the Social Democrats and overthrow the republic.[109] The reform of the constitution in 1929, of which the anthem decree was part, was Seipel's idea, and he hoped that it would lead to the "strengthening of the authority of the state."[110] "Austria's consolidation is not only an economic, but also a psychological problem," an article in the *Reichspost* asserted. The piece went on to say that the return to Haydn's melody would help persuade Austrians "not to lose faith in Austria," thereby preserving the country's existence.[111] For this wing of the Christian Social Party, the Haydn melody was to be a symbol of traditional, conservative, Austrian values.

Members of the Social Democratic Party protested their opponents' anthem measures. They challenged the old-new music on political, not aesthetic, grounds. The change in the lyrics of the old Habsburg melody did not, in their eyes, make the reintroduction of the Haydn tune suitable for the republic. Indeed, the *Arbeiter-Zeitung* contended that the Christian Socials were conscious of the inability of Austrians to disassociate the tune from its imperial origins. "It is adopted," the article argued, "so that the republic can appear to be the continuation of the old state."[112] For the socialists, who were the only political party as a whole still defending the democratic system by this point, the anthem change amounted to a provocation.

Additionally, the Social Democrats contested the conservative claim that the new anthem was already a "people's anthem." The very fact of the melody's dynastic origins, according to the socialists, meant that it could not be a popular anthem. In an article printed in both a socialist publication for soldiers and the *Arbeiter-Zeitung*, the author provided a history of the melody in the imperial era.

---

108. On the attempts to create a stronger sense of Austrianness see Haas, "Staats- und Landesbewußtsein," 479–481; Suval, *Anschluss Question*, chap. 12; Steinberg, *Austria as Theater and Ideology*.

109. von Klemperer, *Ignaz Seipel*, esp. chaps. 5–7.

110. Ibid., 362. Also see Boyer, *Karl Lueger*, 422–430.

111. "Sei gesegnet ohne Ende!," *RP*, 22 December 1929, in WB, TA, Nationalhymne 342.228.

112. "'Gott erhalte!'" *AZ*, 29 January 1930, in WB, TA, Nationalhymne 342.228.

After all, the anthem was created at the insistence of the police official Franz Josef Graf von Saurau in order to create popular support for Emperor Franz II in the war against Napoleon.[113] With the addition of lyrics by a priest, the socialists insisted, the song could never become a meaningful symbol for the population at large. As the Social Democratic mayor of Vienna, Karl Seitz, proclaimed during a meeting of the city council, the anthem was simply "a Christian Social song," a comment that caused a heated argument among the representatives.[114]

Not all supporters of the republic concurred with the socialist assessment. The left liberal newspaper the *Neue Freie Presse* agreed with the socialists on the need to be vigilant against antidemocratic tendencies. "The Social Democrats have every reason," the article read, "to impede the creeping in of monarchist interpretations and the enlistment of the federal anthem by antirepublican forces for their own use." However, the *Neue Freie Presse* did not see the use of Haydn with the changed lyrics as inherently incompatible with the republic, especially since Kernstock's lyrics "correspond to the republic."[115] Even some Christian Socials highlighted the ability of the old melody to be used as a way to win the republic further support. Max Freiherr von Hussarek-Heinlein, a legal scholar and the last minister-president of the Austrian half of the Habsburg monarchy, wrote in January 1930 that he thought it was a mistake that the new republican government had not kept the Haydn melody after the war. "The taking over of such traditions," he insisted, "is well suited to pioneer feelings for the republic in circles that are rather indifferent to the current form of government." Like the anonymous "republican" in 1923, Freiherr von Hussarek-Heinlein maintained that the reinstatement of Haydn was not an attack on the republic, but a way to win it supporters.[116]

And, once again signaling the importance of transborder connections in these debates about symbols, the various backers of "Be Blessed without End" underlined the fact that the Weimar Republic used the same Haydn melody for its anthem, the "Deutschlandlied" ("Deutschland, Deutschland über alles"). In light of this situation, the champions of Kernstock-Haydn made two more arguments in favor of their anthem. First, it was lamentable that another country was using "the wonderful anthem of the Viennese Haydn" while it was exiled from

---

113. "Vom Kaiserlied 1797—zur Bundeshymne 1929," *Auf Vorposten: Schulstunden des Freien Soldaten*, 1 March 1930, and "Gott erhalte ohne Ende . . . Die Geschichte des Kaiserliedes," *AZ*, 2 March 1930, both in WB, TA, Nationalhymne 342.228.

114. "Lärmszenen im Gemeinderat," *NFP*, 26 April 1930, in WB, TA, Nationalhymne 342.228.

115. "Hymnenchaos," *NFP*, 14 February 1930, in WB, TA, Nationalhymne 342.228.

116. Ministerpräsident a.D. Dr. Max Freiherr v. Hussarek-Heinlein, "Pflichten der Oeffentlichkeit gegenüber," *Neues Wiener Journal*, 30 January 1930, in WB, TA, Nationalhymne 342.228.

its birthplace.[117] Second, the decision by the Social Democratic president of the Weimar Republic, Friedrich Ebert, to declare the "Deutschlandlied" the official anthem in 1922 was proof that Haydn's tune could be used in the changed, post-war political circumstances. The *Reichspost* seized upon this point, remarking that the Austrian socialists should be aware "that their political comrades in the German Reich enthusiastically foster the singing of the Haydn melody, which they played a leading role in selecting at the time."[118] Moreover, as Leopold Kun-schak, a pro-democracy member of the Christian Social Party and the leader of the Christian Social Workers' Association, pointed out, the socialist mayor of Vienna Karl Seitz had no problem singing "Deutschland, Deutschland über alles," and thus Haydn, at the seventy-fifth anniversary of the Frankfurt Parliament in 1923.[119] Socialist opposition to the reinstatement of Haydn in Austria was there-fore groundless, according to the CSP.

The Haydn melody, from the viewpoint of its supporters, had proved its po-litical flexibility, and consequently there should be no problems using it for the First Austrian Republic. Referencing the many uses of the British national an-them, the *Neues Wiener Tagblatt*, a proponent of the Heimwehr and the CSP's authoritarian turn, stated, "A well-devised melody has such a large psychological terrain that the most diverse political ideas can find a place on it. Haydn's eternal melody has certainly shown the same thing: between praise for the 'good Kaiser Franz' and 'Deutschland, Deutschland über alles' there are at least a few differ-ences. Both texts give Haydn's music luster. And so too will Kernstock's poem."[120] Yet precisely what the article identified as the strength of Haydn's music would, in the political climate of early 1930s Austria, prove to be a great weakness. The fact that the lyrics for the imperial anthem, the "Deutschlandlied," and now "Be Blessed without End" could be sung to the same Haydn melody only intensified the contest over the anthem, politics, and Austrian identity.

Within a couple of weeks of the cabinet's decision to declare Kernstock-Haydn as Austria's new anthem, an Austrian newspaperman wrote to the chancellor both to express his concerns about the government's resolution and to propose a new anthem. Upon hearing the music played at official occasions, warring politi-cal groups would simply choose which set of lyrics to sing, the man cautioned, and "it would surely often come to alarming political demonstrations that would

---

117. "Sei gesegnet ohne Ende!," *RP*, 17 October 1929, in WB, TA, Nationalhymne 342.228.

118. "Sei gesegnet ohne Ende!," *RP*, 22 December 1929, in WB, TA, Nationalhymne 342.228.

119. Leopold Kunschak, "Seitz kann auch anders!," *Neues Wiener Journal*, 28 January 1930, in WB, TA, Nationalhymne 342.228.

120. "Die neue alte Hymne," *Neues Wiener Tagblatt* (*NWT*), 17 October 1929, in WB, TA, National-hymne 342.228.

disturb public peace and order and eventually to clashes between the different parties and groups!"[121] Although the government dismissed his warning, this individual foresaw the very issues that would arise with the new anthem. With the shift to Haydn, a different form of civic engagement emerged. Whereas previously citizens sent letters to the government to make their views known, many others would now literally voice—sing—their opinions with regard to the pressing questions related to the Austrian state and identity.

Although some contemporary observers mentioned the imperial lyrics as a contributing factor to the "anthem chaos,"[122] this text would be negligible in the public debate over the anthem. This was perhaps because there was little worry about a monarchist restoration in Austria by the 1930s and there was a "spiritual affinity" between the monarchists and many Christian Socials.[123] Rather, the burning political questions of the day related to the conflict among radical German nationalists, conservatives, and socialists over what form of government and primary identification best suited Austria. Whereas the imperial anthem thus had very little public impact because of its remove from the critical issues of the day, the same could not be said for the third set of lyrics set to Haydn: "Deutschland, Deutschland über alles." Penned by Hoffmann von Fallersleben in 1841, the song epitomized the liberal demands for political reform and national unity in the first half of the nineteenth century with its proclamation of "unity and justice and freedom for the German fatherland!" The "Deutschlandlied" thus directly related to the fraught issue of Austrianness after the First World War. Although the Christian Socials had pointed out the common melody between the Weimar Republic's "Deutschlandlied" and "Be Blessed without End" in their efforts to undermine socialist protests, they appear to have overlooked that this shared tune could provide a basis to challenge them and their newly selected symbol. Now that the Haydn melody was once again back in use as Austria's official anthem, the option existed to sing "Deutschland, Deutschland über alles" when it was played. Already during the cabinet meeting in which the Kernstock-Haydn combination was declared the official anthem, Franz Slama, a member of the GDVP and the justice minister at the time, raised the possibility that members of his party would rather sing Hoffmann von Fallersleben's lyrics.[124]

---

121. Letter from Anton Ello to the Bundeskanzler, Vienna, 28 December 1929, in ÖStA, AVA, U.Allg. 3258, 417/1930.

122. "Hymnenchaos," NFP, 14 February 1930, in WB, TA, Nationalhymne 342.228.

123. Steinbauer, Land der Hymnen, 104. Also see Wasserman, Black Vienna, chap. 5.

124. MRP Nr. 603, 13 December 1929, "Einführung einer neuen österreichischen Bundeshymne," in ÖStA, AdR, BKA, MRP, Kt. 150.

A number of political groups and individuals agreed with Slama's opinion and proceeded to make their views known on issues ranging from the anthem to an Anschluss. The education system, a main issue of contention between the political parties, was one of the primary sites where the contestation of the anthem and its Christian Social supporters took place. In January 1930, the cabinet passed another resolution making "Be Blessed without End" the "official text of the federal anthem" for schools.[125] On January 31, the education minister sent a notice to all school boards, informing them of the government's decision.[126] The very same day, a group of students at the University of Vienna sang their dissenting opinions loud and clear. An Evening of Song for the Care of the German Folk Song concluded with the playing of the Haydn melody. Instead of singing Kernstock, a number of right-wing students sang "Deutschland, Deutschland über alles."[127] Shortly thereafter, similar incidents occurred, but this time in the presence of Chancellor Johann Schober, whose cabinet had enacted the new anthem. At ceremonies in Vienna and Graz to confer honorary degrees on Schober, students "who do not stand far from the Greater German camp [Lager]" again sang Hoffmann von Fallersleben when Haydn was intoned, much to the surprise of the other guests.[128]

Such occurrences continued throughout the remainder of the republic's life. On the occasion of the thirteenth anniversary of the republic, one thousand youths attended a Völkisch Rally of the Catholic German Middle School Youth in Graz. About one hundred students affiliated with the Nazis caused a disruption of the ceremony when, upon the playing of Kernstock-Haydn, they sang the "Deutschlandlied" and gave the Hitler salute.[129] And, in the spring of 1933 in Salzburg, at the beginning of a celebration for the Day of Fostering Music, students from the upper classes sang "Deutschland, Deutschland über alles" upon hearing the Haydn melody. The teachers had to stop the singing and proceeded

---

125. MRP Nr. 610, 23 January 1930, "Erklärung der Haydn'schen Hymne zur offiziellen Bundeshymne," in ÖStA, AdR, BKA, MRP, Kt. 151.

126. Letter from the Bundesministerium für Unterricht to alle Landesschulräte, den Stadtschulrat für Wien und an die Aemter aller Ld.Regn. (mit Ausnahme der LR.für Wien und N.Oe.), Vienna, 31 January 1930, enclosed as Beilage D zu Punkt 3 des MRP Nr. 611 von 1930, in ÖStA, AdR, BKA, MRP, Kt. 151.

127. "Die deutsche Studentenschaft Wiens und die Bundeshymne," Welt-Blatt, 4 February 1930, in ÖStA, AdR, Parteiarchive, GDVP, Zeitungsausschnitte, Mappe 24a, 02/c.

128. Description of the students at the Viennese ceremony is from "Kernstock oder Hoffmann von Fallersleben?," Neuigkeitsweltblatt, 14 February 1930, in WB, TA, Nationalhymne 342.228. Also see "Das Deutschlandlied—ein Zwischenfall," AZ, 13 February 1930, in ÖStA, AdR, Parteiarchive, GDVP, Zeitungsausschnitte, Mappe 24a, 02/c.

129. Gestrige Sicherheitswachekommandierungen: 1/48, Frührapport der Abt. I am 13. November 1931, in Steiermärkisches Landesarchiv (StLA), Zeitgeschichtliche Sammlung (ZGS), Kt. 132, Polizeidirektion Graz: Vorfallenheitsberichte, Versammlungen, Veranstaltungen, 1.6.1931–31.5.1932.

to forbid the students from singing while the anthem was played again.[130] These incidents demonstrate the active political engagement on the part of Austrian youths, highlighting how widespread the politicization of Austrian society was at the time. Furthermore, they point to the conflicting ideas about what it meant to be Austrian in the interwar period. Students sympathizing with extremist German nationalism rejected the CSP's project to make Catholic and Habsburg traditions as constitutive characteristics of Austrianness; Austrians, for these students, were instead Germans who needed to become a part of the Reich.

For the Christian Socials, the students' actions were alarming because of their implications for the current government. Reporting on the "regrettable" first incident, the *Welt-Blatt* questioned how the youth could feel "so little connected with the Austrian tribe [*Stamm*] and state." It further asked, "Must the student body really also place itself in a position that opposes that political direction that seeks to strengthen Austria's faith in itself?" The students' decision to sing the "Deutschlandlied" instead of Kernstock had amounted to a display of a lack of loyalty both to the Austrian state and to the Austrian people, and, as such, a threat to the stability of the country and the current federal government.[131] An article addressing the disruptions of the honorary ceremonies for Schober similarly concluded that the students' preference for Hoffmann von Fallersleben was a direct challenge to the government. It was a "demonstration against the chancellor himself," who was an "embodiment of the Austrian state's authority." These students "do not allow themselves to be led by aesthetic concerns, but only political ones, which do not recognize an Austrian state consciousness [*Staatsbewusstsein*]."[132] One individual was so upset by the students' musical protests that he wrote the government asking that the text of the "Deutschlandlied" be taken out of all schoolbooks and that children be forbidden from singing it.[133] In singing "Deutschland, Deutschland über alles," the students were seeking to subvert an already fragile state by defying the government and its increasingly Austrofascist aims.

Völkisch groups were not the only ones advocating the singing of "Deutschland, Deutschland über alles." In addition to criticizing the Christian Socials'

---

130. Präsidial-Büro, Salzburg, 13 May 1933, in Salzburger Landesarchiv (SLA), Rehrl-Brief 1933/1044.

131. "Die deutsche Studentenschaft Wiens und die Bundeshymne," *Welt-Blatt*, 4 February 1930, in ÖStA, AdR, Parteiarchive, GDVP, Zeitungsausschnitte, Mappe 24a, 02/c.

132. "Kernstock oder Hoffmann von Fallersleben?," *Neuigkeitsweltblatt*, 14 February 1930, in WB, TA, Nationalhymne 342.228.

133. Letter from Mjr,d,R Raoul von Sziegethy to the Bundesministerium für Unterricht, Graz, 15 November 1931, in ÖStA, AVA, U.Allg. 4943, 36211/1931. The government dismissed the request.

adoption of Kernstock-Haydn, the socialists encouraged the singing of Hoffmann von Fallersleben. This tactic on the part of the socialists aimed not only at mounting a challenge against their political opponents, but also at expressing their *großdeutsch* sentiments. Otto Glöckel—a leading member of the Social Democratic Party, an influential education reformer, and the head of the Viennese school board—retaliated against the cabinet's anthem measures by releasing his own anthem edict for the capital's school district. He ordered "Deutschland, Deutschland über alles" to be sung at school celebrations. In contrast with the earlier socialist claims that the Haydn tune was tainted by its imperial associations, Glöckel maintained that this connection between Haydn and the empire could be broken because "after more than a decade, the republican form of government has dulled this memory." The "pretty Austrian melody" could be saved by using it in conjunction with Hoffmann von Fallersleben's text, which provided "the official expression of the consciousness of unity of the entire German Volk." By ordering the song to be sung in schools, Glöckel wished to "cultivate the national and republican education of the youth."[134] Just as Reich German republicans saw *großdeutsch* nationalism as central to the attempts to defend the democratic republic, so too did the Austrian socialists.

And, one can imagine, the fact that the "Deutschlandlied" became the official anthem of Germany owing to a 1922 decree by Glöckel's fellow socialist Friedrich Ebert may have played a part in Glöckel's decision. Despite the association of the song with the radical right before 1922, Ebert had been able to persuade other republicans to accept the "Deutschlandlied" by stressing its origins as a song supporting a free and democratic Germany.[135] Indeed, Austrian socialist Theodor Körner wrote an unattributed article for the Reichsbanner's journal in order to inform republicans in the Reich about the struggle over the anthem (and the Austrian political system). He concluded that "for all the upstanding Germans and republicans in German-Austria, there is but one battle cry: 'If already Haydn—then the Deutschlandlied!'"[136] Once again, republicans appealed not only to the *großdeutsch* idea, but also sought cross-border support in their political struggles.

Thus, the crux of the debate about the "Deutschlandlied" in Austria was the question of whether Austrians were looking for a state symbol ("Be Blessed

---

134. "Wenn schon Haydn—dann das Deutschlandlied," *AZ*, 13 February 1930, in ÖStA, AdR, Parteiarchive, GDVP, Zeitungsausschnitte, Mappe 24a, 02/c; "Die Haydn-Melodie in den Schulen," *NFP*, 13 February 1930, in WB, TA, Nationalhymne 342.228.

135. Buchner, *Um nationale und republikanische Identität*, 159–167. For primary documents on the topic see BAB, R1501/116880.

136. "Deutsch—trotz allem!," *DR*, 1 March 1930, 65–66, here 66, in VGA, NL Theodor Körner, Kt. 24, Mappe 1/8.

without End") or a national symbol ("Deutschland, Deutschland über alles").[137] As was the case with the students' musical demonstrations, Glöckel's ordinance raised the ire of the proponents of Kernstock-Haydn. In accordance with the Christian Social project of creating a stronger sense of Austrianness, the *Reichspost* argued that the Austrian state needed a *Staatshymne* (state anthem) as opposed to a *Nationalhymne* (national anthem). The paper did not insist that the "Deutschlandlied" should never be sung, for even the Christian Socials wanting to maintain Austrian independence believed themselves to be German in a national sense. Rather, it maintained that the song was appropriate for "national rallies, which wanted to give expression to the feeling of community and togetherness of all Germans regardless of citizenship."[138] However, "Deutschland, Deutschland über alles" was not suitable "as a state anthem" precisely because the boundaries mentioned in the song did not coincide with the current geopolitical situation and would therefore also upset Austria's eastern neighboring countries. Even the *Neue Freie Presse*, which supported the teaching of the "Deutschlandlied" and was more sympathetic to it, regretted that "the children would themselves be drawn into the party politics controversy." "Nothing [could be] more pernicious," the article lamented, "as when one harms youthful enthusiasm through the conscious pitting of one text against the other one, of the national idea against the Austrian one."[139] The struggle between the proponents of a *Staatshymne* and the supporters of a *Nationalhymne* therefore demonstrates the crisis of Austrianness after the Great War: state and nation were not aligned for Austrians; they were citizens of an independent state, but felt themselves to be members of a German nation.

Thus, in both Germany and Austria, the resonance of certain symbols across the Austro-German border played a role in shaping each debate and served as an important aspect in republicans' efforts to legitimize the new form of government. In both cases, *großdeutsch* nationalism was central to republicans' endeavor both to ward off attacks on the republics and their symbols, and to mobilize enthusiasm for them. While this chapter has highlighted the significance of the cross-border elements of these struggles, it has also drawn attention to differences between the countries. Unlike the Reich Germans and their *Flaggenstreit*,

---

137. Steinbauer uses this terminology to describe the debates about the "Deutschlandlied." Steinbauer, *Land der Hymnen*, 21.

138. "Die Zwei Texte," *RP*, 19 February 1930, in WB, TA, Nationalhymne 342.228. This view fit with the cabinet's announcement in late January 1930 that the introduction of Kernstock-Haydn did not mean that the "Deutschlandlied" was forbidden. The cabinet said the song could be used at unofficial occasions. See MRP Nr. 611, 31 January 1930, "Einführung der neuen Oesterreichischen Bundeshymne," in ÖStA, AdR, BKA, MRP, Kt. 151.

139. "Hymnenchaos," *NFP*, 14 February 1930, in WB, TA, Nationalhymne 342.228.

Austrians were unable to reach a consensus about the purpose of this musical symbol: Should it represent the nation or the state? Should it make reference to Austria's prewar past, or should it be firmly rooted in the democratic present? As the anthem debate demonstrates, these were problems for which Austrians were unable to find a solution that would be amenable to a cross-section of the population.[140] By the late 1920s, Austrians could not reach any form of compromise over the state symbol, in contrast to the flag debate in Germany, where at least each side had individuals from across party and class lines. The problematic relationship between Austrians and the state itself can in part account for the more divisive nature of the anthem debate. Because of these different political contexts, republicans faced unique challenges in their endeavor to popularize their political and national views at home, a topic to be addressed more fully in the next chapter's exploration of the attempts to create and stage state holidays.

---

140. See Hanisch, "Politische Symbole," esp. 424; Gustav Spann, "Fahne."

3

REPRESENTATIVE DEMOCRACY
Commemorating the Republics

On April 24, 1919, a proposal was brought before the Austrian Constituent National Assembly regarding holidays. Originating from the State Chancellery, then headed by the socialist Karl Renner, it suggested that November 12 (the declaration of the Austrian republic) and May 1 (International Workers' Day) be declared legal holidays. The next day, the issue came up for discussion in the National Assembly, with Representative Adelheid Popp of the SDAP giving a short speech in favor of the two dates. While she felt the need to make a plea for May 1 because of its party-specific nature, she indicated that November 12 was a more clear-cut case. "There is not much to say about how important, how beautiful and noble it is to consecrate the inception of the republic with a holiday," Popp stated. "I believe I find myself in agreement with the house when I express the conviction that we also give expression to the needs, wishes, and ideals of the broadest sectors of society by proclaiming November 12 as a state holiday."[1] With no further comment, the representatives approved both dates.

In contrast to the ease with which Austrian politicians chose a day to commemorate the new state, Reich Germans were never able to agree on legal holidays in the Weimar Republic. Coming up for debate in the Reichstag numerous times, the issue of an official celebration for the republic always led to deadlock. According to contemporaries, as well as scholars, the failure of parliament to pass

---

1. "11. Sitzung der Konstituierenden Nationalversammlung für Deutschösterreich am 25. April 1919," in *Stenographische Protokolle über die Sitzungen der Konstituierenden Nationalversammlung der Republik Österreich*, vol. 1 (Vienna: Österreichische Staatsdruckerei, 1919), 271–273, here 273.

a law declaring any number of suggested dates as a national holiday—January 18 (the founding of the Reich in 1871), November 9 (the day the Kaiser abdicated and a republic was declared in 1918), May 1 (the traditional labor holiday), August 11 (the signing of the Weimar Constitution in 1919), to name just a few—highlighted the extreme fragmentation of Weimar political culture and the inability to find a resonant democratic consensus.[2] Yet, as we will see, the ability to create a legal holiday, while revealing, was not necessarily indicative of republicans' success in using the holiday to garner support for the new republics.

Taking a step back from the focus on republicans' *großdeutsch* nationalism, this chapter explores the specific obstacles and prospects that republicans faced in legitimizing the republican form of government in their respective countries. Given that republicans had to deal with distinctive political contexts, they had to figure out how to make democracy acceptable to both the Reich German and Austrian populations before they could create a republican Greater Germany. Furthermore, as we will see in the next chapter, the differing political situations at home affected both the opportunities and challenges that a transborder partnership offered republicans.

To examine the differences between the countries, this chapter concentrates on the attempt to establish and stage holidays for the republics. Commemorations, as both contemporaries and scholars have indicated, were an important way to debate the legitimacy of the political system, as well as to define (or redefine) and concretize a national community. Ideally, commemorations can serve as a means of showcasing unity and consolidating existing power relations. Yet commemorations also risk becoming occasions that highlight divisiveness and unrest.[3] In a time of immense political and social change, the creation of new state holidays in Germany and Austria therefore had the potential not only to aid in forging a community of loyal republicans, but also to become part of the vitriolic and violent political struggles.

With regard to a republican commemoration in Germany, we will see that focusing too much on the lack of a legal holiday obscures the energetic and innovative efforts made to win over the hearts and minds of Germans to the republican cause.[4] Republicans coalesced around August 11, the date on which Friedrich Ebert crossed out the words "draft of" and appended his signature to the Weimar

---

2. Lehnert and Megerle, *Politische Identität*; Lehnert and Megerle, "Problems of Identity," 43–59.

3. Kertzer, *Ritual, Politics, and Power*; Gillis, *Commemorations*; Bucur and Wingfield, *Staging the Past*; Brix and Stekl, *Der Kampf*; Friedrich, *Festive Culture*; Behrenbeck and Nützenadel, *Inszenierungen des Nationalstaats*.

4. Achilles, "With a Passion for Reason"; Rossol, *Performing the Nation*, chaps. 3 and 7; Buchner, *Um nationale und republikanische Identität*; Bryden, "In Search of Founding Fathers"; Ziemann, *Contested Commemorations*.

Constitution in 1919, as the best option for a celebration of the fledgling democracy. Hence, although never legally established, Constitution Day (*Verfassungstag*), became a de facto state holiday. Reflecting the middle ground occupied by the parties of the Weimar Coalition (the Social Democratic, the German Democratic, and the Catholic Center Parties), republicans of varying stripes shared a desire to create a *Volksstaat* (people's state) and a *Volksgemeinschaft* (national community), as well as to reconcile the two, through the staging of a *Volksfest* (popular celebration). Government officials and private organizations, while drawing on older traditions, made a concerted effort to stage new forms of commemoration that would forge a democratic and national community of loyal citizens.

The situation looked wholly different in Austria, where the lack of debate over the legislative aspect of the holiday was not duplicated in the celebrations. As the few scholars who have examined the topic have rightly pointed out, the celebrations on November 12 often mirrored the divisions between the major political "camps" (*Lager*)—the SDAP and the groups on the political right—in Austrian society.[5] Although the major parties pledged their support to the state with the current form of government, they disagreed at a fundamental level on the meaning of the history of November 12, as well as concepts such as democracy, the republic, freedom, and Austria. With few exceptions, the commemorative activities replicated this political conflict. After 1920, mostly halfhearted festivities organized by the Christian Social–controlled federal government came into sharp, and at times violent, conflict with the socialist celebrations. In contrast to the commemorations in Germany, after the early years of the republic the parties made no attempt to create a popular and unified celebration. As we will see, despite its lack of a legal holiday, the Weimar Republic presented more possibilities to fashion a pro-republican consensus than did Austria. This difference between the two states was due to the fact that Austrians, unlike Reich Germans, faced the

---

5. In the 1950s, Adam Wandruszka argued that interwar Austria was divided into three *Lager*: the socialist, Catholic, and nationalist camps. Superseding parties and milieu, these "camps" meant that a worldview governed the way people lived almost every facet of their lives "from birth until death." More recently, historians have proposed that ideological affinities among the parties and associations on the political right mean that there were really two camps: the socialist and the anti-Marxist camps. Adam Wandruszka, "Österreichs politische Struktur: Die Entwicklung der Parteien und der politischen Bewegungen," in *Geschichte der Republik Österreich*, ed. Heinrich Benedikt (Vienna: Verlag für Geschichte und Politik, 1954), 289–485. For further discussions of the term *Lager* see Hanisch, *Der Lange Schatten des Staates*, 117–153; Diamant, *Austrian Catholics*, 73–80. The two-camp theory can be found in Edmondson, *Heimwehr*; Thorpe, *Pan-Germanism*; and Wasserman, *Black Vienna*. On the *Lager* during the holidays see Ernst Hanisch, "Das Fest in der fragmentierten politischen Kultur: Der österreichische Staatsfeiertag während der Ersten Republik," in *Politische Teilkulturen zwischen Integration und Polarisierung: zur politischen Kultur in der Weimarer Republik*, ed. Detlef Lehnert and Klaus Megerle (Opladen: Westdeutscher Verlag, 1990), 43–60; Hanisch, "Politische Symbole"; and Spann, "Der österreichische Nationalfeiertag."

double task of coming to terms not only with the new political system, but also an entirely new (and oftentimes unwanted) state.

Constitution Day in the Weimar Republic

The decision on the part of Reich republicans to use the signing of the Weimar Constitution as an occasion to celebrate initially came in response to a 1919 inquiry from the Finnish foreign office regarding the date of Germany's national holiday. Hermann Müller of the SPD, the German foreign minister at the time, proposed August 11 as a way to "dispel the doubts arising abroad about the continued existence of the German Reich's democratic form of government."[6] While this first consideration of this date largely concerned foreign opinion, subsequent discussions, debates, and planning focused on generating domestic support for the new republic through an annual commemoration. By choosing August 11, the backers of a Constitution Day aimed (unsuccessfully) to avoid a multitude of problems associated with the other leading dates proposed for a national holiday.[7] May 1 would be unable to generate widespread support, for it was directly connected to one social milieu, the labor movement, and was an international celebration ill-suited for a "national" holiday. Constitution Day also avoided the political liability associated with November 9, which the political right and many members of the middle and lower middle classes viewed as a day of shame and instability. And, unlike January 18, August 11 had no association with the monarchical past and could therefore appeal to committed republicans of all parties.

With the choice of August 11 as the potential holiday for the new republic, republicans worked hard to transform the constitution from being merely a legal document into a meaningful symbol. Legal scholar Ralf Poscher has argued that constitutions do not usually make for successful symbols because they are "complex, based on compromise and at least in their organizational component strictly rational objects, which are subject to historical change." Yet, as historian Manuela Achilles has illustrated, Weimar republicans aimed to arouse passion for the constitution.[8] To accomplish this feat, republicans highlighted a

---

6. Auswärtiges Amt, 28 November 1919, Berlin, Nr. A 29570/10370, in BAB, R43I/566, Bl. 34.

7. Fritz Schellack, *Nationalfeiertage in Deutschland von 1871 bis 1945* (Frankfurt am Main: Peter Lang, 1990), chap. 3; Buchner, *Um nationale und republikanische Identität*, chap. 5.

8. Ralf Poscher, "Verfassungsfeier in verfassungsfeindlicher Zeit," in *Der Verfassungstag: Reden deutscher Gelehrter zur Feier der Weimarer Verfassung* (Baden-Baden: Nomos Verlagsgesellschaft, 1999), 21; Achilles, "With a Passion for Reason."

few key aspects of the constitution in their endeavor to build political consensus around it. In what can be seen as the attempt to attract liberals, conservatives, and skeptics, proponents of August 11 emphasized that the constitution was an instrument of order because it had prevented the complete collapse of Germany, maintained the unity of the Reich, and stemmed the westward spread of bolshevism. "The worst enemy of the work from Weimar also cannot deny that, with our new constitution for the Reich, our Volk has had its state and political life restored," Heinrich Krone of the Center Party asserted.[9] By pointing to the constitution's role in saving Germany from ruin and dismemberment, republicans stressed "the national meaning of this constitution for the German future."[10] Republicans thereby tried to dispute the notion that the constitution was un-German or a foreign imposition.

For those citizens who were more likely to support the parties of the Weimar Coalition, republicans held up the constitution as the symbol of freedom for and equality of all Germans, regardless of religion or class. Wilhelm Marx, who twice served as chancellor and was a member of the Center Party, pointed out that the Weimar Constitution guaranteed freedom of religion and for the first time "has given the Catholics here freedom, to which they in many ways had a formal as well as earlier constitutional right, but a right that was time and again limited" in the imperial era.[11] In his role as minister of the interior, Carl Severing of the SPD emphasized that the workers could now feel "that this new state is their state," which would in turn lead to a "feeling of a community of fate [*Schicksalsgemeinschaft*] with all sectors of the Volk."[12] Given that both the Center Party and the SPD had experienced repression in the *Kaiserreich*, such statements about equal rights tried to cement the loyalty of Catholics and workers to the new political system, as well as helped to forge a common cause between the two parties.

---

9. Heinrich Krone, "Zum 11. August 1926," in *Reichsbanner Schwarz-Rot-Gold, Festschrift zur Reichs-Verfassungsfeier am 14. und 15. August 1926 in Nürnberg*, ed. Gauleitung Franken (Nuremberg: Fränkische Verlagsanstalt & Buchdruckerei, 1926), 39–41, here 39, in AdsD, Reichsbanner Schwarz-Rot-Gold. Also see Otto Hörsing's "Die Tat von Weimar," in the same publication, 10–11.

10. Copy of "Die Rede des badischen Staatspräsidenten Dr. Hummel bei der Reichstagsfeier des Verfassungstag," 1922, in BAB, R1501/116864, Bl. 40–46, here 41.

11. Reichskanzler a.D. Dr. Marx, "Ethisches in der Reichsverfassung," *Festschrift zur Verfassungs-feier 1925, Berlin, 8. und 9. August* (Berlin: Warenvertrieb des Reichsbanners Schwarz-Rot-Gold, 1925), 16, in AdsD, NL Willy Müller, Abteilung V, box 8, Fasz. 249.

12. Quoted in "Feier der Reichsregierung," *Westfälische Neueste Nachrichten*, 12 August 1929, in AdsD, NL Carl Severing, Abteilung 1, Mappe 15. Marx also discusses the constitution with regard to the creation of a welfare state. Marx, "Ethisches in der Reichsverfassung," 15. On equal rights as an important aspect of the constitution see "K. Müller / Die Notwendigkeit eines nationalen Feiertages," *Die Hilfe*, 5 September 1921, in BAB, R1501/116861, Bl. 120.

This anniversary was organized not simply as a celebration of the constitution, but also (and even more so) as a celebration of the Volk, understood here in a civic sense as the citizens of the republic. As the German Democratic mayor of Hamburg, Carl Petersen, explained in his 1924 Constitution Day speech in the Reichstag, "We chose August 11 as such a day of reflection because this August 11 is connected to the memory of the first formation of a system of German communal life, which the German Volk . . . has created itself."[13] In other words, as creator of the constitution (by way of elected representatives) and the source of the state's power, the Volk was to be a key motif of this anniversary.[14] The centrality of the Volk to the new republic was especially seen in the prevalent use of the concept of the *Volksstaat* among republicans.

However, as we saw in the previous chapters, republicans did not simply use civic ideas to define the Volk or *Volksstaat*; equally important for the supporters of the republic was a national understanding of the Volk. Nationalism for republicans, as chapter 1 highlighted, differed from the racialized, totalizing idea of the *Volksgemeinschaft* promoted by the political right. Rather, republicans saw nationalism as compatible with democracy and sought to reconcile the *Volksstaat* with the *Volksgemeinschaft*.[15] As a suggested text for a Constitution Day speech published by the government explained, "Unity and justice and freedom [*Einigkeit und Recht und Freiheit*] are the three seeds of the German rebirth, are the pillars of German state life, the bands that hold the German *Volksgemeinschaft* together."[16] And in his 1924 speech for Constitution Day, Petersen exclaimed, "There is no other way to national freedom and national strength than that through the German republic!"[17] Socialists also stressed the intimate connection between the nation and the republic in their celebratory speeches and publications.[18] "The republic has achieved this," Severing of the SPD declared on the tenth anniversary of the constitution. "It has

---

13. "Ansprache des Herrn Bürgermeister Dr. Petersen bei der Verfassungsfeier im Reichstag am 11. August 1924," in BAB, R32/527, Bl. 22.

14. "Verfassungsrede gehalten von Prof. Dr. Gustav Radbruch bei der Feier der Reichsregierung am 11. August 1928," in BAB, R32/527, Bl. 72–80, here 74 and Rs.

15. In his book on the "ideas of 1914," Steffen Bruendel argues that German intellectuals grew increasingly divided during the war about what future form Germany should take, with the ideas of the *Volksgemeinschaft* and the *Volksstaat* being the bases of the two opposing camps. Bruendel, *Volksgemeinschaft oder Volksstaat: Die "Ideen von 1914" und die Neuordnung Deutschlands im Ersten Weltkrieg* (Berlin: Akademie Verlag, 2003).

16. "Warum feiern wir den Verfassungstag?," in *Zum Verfassungstag: Eine Materialsammlung* (Berlin: Reichszentrale für Heimatdienst, 1928), 18, in BAB, R32/426, Bl. 109.

17. Ansprache des Herrn Bürgermeister Dr. Petersen bei der Verfassungsfeier im Reichstag am 11. August 1924, in BAB, R32/527, Rs. of Bl. 25.

18. Buchner, *Um nationale und republikanische Identität*, 343–344.

saved German territory [*Boden*] and the German Volk!"[19] According to this republican line of thinking, democracy was a German value and characteristic, and Germanness was democratic at its core. The contentions of the political right that the constitution and the republic were un-German were therefore wrong, republicans insisted. After all, power now emanated from the Volk, understood in a national sense, which meant that the democratic republic was a truer expression of the national community than a monarchical or authoritarian regime could be.

In order to impart these messages and try to anchor them in the hearts and minds of the population at large, republicans worked to create an annual holiday specifically devoted to the infant republic. Such a commemoration, the supporters of the republic contended, would provide an invaluable opportunity to educate Germans about the merits of the new state. "The implementation of a national holiday is an issue of far-reaching importance," the German Teachers' Association, which supported August 11 as a day of commemoration, wrote in a letter to the Reich Ministry of the Interior in the early 1920s. "Not least of all, the younger generation's education in the idea of the *Volksstaat* requires a visible focus around which all national comrades [*Volksgenossen*] rally. The avowal to the Reich and to the principles of its constitution necessitates a regularly recurring celebratory form, which can best be created in the shape of a general national holiday."[20] Coming from a teachers' organization, which could just as easily have advocated the use of civics lessons in school, this letter shows that supporters of the republic attached a special importance to the role of a state holiday in winning over the public to the democratic state.

The creation of a holiday specifically for the republic necessitated, in the eyes of Constitution Day organizers, a form of state commemoration that befitted the now more intimate relationship between state and society following World War I. One of the most important figures in developing a suitable holiday was Edwin Redslob, the head of the newly created office of the Reichskunstwart (federal art expert). While various ministers of the interior dealt with the organizational aspects of August 11, Redslob was in charge of staging the federal government's celebrations. Furthermore, he was the one federal government official who consistently dealt with August 11 during the entire Weimar Republic. Redslob had trained as an art historian and served as a museum curator before his appointment in 1920 to this post within the Reich Ministry of the Interior. Although

---

19. Quoted in "Feier der Reichsregierung," *Westfälische Neueste Nachrichten*, 12 August 1929, in AdsD, NL Carl Severing, Abteilung 1, Mappe 15.

20. Letter from the Deutscher Lehrerverein to the Ministry of the Interior, Tgb.Nr.2019/22, Berlin, 21 November 1922, in R1501/116861, Bl. 330.

the actual power of the office has been debated by historians, he both theorized about and engaged in a wide array of artistic and cultural activities, ranging from taxes on works of art to the problems faced by traditional handicrafts to the creation of new symbols for the Reich.[21] For the purposes of this chapter, the focus will be on Redslob's theories regarding the role of commemoration in German society. "A new search for community in our immediate present," wrote Redslob for a radio address on the occasion of the tenth anniversary of the constitution, "clearly follows from the dissolution of all forms of state brought about by the revolution."[22] In his view, commemorations played a key role in this search: "Festivals are the formed experience of the community."[23]

To create a community of loyal republicans, Redslob proposed to craft a new type of state commemoration that would be radically different—in both content and form—from the commemorations of the *Kaiserreich*. In line with republicans' desires to show the intimate connection between nationalism and democracy, he criticized the imperial festivities for promoting dynastic particularism over German unity. Imperial Germany "honored the Prussian crowning of the king but not the crowning of the emperor, just as the Siegesallee [the Victory Avenue in Berlin] portrayed Prussian history emanating from the Margraviate of Brandenburg rather than German history."[24] Furthermore, not only did the Volk not figure as the object of celebration, but it was also made into a passive audience at these ostentatious festivities.[25] The government celebrations of the imperial era therefore "became more and more a conscious display of the power of the state."[26] Such styles of commemoration, which privileged the state over its citizens, would not suit the new *Volksstaat*. However, what Redslob referred to as "the movement to a new festival culture" did not entail a complete rejection of preexisting traditions.[27] In seeking to create a popular celebration that would be more in line with democratic politics, he looked back to the popular festivals of the first half of the nineteenth century. This form of commemoration was created by the Volk to celebrate itself and often in opposition to reactionary,

21. Annegret Heffen, *Der Reichskunstwart, Kunstpolitik in den Jahren 1920–1933: Zu den Bemühungen um eine offizielle Reichskunstpolitik in der Weimarer Republik* (Essen: Verlag Die Blaue Eule, 1986); Achilles, "Re-forming the Reich," 122–139.

22. Edwin Redslob, Draft of "Die Verfassungsfeier als Ausdruck deutscher Festeskultur," in BAB, R32/426, Bl. 79–96, here 79. For another copy of Redslob's essay see R32/499, Bl. 263–280.

23. Untitled page at the end of Edwin Redslob, "Feste und Feiern des Volkes," in BAB, R32/499, Bl. 261.

24. [Redslob], Draft of "Akademie-Vortrag," BAB, R32/499, Bl. 331–332.

25. Redslob, "Feste und Feiern des Volkes," in BAB, R32/499, Bl. 252.

26. [Redslob], Draft of "Akademie-Vortrag," BAB, R32/499, Bl. 332.

27. Redslob, "Feste und Feiern des Volkes," in BAB, R32/499, Bl. 255.

particularistic governments.[28] Redslob posited that in Imperial Germany a division had developed between *Staatsfeste* (state celebrations) and *Volksfeste* (popular celebrations), and his goal was to erase this historical split.[29]

In order to achieve a popular state celebration, organizers both within and outside the government stressed the involvement of ordinary citizens in the holiday. Just as citizens were now active participants in the state's power, they too should play an active role in the celebration of the state. According to Redslob, the various sorts of events developed needed to "overcome the sharp division between participants [*Mitwirkenden*] and onlookers [*Zuschauern*]," an important aspect of traditional popular festivals and a sharp difference from the pompous celebrations of the Wilhelmine period.[30] Whereas Redslob aimed primarily to forge a community loyal to the democratic state through the active involvement of individuals, others made similar proposals in order to teach the individual about his or her role in the nascent republic. Fritz Koch, a leader of the Reichsbanner, argued that the Constitution Day celebration needed to be a *Volksfest* in which people were more than simply spectators. "The attempt must be made to interest old and young, man and woman to take part themselves to the best of their ability," Koch proposed. "Thereby will all those, who today still stand aside uninterested, become aware and thus be won for us. . . . We will achieve the growing feeling of responsibility of the German citizen and thereby also the self-confident feeling of being a free citizen in a free state."[31] The push to create participatory celebrations was therefore not only a reflection of the new power relations in the state, but also an instrument to instruct Germans of their new function in politics.

This shift in goals and content—to have the Volk as a central object of celebration as well as the active agent of the event— did not automatically transform Constitution Day into a *Volksfeiertag* (people's holiday). An important aspect of creating a real *Volksfeiertag* was getting people to participate. The creation of a popular holiday was a process in which every year organizers tweaked the program and created new events in response to previous years' successes and failures. After all, in 1920, when asked whether the government would decorate with flags for

---

28. Dieter Düding, Peter Friedemann, and Paul Münch, eds., *Öffentliche Festkultur: Politische Feste in Deutschland von der Aufklärung bis zum Ersten Weltkrieg* (Reinbeck: Rowohlt, 1988).

29. Fritz Herbert Lohe, "Staatliche Feiern—Volksfeiern: Ein Vortrag des Reichskunstwarts," *Deutsche Allgemeine Zeitung*, November 1930, in BAB, R32/499, Bl. 312.

30. Edwin Redslob, Draft of "Die Verfassungsfeier als Ausdruck deutscher Festeskultur," 1929, in BAB, R32/426, Bl. 79–96, here 96.

31. Fritz Koch, "11. August oder 18. Januar," in *Festschrift zur Verfassungsfeier 1925, Berlin, 8. und 9. August* (Berlin: Warenvertrieb des Reichsbanners Schwarz-Rot-Gold, 1925), 8, in AdsD, NL Willy Müller, Abteilung V, box 8, Fasz. 249.

the first anniversary of the constitution, the Reich Ministry of the Interior under Erich Koch-Weser of the DDP ruled out the idea because "one cannot well hang flags in a time of national humiliation."[32] And when the government did stage the first Constitution Day festivities in 1921, they were far from being a *Volksfest*. Concerned about provoking opponents of the republic, especially those recently elected to the Reichstag, the government limited celebrations to a ceremony in the State Opera House in Berlin, which included musical performances and a speech about the meaning of the day given by Chancellor Joseph Wirth of the Center Party. Furthermore, Redslob was told to refrain from decorating the room with the republic's controversial colors of black-red-gold. This Constitution Day was, in Redslob's later estimation, an "academic, cool ceremonial act of the Reich authorities."[33] Yet, already during the ceremony, Wirth expressed his hopes that in the future the *Volksstaat* would be celebrated by the entire Volk.[34] And in the years that followed, the Constitution Day festivities would continually come closer to this ideal of a *Volksfest* celebrating the democratic state (at least until 1931, when the political and economic crisis prevented elaborate celebrations).

The mild success of the 1921 commemoration and the unexpected outpouring of support for the republic at Walther Rathenau's state funeral after his assassination by members of the right-wing Deutschvölkischer Schutz- und Trutzbund led the government to start taking measures to turn the *Verfassungstag* into a *Volksfeiertag*.[35] Such efforts began in earnest when in early July 1922 the Reich minister of the interior, Adolf Köster of the SPD, suggested that the federal government's main ceremony be moved to the Reichstag "as the real house of the people [*Volkshaus*]," that public events should be created (by the government or private initiative) "so that the population itself also plays a part in the celebration," that a military reveille should start the day, that various levels of government should organize a cultural performance, and, lastly, that the provincial governments should be encouraged to hold similar activities.[36] These recommendations would establish the basic framework for all future Constitution Days and demonstrate the push beginning in 1922 to actually make the holiday more popular throughout the entire country.

---

32. Auszug aus dem Protokoll der Sitzung des Reichsministeriums vom 3. August 1920, in BAB, R43I/566, Bl. 55.

33. Edwin Redslob, "Die Staatsfeiern der Reichsregierung," without newspaper title or date, in BAB, R32/499, Bl. 314.

34. Quoted in Untitled [about the celebration on 11 August 1921], 1921, in R1501/116861, Bl. 152.

35. Achilles, "Re-forming the Reich," chap. 4.

36. Copy of a letter from the Reichsminister des Innern to the Herrn Reichspräsidenten, the Herrn Reichskanzler und sämtliche Herren Reichsminister, Berlin, 5 July 1922, in BAB, R1501/116864, Bl. 5.

Over the course of the next nine years, the federal government and some provincial authorities would continue to come up with specific commemorative practices to spread the appeal of the holiday to all citizens.[37] These included festive and torchlight processions by organizations and clubs, open-air concerts by military and police bands, garden parties, sporting events particularly for the youth, the addition of more evening events in larger spaces in Berlin, publications about the meaning of the day, and competitions to come up with poetic and musical works that would pay tribute to the *Volksstaat*. Regardless of what had occurred the previous year, officials during the planning stages of the holiday continually proposed "that the joint Constitution Day celebration in this year still needs to be organized differently and above all should develop into a genuine *Volksfest*"—as a Prussian minister put it when he suggested that more open-air concerts and special activities for children should be held in 1928.[38]

The government was not the only organizer of celebrations for August 11. Private organizations and sporting and singing clubs also played key roles in participating in government events and orchestrating their own activities. After its founding in 1924, the Reichsbanner became the most significant association in this regard and, as Fritz Koch's statement above demonstrates, also had the goal of creating a *Volksfest* for August 11. Choosing one city as the location for its central celebration each year, the Reichsbanner also staged smaller Constitution Day festivities throughout Germany. In the first year of its existence alone, the group's commemorations brought together thousands of people in both major cities and small towns. A sampling of estimated numbers of attendees provides an idea of the extensiveness of this Reichsbanner Constitution Day: 15,000 Reichsbanner members in Weimar; over 1,000 men and women in Münster; thousands of participants in Berlin, with 5,000 uniformed Reichsbanner members; "almost the entire population" in Cottbus, Sommerfeld, Guben, Spremberg, Frankfurt an der Oder, Schneidemühl, Schwiebus, Prenzlau; over 100,000 people in Hamburg; 15,000 to 20,000 in Stettin; 35,000 to 40,000 in Kiel; 30,000 in Magdeburg; "the entire population" in Görlitz; 28,000 to 30,000 people in Breslau; 2,500 to 3,000 spectators and 600 Reichsbanner members in Brieg; 15,000 people in Rostock; 20,000 in Hanover; 8,000 in Goslar; 16,000 in Cassel; 60,000

37. Pamela Swett, "Celebrating the Republic without Republicans: The Reichsverfassungstag in Berlin, 1929–1932," in *Festive Culture in Germany and Europe from the Sixteenth to the Twentieth Century*, ed. Karin Friedrich (Lewiston, NY: Edwin Mellen, 2000), 284–286.

38. Zu Rk.2658, Gemeinsame Verfassungsfeier des Reichs, Preußens und der Stadt Berlin am 11. August 1928, Besprechung im Preußischen Ministerium des Innern am 26. März 1928, Berlin, 28 March 1928, in BAB, R43I/571, Bl. 185.

in Nuremberg.[39] These Reich-wide celebrations also performed an important function in bringing popular Constitution Day events to places such as Bavaria, where the provincial government—conservative and wary of a federal push for centralization—refused to organize official commemorations.

By 1929, the tenth anniversary of the constitution, the Reichsbanner could happily report that it, alongside a number of local authorities, civil servants, and a range of working-class, bourgeois, and Catholic associations, had achieved its goal of creating popular celebrations for the republic. According to *Das Reichsbanner*, the organization's journal, various celebrations had attracted 150,000 Reichsbanner members and hundreds of thousands of others in Berlin; over 15,000 people in Hannover; 100,000 in Hamburg; hundreds of thousands in Düsseldorf; 100,000 in Heidelberg; tens of thousands in Bremen; 21,000 in Karlsruhe; 20,000 in Lübeck; and 20,000 in Minden. Although the publication did not provide specific numbers for Magdeburg, Essen, Kassel, Braunschweig, Darmstadt, Stuttgart, Stettin, Detmold, Bochum, Mannheim, Fürstenwalde, Bonn, Saarbrücken, Nuremberg, Munich, Stralsund, Oppeln, Duisburg, Ulm, Mainz, Frankfurt an der Oder, Küstrin, Koblenz, Cologne, and Ludwigsberg, it remarked that massive crowds participated in and attended parades, firework shows, concerts, and sporting events in these locales.[40]

Such commemorations not only attracted large numbers of Germans to the republican form of government, but they were also able to bridge some political, class, religious, and generational gaps that plagued German society. With a leadership composed of members from the Social Democratic, German Democratic, and Center Parties, the Reichsbanner highlighted that it brought together members of all three parties, as well as Catholics, Protestants, and Jews. "As in the trench," Hermann Grossmann stated on the occasion of the Reichsbanner's 1925 Constitution Day festivities in Berlin, "the Reichsbanner comprises rich and poor; educated and uneducated; farmer and city dweller; Jew, Christian, and atheist; Catholic and Protestant, in short a German person next to the other, so that we understand one another and learn to act justly."[41] Such words were more than mere idealistic rhetoric. For example, in its accounts of the 1929 official and private Constitution Day festivities, *Das Reichsbanner* mentioned how bourgeois

---

39. "Pressestimmen über die Feier in Weimar," "Die Verfassungsfeier in Münster," and "Die Feier in den Bannergauen," all in *Der Fünfte Jahrestag der deutschen Reichsverfassung: Aufmarsch des Reichsbanners Schwarz-Rot-Gold am Verfassungstag 1924*, in R43I/570, Bl. 275–289.

40. "Der Sieg der Weimarer Reichsverfassung," *DR*, 24 August 1929 (Beilage), 283–284. On Berlin see "Der Tag der deutschen Nation," *DR*, 17 August 1929, 269.

41. Dr. Hermann Grossmann, "Gerechtigkeit," in *Festschrift zur Verfassungsfeier 1925, Berlin, 8. und 9. August* (Berlin: Wrenvertrieb des Reichsbanners Schwarz-Rot-Gold, 1925), 24, in AdsD, NL Willy Müller, Abteilung V, box 8, Fasz. 249.

FIGURE 1. Reichsbanner celebrations for the tenth anniversary of the Weimar Constitution in August 1929. "The demonstration of 150,000." *Illustrierte Republikanische Zeitung*, August 17, 1929, 520–521. Reproduced with permission of Verlag J. H. W. Dietz Nachf.

and workers' clubs alike, Catholic youth groups, unions, firemen, policemen, and the army participated alongside the Reichsbanner.[42] These initiatives from private organizations to create an inclusive community of republicans demonstrate that the holiday was indeed developing into a *Volksfest*.

The culmination of the search for a popular state holiday was a new event added for the tenth anniversary of the constitution in 1929 and held again during the 1930 commemoration: the staging of a mass spectacle in the Berlin stadium, which was made possible by the advent of radio, microphones, and loudspeaker systems.[43] The 1929 stadium show, written by Josef von Fielitz and held under the guidance of Redslob, had three main motifs: the attempt to build a bridge (which can only be successfully completed by the youth) to represent the unity of the Reich; "the image of a living Reich flag"[44] made up of children dressed in black, red, and gold; and, finally, sporting competitions and dancing. All in all, 11,500 schoolchildren (under the guidance of their teachers) performed alongside members of the German Workers' Choral League, an athletic club, and the bands of the police and of the Reichsbanner for an audience of about fifty thousand. The 1930 stadium show, titled "Germany's River," was written by Redslob and performed both in Wiesbaden in July 1930 on the occasion of the evacuation of the Rhineland by French troops and in Berlin for Constitution Day. In this spectacle, children clad in different shades of blue and green ran onto the field to represent Germany's rivers—the Pregel, the Vistula, the Oder, the Elbe, the Weser, the Spree, the Havel, and the Danube—accompanied by symbols of the major cities on each of these rivers. The main story line was that the Rhine had to be freed from the chains of foreign oppression before it could join the rest of the rivers. Once again, thousands of schoolchildren performed for an audience of fifty thousand. Both of these stadium shows included the singing of the national anthem, which according to organizers and the press enabled those in the bleachers to become participants.[45] Moreover, according to Redslob, both performances had thousands more participants as a result of radio broadcasts. Listeners across

---

42. "Der Sieg der Weimarer Reichsverfassung," *DR*, 24 August 1929 (Beilage), 283–284. For an example regarding the inclusion of Jews see the 1926 Reichsbanner commemoration in Bonn, where a service was held not only at the Ehrenfriedhof, but also at the Jewish cemetery. "Programm," *Verfassungsfeier 1926 des Reichsbanners Schwarz-Rot-Gold Gau Oberrhein in Bonn, 14. u. 15. August 1926*, in AdsD, Reichsbanner Schwarz-Rot-Gold, Exponate 19.

43. As Nadine Rossol has importantly shown, the Nazis were not the only ones to embrace new technologies and mass spectacle; republicans did so as well. Rossol, *Performing the Nation*, chaps. 3 and 4.

44. Draft of the Spielfolge, in BAB, R32/430, Bl. 70.

45. "Die Jugend im Stadion: Das grosse Festspiel 'Deutschlands Strom,'" *BT*, 11 August 1930, in BAB, R32/437, Bl. 51.

the Reich had "the opportunity . . . to take part in the celebration from afar" through the use of this technology.[46]

The turn to mass spectacle by the organizers of Constitution Day was hailed as a great success in creating a truly popular celebration. As one newspaper headline proclaimed, "Constitution Day—finally a *Volksfeiertag*!"[47] Furthermore, this development in the culture of commemoration did a great deal in achieving its two chief goals: the education of the population on the one hand, and the portrayal and construction of a republican community on the other. In a report on the schools' involvement in the 1930 show, the vice president of the provincial school council concluded that, as in the previous year, the participation of the schoolchildren had an "*educational benefit.*" "In vivid style," he continued, "they experienced the idea of the Reich's constitution, which holds Germany together, they experienced the misery of the occupied borderland, otherwise unknown to central Germany, and the importance of its liberation. Generally they learned to fit into a great whole, and they saw how, despite all opposition, the labor of the many evolved into a gratifying work for all thanks to the energy of the individual."[48] Indeed, according to Redslob, these mass spectacles had "an exceedingly strong effect" and gave "a large number of Germans the feeling of togetherness and unity on Constitution Day."[49]

Although historian Pamela Swett has criticized these performances for lacking a "coherent vision of the Republic," she overlooks how such celebrations mobilized hundreds of thousands of people to partake in events that exemplified republican arguments about the relationship between nationalism and democracy.[50] Republicans, as the themes of the stadium spectacles illustrate, tried to use Constitution Day to highlight their national sentiment in order to fend off their opponents' argument that the republic and its supporters were un-German. As one newspaper exclaimed after the performance of "Germany's River," "It was an hour of a national experience. Republicans also have national sentiment."[51] Nor were these the only events to highlight republican nationalism during Constitution

46. Edwin Redslob, Draft of "Die Verfassungsfeier als Ausdruck deutscher Festeskultur," in BAB, R32/426, Bl. 79–96, here 94.

47. Title of a picture collage from an untitled, undated publication, in BAB, R32/437, Bl. 81.

48. Studiendirektor Roethig-Luckau, Bericht über die Stadionverfassungs- und Rheinlandbefreiungsfeier vom 10. August 1930, in BAB, R32/434a, Bl. 85. Emphasis in original.

49. Letter from Redslob to Oberspielleiter Josef von Fielitz, Berlin, 16 August 1929, in BAB, R32/503, Bl. 136.

50. Swett, "Celebrating the Republic," 290. Anthony McElligott also goes too far in contending that the 1930 performance was characteristic of "cultural authoritarianism." McElligott, *Rethinking the Weimar Republic*, chaps. 3 and 6, here 153.

51. "Verfassungsfeier im Grunewaldstadion," *Westfälischer Courier*, 13 August 1930, in BAB, R32/437, Bl. 37.

Day. Friedrich Ebert, for instance, used the 1922 Constitution Day to declare the "Deutschlandlied" as the national anthem of the republic. And, as we will see in the following chapter, the *großdeutsch* idea would also be a prominent motif at Constitution Day and other republican festivities. While an important motivation in all these actions was to entice skeptics of the republic to participate by employing motifs that would also be dear to their hearts,[52] it would be wrong to see this as the organizers' only purpose. These particular events allowed republicans an opportunity to express their specific version of German nationalism.

Despite these successes, Constitution Day simultaneously drew attention to the fractures within Weimar political culture because of the opposition of many political groups to the republican and democratic form of government.[53] On the political right, critics of August 11 decried the attempt to turn the constitution into a national symbol. Members of the DNVP and the Stahlhelm argued against the republican notion that the constitution grew out of the Volk. Rather, they maintained that it was a foreign imposition. In an effort to prove their point, they cited article 178, paragraph 2 of the Weimar Constitution, which stated that the postwar constitution of Germany could not affect the terms of the Treaty of Versailles. According to their logic, this article demonstrated that the Weimar Constitution was subordinate to the so-called Allied Diktat.[54] Furthermore, as Reichstag representative Friedrich Everling argued, the republican proposals to make August 11 a "national holiday" (*Nationalfeiertag*) misused the term "national." A member of the DNVP and outspoken supporter of the black-white-red tricolor, Everling maintained that "the content of the constitution contradicts the essence of our nation," and "it does not have the ability to unify, which we must at the very least connect with the concept of the 'national.'"[55] For conservatives, republican proclamations concerning the relationship between Germanness and democracy fell on deaf ears.

Right-wing nationalists, as well as communists, also disparaged the proposition by the supporters of democracy that August 11 should be a day of celebration. During a 1927 debate in the Reichstag's Committee for Legal Affairs on proposals to make August 11 an official holiday, August Creutzburg, a member of the

---

52. Schellack, *Nationalfeiertage*, chap. 3.

53. Lehnert and Megerle, *Politische Identität*. Other scholars have noted that the festivities were able to achieve at least a limited consensus among republicans. See Friederike Schubart, "Zehn Jahre Weimar—Eine Republik blickt zurück," in *Griff nach der Deutungsmacht: Zur Geschichte der Geschichtspolitik in Deutschland*, ed. Heinrich August Winkler (Göttingen: Wallstein, 2004), 134–59; Achilles, "With a Passion for Reason."

54. "Um den Nationalfeiertag. Beratungen im Rechtsausschuss," *Börsen-Zeitung*, 7 July 1927, in BAB, R72/1160, Bl. 69; "Gedankliches zur Verfassungsfeier," *Stahlhelm Zeitung*, 11 August 1927, in BAB, R72/1309, Bl. 2.

55. Friedrich Everling, "Nationalfeiertag?—Nationaltrauertag!," *Der Aufrechte*, 15 July 1927, in BAB, R72/1160, Bl. 68.

German Communist Party, remarked that communists "would regard Constitution Day as a day of mourning," for "the Weimar Constitution has only secured the rule of the bourgeoisie." In the same debate, Axel von Freytagh-Loringhoven of the DNVP contended that in a time of national humiliation—that is, while the Treaty of Versailles was still in effect—Germans should not hold festive occasions. Instead the population should hold a national day of mourning on June 28, the day the treaty was signed.[56] Yet the pall of the hated peace treaty was not the only reason why the political right refused to recognize August 11 as a holiday. According to, respectively, Graf Westarp and Wilhelm Bazille of the DNVP, "the national holiday must arise out of the heart of the Volk,"[57] and a "national holiday can only be a day about which the entire Volk is convinced that this day means something great in its life."[58] Both concurred that Constitution Day did not fulfill these requirements because of political cleavages and opposition to the republic within the population.

This antagonism toward legislation regarding August 11 was also reflected in the actions of opponents during the planning and celebration of Constitution Day. From storming out of ceremonies to refusing to stage festivities to providing diminished funds for planned commemorations, adversaries of Constitution Day found ways to make known their dissatisfaction with the de facto holiday. In 1927, for example, soldiers created an uproar when they abruptly left a Constitution Day ceremony in Gießen after the speaker criticized the monarchy. Their actions prompted republicans to decry the "demonstration against the republican political system" by members of the army, who had sworn an oath to protect the democratic constitution.[59] In other cases, organizations opposed to the republic refused from the outset to take part in the festivities on August 11. Much to the dismay of Chancellor Wilhelm Marx of the Center Party, who had hoped to stage a grand apolitical celebration, the Stahlhelm declined an invitation to participate

56. "Um den Nationalfeiertag," *BBZ*, 7 July 1927, in BAB, R72/1160, Bl. 69. Those falling in line with Stresemann's less radical German People's Party proposed that January 18 be the new national holiday. Prof. Dr. R. Hennig, "Sedan-Ersatz," *Tägliche Rundschau*, 8 August 1922, in BAB, R1501/116864, Bl. 106; "Nationalfeiertage: Ein Vorwort zu den Verfassungsfeiern am 11. August," *Tägliche Rundschau*, 2 August 1922, in BAB, R1501/116861, Bl. 286.

57. Auszug aus dem Protokoll der Parteiführerbesprechung vom 4. Juli 1927, in BAB, R43I/567, Bl. 87.

58. Letter from Der Staatspräsident von Württemberg (Bazille) to Reichskanzler Dr. Marx, Stuttgart, 21 June 1927, in BAB, R43I/567, Bl. 76–77.

59. Copy of a letter from the Staatspräsident und Minister des Äussern (Ulrich) to the Reichswehrminister, 17 August 1927, Darmstadt, in BAB, R43I/571, Bl. 162–164, here 163. Also see Bl. 165–173. The police, as well as other local officials, criticized the speech as being too political and unsuited for the occasion of Constitution Day.

in a torchlight parade for the 1927 Constitution Day in Berlin.[60] Similarly, members of the DNVP, the Nazi Party, and the Communist Party of Germany skipped a 1929 session of the Munich city council because the mayor was giving a speech to commemorate Constitution Day.[61] More consistently, Bavarian authorities rejected requests by the Reich Ministry of the Interior to hold annual festivities on August 11, with the exception of the ten-year anniversary of the constitution in 1929. As the Bavarian government explained in 1923, "In Bavaria, one admittedly affirms the constitution, but one does not affirm it happily." The Bavarian government, dominated by Catholic conservatives who were against the republic and rule from Berlin, went on to complain that such a request "transgresses the authority of the Reich government."[62]

Such demonstrations against Constitution Day, although troublesome for the republic's attempt to gain legitimacy, only occasionally devolved into physical conflicts.[63] The relative peacefulness of the de facto holiday in Germany stands in sharp contrast to the state holiday in Austria, which was plagued by violence. Bazille, the DNVP governor of Württemberg, explained in part why this was the case: "I am naturally of the opinion that one should not infringe upon the views and feelings of others. My demonstrations are therefore not directed against the heretofore customary style of the Constitution Day celebration, but simply against the attempt to make this day the legal national holiday of the Germans."[64] Even the Stahlhelm, a paramilitary organization aimed at bringing down the democratic form of government, echoed such sentiments.[65] And, as the historian Bernd Buchner has noted, although President Paul von Hindenburg and interior ministers from the DNVP and DVP were not supportive of the republic, none of these politicians attempted to cancel the August 11 events.[66]

Although Constitution Day surmounted these challenges, it could not weather the increasingly violent clashes between political adversaries, growing economic difficulties, and escalating efforts to dismantle democratic institutions that began with the enactment of emergency decrees in 1930. Although the 1931 Constitution Day activities had to be scaled back owing to the effects of the Great Depression

---

60. See relevant documents in BAB, R43I/571, Bl. 100–121, 126, 134–136.
61. Letter from the Vertretung der Reichsregierung in München to the Reichskanzlei, Munich, 9 August 1929, in BAB, R707/101, Bl. 32.
62. Bericht über die Sitzung im Reichsministerium des Innern mit den Vertretern des Reichsrats über die Verfassungsfeier am 11. August, Berlin, 14 July 1923, in BAB, R43I/570, Bl. 166 and Rs.
63. Swett, "Celebrating the Republic," 294–300.
64. Letter from Der Staatspräsident von Württemberg (Bazille) to Reichskanzler Dr. Marx, Stuttgart, 21 June 1927, in BAB, R43I/567, Bl. 76–77.
65. "Gedankliches zur Verfassungsfeier," Stahlhelm Zeitung, 11 August 1927, in BAB, R72/1309, Bl. 2.
66. Buchner, Um nationale und republikanische Identität, 334–336.

and the presidential cabinets, which led to growing authoritarianism in the government, the speaker at the event, Finance Minister Hermann Dietrich of the DDP, continued to find inspiration in the constitution while recognizing the immense challenges facing Germany.[67] However, a year later, the official Constitution Day speaker, Interior Minister Wilhelm Freiherr von Gayl of the DNVP, dismissed the constitution as a divisive force in German national life and advocated changing it. Furthermore, he maintained that Constitution Day had never developed into a popular holiday.[68] By 1932, therefore, Constitution Day was no longer a celebration of the Weimar Constitution; rather, it had become a "burial of the republic."[69] As Joseph Goebbels sarcastically remarked in a 1932 diary entry, "Last Constitution Day! Let them have a brief bit of joy!"[70] Goebbels was indeed correct. Five months later, Hindenburg appointed Hitler chancellor, which soon brought the democratic experiment to an end.

Yet, until 1931, the general trend was toward the increasing popularity and success of the holiday. Although it is important not to ignore the difficulties that republicans encountered in garnering support for the republic, critiques, such as the one that the historian George Mosse levels against Constitution Day, are overstated. "A government based on discussion and compromise," Mosse argues, "had no real interest in grasping the traditions of a national cult which seemed opposed to rational control of the state."[71] Republicans did, however, appeal to the ideas of the *Volksgemeinschaft* while also trying to inculcate the population with the individual responsibilities of a citizen living in a democratic state. Considering the controversial founding of the republic, as well as the economic and political turmoil during its life span, it is remarkable to see the significant strides made by the government and private organizations in creating a popular republican holiday that bridged at least some of the sociopolitical divisions in Germany. After all, Imperial Germany, which was founded following a victory over France, never had a state holiday. And even the official holidays in countries that had a triumphal beginning for democracy, such as Bastille Day in France or Independence Day in the United States, were contested and took time to develop

---

67. Rede des Reichsministers der Finanzen im Reichstag zur Verfassungsfeier am 11. August 1931, in BAB, R43I/573, Bl. 219–236.

68. [Untitled], in BAB, R43I/573, Bl. 284–297.

69. Buchner, *Um nationale und republikanische Identität*, 304.

70. Quoted in ibid.

71. George Mosse, *The Nationalization of the Masses*, 124–125, here 125. Also see Peukert, *Weimar Republic*, 5–6, 35; Gay, *Weimar Culture*, esp. chap. 2; Swett, "Celebrating the Republic." For works that provide further evidence against this older contention see Achilles, "With a Passion for Reason," and Rossol, *Performing the Nation*, chaps. 3–4.

into an accepted tradition.[72] As the case of Austria shows, the legal declaration of a national holiday to commemorate the infant republic did not necessarily accomplish the desire to stage a true *Volksfest*.

November 12 in Austria

As the anecdote opening this chapter illustrated, Austrians chose a legal holiday for the new republic with little trouble. This initial acceptance would not be without problems in the future. It reflected the political situation of the early years of the republic, when the Social Democrats, Christian Socials, and German nationalists worked together as a coalition government until 1920. Increasingly, the different political parties would disagree about the past events leading to the declaration of the republic, the present state of the country, and the future path Austria should take. Consensus such as that achieved in April 1919 regarding the holiday would become the exception rather than the rule in the future yearly commemorations. Whereas republicans in Germany had not chosen November 9 so as to avoid conflicting sentiments about the meaning of that day, the various political parties in Austria would engage in a hostile dispute over what had actually happened in the autumn of 1918. Although the Constituent National Assembly's "Announcement to the Austrian Volk" of November 12, 1918, had declared that "burgher, farmer, and worker have united in order to found the new German-Austria," the major political parties began to put forth differing interpretations of the republic's creation.[73] As the conflicting narratives of the republic's founding demonstrate, the adherents of the three major parties were unable to create a common collective memory that transcended the social and political divisions within Austria.[74]

Relying on Marxist language and ideas of class struggle, the socialists insisted that workers alone had created the republic. As Ferdinand Hanusch, an SDAP representative to the Nationalrat and a central figure in implementing

---

72. Gillis, *Commemorations*, 8–11.

73. Staatskanzler Karl Renner of the SDAP read the announcement to no objections. "3. Sitzung der Provisorischen Nationalversammlung für Deutschösterreich am 12. November 1918," in *Stenographische Protokolle über die Sitzungen der Provisorischen Nationalversammlung für Deutschösterreich*, vol. 1 (Vienna: Deutschösterreichische Staatsdruckerei, 1919), 69. This initial consensus soon fell apart over questions of a constitution, provincial power, and foreign policy. See John Boyer, "Silent War and Bitter Peace: The Revolution of 1918 in Austria," *Austrian History Yearbook* 34 (2003): 1–56.

74. This inability to do so was not simply a product of the postwar period, as similar accusatory rhetoric occurred in the last decades of the Habsburg Empire among the CSP, Social Democrats, and German nationalists. Unowsky, *Pomp and Politics*, 145–184.

postwar social reforms, pronounced before a like-minded crowd in Graz during the 1922 celebrations, "It is shameful that neither the bourgeoisie nor the
landowners were involved with the founding of the republic. They have left it
solely to the working class."[75] The Social Democrats did not simply take pride
in their role as founders of the new state; they also viewed the actions of the
working class as amounting to a revolution that freed subjects of the empire
from Habsburg oppression. "In the revolution of 1918," Otto Bauer explained
on the occasion of the tenth anniversary of the republic, "Social Democracy
finally chased away the emperor, dissolved the House of Lords and the provincial legislatures and municipal councils elected on the basis of privileged voting
rights, and enforced the democratic republic against the resistance of the still
monarchist bourgeoisie."[76] Hence, in the socialist narrative, November 12 was,
despite the terrible material deprivation of the time, a positive event worthy of
celebration.

Politically conservative Catholics took issue with this socialist interpretation
of November 12. An article in the *Reichspost*, the paper associated with Ignaz
Seipel's increasingly authoritarian wing of the CSP, summed up various aspects
of this viewpoint on the 1925 anniversary. It deserves to be quoted at length:

> The new Austria still has no state holiday which would be, in a posi-
> tive sense, a heartfelt affair of the entire Volk. An accidental histori-
> cal date cannot mean more for the common feeling than Kienzl's
> well-intentioned national anthem for which Dr. Renner has written
> his peculiar text. No great longing of the Austrian Volk, no national
> dream, no high political goal was realized on November 12, 1918. Not
> even for the Social Democrats. Such grand words they also found
> afterward—they supported the old empire's right to exist until the last
> months before the collapse and also did not fail to give personal decla-
> rations of loyalty to the monarch. The Austria of November 12 was for
> no one a constructive work, for no one a victory of positive energies.
> Rather, it was only the result of an insane destructive work in which we
> have played the smallest part. The Republic of Austria was not created
> back then, but left over [*übrig geblieben*].[77]

75. Quoted in "Der Jahrestag der Republik," *Arbeiterwille* (Abendblatt), 13 November 1922, 1.

76. Otto Bauer, "Es lebe die Republik!," in *Zehn Jahre Republik*, ed. Josef Luitpold Stern (Vienna:
Wiener Volksbuchhandlung, 1928), 5, in VGA, Sacharchiv, Lade 16, Mappe 2.

77. "Am 12. November," *RP*, 12 November 1925, in ÖStA, AdR, Parteiarchive, GDVP, Zeitungsausschnitte, Mappe 1, 0/C.

For many Christian Socials, no revolution, socialist or otherwise, had taken place in November 1918. The Austrian republic was simply the outcome of the collapse, not the overthrow, of the Habsburg monarchy. Or, in another interpretation that again sought to undermine the socialists' claims, conservatives suggested that the rump state was the sole doing of the Allies. On the occasion of the third anniversary of the republic, another *Reichspost* article argued that "the harsh will of merciless victors formed" the new state.[78]

The Greater German People's Party advanced its own version of events, which fell in between the SDAP's and CSP's interpretations. Like the Christian Socials, the Greater Germans argued that a revolution did not occur in 1918; however, from this point forward, the two parties' interpretations often differed. Members of the GDVP argued that by the autumn of 1918, the Austro-Hungarian Empire was coming to an end regardless of the actions of the population. In fact, these opponents of the monarchy maintained that the imperial state collapsed because of the strains of the war, the authorities' loss of power and legitimacy, as well as the population's indifference toward the Habsburgs. "Above all and in the first instance," an article in the Greater German–oriented *Wiener Neueste Nachrichten* stated on the 1927 anniversary, the rule of the Habsburgs "had died in the feelings of the broad masses of the Volk already before the resolution of the Provisional German-Austrian National Assembly." The article continued that no revolution had occurred because there was no authority left to revolt against.[79]

Greater Germans did not refute Austrians' role in the formation of the new republic. Decrying the "Marxist-party political falsification of history," the same article emphasized that all sectors of Austrian society—the *Bürgertum*, farmers, and workers alike—had participated in the establishment of the republic.[80] The Greater Germans even went so far as to assert that "the decisive national circles were also the ones, who in the days of the collapse of 1918, long before the Social Democrats, carried the idea of the republic in the Viennese population." To support this claim, they pointed out that a republican form of government was the only way to achieve their desired union with Germany, given the historical

---

78. "Liebe des freien Mannes," *RP*, 12 November 1921, in ÖStA, AdR, Parteiarchive, GDVP, Zeitungsausschnitte, Mappe 24a, 0/c. Also see "Zum Staatfeiertag," *RP*, 11 November 1921, in ÖStA, AdR, Parteiarchive, GDVP, Zeitungsausschnitte, Mappe 24a, 0/c.

79. "Der Tag der Republik," *WNN*, 12 November 1927, in ÖStA, AdR, Parteiarchive, GDVP, Zeitungsausschnitte, Mappe 24a, 02/P.

80. Ibid. Also see Franz Dinghofer, "Zum 12. November," *WNN*, 12 November 1925, in ÖStA, AdR, PrK 7809/1925; "Nationalfeiertag," *WNN*, 12 November 1926, in ÖStA, AdR, Parteiarchive, GDVP, Zeitungsausschnitte, Mappe 1, 0/P.

rivalry between the Habsburgs and Hohenzollerns.[81] And, as fervent supporters of an Anschluss, some members of the GDVP looked back at the declarations of November 12, 1918, as the realization of greater German hopes, although others highlighted the hardships of that period and the eventual Allied prohibition of a political union.

The disputes over the founding of the republic reflected a fundamental disagreement among, and even within, the parties regarding the meaning and practice of democracy, as well as the custodianship of the republic.[82] Members of opposing political parties traded accusations about who could be labeled the supporters and who the enemies of the republic, highlighting an us-versus-them mentality.[83] Whereas the discursive terms and symbols for Constitution Day in Germany possessed a flexibility that enabled the three centrist parties to map their own political definitions on these terms and still find common ground, discussions about the republic and democracy surrounding November 12 furthered the fragmentation of Austrian political culture. The ability of the ideas of the republic and democracy to be filled with different meanings did not, in the Austrian case, enable a consensus to be established among the various parties. With the republic and the revolution at the center of the November 12 commemorations, the annual Austrian holiday therefore reinforced divisions within society, especially among the followers of the two largest parties: the SDAP and the CSP.

Among the major parties, the socialists presented the most consistent message, owing to the highly organized nature of the party and relatively homogeneous party base. At the November 12 celebrations, Social Democrats often talked about "our republic," with the possessive pronoun referring to the workers and not to Austrians. For a party that had not held power at the federal level since 1920, this assertion that the republic belonged to the proletariat was predicated in part on the achievements of the revolutionary period. As the self-anointed founders of the republic, socialists highlighted how their overthrow of the Habsburgs led to political equality and freedoms for workers, who had heretofore been suppressed by a violent monarchy and a political system based on privileges. In addition to

81. Victor Lischka, "So kam die Republik . . . ," *WNN*, 11 November 1928, in ÖStA, AdR, Parteiarchive, GDVP, Zeitungsausschnitte, Mappe 24a, 02/P.

82. Helmut Rumpler, "Parlamentarismus und Demokratieverständnis in Österreich, 1918–1933," in *Das Parteienwesen Österreichs und Ungarns in der Zwischenkriegszeit*, ed. Anna Drabek, Richard Plaschka, and Helmut Rumpler (Vienna: Verlag der Österreichischen Akadamie der Wissenschaften, 1990), 8–9. For an overview of socialist and Christian Social rhetoric see also Hanisch, "Das Fest," 54–58.

83. Hanisch points out that the fear of the "other" became an obsession during the First Republic. Hanisch, "Das Fest," 44.

the democratization of the government, workers benefited from a series of social reforms enacted by the SDAP while it was still part of the governing coalition: the eight-hour workday, unemployment insurance, and vacation time. "It is our republic! The republic of the workers," the *Arbeiter-Zeitung* thus proclaimed on the occasion of the seventh anniversary of the republic. "Because we, the working Volk of city and town, we have created it, we have built it, we have defended it against economic crisis and political danger."[84]

Socialists advanced their claims to the republic based not only on their role as the republic's creators, but also as its sole defenders. They repeated the refrain that they would "do [the] utmost to defend the new democratic state form against all plans of the reaction."[85] From their point of view, an array of domestic and foreign threats endangered the republic, democratic practices, and consequently the political and social advancements made by and for the working class. Viewing the contemporary political situation through a Marxist lens, socialists lamented that "our republic also had to become a bourgeois republic." The crux of the problem was that "the bourgeois republic in this country is an internal contradiction because our bourgeoisie are not republican."[86] A number of dangers arose from this situation, according to supporters of the SDAP: the threat of a monarchist restoration, attempts to reform the constitution in order to create an authoritarian government, the plots of fascist groups to overthrow the republic with the help of Mussolini and Horthy, the increased power of the Catholic Church in political affairs, and the country's submission to international capitalism and domestic stock market barons and landowners.[87]

Precisely because of the co-optation of the republic by reactionary forces, the socialists argued that the republic was not the final goal sought by the working classes. Rather, the republic was a step toward achieving socialism because it served as an important site where the class struggle outlined by Marx was taking place and could finally be won by the workers. An article from a 1932 bulletin for the SDAP in Styria explained that the socialists would march on November 12 to celebrate "the republic as the effective instrument of class struggle, as the barricade that we have erected against the boundless class rule of the bourgeoisie, as the barricade on which we protect ourselves and over which we will rush forward

84. "Auf Felsen gebaut," *AZ*, 12 November 1925, 1.

85. "Am Vorabend des Jahrestages," *Arbeiterwille*, 11 November 1919, 2.

86. "Der Tag der Republik," *AZ*, 12 November 1920, 1. Such accusations were already being made in 1919 when the socialists were still in a coalition with the bourgeois parties. See "Am Vorabend des Jahrestages," *Arbeiterwille*, 11 November 1919, 2.

87. "Gegen den Faschismus! Für die Republik des arbeitenden Volkes!," *Der Abend*, 11 November 1927, in WB, TA, Nationalfeiertag (12 November).

to new victories!"[88] Although in policy and practice the Social Democrats pursued a reformist agenda, they primarily used fiery and uncompromising Marxist rhetoric. Their discursive attempts to claim the republic for the workers and socialism created real fear among the middle classes and farmers, who were terrified that the Bolshevik Revolution would be repeated in Austria. Despite being the only consistent defenders of the democratic republic, the socialists, through their doctrinaire words, nonetheless contributed to the dysfunction of the Austrian republic.[89]

Members of the Christian Social Party vociferously disputed the socialists' contention about who were the supporters and the adversaries of the republic. Speaking material distributed by the General Secretariat of the Christian Social Federal Executive Committee for the tenth anniversary of the republic refuted the socialist accusation that the CSP was "an opponent of the republic."[90] As the pamphlet explained, simply using "the word democracy" did not give one "a right to become called the defender of democracy." Only those "who through their work prove that they think, feel, and also thereafter behave democratic" could be considered to be the supporters of democracy.[91] It was the Christian Socials, the piece continued, who "were represented in the government of the republic and have carried the difficult burden of work and responsibility."[92] Having listed the accomplishments of the party and its leader, Ignaz Seipel, the party's executive committee argued "that the threat to democracy comes from those who always pretend to be the best democrats and the best republicans, from the Social Democrats, who as recently as two years ago at their party congress have declared their strange democratic-republican belief that democracy and the republic are for them actually just the transitional stage to social dictatorship."[93] The

---

88. "Durch die Republik zum Sozialismus empor!," Mitteilungsblatt der Sozialdemokratischen Partei Steiermarks, November 1932, Nr. 11, 1, in StLA, ZGS, Kt. 204, Verschiedenes: Kommunistische Partei.

89. Leser, "Austria between the Wars"; Kitchen, Coming of Austrian Fascism, chap. 1; Melanie Sully, "Social Democracy and the Political Culture of the First Republic," Peter Loewenberg, "Otto Bauer as an Ambivalent Party Leader," and Karl Stadler, "Austrian Social Democracy: The Image and the Facts," all in The Austrian Socialist Experiment: Social Democracy and Austromarxism, 1918–1934, ed. Anson Rabinbach (Boulder, CO: Westview Press, 1985), 57–70, 71–79, and 81–87 respectively; Hanisch, Der Grosse Illusionist, 143–310.

90. Generalsekretariat der christlichsozialen Bundesparteileitung, "Rednermaterial: Die Arbeit der christlichsozialen Partei in der Republik," 3, in SLA, Rehrl Politica, 1929/0006.

91. Ibid., 4.

92. Ibid., 1.

93. Ibid., 4. This statement refers to the 1926 Linz Party Program of the SDAP, which stated that a dictatorship of the working class would be needed in order to secure, not replace, democracy if bourgeois forces should try to overthrow the republic. The radical rhetoric was problematic and provided further evidence for those on the right that the SDAP was really trying to implement bolshevism. Sully, "Social Democracy," 62; Hanisch, Der Grosse Illusionist, 230–240.

Christian Socials therefore reversed the argument made by the socialists. Portraying themselves as the ones seeking to stabilize and save the republic, they used the socialists' rhetoric of class warfare in an effort to prove that the SDAP sought to supplant democracy with bolshevism.

Yet the Christian Social references to democracy did not entail straightforward definitions revolving around the ideas of "government by the people, for the people" or equality. Although Christian Social attitudes toward the republic were divergent and changed over time, Christian Socials collectively and repeatedly infused their idea of democracy with a Catholic worldview. "In the *Volksstaat*, the rigid structure of the disintegrated authoritarian state [*Obrigkeitsstaat*] is doubly supplanted by the Volk's sense of duty. Materialism and socialism cannot offer the foundations. They do not have a lasting conception of the state [*Staatsidee*]," the Christian Social newspaper in Salzburg explained on the third anniversary of the republic. "Only Christian solidarity of the Volk forms the sole basis for the *Volksstaat*."[94] As did the socialists, the Christian Socials assumed a polarizing stance about not only which Austrians could lay claim to the republic, but also which values should underpin it. In seeing Catholicism as the basis for democracy and demanding a role for the Catholic Church in public life, the Christian Socials devised an understanding of democratic values and practices that would be unacceptable to the socialists and even the German nationalist camp.

The desire to link Catholicism and the republic gave way to more troubling presuppositions about how democracy should function in Austria. During his two-year break from being chancellor of the republic, Seipel proclaimed during the 1925 anniversary of the republic that "no state—may it be a monarchy or republic, old or young, big or small—can exist without God. Because we Catholics know this, we therefore expressly declare our belief that in our state as well there can be no authority except for that which comes from God."[95] Repeatedly, members of the party and the Catholic Church used the republic's celebration to assert an idea that stood in direct opposition both to the declaration of the republic ("German-Austria is a democratic republic, all public authorities are to be conferred by the Volk") and to the first article of the constitution ("Austria is a democratic republic. Its laws proceed from the people").[96] For the right wing of the CSP, power came from God, not from the people. Indeed, by the late 1920s, Seipel had reversed his earlier (although reluctant) backing of a democratic form of government and came increasingly to speak of "true democracy," which in

---

94. "Der 12. November," *Salzburger Chronik*, 12 November 1921, 1.

95. "Am Grabe des Landespatrons: Eine hochbedeutsame Predigt Dr. Seipels," *RP*, 13 November 1925, 3.

96. Hanisch, "Das Fest," 50; Diamant, *Austrian Catholics*.

reality amounted to authoritarianism, corporatism, and support for the Austro-fascist Heimwehr.[97]

Christian Social claims to the republic did not simply alienate the majority of the working classes who voted for the socialists; they also excluded Jews. Since the party's founding, anti-Semitism had served as a major plank in its platform, and continued to do so after the Great War. Whereas some members, such as Seipel, were "moderate anti-Semites," others combined older forms of religious anti-Semitism with new racial ideas, leading to radical proposals about how to deal with the Jewish population of Austria.[98] Anton Jerzabek, a member of the CSP and the leader of the League of Anti-Semites, used the occasion of the first anniversary of the republic to proclaim to loud applause, "If we are missing something in the Republic of Austria, it is democracy. So long as the Jewish domination lasts, we must fight for the equality of Christians until the day comes when we can say: we are free from the yoke!"[99] In this case, freedom was equated with freedom from Jews. Indeed, some Christian Socials went so far as to advocate segregating Jews from Christian society and reducing Jews to second-class citizens. Among this group were individuals such as Jerzabek and Leopold Kunschak, the leader of the Christian Social Workers' Association. Kunschak's rabid anti-Semitism, which he continued to voice even after the Second World War, is particularly significant because he was the leader of the CSP's pro-democracy wing, disagreeing with Seipel's alliance with the Heimwehr and seeking to work with the SDAP in the republic's final phase. Hence, while he was willing to see equal rights for all workers regardless of their political allegiances, his notion of democracy and freedom troublingly did not extend to Austrian Jews.[100]

Both reflecting and heightening the irreconcilable understandings of the founding of the republic and the function of democracy were the actual festivities organized for the holiday. In contrast to Germany, there was no central government office in Austria responsible for organizing state celebrations for the November 12 anniversary. Rather, the task of orchestrating various activities fell to different ministries. The federal government under the control of the Christian Socials, however, made very little effort to create the type of popular

---

97. For more on Seipel's ideas see von Klemperer, *Ignaz Seipel*, esp. chaps. 4–7; Diamant, *Austrian Catholics*, esp. 106–116; Diamant, "Austrian Catholics"; Steiner, *Wahre Demokratie?*; Boyer, *Karl Lueger*, 413–435; Deak, "Ignaz Seipel."

98. Bruce Pauley, *From Prejudice to Persecution*, chap. 11.

99. "Ein Jahr Republik," *RP*, 14 November 1919, 4.

100. Pauley, *From Prejudice to Persecution*, 158–163; Diamant, *Austrian Catholics*, 121–124; Angelika Königseder, "Antisemitismus 1933–1938," and Anton Pelinka, "Christliche Arbeiterbewegung und Austrofaschismus," both in *Austrofaschismus: Politik—Ökonomie—Kultur, 1933–1938*, ed. Emmerich Tálos and Wolfgang Neugebauer (Vienna: LIT Verlag, 2005), 54–65 and 88–97 respectively.

republican holiday envisioned and staged by Edwin Redslob in the Reich. Indeed, the celebration of the republic's founding was primarily the domain of the political parties, a factor that contributed to the divisiveness of the holiday and an increasing level of violence during the annual commemoration.

Already in 1919, certain patterns of celebration developed that would continue throughout the republic. From the first anniversary of the republic, the SDAP began to organize party assemblies, marches, torchlight parades, sporting events, concerts, activities for the youth, and plays with inexpensive tickets in urban centers. At the rallies and marches, fiery speeches and placards were filled with the type of rhetoric detailed above: claims that the republic belonged to the workers and invective denouncing those deemed to be reactionary, monarchist, fascist, bourgeois, and/or clerical. Working-class men, women, and children turned out in large numbers to the events. At gatherings held in each Viennese district, as well as in cities throughout the country, they sang a host of songs that were symbols of previous revolutions and international socialism. The most popular were the "Lied der Arbeit," the anthem of Austrian Social Democracy that was first used by the working-class organization in the late 1860s; "La Marseillaise" and Hölderlin's "Hymne an der Arbeit," both celebrating the French Revolution; and "The Internationale," the song of the Second International. They carried the international symbol of socialism, red flags, and wore red armbands and red carnations, a symbol of the socialist movement in Austria since the late nineteenth century. The fact that the symbols of the republic—the Renner-Kienzl anthem before 1929 and the red-white-red flag—were largely missing from the socialist festivities is indicative of the socialists' narrow understanding of the republic as the domain of the workers.[101] For parades, the organizations and groups associated with the Social Democratic Party—ranging from unions to workers' gymnastic organizations to the Schutzbund to postal employees to socialist women's groups—marched in the hundreds, thousands, and even tens of thousands.[102]

Indeed, the socialists quickly came to dominate the celebration of November 12. While they filled the streets of cities like Vienna, Graz, Salzburg, and Linz, the other sectors of Austrian society tended to stay at home—which only confirmed for the socialists their argument that the bourgeoisie was seeking to undermine the republic. The *Arbeiter-Zeitung* pointedly stated as much on the

---

101. As Hanisch has indicated in his piece on the holiday, "The 'transfer of the sacral' to the republic based on a shared constitutional patriotism failed." According to Hanisch, the socialists sacralized their party and the proletariat, while the Catholics politicized the sacred. Hanisch, "Das Fest," 50.

102. This description is based on issues of the *AZ*, the *Arbeiterwille*, and the *Salzburger Wacht* in the days following the November 12 celebrations from 1919 to 1933.

second anniversary of the republic: "How cool, how foreign, how hostile it [the bourgeoisie] faces the republic never shows more clearly than on the legal state holiday of the republic; it does not celebrate the republic. For [the bourgeoisie], the republican November 12 is no less foreign than the proletarian first of May."[103] For the Social Democrats, November 12 amounted to a visual manifestation of the antirepublican attitudes of the CSP, the GDVP, and more generally the bourgeoisie. With the exception, again, of the tenth anniversary of the republic, members of the SDAP emphasized that only the workers turned out for the republic's annual commemoration; the bourgeoisie was conspicuously absent. November 12 therefore became a way for the socialists to denounce their political opponents while demonstrating their own loyalty to the republic and the strength of the working class in Austria. Upon reporting that over twenty thousand workers had marched through the streets of Linz for the third anniversary of the republic, the *Arbeiter-Zeitung* concluded that the "demonstration celebration" was a warning to the bourgeoisie to keep its hands away from the workers' republic because it showed that "Linz is red and remains red, and this red Linz is determined to defend its cause, the socialist cause, until the last man, until the last drop of blood!"[104] For the SDAP, the state holiday had become another May 1, another working-class holiday—a point that socialist newspapers repeatedly brought up.[105]

The Social Democrats' opponents had an explanation as to why much of the population did not turn out to celebrate November 12. According to a 1919 article in the *Tagespost*, a newspaper out of Graz aligned with the German nationalist point of view, "The first anniversary of the proclamation of the republic yesterday became almost exclusively a party holiday of the Social Democrats." Or as the Christian Social *Grazer Volksblatt* put it eight years later, "Since November 12 has been celebrated as the national holiday, it was used by the party- and 'patent'-republicans not as a celebration for the republic, but as a protest against it, as a demonstration for the 'socialist' republic according to the model from Moscow."[106] Both pieces condemned the SDAP for turning what was supposed to be a state holiday into a party holiday, in effect keeping all nonsocialists from participating. Just as the Social Democrats saw the absence of the bourgeoisie as evidence of betrayal of the republic, the other parties interpreted the socialists' alleged seizure of the holiday as proof of the SDAP's undemocratic intentions. Thus, because of the prominence of socialist demonstrations on the republic's

103. "Der Tag der Republik," *AZ*, 12 November 1920, 1.
104. "Linz. 12. November," *AZ*, 14 November 1921, 2.
105. For example, see ibid.
106. "Staatsfeiertag—Schulsonntag," *Grazer Volksblatt*, 12 November 1927, 1.

anniversary, the republic became, in the eyes of the middle classes, inherently linked to socialism, thereby extinguishing their support for it.[107]

Not all Catholics stayed at home on November 12. As a way to link the new Austrian state to older Catholic and imperial traditions associated with the Habsburg Empire, they moved the celebration of the feast day of the patron saint of Austria, Leopold III, from November 15 to November 12.[108] Since 1902, members of the Christian Social Party and church hierarchy had made a pilgrimage on November 15 to the grave of Leopold, who had been a member of the Babenberg dynasty and the margrave of Austria from 1095 until 1136. After the First World War, prominent Christian Social politicians, the archbishop of Vienna, and other members of the clergy, as well as thousands of their followers, now visited his grave at Klosterneuburg, a monastery founded by Leopold and located a short distance from Vienna, on the republic's anniversary. According to Anton Orel, leader of the Christian Social League of Working Youth, a Viennese municipal councilor, and a member of the executive committee of the Anti-Semites' League, Leopold provided "the symbols of our Catholic, German, Austrian culture."[109] And, during the 1930 anniversary of the republic, the *Reichspost* proclaimed that the pilgrimage amounted to the "avowal to the Christian state, the pledge not to rest before this goal is achieved."[110] As with the Social Democrats, the Christian Socials sought to lay claim to the state based on their particular worldview. Moreover, such calls for a Christian state were predicated on the exclusion of both socialists and Jews, who were frequently denounced at the ceremonies at Klosterneuburg.

Amid the aforementioned party commemorations were the festivities organized by the federal government. In the early years of the republic, when Social Democratic leaders still occupied positions of power, the activities involved celebrations to be held in all schools and at sporting events. Cognizant of the difficulties facing the country, Otto Glöckel, then state undersecretary of education, suggested in 1919 that the school celebrations involve "serious and dignified singing" and speeches by the teachers, which should "illuminate the meaning of the day, especially pointing to the consequences of newly won political freedom, foreshadowing the tremendous difficulties with which our young state form had to struggle. They should therefore remind the future citizens [*Bürger und Bürgerinnen*] of German-Austria of the duties that stand before them: working

107. Hanisch, "Das Fest," 57; Diamant, *Austrian Catholics*, 75.
108. Hanisch, "Das Fest," 50–51.
109. Quoted in "Die Versammlung in und vor dem Stiftskeller," *RP*, 13 November 1923, 4. For more on Orel and the Anti-Semites' League see Pauley, *From Prejudice to Persecution*, 183–189; Peter Pulzer, "The Tradition of Austrian Antisemitism in the Nineteenth and Twentieth Centuries," *Patterns of Prejudice* 27, no. 1 (1993): 41–42.
110. "Bekenntnis zum christlichen Staate," *RP*, 13 November 1930, 5.

collaboration on the construction and internal administration of our free state."[111] Yet, following the departure of the SDAP from the coalition government in 1920, such efforts by federal officials decreased.

Additionally, the involvement of the military in the November 12 celebrations began informally as early as the first anniversary. The Volkswehr, the immediate postwar armed forces of German-Austria later disbanded by the Treaty of Saint-Germain, held a celebration in their barracks in 1919.[112] And, in 1920, the socialist leader Julius Deutsch, who had been the defense minister until a month prior, gave a speech to assembled soldiers at the Viennese city hall, praising their defense of the republic from threats mounted by the extreme right and left. He also pronounced the usual party line about the workers being the only founders and supporters of the republic, since, in the early postwar years, the Social Democrats controlled the army, and the soldiers were largely SDAP backers.[113] Upon the suggestion of Josef Wächter, an army officer serving as the defense minister, the first official celebration of the newly formed Austrian army occurred in 1921, with units stationed around the country parading through major thoroughfares and being reviewed by federal, provincial, and local officials.[114] Both the 1921 and 1922 military celebrations earned the approval of the socialists. These celebrations were "stripped of all the pomp and finery from the monarchical period, and thereby proceeded directly in a very dignified manner," the *Arbeiter-Zeitung* commented on the third anniversary of the republic. "The sons of the Volk gathered in unaffected style to celebrate the day of remembrance for the republic that they fought for and to vow that they are ready anytime to sacrifice everything to defend the free *Volksstaat*."[115]

The tenor of the military celebrations soon changed as the army became a political instrument of Carl Vaugoin, a Christian Social in Seipel's circle who served briefly as defense minister in 1921 and then again from 1922 to 1933. The military celebrations, especially those in Vienna, now became a site of conflict during the November 12 festivities. Whereas the Social Democratic and Catholic commemorations for the first four anniversaries of the republic occupied separate geographical spaces in Vienna, the military celebrations orchestrated by

---

111. [Untitled, but earlier version titled "An Alle Landesschulrats, Schulfeier anlässlich des 12. November"], enclosed in Unterricht, Erinnerung, Betreff: Schulfeier am 12. November 1.J., Nr. 20823, 30 September 1919, in ÖStA, AVA, U.Allg. 4214, 20823/19.

112. "Die Feier des 12. November," *NFP*, 13 November 1919, 5.

113. "Der Gedenktag der Republik: Die Feier der Wehrmacht," *AZ*, 13 November 1920, 3.

114. MRP Nr. 138 vom 8. November 1921, "11. Militärische Feier anläßlich des Staatsfeiertages am 12. November 1921," in ÖStA, AdR, BKA, MRP, Kt. 51.

115. "Der Festtag der Republik," *AZ*, 14 November 1921, 2; "Die militärische Feier," *AZ*, 13 November 1922, 2.

Vaugoin now brought the socialists and Christian Socials into a direct confrontation with one another beginning in 1923.[116] Just as the Christians Socials sought to establish a link to older Catholic and imperial traditions through the pilgrimage to Klosterneuburg (or the restoration of the Haydn melody), Vaugoin set about reintroducing Habsburg symbols to the army. Hence, for the 1923 holiday, the order went out from the Ministry of Defense that imperial songs, including the "Prince Eugene March," the "Deutschmeister Regimental March," and the "Radetzky March," were to be played as the army marched, for the first time after the war, on Vienna's Ringstrasse.[117] Complementing the use of imperial songs, a number of officers in the Second Squadron turned up wearing imperial medals that they had earned during the First World War. Furthermore, in addition to the president, parliamentary representatives, Viennese city councilors, ambassadors, and foreign military attachés, Vaugoin invited the generals and field marshals of the old imperial army to watch the parade.[118]

In response, workers, identifiable by their red flags and carnations, began to whistle and yell. According to military reports, they insulted the troops, calling out, "famished Nazis, monarchist skulls."[119] An account of the incident in the *Reichspost* claimed that they had screamed, "Three cheers for the red army! Three cheers for the proletarian soldiers!"[120] The *Arbeiter-Zeitung* maintained that the workers had shown up to support the army but yelled out "Three cheers for the republic!" "Three cheers for the republican army!" and "Boo Vaugoin!" upon hearing the imperial marching tunes, and whistled only at those soldiers wearing their war medals.[121] The socialists viewed Vaugoin's staging of the ceremony as a direct provocation. "If [Vaugoin and Seipel] already have to celebrate the national holiday," the *Arbeiter-Zeitung* proclaimed when it learned that imperial officers would be given a special place from which to observe the ceremony, "they would like still to take the soul of the day, which is dedicated to the tradition of revolution that gave birth to the republic, and dedicate it to the tradition of the *k. und k.* [*kaiserlich und königlich* (dual monarchy)] army!"[122] For the Social

---

116. Hanisch, "Das Fest," 49–50.

117. 2. Brigadekommando (Stadtkommandant) in Wien, Tagesbefehl Nr. 47, MA. Zahl 2063/ Stkmdt., Paradeausrückung am 12. November 1923, Vienna, 8 November 1923, in ÖStA, AdR, BMfHW, 1.A.39–17. Präs. 3270.

118. PrK 7455/1923, Amtsveranlassung, Parade am 12. November 1923, in ÖStA, AdR, PrK 9147/1926.

119. See military reports of the incidents in ÖStA, AdR, BMfHW, 1923, 1.A.39–17/8. The quote comes from Radfahrbataillon Nr. 4, Meldung über Störung der Truppenparade am 12. November 1923, E.No. 357, 19 November 1923.

120. "Parade der Wiener Garnison," *RP*, 13 November 1923, 4.

121. "Der Tag der Republik," *AZ*, 13 November 1923, 1.

122. "Wie Seipel und Vaugoin den Nationalfeiertag feiern," *AZ*, 11 November 1923, 2.

Democrats, the staging orchestrated by Vaugoin, and the workers' response, fit into their narrative that the workers had to defend the republic against a hostile clerical, bourgeois government. The Christian Socials, on the other hand, saw the workers' demonstration as a sign of their disloyalty to the republic, for it was "completely unseemly, tactless, and equally harmful to the reputation of the army and the republic."[123] Once again, the actions of the two major parties in the First Republic, as well as their interpretations of events, pointed to the increasingly hardening lines between the different political camps.

In 1923 the Viennese celebration was limited to a war of words, but the situation escalated to physical conflicts the following year. The military celebration again drew the ire of the workers. Habsburg army officers had prominent seats among the government officials viewing the parade, the military band played imperial tunes, and more soldiers wore their imperial war medals, or, as the *Arbeiter-Zeitung* called them, "symbols of the monarchy's mass murder."[124] When the cavalry were leaving the Ringstrasse to return to their barracks, they encountered a large group of youths at the top of Mariahilferstrasse who proceeded to boo them. The police stepped in to provide protection for the military riders, but more demonstrators continued to gather. At this point a socialist city councilman, Franz Kurz, was arrested by the police for leading the demonstration, which further angered the protesters. (Kurz, upon identifying himself, was let go.) More police were brought in to break up the crowds, as ever more protesters joined in when the procession reached the Gürtel. A man rushed at one of the riders, seeking to make him fall from his horse, and was arrested by the police. As the cavalry neared the barracks, two thousand more workers awaited them. Because of the demonstrators' numbers, the police failed to prevent them from throwing stones at the riders. By the end of this incident, the police had detained seventeen people and charged two of them.[125] According to the statements gathered from the soldiers involved, the angry crowd had been composed of both younger and older people wearing red armbands, streetcar and railway workers, and members of the Schutzbund, who shouted insults, spat at the soldiers, and inflicted injuries by throwing stones, bottles, and hardware.[126] Thereafter, the military parade was canceled in Vienna (although not in other cities), and the troops stationed in the capital held a ceremony in their barracks instead. Even though only low-level

---

123. "Parade der Wiener Garnison," *RP*, 13 November 1923, 4.

124. "Der Pöbel und die Habsburgerpletschen," *AZ*, 14 November 1924, enclosed in PrK 7256/1924, in ÖStA, AdR, PrK 9147/1926.

125. Report sent from the Polizeidirektion Wien to the BMfHW, Pr.Zl.IV-47 Exp., Paradeausrückung der Truppen der Garnison Wien am 12. November 1924, Vienna, 12 November 1924, in ÖStA, AdR, BMfHW, 1924, 23 1/1, 69018/1.

126. See the various Protokolle in ÖStA, AdR, BMfHW, 1924, 23 1/1, 69018/1.

violence had occurred, it was indicative of the growing violence within Austrian society that would come to a head in the July 1927 riots in Vienna and the brief civil war of 1934.

Not all events in the years leading up to the tenth anniversary were so divisive. There were some military celebrations that occurred peacefully without disturbances: the 1924 celebrations in Graz and Linz went smoothly, for example.[127] And, in rare moments, some politicians sought to achieve a degree of consensus in support of the republic. In Krems, on the occasion of the third anniversary, all three of the major parties came together for a "powerful rally" and "carried out in unity the oath of allegiance to the republic and let ring out the warning call for all those who should want to infringe upon our free state, the democratic republic of German-Austria."[128] Moreover, Michael Hainisch, the partyless Austrian president from 1920 until the end of 1928 who was committed to democracy, gave addresses on the November 12 holidays that sought to engender support for the republic and to find common ground among all citizens regardless of their party affiliations. And when he hosted receptions in 1925 and 1927 for the chancellor and the presidents of the Nationalrat and Bundesrat, the speeches given by these leaders, even though they belonged to either the SDAP or CSP, encouraged both harmony and support for democracy.[129]

But even the more conciliatory celebrations held by government officials still pointed to a fundamental problem with the Austrian state commemoration: the federal government's lack of effort in trying to create a popular holiday. In addition to the presidential reception of the country's top politicians, beginning in 1925, the president invited representatives serving in the Nationalrat and the Bundesrat, diplomats and consular officials, and journalists to high tea.[130] However, the government made no attempt to organize these events every year.[131] Although the presidential reception resulted in speeches that were carried by the major newspapers for the public to read, both these events were limited to elites.

---

127. See coverage of the Graz ceremony in ÖStA, AdR, BMfHW, Kanzleistelle A, 1924, 23 1/1, 60933/1. For Linz see "Die Parade der Garnison Linz," *Tagblatt*, 15 November 1924, in ÖStA, BMfHW, 1924, 23 1/1, 70425/1.

128. "Der Tag der Republik," *Land-Zeitung*, 17 November 1921, enclosed in a letter from the Ortskommando in Krems a.d.D. to the BMfHW, Zahl 498 res., Bericht über die Nationalfeier am 12. November 1921, Krems, 18 November 1921, in ÖStA, AdR, BMfHW, 1.A.39–11/10, 1921. Also see "Tiroler Landtag: Ein Bekenntnis zur Republik," *Grazer Volksblatt* (Morgenblatt), 9 November 1921, 3.

129. See summary in Hanisch, "Das Fest," 46.

130. PrK 7859/1925, Amtsveranlassung, Tee aus Anlass des Nationalfeiertages am 12. November 1925, in ÖStA, AdR, PrK, 7859/1925.

131. PrK 9286/1926, Amtsveranlassung, Anfrage des Abg. Austerlitz über unterbliebene Regierungsgratulation am Jahrestag der Republik, in ÖStA, AdR, PrK 9286/1926.

The president's office never looked into creating an event that would involve popular participation. Even the military parades throughout Austria, which attracted large crowds of onlookers, were not created with the idea of a *Volksfest* in mind. Despite Vaugoin's choosing to move the military parade to the Ringstrasse from the Heldenplatz in 1923 "because [there is] more freedom of movement and the public sees more,"[132] there was no further talk of using this event to create a more participatory form of commemoration. Indeed, the purpose of the military ceremony was to allow soldiers to demonstrate "the public expression of the loyalty of the army to the constitution."[133] Unlike Redslob, who wanted to erase the division between onlooker and participant in order to create a more democratic form of commemoration, Christian Social officials paid little attention to public involvement and certainly did not seek to capture the imagination of the population. They showed no initiative in creating rituals or traditions to honor the republic.

The tenth anniversary of the republic was exceptional in that the federal government and citizenry alike celebrated with great fanfare, although not without a repeat of the difficulties that plagued previous years. In Vienna, on the evening of November 11, military musicians played a "monster concert" on the Heldenplatz; troops helped to illuminate the parliament building, the Heldenplatz itself, and the tower of St. Stephen's Cathedral with spotlights, while the Viennese government did the same for the city hall; troops conducted celebratory ceremonies in the barracks; and government buildings were festively decorated with the flags bearing the country's colors of red-white-red. On the day of the anniversary, a platoon of soldiers with flags made its way in the morning to the president's and chancellor's offices with musical accompaniment; numerous government officials, including Hainisch, Seipel, and Vaugoin, and members of the diplomatic corps attended a High Mass led by the archbishop of Vienna; and the military companies stationed outside the church then paraded through the streets back to the barracks. Additionally, the president held receptions for the presidents of the Nationalrat and the Bundesrat, for the federal government, and for foreign officials; and the Nationalrat conducted a celebratory session.[134] Around the country, there were military parades, cultural offerings, celebratory Masses, and special sessions of provincial assemblies and city councils to celebrate the tenth

132. Vortrag für den Ministerrat betreffend die Feier am 12. November, in ÖStA, AdR, BMfHW, 1923, 1.A.39–17, Präs. 3720.

133. BMfHW, Präs. Zahl 3720 von 1923, Gedenkfeier am 12. November, 2 November 1923, 1 in ÖStA, AdR, BMfHW, 1.A.39–17, Präs. 3720.

134. "Programm," in PrK 8999/1928, Amtsveranlassung, Bericht über die Feierlichkeiten am 11. und 12. November 1928, in ÖStA, AdR, PrK 8999/1928.

anniversary. Events such as the "monster concert" and the festive lighting of major landmarks in Vienna, as well as the military celebrations in the provinces, drew sizable crowds, prompting the *Reichspost* to observe, "It needs to be entered as proof of the advancing consolidation of our political system despite all inhibitions: yesterday, on the tenth anniversary of the declaration of the republic, the population in its entirety has expressed a more vivid inner sympathy with the day of remembrance for the first time."[135]

Not only did the tenth anniversary draw out large swaths of the population who had previously stayed home, but, as with some of the earlier observances, there were also glimpses of conciliatory politics. In Salzburg, the newspapers aligned with the Social Democrats, and the Greater German People's Party praised a performance of Schiller's *Wilhelm Tell* for the occasion because the audience had included people from the different sociopolitical camps. As the socialist *Salzburger Wacht* declared, "Here the common people's republic was already carried out. . . . All sections of the Volk, all secular and church authorities of the city and province (including the archbishop) met together peacefully by the Rütli oath: 'We want to be a single Volk of brothers.' In league with Friedrich Schiller, who lives in all the hearts of the German Volk, the question of the republic would therefore already be solved."[136] And the numerous speeches given by officials of the three major parties at the presidential receptions and the celebratory sessions of the legislative bodies took a more subdued tone than the speeches given to their party bases.

The widespread participation of all sectors of the Austrian population in the tenth anniversary celebrations should not, however, be mistaken for consensus.[137] Although the German ambassador to Austria, Hugo Graf von und zu Lerchenfeld, concluded his report on the commemoration with the following line—"All in all the day from November 12 proves a decisive strengthening of the Austrian state idea and of the willingness of all sectors of the Volk to work together on this state"—his full account belied such a rosy outlook. He began his description of events by explaining how the November 12 celebrations had, in the past, been "a party affair of the Social Democrats" and that the federal government was seeking to give the tenth anniversary "the meaning of an occasion for the entire Austrian Volk." Yet the following sentence pointed to the limits of the attempt to surmount sociopolitical divides and include the "entire" population. Lerchenfeld quoted Seipel as personally telling him that "the people should see that we

---

135. "Dissonanz am Staatsfeiertag," *RP*, 13 November 1928, 1.

136. "Die Republikfeier im Stadttheater," *Salzburger Wacht*, 13 November 1928, 5. Also see "Wilhelm Tell," *Salzburger Volksblatt*, 13 November 1928, 6.

137. For the argument on consensus in 1928 see Hanisch, "Das Fest."

are not a socialist republic." Seipel's desire was therefore not to create a popular celebration shared by all citizens, but to encourage the participation of Catholics in an effort to reclaim the republic from the Social Democrats. Lerchenfeld went on to detail how the Bundesrat, the upper chamber of parliament, failed to have a commemorative ceremony because of the SDAP's refusal to participate. The Social Democrats in the Bundesrat argued that the president of the chamber, Richard Steidle, was unfit to give a celebratory speech for the republic owing to his leading role in the Heimwehr. Lerchenfeld also mentioned how before and after the University of Vienna's celebrations, there were skirmishes between Austrian Nazi and "radical leftist" students.[138] Thus, the greater number of activities organized to celebrate the holiday and the larger numbers of people participating did not surmount the increasing conflicts by various political parties to control the image and governance of the republic.

As in previous years, the parties continued to employ highly charged rhetoric and still held their own festivities; skirmishes between political opponents also persisted. Throughout the country, the socialists held their annual assemblies and marches. And in the capital they unveiled before a large crowd of supporters the "Monument of the Republic," which carried the inscription "To the memory of the establishment of the Republic on 12 November 1918" above the busts of three deceased Austrian socialist leaders: Victor Adler, Ferdinand Hanusch, and Jakob Reumann. Months earlier, the monument had already provoked a heated debate in the Vienna city council. Members of the CSP and GDVP protested that the memorial was not a "monument of the republic" but a "party monument." These councilmen asserted that the socialists were using the monument to falsify history in an effort to lay sole claim to the republic.[139] Additionally, the Schutzbund disrupted military celebrations in Klagenfurt,[140] and workers in Vienna booed the army, its supporters, and the police as the troops made their way from St. Stephen's back to the barracks.[141]

---

138. Letter from the Deutsche Gesandtschaft Wien (Lerchenfeld) to the Auswärtige Amt Berlin, Vienna, 14 November 1928, in PAAA, R73378, IIOe1874.

139. Quote is from Karl Rummelhardt, who was also the president of the Christlichen Gewerkschaft. The debate can be found in Stenographisches Bericht über die öffentlichen Sitzung des Gemeinderates der Bundeshauptstadt Wien vom 22. Juni 1928, 1968–1983, in Wiener Stadt und Landesarchiv, Zahl 2322, Präs. 30.6.1928.

140. Letter from the Deutsches Konsulat Klagenfurt to the Deutsche Gesandtschaft in Wien, Tgb. Nr. 2381, Klagenfurt, 12 November 1928, in PAAA, R 73378, IIOe1879.

141. Report sent from the Bundes-Polizeidirektion in Wien to the Bundeskanzler, Pr.Zl.IV-4196/18/28, Vienna, 12 November 1928, Veranstaltungen anlässlich des 10 jährigen Bestandes der Republik am 12. November 1928, in ÖStA, AdR, BKA, Berichte der Wiener Polizeidirektion, Jan-Dez 1928, Kt. 12.

The tenth anniversary celebration also had the ignominious distinction of being the first time that the Heimwehr and the Austrian Nazis, both of which were intent on destroying the republic, took part in the November 12 observances. Around eighteen thousand members of the Heimwehr descended on Innsbruck, the site of the largest Heimwehr gathering that year, with smaller assemblies and marches occurring in places like Graz, Leoben, and Bruck an der Mur.[142] The leading figures of the Heimwehr used the republic's holiday to announce that while their organization was loyal to the Austrian state, "the best parts of the Volk reject the state in its present form."[143] The Nazi Schutzstaffel (SS) also held a celebration in Innsbruck,[144] while the Viennese district of the Hitler Youth organized a rally later in the month under the heading "We have experienced betrayal and deception by the Marxist leaders in the ten years of the republic."[145] Clashes between the socialists and the extreme right, which had been occurring throughout the country, now became a fixture of the November 12 celebrations. In Innsbruck, fights occurred between the Social Democrats and the Heimwehr, with one member of the Heimwehr suffering a stab wound in the back.[146] A shouting match of "Heil!" and "Freundschaft!" occurred in Vienna between small groups of Nazis and workers, at which point the police stepped in and arrested some of the workers.[147]

Although the government continued to hold military celebrations and presidential receptions and teas, the focus of the November 12 holiday in the following years was the conflict between the socialists and a diverse group of anti-Marxist and antirepublican forces, which included the Heimwehr, the Christian Socials,

---

142. "Imposanter Verlauf der Innsbrucker Heimwehrtagung," *RP*, 13 November 1928, 5; "Der 12. November in Innsbruck," *WNN*, 13 November 1928, 2; "Heimwehrkundgebung in Innsbruck," *Salzburger Chronik*, 13 November 1928, 3; "Republikfeier und Heimwehrprovokation in Innsbruck," *AZ*, 13 November 1928, 4; "Die Heimwehrterror in Innsbruck," *AZ*, 17 November 1928, 2. For police reports and newspaper coverage of the Heimwehr and socialist commemorations in Styria see Feier des 12. November 1928 (Republikfeier), in StLA, L. Reg. 384 R 21/1928.

143. "Heimwehrkundgebung in Innsbruck," *Salzburger Chronik*, 13 November 1928, 3. Walter Pfrimer and Richard Steidle delivered speeches.

144. Report sent from the Ortskommando Innsbruck to the BMfHW, Exh.N 361/1928, Verstärkte Bereitschaft am 12./XI, Innsbruck, 13 November 1928, in ÖStA, AdR, BMfHW, A, 1928, 23–1/3, 54569/Präs./1928.

145. Three thousand copies of the flyer announcing this event were confiscated by the police. Enclosed in Bundes-Polizeidirektion in Wien, G.P. 2211/28, Flugschrift: "Verrat und Betrug" . . . Beschlagnahme gemäß § 15 PrG, Vienna, 23 November 1928, in ÖStA, AdR, BKA, Berichte der Wiener Polizeidirektion, Kt. 12.

146. "Zusammenstöße in Innsbruck," *6-Uhr-Blatt* (Abendausgabe des *Grazer Volksblattes*), 13 November 1928, 3; "Heimwehrkundgebung in Innsbruck," *Salzburger Chronik*, 13 November 1928, 3.

147. "Zwischenfälle," *AZ*, 13 November 1928, 3. The article noted that the police gave the Nazis preferential treatment.

the Greater Germans, and the Nazis. Indeed, what was supposed to be a day to celebrate the republic's founding increasingly became an occasion to call for its destruction, as well as the annihilation of the Social Democratic Party. The Austrian Nazis, who opposed the socialists, the Christian Socials, and the Heimwehr, used the 1932 holiday to stage a march of nine thousand party adherents through the thoroughfares of Vienna and to call for an Anschluss and the "finale" of the republic.[148] In a collage titled "14 Years of the Republic" that ran in *Der Notschrei*, the Nazis presented their argument as to why the republic needed to be destroyed. Pictures of "Jews," murdered Nazis, and economic desperation contained text screaming, "Hunger," "Red culture," "Jewish Menace," "Murder," "Misery," "Homelessness."[149] Likewise, the Heimwehr also saw the November 12 holiday as a platform to announce their views on what the Austrian state should look like. At a Heimwehr rally in Graz for the 1929 anniversary of the republic, Ernst Rüdiger Starhemberg, the leader of the Upper Austrian Heimwehr, announced to over seventeen thousand followers, "Today we demand that the current constitution, which the year 1918 has bestowed upon us, vanish and demand that we are given a constitution that is worthy of a Christian and German Volk. If the Marxists are not agreed, Chancellor Schober should call us. Then we will teach them and make them good Germans and Catholics."[150]

With many Christian Socials in the government directly lending their support to the Heimwehr, and with the publications of both the CSP and the GDVP heaping praise on the Heimwehr rallies from 1928 onward, the socialists were no longer overstating the claim that they were the only defenders of the republic. As the Heimwehr used its marches to show that the socialists' "monopoly on the streets and plazas is broken,"[151] the Social Democrats continued to stage large rallies on November 12. According to the report of the party leadership for Styria, it had staged the largest rally Graz had ever seen since the 1918–1919 revolution with around twenty-five thousand workers and members of the Schutzbund attending the 1929 celebration.[152] And when the Nazis paraded through Vienna in 1932, the socialists assembled a contingent of around sixty thousand workers as

148. Quote is from Dr. Alexander Schilling-Schletter, "14 Jahre Republik," *Der Notschrei*, 12 November 1932, 4 and 6, here 6. For coverage of the march see "60.000 Sozialdemokraten, 9000 Nazi," *Wiener Sonn- und Montagszeitung*, 14 November 1932, in WB, TA, Nationalfeiertag (12. November).

149. "14 Jahre Republik," *Der Notschrei*, 12 November 1932, 8–9.

150. "Die Fahnen- und Wimpelweihe des Heimatschutzes," *6-Uhr-Blatt* (Abendausgabe des *Grazer Volksblattes*), 13 November 1929, 4.

151. "Der Staatsfeiertag kein Monopol mehr," *6-Uhr-Blatt*, 13 November 1929, 1.

152. Bericht des Landesparteioberstandes der Sozialdemokratischen Partei Steiermarks an den Landesparteitag für das Jahr 1929, 4–5, in StLA, ZGS, Kt. 187, Verschiedenes 1918–, Sozialdemokratische Partei 1918–1931.

a counterdemonstration.[153] The SDAP also interpreted the federal government's decision to reverse its earlier ban on all marches during the 1932 holiday as a victory for the workers. It was, according to the *Arbeiter-Zeitung*, "in view of the resolute will of the Viennese working class, which would in any case celebrate the birthday of the republic in its own style, [that] the government has rescinded the ban on marches."[154] Yet, in the end, the sizable armies of workers marching on November 12 deceived the socialists about their real strength against the growing power of the political right.[155]

The very next year, the federal government, which had been led by the Christian Social Engelbert Dollfuss upon his assumption of the chancellorship in May 1932, banned all forms of commemoration for the fifteenth anniversary of the republic. By this point, Dollfuss had used a technicality to disband the parliament in March, and was seeking ways to destroy the Social Democratic Party in order to establish an Austrofascist state. Therefore, not only did the government cancel all government festivities except for a Mass in St. Stephen's Cathedral, but it also forbade any political demonstrations from taking place on November 12 by enacting a law regarding the maintenance of "public safety and the welfare of the public."[156] Although there was certainly reason to worry about violence breaking out on November 12, the use of this law was entirely cynical.

Only two months before, the government had helped to stage mass commemorations for the joint occasion of the Allgemeiner deutscher Katholikentag (General German Catholic Congress) and the 250th anniversary of the Battle of Vienna. The Katholikentag took place September 7–12, and the government officials declared September 12, the day on which an army of Austrian, Polish, and Bavarian troops defeated the Ottoman soldiers in 1683, an official state holiday. On September 12 alone there was a Mass led by Polish clergy on the Kahlenberg, the place from which Jan Sobieski launched his attack on the Ottoman forces, that was attended by four thousand people; the Ceremony of the Federal Government for the Memory of the Liberation of Vienna from Turks at the Heldenplatz, in which twelve thousand took part; the third general assembly of the

153. "60.000 Sozialdemokraten, 9000 Nazi," *Wiener Sonn- und Montagszeitung*, 14 November 1932, in WB, TA, Nationalfeiertag (12. November).

154. "Wir marschieren am 12. November!," *AZ*, 10 November 1932, in WB, TA, Nationalfeiertag (12. November).

155. Hanisch, "Das Fest," 54; Rabinbach, *Crisis of Austrian Socialism*.

156. PrK 10922/1933, Amtsveranlassung, 12. November, Nationalfeiertag des Jahres 1933, in ÖStA, AdR, PrK 10922/1933; Bundes-Polizeidirektion in Wien, V.B.2/66/1933, Vienna, 2 November 1933, Untersagung einer Kundgebung der Organisation der Sozialdemokratischen Partei auf der Ringstrasse am 12. November 1933, in ÖStA, AdR, BKA, Berichte der Wiener Polizeidirektion, 1933/November, Kt. 34.

Katholikentag in the Viennese stadium with fifteen thousand participants; the Austrian Heimatschutz's Celebration of the Liberation from the Turks on the plaza before city hall with seventeen hundred Heimwehr men and five thousand onlookers; and a closing ceremony for the Katholikentag in and around St. Stephen's, which drew a crowd of ten thousand. Government leaders, the army, and the clergy took part in these events. Speakers at the various gatherings addressed themes such as "Austria's mission as the bulwark of the Catholic faith" and "German *Volkstum* from the strength of Christianity."[157] These festivities, celebrating Catholicism, corporatism, conservatism, authoritarianism, and Austria's imperial past, amounted to a preview of the Austrofascist regime, which would fully assume power after the forces of the political right defeated the Social Democrats in a brief civil war in February 1934.[158]

The November 12 anniversary in 1933 therefore stood in stark contrast to the September celebrations. In an attempt to circumvent the ban on parades and gatherings, the SDAP organized "walks" in various cities. Workers were to wear red carnations, carry red flags, and release red balloons as they walked through the city as a way to protest the current government and show their support for the republic. This action resulted in the police moving against the walkers. Officers made numerous arrests, including 225 people in Vienna alone. Among those detained by the police were Karl Renner and Friedrich Adler. Moreover, the police used force and beat the socialist protesters with their batons, causing many injuries.[159] In Linz, members of the Heimwehr attacked the sixty-seven-year-old socialist mayor during the "walks" there. According to the *Arbeiter-Zeitung*, the police did nothing, and the mayor had to be saved by socialist youths.[160] The fifteenth and final anniversary of the republic should therefore be seen as one of many steps taken by the Christian Social–led government to deliberately undermine the SDAP and the republic.

Thus, the state holiday for the republic in Austria looked quite different from the de facto Constitution Day in Germany. Indeed, the two celebrations point to a number of key distinctions between the political cultures of interwar Germany and Austria. The desire and the ability to stage a popular holiday for the Weimar Republic were due to a democratic consensus created by the parties of

---

157. Bundes-Polizeidirektion in Wien, Pr.Zl. IV-6566/22/33, Vienna, 12 September 1933, in ÖStA, AdR, BKA, Berichte der Wiener Polizeidirektion, September 1933, Kt. 32.

158. For more on Dollfuss's "Austrian ideology" see Anton Staudinger, "Austrofaschistische 'Österreich'-Ideologie," in *Austrofaschismus*, ed. Tálos und Neugebauer, 28–52.

159. "Der zwölfte November," *AZ*, 13 November 1933, in WB, TA, Nationalfeiertag (12. November).

160. "Der 12. November," *AZ*, 14 November 1933, in WB, TA, Nationalfeiertag (12. November).

the Weimar Coalition. Their members were willing to work across class, political, and confessional divisions to support and celebrate the republic. In seeking to create a *Volksfest*, they sought to be inclusive of all Germans in their attempts to win over skeptics and opponents of the republic. Although a number of political groups on both the right and left of the political spectrum refused to support the republic and celebrate its constitution, the republicans, until 1931, made progress in achieving their goals. Austrians, on the other hand, not only remained within their particular *Lager*, but also purposefully sought to antagonize their political opponents. Rather than a popular holiday, the republic's birthday became a site where the various parties and paramilitary groups fought over the current and future form of the state. On the last *Republikfeier*, the socialists and Christian Socials accused one another of having prevented the creation of a popular commemoration, again displaying the primary reason why the holiday had never become a *Volksfest*.[161]

Yet these political fractures were not the only problems highlighted on November 12. The republic's anniversary also became a day to express the desire for the dissolution of the very state being commemorated. For socialists, the GDVP, the Nazis, and nationalist wing of the CSP, November 12 became an occasion to once again demand an Anschluss. This situation should not be surprising, given that the "Law from 12 November 1918 about the Form of the State and Government of German-Austria" declared that "German-Austria is a constitutive part of the German republic."[162] For example, on the tenth anniversary of the Austrian republic, the Österreichisch-Deutscher Volksbund in Vienna sent postcards to numerous politicians of all parties, government officials, bureaucrats, public intellectuals, artists, and academics, asking them to sign in support of the 1918 law. The Volksbund then reproduced the signatures and ran them in a commemorative issue of its publication, *Der Anschluss*. Over four hundred prominent Austrians from the fields of politics, the civil service, culture, and economics stated that they "remain[ed] true to this resolution" from November 12, 1918.[163] As with the paradoxical proclamation of the republic itself, Austrians at times used the anniversary of the republic to call for the elimination of that republic's sovereignty. Austrians, however, were not alone in seeing political

---

161. "Staatsfeiertage," *AZ*, 4 November 1933, and "Staatsfeiertag und Sozialdemokratie," *RP*, 5 November 1933, both in WB, TA, Nationalfeiertag (12. November).

162. "Nr. 5/1918, Gesetz vom 12. November 1918 über die Staats- und Regierungsform von Deutsch-Österreich," in *Staatsgesetzblatt für den Staat Deutschösterreich*, Jahrgang 1918 (Vienna: Deutschösterreichische Staatsdruckerei, 1918), 4.

163. *Der Anschluß*, 2. Jahrgang, Folge 11, 12 November 1928, in PAAA, R 73303, IIOe1874.

holidays as times to demonstrate Austro-German togetherness. As we will see in the next chapter, the transborder relationship between Reich Germans and Austrians became a recurring feature of republican commemorations and rallies. Only by examining republican celebrations from a transnational perspective can we fully grasp the attempts to legitimize and defend the republics.

4

STAGING A GREATER GERMAN REPUBLIC

Cross-Border Republican Rallies

All Berlin appeared to be out enjoying the sunny Sunday in August. Over two million people rode the streetcars, while the bus system transported over seven hundred thousand individuals and the subways carried nearly five hundred thousand riders around the city. Traffic was certainly higher, by at least six hundred thousand people, than any other Sunday that month. It was not the glorious weather alone, however, that brought people into the streets. Rather, it was the numerous events being held to commemorate the tenth anniversary of the Weimar Constitution. In addition to the government's commemorations before the Reichstag and in the stadium, the Reichsbanner had elected to hold its central Constitution Day festivities in Berlin that year. To honor the occasion, the Reichsbanner organized sporting activities, a rally for railway workers, a festive ceremony in the Kroll Opera, and a rally in the Lustgarten followed by a five-hour parade along Unter den Linden. Based on sales of special badges produced for the weekend, the Reichsbanner estimated that eight hundred thousand people took part in its activities.[1]

Although Constitution Day was a celebration of the republican state, as we saw in the previous chapter, it was also a celebration of the German Volk. Consequently, the Reichsbanner journal's main report on the festivities carried the title, "The Day of the German Nation." For the Reichsbanner and other republicans, the nation was, of course, a *großdeutsch* one. Consequently, a contingent

---

1. "Der Tag der deutschen Nation," *DR*, 17 August 1929, 269.

of fifteen hundred Austrian socialists from the Schutzbund traveled to Berlin to help the Reichsbanner celebrate the Weimar Republic. According to the *Berliner Montagspost*, the inclusion of the Austrian delegation in the parade was "the high point" of that event.[2] Over the course of the Reichsbanner celebrations, the Austrians received an enthusiastic welcome from Berliners, and republican leaders emphasized that they hoped the Weimar Republic would become a *großdeutsch* republic.[3] To "loud applause," Julius Deutsch, the head of the Schutzbund, declared, "As we departed Vienna, we were of the opinion that we travel to another country. As we crossed the state border, however, then we knew: It is no border! We return to our fatherland."[4]

The 1929 Constitution Day, as well as the first anniversary of the Reichsbanner described at the opening of this book, were not singular events during the Weimar era. As Otto Hörsing, the socialist leader of the Reichsbanner, remarked during the parade, "Who can even think of a grand demonstration of the Reichsbanner without our friends from Vienna."[5] Whether celebrating Constitution Day or November 12, or staging pro-republican demonstrations for the Reichsbanner or the Schutzbund, German and Austrian republicans frequently used *großdeutsch* motifs and cross-border visits to demonstrate their two central, interconnected arguments: a *Großdeutschland* could be achieved only through a republican form of government, and an Anschluss would help to strengthen democracy in Central Europe. Whereas the previous chapter examined the attempts to use commemorations to legitimize (or protest) each republic, this chapter looks at the transborder aspects of those holidays and others. To date, the importance of these Austro-German republican celebrations has been completely overlooked by scholars writing about Weimar symbolism.[6] By bringing these transborder events into the story about republican efforts to support democracy, this chapter further emphasizes the importance of Austro-German connections to the debates about political legitimacy in interwar Central Europe. It highlights once again the high level of commitment that republicans had to their *großdeutsch* nationalism. Moreover, this chapter will demonstrate that the Anschluss idea was

---

2. "Gewaltiger Aufmarsch des Reichsbanners," *Berliner Montagspost*, 12 August 1929, in BAB, R72/1942, Bl. 15, here Rs. of 15.

3. Ibid. Also see *DR* issue from 17 August 1929, 270–275.

4. "Die Eisenbahner im Zirkus Busch," *DR*, 17 August 1929, 275.

5. "Gewaltiger Aufmarsch des Reichsbanners," *Berliner Montagspost*, 12 August 1929, in BAB, R72/1942, Bl. 15.

6. Achilles, "Re-forming the Reich" and "With a Passion for Reason"; Buchner, *Um nationale und republikanische Identität*; Bryden, "In Search of Founding Fathers"; Rossol, *Performing the Nation*, chap. 3; Ziemann, *Contested Commemorations*.

not simply limited to party leaders, but also extended to the rank and file of these organizations.

While republicans from both sides of the border came together to support parliamentary democracy, their relationship was not without problems. As the previous chapter demonstrated, republicans were dealing with vastly different domestic situations in their struggle to defend the republics. Whereas Catholics, socialists, and left liberals in Germany were willing to collaborate with one another, Austrian socialists were the only consistent republicans in the rump state. The Schutzbund delegation at the 1929 *Verfassungsfeier* (Constitution Day celebration) made this clear, calling out, "We from Red Vienna greet you in Berlin!"[7] Adding to the difficulties was the fact that the Social Democrats in Austria had acrimonious relations with the other domestic parties, especially the Christian Socials. The SDAP's revolutionary rhetoric and attacks on their Catholic political opponents at home resulted in tensions between the Schutzbund and the Reichsbanner, as well as strains between the Center Party and the Reichsbanner. These disagreements, however, did not simply originate within the republican coalition. Conservatives and the radical right in both states endeavored to break up the republican alliance. The political right's effort to do so was another sign of the importance of the cross-border republican partnership to the defense of democracy.

Forging a *Großdeutsch* Republican Community

"Because what more strongly ties the *Auslandsdeutschen* [Germans outside the Reich] to their tribes [*Stämme*] and to the territory of their homeland [*Heimatgebiet*] than the community of festivals and the forms in which the German celebrates his festival," wrote Edwin Redslob in a piece titled "Constitution Day as the Expression of German Festival Culture."[8] Commemorations played an important role in imagining a transborder German community during the interwar period, as Redslob's quote suggests. Unable to create a state that included all German speakers because of the restrictions of the peace treaties, German speakers used commemorative activities both to present their particular understandings of nationhood and to help foster a sense of national togetherness that extended beyond the boundaries of the Reich. While republicans expressed concern for German minorities in Eastern Europe and hoped to whip up support among

---

7. "Die Feier des Reichsbanners," *AZ*, 12 August 1929, 1.
8. Edwin Redslob, Draft of "Die Verfassungsfeier als Ausdruck deutscher Festeskultur," in BAB, R32/426, Bl. 79–96, here 90.

Germans overseas, they limited their demands for the redrawing of territorial boundaries, as we have seen. Given that their major vision for the reorganization of Europe was an Anschluss, the *großdeutsch* idea became a central motif in their festivities and rallies. In promoting the *großdeutsch* idea at public events, republican leaders endeavored to instill their version of nationalism in their supporters while generating enthusiasm for the republics. As an uncontested ideal among republicans in Germany and Austria, *großdeutsch* nationalism also served to cement the bonds among the four republican parties, thereby bolstering their fight against the threats of monarchism and fascism. Moreover, republicans hoped their proclamations in favor of an Anschluss would offer proof of their national convictions. By countering the political right's arguments that the republics and their proponents were un-German, they sought to win over skeptics.

One way that republicans spread a *großdeutsch* conception of nationhood was to single out Austria when pointing to the connections between democracy and Germanness. Although, as the previous chapter demonstrated, the political cultures of Germany and Austria were vastly different, republicans in both states viewed political celebrations and demonstrations as platforms to voice their support for the *großdeutsch* idea and an Anschluss. In Austria, calls for a "speedy return to the common mother: to the free democratic republic of *Groß-Deutschland*" surfaced even before the war ended and elicited great enthusiasm when proclaimed at a socialist rally for a republican form of government in early November 1918 in Graz.[9] In the following years, Austrian socialists voiced similar sentiments during a range of occasions, including the November 12 celebrations, the 1927 and 1930 Nationalrat elections, and the debate about the national anthem.[10] Likewise, in Germany, republicans used Constitution Day festivities and Reichsbanner gatherings to express their wish for a "German republic from Aachen to Vienna," to use the words of Walter Kolb at a 1926 Reichsbanner *Verfassungsfeier* in Bonn.[11]

The republican press in both countries also helped to disseminate the *großdeutsch* message beyond the participants at holidays and rallies. In addition to reporting on pro-republican events and reprinting the speeches of prominent politicians, newspapers and pamphlets printed articles concerning the Anschluss

---

9. "Massenkundgebung am Franzensplatz," *Tagespost*, 4 November 1918, in WB, TA, Anschluss bis 1926.

10. For examples see "Der Tag der Republik," *AZ*, 12 November 1920, 1; "Der Gedenktag der Republik," *AZ*, 13 November 1920, 3; "Arbeiter und Arbeiterinnen!," *AZ*, 6 November 1921, 1; "Hernals," *AZ*, 13 November 1922, 2; "Der Tag der Republik," *AZ*, 13 November 1922, 1; "Leopoldstadt," *AZ*, 13 November 1925, 2; "Sie war unser! Sie wird unser sein!," *AZ*, 12 November 1927, 2; "Ein neues Zeitalter soll kommen!" and "Wähler und Wählerinnen!," in VGA, Parteistellen, Kt. 216, Mappe 1456.

11. Walter Kolb, "Frei Heil!," in *Verfassungsfeier 1926 des Reichsbanners Schwarz-Rot-Gold Gau Oberrhein in Bonn, 14. u. 15. August 1926*, in AdsD, Reichsbanner Schwarz-Rot-Gold, Exponate 19.

idea and the situation of republicans in the neighboring country. For instance, the Reichsbanner published an eponymous journal that ran articles on such topics as the differences between *großdeutsch* and *alldeutsch* nationalisms, the Schutzbund, the threats posed by fascism and monarchism in Austria, the collapse of Austria-Hungary, the problems of the Austrian military, the Anschluss idea in Germany, and an Austro-German customs union. The *großdeutsch* idea also merited mention in articles related to the advantages of a centralized state (*Einheitsstaat*) over a federal state (*Bundesstaat*), *Grenzlanddeutschtum* (borderland Germandom), foreign policy, pacifism, the Weimar Constitution, the reasons why January 18 should not be a national holiday, and an upcoming meeting of the youth section of the Reichsbanner.

While Reich Germans penned some of these articles, the Reichsbanner sought to reinforce these cross-border ties and satiate its membership's interest in Austria by asking Austrian politicians to write for its journal. "By the way, it seems that we have once again entered a period in which it is up to us to emphasize regularly the idea of German-Austrian togetherness and to keep alive among us the interest in the preservation and stabilization of democracy in this German country," the editorial staff of *Das Reichsbanner* wrote to Julius Deutsch in a request for an article on military politics.[12] Over the course of its existence, the journal featured pieces by the likes of Deutsch, Karl Renner, and Fritz Brügel that informed Reich German readers about the Schutzbund, the Heimwehr, the Anschluss idea, the reaction of Austrians to the election of Hindenburg, and the general political situation in Austria. Similarly, Austrian pro-republican papers featured Reich German authors and frequently covered republican events in Germany. By educating their readers about a shared nationality and common struggle for democracy, these publications sought to strengthen the bond between republicans in both countries.

These efforts at promoting republican *großdeutsch* nationalism extended beyond the written and spoken word. Republicans on both sides of the Austro-German boundary made symbolic gestures to acknowledge and reinforce their cross-border relationship. Members of the Reichsbanner frequently pointed out that the inspiration for its name, the official colors of the republic, was "the symbol of *großdeutsch* Germany."[13] The local Reichsbanner group in Weimar decided

---

12. Letter from the Reichsbanner Schwarz-Rot-Gold (Redaktion der Bundeszeitung *Das Reichsbanner*) to Julius Deutsch, Magdeburg, 20 February 1930, in VGA, Parteiarchiv vor 1934, Mappe 35. Also see Letter from the *Illustrierte Reichsbanner-Zeitung* to Karl Heinz, Berlin, 5 April 1929, in VGA, Parteiarchiv vor 1934, Mappe 35.

13. Speech by Willy Hellpach in "Reichsbannertage in Süddeutschland," *DR* (Beilage), 1 April 1925, o.S.

to show the connections between Germany and Austria even more demonstratively by creating a chapter flag that contained the black-red-gold flag of the Reich and the red-white-red flag of the "German-Austrian republic."[14] Further underscoring the importance of the *großdeutsch* idea to Reich German republicans, the Reichsbanner used the title "*Großdeutsch* Day" for events ranging from a 1925 flag consecration in Aurich to a 1926 Constitution Day in Frankfurt.[15] Additionally, Redslob's mass spectacle "Germany's River," staged on the occasion of the liberation of the Rhineland and the Constitution Day in 1930, highlighted that Reich republicans were not merely concerned with Germany's western border. When the children embodying the Danube ran out onto the field, the accompanying musicians played Strauss's "Blue Danube." The director did not, however, leave any doubt that the Danube was a symbol of Austria's inclusion in Germany; the major "German" city he chose to represent the river was Vienna, symbolized by St. Stephen's Cathedral. In its coverage of the spectacle in the Berlin stadium, the liberal *Berliner Tageblatt* gushed, "The cheers increased to enthusiasm, which also spread to the spectators, as the river of our Austrian brotherland flowed in: the Danube, accompanied by music from dear Johann Strauss!"[16]

Socialists in Austria were keen to show that "Red Vienna" was black-red-gold Vienna as well. The chief symbol of "Red Vienna" was the municipal housing projects constructed for workers. While the most famous of these carried the name "Karl-Marx-Hof," leaders in the city decided in 1926 to name one of the buildings for the recently deceased Friedrich Ebert, a leader of the SPD and the first president of the Weimar Republic. Lest an observer simply view this act as a demonstration of the link between two socialist parties, the main speaker at the event and news coverage of it made clear that the *großdeutsch* idea was a motivating factor in the name choice. Reporting on the "rally for the Anschluss" that had taken place at the opening of the Ebert-Hof, the *Arbeiter-Zeitung* concluded, "With this naming, the municipality not only wanted the Viennese population always to hold on to the memory of Ebert, who emerged from the working class, but also desired above all else to erect a visible symbol of the will to Anschluss of the overwhelming majority of the Volk."[17]

---

14. Letter from the Reichsbanner Gau Großthüringen to Julius Deutsch, 17 August 1927, in VGA, Parteiarchiv vor 1934, Mappe 35.

15. "Aus den Gauen," *DR* (Beilage), 1 May 1925, o.S.; *Großdeutscher republikanischer Volkstag für Südwestdeutschland in Frankfurt a.M., Samstag, den 8., Sonntag, den 9. u. Dienstag (Verfassungstag), den 11. August 1925, Programm und Liedertexte,* 1, in AdsD, Reichsbanner Schwarz-Rot-Gold, Nummer 145.

16. "Die Jugend im Stadion: Das grosse Festspiel 'Deutschlands Strom,'" *BT*, 11 August 1930, in BAB, R32/437, Bl. 51.

17. "Die Gemeinde Wien dem Andenken des ersten deutschen Reichspräsidenten," *AZ*, 25 October 1926, in WB, L121260, Bd. 2, Fasz. I, Untermappe I, 151.

For republicans, such symbolic acts within one's own country did not go far enough. To prove the seriousness of their commitment to a *großdeutsch* republic, republicans traversed the boundary between the two states. In doing so, they could demonstrate the porousness of a border they hoped would one day be erased. The trips also served as a way to illustrate to lay republicans that Germans and Austrians both belonged to the same Volk and were engaged in a joint fight for democracy. This cross-border activity for republicans took off with the establishment of the two republican defense organizations: the Republikanischer Schutzbund in February 1923 and the Reichsbanner in February 1924. Within months of the Reichsbanner's founding, its leaders expressed a desire to establish "a lasting political relationship" with the Schutzbund. The leadership of the Austrian formation enthusiastically responded, saying it wished "to enter into not only a friendly collaboration, but rather a relationship of brotherly cooperation" with the Reichsbanner.[18] Highlighting the collaboration between the two groups was the fact that Otto Hörsing, the head of the Reichsbanner, served as an honorary chairman of the Schutzbund, while Deutsch and Theodor Körner of the Schutzbund were members of the Reichsbanner Reich Committee. In fact, the Schutzbund was the only pro-republican organization outside the Reich with which the Reichsbanner chose to establish relations.[19]

The cross-border journeys began when the Reichsbanner wanted to stage a "powerful demonstration for the republican and *großdeutsch* ideas" at its 1924 Constitution Day celebration in Weimar. Consequently, the Reichsbanner executives asked the Schutzbund to send a representative to the festivities.[20] Theodor Körner, a general in the Austro-Hungarian and Austrian armies until 1924 who then became a socialist representative in parliament, made the trip to the birthplace of the German constitution and brought "the greetings of my friends, the

---

18. Unsigned letter [from Schutzbund] to the Bund "Reichsbanner Schwarz-Rot-Gold," 18 July 1924, in VGA, Parteiarchiv vor 1934, Mappe 35. As this quote and the other actions of the Schutzbund explored in this chapter suggest, the Schutzbund was not merely committed to "proletarian-international" ideas, as Karl Rohe has suggested. While a purely socialist organization that hoped to achieve socialism, it also promoted republican *großdeutsch* nationalism. Nor were Austrian socialists primarily committed to an Anschluss for revolutionary reasons, as their various statements throughout this book demonstrate. Rohe, *Das Reichsbanner*, 228, 238–239.

19. "Im Herrenkrug," *DR*, 15 May 1926, 76. Only in October 1932 did the Reichsbanner finally agree to join the International Conference of Disabled Soldiers and Ex-Servicemen (CIAMAC), an organization that focused on international reconciliation. "Beitritt des 'Reichsbanners Schwarz-Rot-Gold' zur Kriegsopfer-Internationale," enclosed in a letter from the Kriegsinvaliden und Kriegerhinterbliebenen, Landesverband für Wien, Niederösterreich und Burgenland to Karl Heinz, Vienna, 28 October 1932, in VGA, Parteiarchiv vor 1934, Mappe 35.

20. Letter from the Reichsbanner Schwarz-Rot-Gold Bundesvorstand to the Republikanischer Schutzbund (Deutsch), Magdeburg, 3 July 1924, in VGA, Parteiarchiv vor 1934, Mappe 35.

upright republicans of the Austrian *Stamm* of the Germans."[21] From this point forward, the two organizations sought to bolster republican nationalism by visiting the neighboring country. Moreover, in the future, not only prominent leaders, but also ordinary members of the two associations made the trip across the Austro-German boundary.

Just six months after Körner's initial visit to Germany, Austrian socialists thus returned to the Reich to help the Reichsbanner celebrate its first anniversary. Led by Julius Deutsch and Josef Püchler, the socialist vice-mayor of Wiener Neustadt, a division of thirty-nine Schutzbund members attended the festivities in Magdeburg. As the vignette at the opening of this book illustrated, their presence was intended to highlight the centrality of the *großdeutsch* idea to the defense of a republican form of government. "Through this [republican] Anschluss," Deutsch pointed out in one of his speeches, "all republican, democratic, peaceful, and conciliatory ideas would be supported."[22] Until that time came, both defense leagues would work together to support democracy. Such proclamations were met with "unending applause" from the Reichsbanner audience. The appearance of Deutsch and the other Schutzbund affiliates was enough to cause "an indescribable elation" and lent the "event a distinctive character," according to republican publications in the Reich.[23] A reporter for the *New York Times* affirmed these accounts, describing the presence of the Austrians as "the feature of the celebration."[24]

Yet it was not simply prominent politicians who embraced the *großdeutsch* idea at the celebration. At the arrival of the Schutzbund delegation, crowds stood "tightly packed" to welcome the Austrians. Even more remarkable was an "overwhelmingly beautiful and incredibly stunning rally" that spontaneously occurred at the departure of the Schutzbund. Although only a small notice about the Austrians' departure appeared in the press, thousands turned up to wish the Austrians well. Mothers carried their children on their shoulders, crowds heartily cheered, while still others waved handkerchiefs and handed flowers to the Austrians. "All of Magdeburg was on its feet!" exclaimed *Das Reichsbanner*, while it also pointed out that *völkisch* groups, the Stahlhelm, the DNVP, and the DVP were missing from the celebration of the Austrians. Contrasting republican enthusiasm with

21. "General Körner," *DR*, 15 August 1924, o.S.

22. "Das Reichsbannerfest in Magdeburg," *AZ*, 24 February 1925, in WB, TA, Republikanischer Schutzbund.

23. First quote is in "Trommerschlag und Hörnerklang: Nationalrat Deutsch," *DR*, 1 March 1925 (2. Beilage), o.S; second quote is from "Ein Jahr Reichsbanner," *Germania* (Abendausgabe), 23 February 1925, o.S.

24. T. R. Ybarra, "Burn Boundary Posts of All the Reich States and of Austria at German Republican Rally," *New York Times*, 23 February 1925, 1.

the political right's absence, the article raised the question of who were the best Germans. Given their failure to attend, conservatives and right-wing activists had "no right to call themselves Germans." Rather, the article concluded that the republican population, those who resided in the side streets and the working-class suburbs, were the "true German national comrades [*Volksgenossen*]."[25] Once more, republicans saw their *großdeutsch* nationalism as a way to question the national credentials of their opponents while proving their own commitment to the German cause. Additionally, the reporter observed a noteworthy feature that would continue to appear at most of these cross-border exchanges: in addition to the *großdeutsch* rhetoric of the republican leaders, a genuine popular enthusiasm for a *großdeutsch* republic was evident as well.

Nor was this excitement limited to Austrian visitors to the Reich. The year 1925 also marked the first visit of a Reichsbanner member to Austria. In July, the Schutzbund organized a marshals' convention paired with an Anschluss rally in St. Pölten that drew twenty thousand of its supporters. "Needless to say," explained the Schutzbund secretary Karl Heinz, "a representative of the combat-ready republicans of Germany could not be left out of such a rally, which has had a political effect that has exceeded all expectations."[26] The presence of Karl Kunzemann, the secretary of the Reichsbanner, ensured the demonstration was a "*Verbrüderungskundgebung*," a rally for the avowal of brotherhood. To further prove this point, republican publications mentioned that his speech on the fight against reactionary forces and desire for an Anschluss received enthusiastic applause.[27]

The next occasion at which the two groups met was the Reichsbanner's 1925 Constitution Day festivities in Berlin. As opposed to just sending one representative, as had occurred with the 1924 Constitution Day, the Schutzbund dispatched two hundred individuals to the anniversary celebration.[28] Once again, the presence of Austrians delighted the Reich German crowds. Thousands gathered with black-red-gold flags to witness the arrival of the Austrians, cheering both the appearance of the Schutzbund and the *großdeutsch* comments of the speakers.[29] At the showpiece of the weekend—a parade and a rally in Treptow Park—participants and onlookers "stormily greeted" the Schutzbund delegation, and various Reichsbanner speakers underlined the importance of the Austrians' involvement in the *Verfassungsfeier*. When a representative of the Schutzbund,

25. "Empfang der Oesterreicher" and "Der Triumphzug," *DR*, 1 March 1925 (1. Beilage), o.S.

26. Karl Heinz, "Oesterreich im Kampfe," *DR*, 15 July 1925 (Beilage), o.S.

27. "Der Ordnertag des Republikanischen Schutzbundes," *AZ*, 15 June 1925, 1–2; Karl Heinz, "Oesterreich im Kampfe," *DR* (Beilage), 15 July 1925, o.S.

28. "Die Verfassungsfeier im Reiche," *DR*, 15 August 1925 (Beilage), o.S.

29. "Die Verfassungsfeier," *Vorwärts*, 8 August 1925 (Morgenausgabe, 1. Beilage), o.S; "Empfang der österreichischen Gäste," *Germania* (Abendausgabe), 8 August 1925, o.S.

Hans Lagger, announced that "we Austrians are and remain German and republican" and that "the inner Anschluss of Austria with Germany has already been accomplished," he received "roaring applause."[30] The Austrians enjoyed another warm welcome from republicans in Potsdam, where they spent a day before returning home.[31]

Further cementing the close ties between the two organizations that year was the attendance by Deutsch at the Reichsbanner Parliament in October and Hörsing's participation in the Schutzbund Reich Conference, which was held in conjunction with the party's commemoration for November 12. At the Reichsbanner Parliament, Deutsch received "stormy applause" when he declared that only the republic and its supporters could pave the way for an Anschluss.[32] Likewise, Hörsing garnered an enthusiastic response to his speeches given to the Schutzbund during its November 12 celebration and its meeting the following day. Hörsing's presence was not the only representation of the *großdeutsch* idea at the anniversary of the Austrian republic. For the first time, the Schutzbund carried black-red-gold flags alongside their customary red banners.[33] The activities of "the two republican defense associations have not only powerfully invigorated the republican movement, but also the Anschluss movement," concluded the report of the SDAP's party congress.[34]

The following year saw an increase in the number of republicans visiting their German-speaking neighbors. In February, around five hundred members of the Schutzbund were among the 120,000 people who celebrated the second anniversary of the Reichsbanner in Hamburg. As with their previous visits to Germany, the Schutzbund delegates received a joyous response from the Reich population. On their way to Hamburg, the delegates stopped in Berlin, where two thousand Reichsbanner members feted them in Schloss Belvue.[35] In Hamburg, pouring rain failed to prevent thousands of men and women from gathering to greet the Austrians in "such a stunning reception, the likes of which Hamburg has never experienced."[36] Calls for an Anschluss also occupied an important part in the various speeches given at the official ceremony, a gathering of the railway workers

---

30. "Die Verfassungsfeiern im Reiche," *DR*, 15 August 1925 (Beilage), o.S.

31. "Fackelzug in Potsdam," *DR*, 15 August 1925 (Beilage), o.S.

32. "Reichsbanner-Parlament," *DR*, 15 October 1925 (Beilage), o.S.

33. "Die Feier des republikanischen Schutzbundes," *NWT*, 13 November 1925, in ÖStA, AdR, Parteiarchive, GDVP, Zeitungsausschnitte, Mappe 267, 63/s; "Die Schutzbundparade auf dem Karlsplatz," *AZ*, 13 November 1925, 1.

34. "Protokoll des sozialdemokratischen Parteitages 1925," in WB, TA, Schutzbund.

35. "Fünfhundert Mitglieder des Republikanischen Schutzbundes in Berlin," *NFP*, 21 February 1926, in WB, TA, Schutzbund.

36. "Die Delegation des Republikanischen Schutzbundes in Hamburg," *AZ*, 23 February 1926, in WB, TA, Schutzbund.

FIGURE 2. The Schutzbund at the second anniversary of the Reichsbanner in Hamburg in February 1926. "The Austrian comrades were enthusiastically greeted at their departure from the Alte Markt," *Illustrierte Reichsbanner-Zeitung*, March 6, 1926. Reproduced with permission of Verlag J. H. W. Dietz Nachf.

at the Trade Union House, and a giant rally where "an inestimable crowd had gathered."[37] Unlikely sources, such as the Stahlhelm, begrudgingly praised the festivities and admitted that the celebration had "an enduring promotional effect."[38] The Austrian consulate similarly concluded that the anniversary was a "political experience of not unimportant significance" and that the Reichsbanner "as the bearer of the republican consciousness and the *großdeutsch* idea has become in politics a power of the first degree."[39] Before returning home from the successful weekend in Hamburg, the Austrians had a stopover in Magdeburg, where once again "densely packed" crowds turned out to see the Schutzbund representatives march through the streets.[40] While the Schutzbund contingents traveling to the Reich consisted mainly of individuals from Vienna and Linz, delegations from Tyrol and Vorarlberg made a voyage to Konstanz that summer in order to participate in a Republican Day staged by the Gau (district) Baden of the Reichsbanner. "Never before were so many people here at the harbor as now," an older member of the Reichsbanner exclaimed while awaiting the arrival of the Austrians' boat. As the ship neared the shore, the Schutzbund band aboard began to intone "Deutschland, Deutschland über alles."[41] Time and time again, lay republicans and their leaders were eager to show their interest in the *großdeutsch* and republican causes.

The summer of 1926 also marked the first and one of the only times that large numbers of Reichsbanner men made the trip to Austria. In July, the Austrian Workers' League for Sport and Physical Culture (Arbeiterbund für Sport- und Körperkultur) put on a Workers' Gymnastics and Sport Festival in Vienna that included working-class athletes from Czechoslovakia, Poland, France, Switzerland, Hungary, Yugoslavia, Belgium, and Lithuania, in addition to Germany. The Reich had the largest delegation from outside Austria, consisting of four thousand Reichsbanner members who hailed from all the organization's 32 districts and 250 local chapters.[42] Demand to go among the Reichsbanner rank and file was

---

37. Letter from the Generalkonsulat der Republik Oesterreichs in Hamburg to the BKA–AA, Hamburg, 22 February 1926, Zl. 11089, in ÖStA, AdR, BKA, AA, NPA, Kt. 154, Liasse Deutschland 19/1, Reichsbanner Schwarz-Rot-Gold, Bl. 5–7, here 7. Also see "Reichsbannertagung in Hamburg," *Germania* (Abendausgabe), 22 February 1926, o.S.; "Begründungstag des Reichsbanners," *Hamburger Nachrichten*, 22 February 1926, in BAB, R72/1941, Rs. of Bl. 35.

38. "Der Stahlhelm" Bund der Frontsoldaten Ortsgruppe Hamburg-Mitte, Gesamtbericht über die Reichsbannertagung am 20. und 21. Februar 1926 in Hamburg, 21 February 1926, in BAB, R72/1941, Bl. 10–15, here 12.

39. Letter from the Generalkonsulat der Republik Oesterreichs in Hamburg to the BKA–AA, Hamburg, 22 February 1926, Zl. 11089, in ÖStA, AdR, BKA, AA, NPA, Kt. 154, Liasse Deutschland 19/1, Reichsbanner Schwarz-Rot-Gold, Bl. 5–7, here 5.

40. "Die Oesterreicher in Magdeburg," *DR*, 1 March 1926, 33.

41. O. Hörsing, "Republikanische Tage in Konstanz," *DR*, 15 June 1926, 94.

42. "Der rote Sonntag," *AZ*, 12 July 1926, 2–3; "Das 'Reichsbanner Schwarz-Rot-Gold,'" *NFP*, 12 July 1926, in WB, L121260, Bd. 2, Fasz. I, Untermappe 1, 38.

even greater than the thousands who made the journey; numerous unemployed members discussed cycling or walking to Vienna, prompting the leadership to send out a warning against doing so.[43] Although the event was designed to be a "demonstration of proletarian strength,"[44] the German and Austrian participants signaled beforehand that the visit to "the capital of our German-Austrian brother state" would be "an avowal to the *großdeutsch* republican idea."[45] Thus, during the various activities—including a mass rally on the Heldenplatz, a torchlight parade, a gathering of the various socialist paramilitary groups, a meeting of republican students, and a four-hour parade along the Ringstrasse to the Prater—speakers such as Otto Bauer, Julius Deutsch, Karl Höltermann (a socialist journalist who would become the chairman of the Reichsbanner in 1931), Walter Kolb, Paul Löbe, and Horst Bärensprung (a police president in Magdeburg and secretary of the Reichsbanner) proclaimed socialist sayings alongside expressions of *großdeutsch* nationalism.[46] Over the course of the weeklong gathering, participants used more general republican slogans such as "against international fascism, for the republic, and for the Anschluss of Austria with Germany," while also calling out, "Cheers to the International!"[47]

And, in reactions mirroring other events bringing German and Austrian republicans together, Austrian workers expressed excitement upon seeing the Reichsbanner. During the parade, the German delegation received the warmest welcome.[48] Moreover, a spontaneous Anschluss rally occurred during the departure of the Reichsbanner members from the Gau Magdeburg-Anhalt, Leipzig, and Hamburg, despite only a short notice about it in the newspaper. That Austrian workers would rally behind the Anschluss idea should not be altogether surprising, given that some members of the working class displayed interest in nationalism even before the First World War.[49] Thousands of men and women gathered at the Rathausplatz as the Reich Germans assembled to march to the train station, giving the Reichsbanner men flowers, carrying their luggage, and cheering loudly for socialism and an Anschluss. As the Reichsbanner representatives made their way down Mariahilferstrasse, the windows of buildings flew

---

43. "Mitteilungen des Bundesvorstandes," *DR*, 1 June 1926, 86.

44. "Aufmarsch der proletarischen Wehrorganisation," *AZ*, 11 July 1926, 1.

45. W. Nowack, "Deutschösterreich," *DR*, 1 July 1926, 100–101.

46. "Loebe beim Arbeiterturnfest," *Volkszeitung*, 8 July 1926, in WB, L121260, Bd. 2, Fasz. I, Untermappe 1, 31; "Der erste Reichsordnertag," *AZ*, 11 July 1926, 7; "Eine Anschlußkundgebung der republikanischen Studentenschaft," *AZ*, 11 July 1926, 13.

47. "Für den Anschluß," *Berliner Börsen-Courier*, 12 July 1926, in WB, L121260, Bd. 2, Fasz. I, Untermappe 2, 120; numerous articles in *AZ*, 11 July 1926, 1–2, 13.

48. "Der rote Sonntag," *AZ*, 12 July 1926, 2–4; "Im roten Wien," *DR*, 15 July 1926, 103.

49. Jakub Beneš, "Socialist Popular Literature and the Czech-German Split in Austrian Social Democracy, 1890–1914," *Slavic Review* 72, no. 2 (2013): 327–351.

FIGURE 3. The Reichsbanner at the Workers' Gymnastics and Sport Festival in Vienna in July 1926. "The Reichsbanner in Vienna. Rousing welcome at the parade in front of the Austrian parliament," *Illustrierte Reichsbanner-Zeitung*, July 24, 1926. Reproduced with permission of Verlag J. H. W. Dietz Nachf.

open, people ran out of the coffeehouses and stood on chairs to catch a glimpse of the Germans, onlookers filled the sidewalks, traffic came to a standstill, and the Viennese cried out, "Cheers to Germany!" "Cheers to the Anschluss!" "Cheers to the great German republic!" Individuals from the Schutzbund had to close access to the train station because too many people were trying to gain entry to the platforms in an effort to say goodbye to the Germans. While maintaining order, the Schutzbund men also gave the Reichsbanner members their insignia as a memento. When the Reichsbanner contingent boarded the train, the spectators unleashed a hail of flowers and waved handkerchiefs.[50] Parallel scenes played out when the Reichsbanner groups from Berlin and Breslau stopped in Linz on their way back home.[51] Republican *großdeutsch* nationalism thus not only elicited an enthusiastic response from ordinary workers in Vienna, but it also was a topic that republican publications made sure to highlight in their coverage of these cross-border events.

That same month, two hundred members of the Austrian Typographia, the socialist book printers' choral group, traveled to Berlin and Nuremberg, where the Reichsbanner and various Social Democratic groups greeted them, and speakers called for the creation of a *großdeutsch* republic.[52] Just a couple of weeks later, the Schutzbund sent over one thousand members to the Reichsbanner Constitution Day celebrations in Nuremberg. While the Austrians were only a small fraction of the two hundred thousand people who attended the festivities, they once more garnered special attention. Interest in the *großdeutsch* idea was high among the local population, with giant crowds converging on the train station hours before the Austrians' arrival.[53] Speeches calling for an Anschluss by the likes of Püchler, Renner, Hans Vogel (a socialist Reichstag delegate), Höltermann, Hermann Müller-Franken (a member of the SPD who twice served as chancellor of Germany), and Heinrich Krone (a Reichstag representative from the Center Party) received a warm response, as did Körner's address at the Reichsbanner Constitution Day in Munich.[54] To create a lasting memory of this demonstration

---

50. "Der Abschied vom Reichsbanner und von den deutschen Sportlern," *AZ*, 14 July 1926, in VGA, Sacharchiv, Lade 1, Mappe 41, A, Anschluss.

51. "Eine Kundgebung für die deutschen Reichsbannerleute," *Steyr Tagblatt*, 17 July 1926, in WB, L121260, Bd. 2, Fasz. I, Untermappe 2, 8; "Reichsbanner Schwarz-Rot-Gold," *Linzer Tagblatt*, 18 July 1926, in WB, L121260, Bd. 2, Fasz. I, Untermappe 2, 11.

52. "Die Wiener 'Typographia' in Berlin," *DR* (Gaubeilage Berlin-Brandenburg), 1 August 1926, o.S; "Die Typographia in Nürnberg," *AZ*, 31 July 1926, in WB, L121260, Bd. 2, Fasz. I, Untermappe 1, 55.

53. "Der österreichische Schutzbund in Nürnberg," *AZ*, 14 August 1926, in WB, L121260, Bd. 2, Fasz. I, Untermappe 1, 74.

54. "Der Massenaufmarsch des Reichsbanners und die Massenkundgebung im Luitpoldhain," *AZ*, 16 August 1926, in WB, L121260, Bd. 2, Fasz. I, Untermappe, 1, 83; "Die Feier in Nürnberg,"

of Austro-German togetherness, republicans in Nuremberg gave the Schutzbund delegates black-red-gold emblems, cockades, Reichsbanner eagles, and flags that the Austrians waved out of the windows of the train to the many onlookers who had gathered to see them off.[55]

The Reichsbanner chapters located in Schleswig-Holstein also invited Deutsch to make a lecture tour in September of that year. Recognizing that the main challenge to the republics was no longer being mounted by legitimists but by fascists, Reichsbanner leaders in this northern region asked Deutsch to come speak about the "fight against fascism."[56] Deutsch's presence attracted one thousand Reichsbanner members to a rally in Flensburg, another thousand people to his lecture in Altona, thousands for a torchlight parade and a gathering in the Trade Union House in Kiel, and an audience of ten thousand Reichsbanner members, workers, farmers, and the unemployed at a parade and rally in Neumünster.[57] Among the Reichsbanner men participating in the events in Neumünster was a group who had traveled to the workers' sport festival in Vienna a couple of months prior and consequently knew to welcome Deutsch with the Schutzbund greeting of "Friendship!"[58] In his lectures, Deutsch argued that a crisis of capitalism, not a crisis of democracy, was the root cause of fascism. He also pointed out that fascism was an international movement and likewise needed to be countered by democrats from various lands. Yet he did not simply limit his focus to contemporary political struggles; he also took time to emphasize Austrians' and Germans' national bond. "If an Austrian comes here, he feels himself not to be a foreigner but a German, connected with the national comrades [*Volksgenossen*] of a united Germany from the Elbe to the banks of the Danube," explained Deutsch.[59]

The year 1927 marked a sharp downturn in the cross-border travels of Austrian and German republicans. This drop-off in activity was most likely due to

Sportzeitung, 18 August 1926, in ÖStA, AdR, BKA, AA, NPA, Kt. 160, Liasse Deutschland 19/12, Bl. 9; Letter from the Vertretung Reichsregierung in München to the Reichskanzlei Berlin, Munich, 10 August 1926, A. Nr. 394, in R43I/571, Bl. 48.

55. R., "Die Gewalt der Idee," *DR*, 1 September 1926 (Beilage), 131; "Die Ankunft der Nürnbergerfahrer in Wien," *AZ*, 16 August 1926, in WB, L121260, Bd. 2, Fasz. I, Untermappe, 1, 83.

56. Letter from the Reichsbanner Gau Schleswig-Holstein to Deutsch, Kiel, 16 August 1926, in VGA, Parteiarchiv vor 1934, Mappe 35.

57. "Eine Anschlußkundgebung in der nördlichsten Stadt Deutschlands," *AZ*, 21 September 1926, and "Anschlußkundgebung in Schleswig-Holstein," *AZ*, 24 September 1926, both in WB, L121260, Bd. 2, Fasz. I, Untermappe 1, 110 and 112; "Anschlußbegehr und Faschismusabwehr," *Innsbrucker Volkszeitung*, 25 September 1926, in WB, L121260, Bd. 2, Fasz. I, Untermappe 2, 67.

58. "Anschlußkundgebung in Schleswig-Holstein," *AZ*, 24 September 1926, in WB, L121260, Bd. 2, Fasz. I, Untermappe 1, 112.

59. "Anschlußbegehr und Faschismusabwehr," *Innsbrucker Volkszeitung*, 25 September 1926, in WB, L121260, Bd. 2, Fasz. I, Untermappe 2, 67.

the deteriorating situation in Austria. In July, a court had found three members of the right-wing Frontkämpfervereinigung (the Front Veterans' Association) not guilty of the murders of a Schutzbund member and a boy in the town of Schattendorf. Upset by the verdict, workers spontaneously began rioting in Vienna (against party wishes), eventually setting fire to the Ministry of Justice building. Federal police (that is, police controlled by the Christian Social government) fired on the protesters, resulting in the deaths of eighty-five workers and four policemen. As the next section will demonstrate, Hörsing's avowal of support for the Schutzbund following the July Revolt led to problems within the transborder republican coalition. Consequently, the only time that members of either group traversed the boundary that year appears to be Höltermann's attendance at two Schutzbund conferences in May and October, during which he pledged that the Reichsbanner would continue to work with the Schutzbund.[60]

It took almost a year for the transborder visits to pick up again. The Republican German Auto Club traveled to Austria in April 1928, and sixty-one Reichsbanner members from Berlin went on a ski trip to Tyrol in December 1928, demonstrating a commitment to the republican *großdeutsch* idea.[61] That summer and fall the Schutzbund sent a number of groups to the Reich. In June, members of the Austrian paramilitary organization from Vienna and Linz attended a Reichsbanner festival in Brandenburg. During a speech at the event, Johannes Stelling, a member of the SPD later murdered by the Nazis in 1933, argued that the recent success of the Weimar Coalition in the Reichstag elections should give new impetus to the fight for "the unification with our brothers from Austria, with all those who speak German."[62] The main demonstration for republican *großdeutsch* nationalism in 1928 occurred at the Reichsbanner's Constitution Day activities in Frankfurt. A couple of months before the event, the executive committee of the Reichsbanner wrote to Deutsch asking the Schutzbund to send a speaker and small delegation to the celebration "in order to characterize the avowal of friendship and brotherhood between Austria and us."[63] As had occurred at previous events, the Austrians, led by Körner and Renner, received "endless jubilation" from the thousands who gathered at the train station and in the streets. Frequently interrupted by cheers of approval, Körner gave a speech praising the Weimar Constitution

---

60. "Die Reichskonferenz des Republikanischen Schutzbundes," *AZ*, 22 May 1927, and "Fünfte Reichskonferenz des Republikanischen Schutzbundes," *AZ*, 16 October 1927, both in WB, TA, Schutzbund.

61. "Osterfahrt nach Wien," *DR*, 29 April 1928 (Beilage), 85–86; "Zweiter Tiroler Reichsbanner Skifahrt," *DR*, 26 January 1929 (Beilage für die Gaue Berlin-Brandenburg und Pommern), o.S.

62. "Schwarzrotgoldene Pfingsten," *DR*, 17 June 1928 (Gaubeilage Berlin-Brandenburg), o.S.

63. Letter from the Reichsbanner Vorstand to Deutsch, Magdeburg, 1 June 1928, in VGA, Parteiarchiv vor 1934, Mappe 35.

for leaving "open our return to the Reich."[64] Schutzbund secretary Karl Heinz was also slated to attend a Reichsbanner gathering in Hanover in October.[65] Viewing these transborder visits as an important way to make their *großdeutsch* nationalism concrete, republicans thus worked to maintain the links across the border despite the recent challenges to the transborder partnership.

The following year was the last time that Reichsbanner members beyond the leadership traveled to Austria. As part of a tour of "*Großdeutschland*," 105 individuals from the Berlin chapter of the Reichsbanner visited Prague, Iglau, Vienna, Leoben, Salzburg, Munich, Nuremberg, Bayreuth, and Leipzig in the summer of 1929. The use of the word *Großdeutschland* to describe a trip that included cities in Czechoslovakia points to the expansiveness of republican ideas about Germanness. Yet, as we have seen, although these ideas included areas aside from Germany and Austria in a German nation, most republicans' statements specifically pertaining to the borders of a future *Großdeutschland* excluded Czechoslovakia. Indeed, the report on the trip in *Das Reichsbanner* only briefly mentioned the Czechoslovakian stops on the itinerary; they did not get the detailed descriptions merited by the destinations in Austria, which were said to demonstrate "genuine joy, republican solidarity, *großdeutsch* longing!" The stop that garnered the most attention was Vienna. There, the Reichsbanner group made time to see the associational house of the Schutzbund, the city hall, the memorial in the Zentralfriedhof to the victims of the July Revolt, public works projects, the Prater, and the wine taverns in Grinzing. The "high point of our Viennese stay," according to a writer for *Das Reichsbanner*, was an Anschluss rally held at the symbolic site of the Ebert-Hof. Although there had been only a short notice printed in the *Arbeiter-Zeitung* about the event, around ten thousand Viennese showed up in addition to the Schutzbund delegation and residents of the building because they "wanted to profess a belief in the *großdeutsch* social republic together with us."[66] In their speeches, Deutsch and Heinz Löwy of the Reichsbanner signaled the bond of the two "antifascist defense organizations," as well as the "inner togetherness" of Germans and Austrians.[67]

In addition to this Anschluss rally in Vienna, seventy members of the Berlin chapter made a repeat ski trip to Tyrol in December 1929.[68] While there, the

---

64. "Empfang der Oesterreicher und des Bundesvorstandes," *DR*, 19 August 1928, 218.

65. Letter from the Reichsbanner Bundesvorstand to Karl Heinz, Magdeburg, 19 September 1928, in VGA, Parteiarchiv vor 1934, Mappe 35.

66. "Durch Großdeutschland," *DR* (Beilage Jungbanner), 6 July 1929, 216.

67. "Eine Anschlußkundgebung im Ebert-Hof," *AZ*, 23 May 1929, in WB, TA, Anschluss 1929–1931. Film of the event can be found at "Anschlusskundgebung im Ebert-Hof," 1929, StadtFilmWien: http://stadtfilm-wien.at/film/133/.

68. "Reichsbannerfahrt nach Tirol," *DR*, 11 January 1930, 16.

Schutzbund and Eisenbahner und Telegraphen Ordner (Railway and Telegraph Guards) held a well-attended Comrade Evening complete with men and women dressed in folk costumes performing traditional dances. To the approval of the audience, the speeches by a representative of each group highlighted how the republicans maintained unwavering support for an Anschluss.[69] The other two cross-border trips were confined to Reichsbanner leaders making a show of support for their allied paramilitary organization. A representative from the Reichsbanner in Schleswig-Holstein, the socialist Richard Hansen, went to an anti-Heimwehr rally in Purkersdorf in August, where both he and Deutsch called for Austro-German unity. Unlike the Austrofascist Heimwehr, which allied itself with Mussolini's Italy and Horthy's Hungary, the republicans represented the "true Volk," according to a speech by Deutsch. Their "only political aim" was consequently an Anschluss.[70] On both occasions, speakers made the repeated republican suggestion that the forces behind democracy were better Germans than those on the political right. That fall Höltermann went to the Schutzbund conference in Vienna, where he focused on the two associations' political struggles. Avoiding any direct mention of the *großdeutsch* idea, he assured those gathered of the Reichsbanner's continued support.[71]

Austrian socialists made a number of journeys to Reichsbanner events in 1929 to demonstrate the same sentiment voiced by Höltermann. In May, a delegation of Schutzbund troops went to a South Bavarian Republican Day that attracted ten thousand Reichsbanner members and onlookers. A socialist editor from Innsbruck used the occasion to emphasize "that a strong feeling of togetherness dwells particularly in the Austrian working class," and Hörsing vowed to support the Schutzbund in its fight against the Heimwehr.[72] The following month, Deutsch delivered a series of lectures in Leipzig about fascism, the close relationship between the Schutzbund and the Reichsbanner, and the desire for an Anschluss on republican grounds. One attendee praised Deutsch's speaking capabilities but expressed disappointment that no republicans beyond his fellow Reichsbanner members came to hear Deutsch.[73]

This lack of interest in an Austrian visitor was, however, an aberration. That same month, Renner attended a Wartburg festival of the Reichsbanner and other

---

69. "Reichsbanner-Kameradschaftsabend und Anschlußkundgebung," *Innsbrucker Volkszeitung*, 23 December 1929, in WB, L121260, Bd. 20.

70. "Die innere Spannung in Oesterreich," *Frankfurter Zeitung*, 19 August 1929, in WB, L121260, Bd. 21.

71. "Reichsbanner und Schutzbund," *Vorwärts*, 20 October 1929, in BAB, R72/1959.

72. "Der Reichsbannertag in München," *AZ*, 27 May 1929, 1.

73. "Kamerad Dr. Deutsch (Wien) im Gau Leipzig," *DR*, 6 July 1929 (Beilage Jungbanner), 216.

republican organizations in Eisenach, where he received a warm welcome.[74] And, as detailed at the beginning of this chapter, Berliners cheered the appearance of the fifteen hundred Schutzbund men at the tenth anniversary celebrations for the Weimar Constitution. The enthusiasm for Austro-German unity remained until the Austrians left the German capital. A rank-and-file member of the Reichsbanner observed, "I have never before in my life seen such enthusiasm as at the departure of the Austrians."[75] And unlike the reception given to Deutsch just a couple of months earlier, his appearance at the railway workers' rally during the Constitution Day festivities caused "a storm of excitement suddenly to break out."[76] Moreover, Reichsbanner groups remained eager to secure Deutsch as a speaker at their rallies, with Gau Baden, Gau Central Silesia, the chapter in Dresden, and the chapter in Gelsenkirchen asking Deutsch to come to events in the fall and winter of 1929.[77]

Cross-border travel significantly fell off after this point owing to increasing financial difficulties with the onset of the Great Depression and the growing political crises in both states. In 1930, it appears that the Reichsbanner sent no members to Austria. The Reichsbanner, however, still expressed interest in maintaining this transborder relationship by inviting Austrian socialists to the Reich. Once again Deutsch was the preferred speaker among the German republicans. Not only did the executive committee request his presence, but so too did the districts of East Saxony and Chemnitz.[78] Deutsch did not travel alone on all his trips to Germany in 1930. For its national meeting in June in Magdeburg, the Reichsbanner scheduled the main event—a gathering in a new stadium—to be an Anschluss rally. The leadership of the Reichsbanner was pleased that it had engaged Deutsch as a speaker and that he would be accompanied by one hundred other

---

74. "Wartburgfest der Republik," *DR*, 1 June 1929, 171.

75. Letter from Karl D. to the *Demokratische Post* reprinted in "Dank an die Quartiergeber," *DR* (Beilage für Berlin-Brandenburg), 5 October 1929, o.S.

76. "Die Eisenbahner im Zirkus Busch," *DR*, 17 August 1929 (Beilage), 275.

77. Letter from the Reichsbanner Bundesvorstand to Deutsch, Magdeburg, 3 August 1929, in VGA, Parteiarchiv vor 1934, Mappe 35; Letter from the Reichsbanner Gau Mittelschlesien to Deutsch, Breslau, 4 September 1929, in VGA, Parteiarchiv vor 1934, Mappe 35; "'Kein Stein bleibt auf dem anderen' wenn der Schutzbund in der Kampf zieht," *BBZ*, 7 November 1929, in BAB, R72/1959; Letter from the Reichsbanner Ortsgruppe Gelsenkirchen to Deutsch, Gelsenkirchen, 27 November 1929, in VGA, Parteiarchiv vor 1934, Mappe 35. The chapter in Dresden, as well as the local branch of the SPD, had also arranged for Deutsch to be a speaker at a rally in November. Owing to the increasing political problems in Austria, Deutsch was unable to go and sent Heinz in his place.

78. Letter from the Reichsbanner Bundesvorstand to Deutsch, Magdeburg, 20 February 1930; Letter from the Reichsbanner Gau Ostsachsen to Deutsch, Dresden, 18 December 1929; Letter from the Reichsbanner Gau Chemnitz to Deutsch, Chemnitz, 20 March 1930, all in VGA, Parteiarchiv vor 1934, Mappe 35.

Schutzbund members.[79] As had been the case in previous years, the Schutzbund caused a sensation among the republicans in the Reich. Thousands gathered to cheer on the Austrians upon their arrival, calling out "Friendship!" Wherever the Schutzbund appeared that weekend, onlookers greeted them enthusiastically. Using loudspeakers at the rally in the stadium, the Prussian interior minister Heinrich Waentig of the SPD and Deutsch proclaimed republicans' support for an Anschluss to the tens of thousands of people in the audience. Upon the conclusion of Deutsch's speech, the crowd broke out into "thunderous" applause. Various groups carrying provincial flags and symbolizing the "German Volk's tribes [*Volksstämme*]" then filled the field, with the Austrians marching in, amid great fanfare, as the last of the missing tribes. An announcer called out, "Hail to you, O messengers from Austria, you shall be connected with us for now and all time! . . . *Großdeutschland* . . . Its greatness is justice, is freedom, human dignity, work, brotherliness!" Drummers proceeded to play as a giant black-red-gold flag was raised and thousands sang the third stanza of the "Deutschlandlied." Fireworks provided an explosive end to the ceremony.[80] The rally, concluded the *Arbeiter-Zeitung*, was able "to bear witness to the vivid strength of the Anschluss idea."[81]

As the crises engulfing both countries worsened, the transborder activities tapered off. The 1930 national meeting of the Reichsbanner was the last mass event of this nature. Only Renner made the journey to a Reichsbanner celebration, styled as a Day of March Readiness in Nuremberg in February 1931. The focus of Renner's speech was the struggle against fascism, and mention of the Anschluss idea was missing.[82] Later that year, the Schutzbund did manage to send a contingent of its members from Tyrol and Carinthia to the Reichsbanner Constitution Day observance in Koblenz.[83] "In this difficult time of reckoning for the German Volk, it is for the republicans on the southern border of the German-language area a heartfelt desire to reach the brotherly hand across all boundary posts to their brothers in the Reich," explained Hans Lagger, a Schutzbund leader from Klagenfurt, once again calling attention to the *großdeutsch* idea. "We feel solidarity between ourselves and the republicans in the German Reich in the fight against the violent fascism and hateful chauvinism, which threatens

79. Letter from the Reichsbanner Bundesvostand to the Republikanischer Schutzbund Zentralleitung, Magdeburg, 2 May 1930, in VGA, Parteiarchiv vor 1934, Mappe 35.

80. "Schutzbund und Reichsbanner Schwarz-Rot-Gold," *AZ*, 11 June 1930, in WB, TA, Reichsbanner; "Das Volksfest in der 'Neuen Welt,'" *DR*, 14 June 1930, 191–192. Ellipses in original.

81. "Schutzbund und Reichsbanner Schwarz-Rot-Gold," *AZ*, 11 June 1930, in WB, TA, Reichsbanner.

82. "Tag der Marschbereitschaft," *AZ*, 23 February 1931, in WB, TA, Reichsbanner.

83. "Reichsbanner am Rhein," *DR*, 15 August 1931, 257–258.

the freedom of the German Volk, desecrates nations, and conjures new dangers of war."[84] Many Reichsbanner members also wished to use this *großdeutsch* bond in the defense of democracy by attending a sport olympiad in Vienna during the summer of 1931. Despite the numerous requests about attending, the leadership stated the organization could not afford to send an official delegation to Austria.[85] By the 1930s, financial constraints made the concretization of this bond difficult. Indeed, it was remarkable how many members of these defensive organizations had managed to make the trip before the economic downturn. After all, most of those embarking on these journeys were from the working class and, as contemporary observers pointed out, had limited means. A number of commentators noted that many more workers wished to make these trips but were unable to do so because of financial constraints.[86] The fact that so many workers undertook these border crossings illustrates that the republican *großdeutsch* idea had an emotional resonance among rank-and-file republicans.

During the last year of the Weimar Republic, there were only a few instances of leaders traversing the Austro-German border for the republican cause. The precipitous decline in these activities was due not only to the economic crisis, but also to a number of foreign policy setbacks that made the possibilities of an Anschluss seem increasingly remote. Of particular importance was the decision by the International Court in The Hague in the fall of 1931 to ban a customs union between the two countries. In May of that year, the Austrian and Reich governments revealed that they were seeking an economic union as one way to overcome the effects of the Great Depression. France and Czechoslovakia immediately sounded the alarm that a customs union was merely a pretext for creating a political union. As a result of these protests, the matter was brought before the International Court. By a one-vote majority, the Hague court found that the economic merger violated not the peace treaties, but the Geneva Protocols of 1922, an agreement that gave Austria loans from the West. The union was thus declared illegal. Republicans' conviction that an Anschluss must happen with League approval led a number of them to question whether this was still possible, given the court's ruling.[87] Thus, in 1932 only two individuals made the trip across the border on behalf of the republican movement. That spring, when the Reichsbanner directors expressed optimism that the republican movement was on an upswing,

84. "Warum fahren wir nach Koblenz?," *DR*, 8 August 1931, 250.

85. "Mitteilungen des Bundesvorstandes," *DR*, 11 April 1931, 116.

86. "Empfang der Deutsch-Oesterreicher fuer Verfassungsfeier," *Vorwärts* (Abendausgabe), 8 August 1925, o.S.

87. Abschrift eines Schreibens des Presseattachés Sektionsrates Dr. Erwin Wasserbäck to Gesandten Ludwig, Berlin, 31 October 1931, enclosed in BKA, 26322–13/pol., in ÖStA, AdR, BKA, AA, NPA, Kt. 154, Liasse Deutschland 19/1, Bl. 175–185, here 180.

Deutsch spoke to a rally of the Iron Front (a new coalition of the Reichsbanner, socialists, and free unions) in Halle and to a well-attended Reichsbanner gathering in Naumburg.[88] A leader of the Reichsbanner youth movement also went to a Schutzbund rally in Vienna in October 1932, only to be threatened with expulsion by the increasingly authoritarian Austrian government for criticizing its representatives. As the left liberal *Vossische Zeitung* noted, Austrian officials had made no move against Reich Germans from the political right. Joseph Goebbels, Hermann Goering, and Ernst Röhm were able to speak freely at a Nazi rally in Vienna only one month earlier.[89] In the context of economic and political crises, as well as foreign policy setbacks, the opponents of the republics had gained the upper hand.

While the October trip to Vienna marked the last time a Reich German traveled to Austria in the name of the cross-party coalition, it was not the final trip of a Reich republican across the Austro-German boundary. On the occasion of the November 12 celebrations in 1932, Paul Löbe traveled to the Austrian capital. However, this time he went in his capacity "as a representative of German Social Democracy," and his speech reflected this. "Only the violence of capitalist governments prevents us from being one state and one unified party," he declared. To loud applause, he concluded his speech by explaining, "No one holds the Anschluss idea in such high esteem in these dismal and difficult days as the German and Austrian Social Democrats."[90] His decision to deliver a speech from a socialist perspective was in part due to the changed political situation. The fight against fascism in Germany was no longer primarily being conducted by the Reichsbanner, but by the Iron Front, an amalgamation of mainly socialist groups of which the Reichsbanner was simply one member. This shift stemmed from the collapse of the DDP in 1930 and the rightward turn of the Center Party's leadership. Yet his choice also reflected the fact that the two socialist parties formed the basis of the cross-border republican coalition during the existence of the Weimar and First Austrian Republics.

Socialists thus did not only traverse the border to attend general republican rallies; they traveled to the other country to help their sister party in elections, to attend party conferences, and to speak at exclusively socialist events. Consequently, Otto Glöckel spoke at a socialist cultural week in Duisburg in 1925; a number of prominent Austrian Social Democrats attended campaign rallies

---

88. Letter from the Reichsbanner Bundesvorstand (Gebhardt) to Deutsch, Berlin, 24 February 1932, and Letter from Deutsch to Gebhardt, 29 February 1932, both in VGA, Parteiarchiv vor 1934, Mappe 35; "Aus den Ortsvereinen," *DR*, 16 April 1932 (Gaubeilage Berlin und Halle), o.S.

89. "Notizen zur Außenpolitik," *VZ*, 27 October 1932, in WB, L121260, Bd. 53.

90. "Die Aufmärsche in Wien," *Kleine Volks-Zeitung*, 14 November 1932, in WB, L121260, Bd. 50.

during the 1925 Reich presidential elections; Renner went to the SPD party conference in Heidelberg in 1925; Josef Püchler traveled to Bremen in 1926 to speak at a gathering of the Workers' Gymnastics and Sport Movement; soccer players from the Austrian Workers' Association for Sport and Physical Culture traveled to Germany to play a match against a team from the German Workers' Gymnastics and Sport League in 1928; Wilhelm Ellenbogen attended the 1929 SPD party conference in Magdeburg; and a representative of the Viennese Workers' Chamber delivered a speech at a conference organized by the Allgemeiner Deutscher Gewerkschaftsbund (General Federation of German Trade Unions) in Cologne in 1929. Likewise, Hermann Müller spoke at campaign rallies for the 1927 Nationalrat elections in Austria; a delegation of German workers and socialist politicians participated in a Workers' Sport Festival held in Vienna in 1927; socialist choral groups traveled to Vienna for a worker singers' festival in 1930; prominent SPD members such as Rudolf Breitscheid, Arthur Crispien, and Löbe addressed SDAP rallies before the 1930 Nationalrat elections; and Müller returned to Vienna for a commemoration of the twelfth anniversary of the declaration of the Weimar Republic in 1930.

Like Löbe's 1932 appearance in Vienna, many of the socialist cross-border visits also turned into Anschluss rallies. Alongside cheers for the International was thus applause for the *großdeutsch* idea. At the 1926 workers' sport gathering in Bremen, Püchler called for a *großdeutsch* republic and pointed out that the socialist athletes had already partly accomplished this goal, since the Austrian workers' sport organization was a member of the German Workers' Gymnastics and Sport League.[91] During the 1927 Nationalrat campaign, the SDAP made the Anschluss idea a focus of its propaganda. When Müller went to assist the SDAP in winning votes, he told his audience, "Vote red on April 24 and vote for the rallying cry of the Anschluss too!" Occurring simultaneously with this electioneering was the workers' sport competition. The Viennese workers heartily greeted the German delegation with cheers of "*Frei Heil!*"—the Reichsbanner salutation—and decorations of red and black-red-gold flags. Employing a loudspeaker system for the first time in Vienna, Julius Deutsch was able to tell the thirty-five thousand spectators gathered in the stadium at Hohe Warte, "Whoever votes for Social Democracy in the election also fights for the Anschluss."[92] Similar scenes played out at the football game between the German and Austrian workers' teams in

---

91. "Eine Anschlußkundgebung der Arbeitersportler in Bremen," *Volksstimmen*, 18 September 1926, in WB, L121260, Bd. 2, Fasz. I, Untermappe 2, 60.

92. "Der Osterfest des Arbeitersports," *AZ*, 19 April 1927, in PAAA, R73299; Report from the Deutsche Gesandtschaft Wien to the Auswärtige Amt Berlin, 20 April 1927, A. 209, in PAAA, R73299, IIOe627/27.

1928. Deutsch received a lively bravo and loud clapping when he proclaimed to the players and soccer fans, "We would rather play as Germans, as northern and southern Germans!" Arthur Crispien and Franz Künstler of the SPD, also at the match, called for an Anschluss as well.[93] The fact that socialists chose to extol the virtues of an Anschluss at purely party events underscores their commitment to the *großdeutsch* idea.

This party collaboration across borders did not, however, extend to the other members of the Weimar Coalition. For one, there was no equivalent of the DDP in Austria. Although left liberal views continued to be represented in such prominent publications as the *Neue Freie Presse* and the *Österreichische Volkswirt*, individuals harboring such beliefs no longer had a political home following the liberal movement's transformation during the imperial period. As historian Pieter Judson has shown, liberal politicians in the Habsburg monarchy attempted to maintain political relevancy in an age of mass politics by relying on radical nationalism.[94] Thus, the party that was heir to the nineteenth-century liberal tradition was the anti-Semitic and anti-Marxist GDVP. And despite both countries having Catholic political parties, a cross-border cooperation between Seipel's wing of the CSP and the left wing of the Center Party would have been difficult, given their opposing attitudes to the democratic republics.

Many contemporaries noted these differences in trying to explain why the Reichsbanner was allied with a purely socialist organization. According to the *Arbeiter-Zeitung*, it was not that the Schutzbund wanted to be a socialist group, but that it had no possible partners for a republican coalition at home. Whereas Germany had "genuine, dependable republicans in the bourgeois parties too," the same could not be said of Austria. "My God, with whom could we be united here in the defense of the republic? With the black-yellow Christian Socials? Or with the Nazi-related Greater Germans?" Given the reactionary tendencies of the CSP and the right-wing leanings of the GDVP, there was no republican party aside from the SDAP, the publication concluded.[95] Members of the Reichsbanner affirmed this situation and equated the Christian Social Party and the Greater German People's Party with two staunchly antirepublican parties in the Reich: the Catholic Bavarian People's Party and German National People's Party respectively.[96] As we will see, the fact that the Reichsbanner found an ally only

---

93. "Wir wollen als Deutsche spielen! Anschlußkundgebung beim deutsch-österreichischen Länderspiel," *Vorwärts*, 17 December 1928, in BAB, R72/914, Bl. 55.

94. Pieter Judson, *Exclusive Revolutionaries: Liberal Politics, Social Experience, and National Identity in the Austrian Empire, 1848–1914* (Ann Arbor: University of Michigan Press, 1996).

95. "Der Schutzbund," *AZ*, 28 November 1925, in WB, TA, Schutzbund.

96. W. Nowack, "Deutschösterreich," *DR*, 1 July 1926, 100–101, here 101.

in the socialist Republikanischer Schutzbund would create problems not only between the Austrian and German organizations, but also within the Reichsbanner itself.

Troubles within the Transborder Republican Community

Although the two republican organizations maintained strong ties in their efforts to prove both the vigor and the Germanness of the republics, issues arose between the groups because the Reichsbanner, while largely socialist, included members of the German Democratic Party and the Center Party, whereas only socialists composed the Schutzbund. The Schutzbund not only sought to defend the republic against monarchists and fascists, but also sought to realize the "ascendancy of the working Volk, which views the fulfillment of its highest aspiration in liberating socialism."[97] As this statement by Deutsch in *Das Reichsbanner* illustrates, the Schutzbund would not confine its socialist inclinations to events that included only the two socialist parties. Consequently, when the Schutzbund traveled to the Reich, it continued to use its socialist symbols and slogans. At the 1925 Constitution Day celebration, the Schutzbund wore red carnations alongside black-red-gold ribbons and carried a red flag.[98] To a resounding cheer of bravo, a representative of the Schutzbund explained that the Austrians had brought "the banner of Social Democracy" because the socialists were "the only dependable, true republican party" in the rump state.[99] While in Hamburg for the second anniversary of the Reichsbanner, the Schutzbund band played "The Internationale," the anthem of the socialist movement around the world.[100] Similarly, at the Reichsbanner annual festival in 1930, the Schutzbund participants wore red roses on their uniforms.[101] Aware that they were taking part in multiparty events, the Schutzbund tended to underplay, although not completely disregard, their socialist inclinations while in Germany.

The same was not true when the Schutzbund hosted events in Austria that included the Reichsbanner. Thus, when Hörsing went to the November 12 commemoration in Vienna in 1925, he saw red flags next to black-red-gold ones and

---

97. Julius Deutsch, "Oesterreichs Schutzbund," *DR*, 1 November 1924, o.S.

98. "Empfang der österreichischen Gäste," *Germania* (Abendausgabe), 8 August 1925, o.S.

99. "Empfang der Deutsch-Oesterreicher," *Vorwärts* (Abendausgabe), 8 August 1925, o.S.

100. "Die Delegation des Republikanischen Schutzbundes in Hamburg," *AZ*, 23 February 1926, in WB, TA, Schutzbund.

101. "Der große Kommen," *DR*, 14 June 1930, 190.

heard Deutsch call out, "Long live the shared fight for socialism; long live the great and unified German republic!"[102] Even more controversial was the attendance of the four thousand Reichsbanner members at the Workers' Gymnastics and Sport Festival in Vienna in 1926, when red flags abounded, cries of "Long live socialism!" and "Cheers to the International!" rang out, and the "Lied der Arbeit," "La Marseillaise," and "The Internationale" filled the air. On this occasion, the Schutzbund was not alone in elevating the socialist cause. The Reichsbanner marched with red streamers attached to their black-red-gold flags and cheered for "Red Vienna."[103] Höltermann even went so far as to say, "We defend not only the black-red-gold flag, but also the red flag of the working class."[104] As a German diplomat in the Austrian capital quipped, the attendance of the Reichsbanner at an overtly socialist celebration "has caused astonishment for many." Although he posited that the Reichsbanner did not know it was taking part "in a purely socialist party demonstration," the actions of some socialist Reichsbanner leaders like Höltermann indicated otherwise.[105] In similar fashion, the Reichsbanner members who went to the Anschluss rally in the Ebert-Hof in 1929 not only listened to the Schutzbund band play the "Lied der Arbeit," but also took it upon themselves to perform "The Internationale."[106] That same year, Höltermann once again transgressed the Reichsbanner's nonpartisan stance and offered the support of the workers in the Reich to the Schutzbund in its fight against reactionary forces.[107]

Association with a purely socialist organization also encouraged a small number of socialists in the Reichsbanner to ask that the German formation be remade in the image of the Austrian one. The desire on the part of some Reichsbanner socialists to end cooperation with the bourgeois democrats was not entirely attributable to the relationship with the Schutzbund. From the earliest days of the Reichsbanner, which grew out of workers' defense organizations, Social Democrats were reticent about working with members of other parties.[108] Additionally, despite an initial hesitancy about collaborating with bourgeois republicans in the Reich,

102. "Der Tag der Republik," *AZ*, 13 November 1925, 1–2, here 2.

103. "Aufmarsch der proletarischen Wehrorganisation," *AZ*, 11 July 1926, 1; "Wir sind die Kraft," *AZ*, 12 July 1926, 1–2; "Der rote Sonntag," *AZ*, 12 July 1926, 2–5; "Im roten Wien," *DR*, 15 July 1926, 103; "Der Abschied vom Reichsbanner und von den deutschen Sportlern, *AZ*, 14 July 1926, in VGA, Sacharchiv, Lade 1, Mappe 41, A, Anschluss.

104. "Der erste Reichsordnertag," *AZ*, 11 July 1926, 7; "Im roten Wien," *DR*, 15 July 1926, 103.

105. Report from Dönhoff to the Auswärtige Amt Berlin, Vienna, 24 July 1926, B.1428, in PAAA, R73297.

106. "Eine Anschlußkundgebung im Ebert-Hof," *AZ*, 23 May 1929, in WB, TA, Anschluss 1929–1931.

107. "Reichsbanner und Schutzbund," *Vorwärts*, 20 October 1929, in BAB, R72/1959.

108. Rohe, *Das Reichsbanner*, 17–80.

Deutsch and others within the Schutzbund categorically rejected the idea of transforming the Reichsbanner into a socialist defense league.[109] Yet this proposal on the part of German socialists continued to resurface from time to time, especially during the crisis years of the early 1930s. By this point, the DDP had collapsed, and a chancellor from the Center Party, Heinrich Brüning, was actively pursuing a policy to undermine Social Democracy and parliamentary government.[110] A cross-party coalition was therefore less attractive.

Needless to say, the expression of outright socialist sympathies created tensions within the Reichsbanner. While such displays caused some concern among the DDP and the partyless left liberals in Austria, they in particular led to problems within the Center Party and between the Center Party and the Reichsbanner. The socialist proclamations heightened the already existing divisions within the Center Party about working with the Reichsbanner. Conservative elements within the party remained resolutely opposed to any alliance with the Reichsbanner precisely because it entailed close cooperation with the SPD.[111] The Center Party members involved in the Reichsbanner—among them Friedrich Dessauer (a professor and Reichstag member), Franz Ehrhardt (a Reichstag delegate), Constantin Fehrenbach (Reich chancellor from 1920 to 1921), Anton Höfle (a Reich postmaster general), Heinrich Hirtsiefer (a Prussian minister of public welfare), Josef Joos (editor of the *Westdeutsche Arbeiterzeitung* and head of the Catholic Workers' International), Rektor Kellermann (head of the Berlin section of the party), Heinrich Köhler (a finance minister of Baden and the Reich), Heinrich Krone (chair of the Windhorstbund), Wilhelm Marx (a Reich chancellor from 1923 to 1925 and 1926 to 1928), Hermann Orth (the chief editor of *Germania*), Carl Spieker (a leader in the Christian union movement), and Joseph Wirth (Reich chancellor from 1921 to 1922)—tried

---

109. Initially a largely middle-class republican organization approached Deutsch about establishing ties with the Schutzbund. Deutsch, unsure of the viewpoints of the Deutscher Republikanischer Reichsbund, rejected such a partnership. Letter from the Reichsvorstand of the Deutscher Republikanischer Reichsbund to Julius Deutsch / Schutzbund, Frankfurt a.M., 25 March 1924; Letter from [Deutsch] to Adolf Braun, Vienna, 5 April 1924; Letter from the Parteivorstand of the Vereinigte Sozialdemokratische Partei Deutschlands (Adolf Braun) to Deutsch, Berlin, 11 April 1924, all in VGA, Parteiarchiv vor 1934, Mappe 35. For statements against transforming the Reichsbanner see "Die Reichskonferenz des Republikanischen Schutzbundes," *Der Abend*, 13 November 1925, in WB, TA, Schutzbund; "Kamerad Dr. Deutsch (Wien) im Gau Leipzig," *DR*, 6 July 1929 (Beilage Jungbanner), 216.

110. Karl Spiecker, "Zur Reichskonferenz des Reichsbanners," *Germania* (Morgenausgabe), 14 October 1925, o.S; "Kamerad Dr. Deutsch (Wien) im Gau Leipzig," *DR*, 6 July 1929 (Beilage Jungbanner), 216; "Reichsbanner und Zentrum," *Tag*, 18 April 1930, in BAB, R72/1954, Bl. 34; "Stimmen aus Kameradkreisen," *DR*, 17 May 1930, 155–156.

111. "Zentrum und Reichsbanner," *Germania*, 28 July 1927 (Abendausgabe), o.S.; Knapp, "German Center Party and the Reichsbanner"; Rohe, *Das Reichsbanner*, esp. 279–303.

to convince their fellow Catholics that a compromise must be concluded with the socialists despite divergent worldviews. As they pointed out, the Reichsbanner played an important role in defending the republic, and as a republican party, the Center should support it.[112] Moreover, they contended that the Reichsbanner would not have a permanent existence; once the threat from right-wing paramilitary groups vanished, the republican association would no longer be needed.[113] In the meantime, as Krone explained, "Everything must be done so that my Center comrades are recruited for active participation in the Reichsbanner."[114]

Their calls, however, fell on deaf ears as the links between the Reichsbanner and the Schutzbund only increased conservative Catholics' antagonism toward the republican organization.[115] Even the Catholic adherents of the Reichsbanner were perturbed by events like the 1926 Viennese Workers' Gymnastics and Sport Festival. *Germania*, the pro-republican Center newspaper, expressed its unease with the Reichsbanner's involvement in "a purely Social Democratic demonstration." An article in the publication read, "For the Reich German, nonsocialist members of the Reichsbanner, it is intolerable that the strong Reichsbanner columns march in a Social Democratic parade with uniforms and flags and thereby awaken the impression that they are a part of the Social Democratic organization. This demonstration, especially in Vienna, had a downright embarrassing effect on the Center people who belong to the Reichsbanner." The article's author resolved that everything must be done to ensure that the "Reichsbanner absolutely adheres to a party-political neutral line."[116] The fact that supporters of the Reichsbanner in the Center Party had repeatedly to remind Reichsbanner socialists of the need to maintain the organization's nonpartisan nature hurt the socialists' effort to convince hostile Center Party members of the merits of working with the republican association.

---

112. Emil van den Boom, "Zentrum und Sozialdemokratie," *Germania* (Abendausgabe), 4 June 1925, o.S.; Karl Spiecker, "Zur Reichskonferenz des Reichsbanners," *Germania* (Morgenausgabe), 14 October 1925, o.S.; "Zentrum und Reichsbanner," *DR*, 1 December 1925, o.S; "Wir und die Sozialdemokratie," *Germania* (Abendausgabe), 30 May 1927, o.S.

113. "Zentrum und Reichsbanner," *DR*, 1 December 1925, o.S.

114. "Im Herrenkrug," *DR*, 15 May 1926, 75.

115. "Zentrum, Reichsbanner und Schutzbund," *Kölnische Zeitung*, 28 July 1927, in BAB, R72/1954, Bl. 63; the Lower Silesian Center newspaper *Der Greif*, quoted in "Zentrumskritik am Reichsbanner," *BBZ*, 21 July 1929, in BAB, R72/1954, Bl. 46.

116. "Der rote Sonntag in Wien," *Germania* (Morgenausgabe), 6 August 1926, o.S. Also see "Im Herrenkrug," *DR*, 15 May 1926, 76; "Reichsbanner und Zentrum," *Deutsche Tageszeitung*, 20 September 1926, BAB, R72/1954, Bl. 69; "Die Tage in Wien," *DR*, 1 December 1926, 182; "Reichsbanner und Preußenpolitik," *Kreuz-Zeitung* (Morgenausgabe), 23 July 1927, o.S.; "Kein Bruch mit dem Reichsbanner," *Germania* (Morgenausgabe), 29 July 1927, o.S.

Further difficulties occurred because the Austrian socialists' main opponent was the Catholic party in Austria, the Christian Socials. Given the close relations between the Schutzbund and the Reichsbanner, the bitter conflict between the Austrian socialists and the Christian Socials complicated the Center Party's involvement in the Reichsbanner. The Schutzbund frequently assailed the bourgeoisie at home, particularly the CSP, for being hostile to both democracy and an Anschluss,[117] views that began to populate the pages of the Reichsbanner's journal. In an effort to avoid alienating the Center Party, republicans on both sides of the border justified these attacks by stressing that the Christian Socials and the Center Party were wholly different from each other, the common argument being that the Center Party supported democracy while the CSP did not. "The Austrian Christian Socials are, just like the Bavarian People's Party, particularistic and above all reactionary to the bone," a 1926 article in *Das Reichsbanner* insisted.[118] Some republicans acknowledged that this claim was in part overstated and pointed out that certain elements within the CSP, especially the provincial branches of the party and the Catholic workers' movement, supported the republic and opposed fascism. However, even then they still attacked the most prominent circle of the party around Seipel.[119] This condemnation of the Austrian Catholic party created problems for the Center members of the Reichsbanner, as the attacks on CSP appeared to be attacks on political Catholicism.

Tensions came to a head during the July 1927 riots in Vienna. Following this episode, the head of the Reichsbanner, the socialist Hörsing, a man prone to rash actions and statements that caused consternation even within his own party, wrote a letter to Deutsch. Composed only a few days after the riots, when the situation was still unclear, Hörsing pledged the Reichsbanner's "steadfast loyalty [to] and friendship" with the Schutzbund. While lending the "full support" of his organization for the Austrian socialists' paramilitary group, he condemned the actions of the federal government, which was controlled by the Christian Socials.[120] In his estimation, the Christian Social authorities were responsible for the escalation of violence in Vienna. At first, it appeared that Hörsing's letter would finally

---

117. "Die Reichskonferenz des Republikanischen Schutzbundes," *Der Abend*, 13 November 1925, in WB, TA, Schutzbund; "Der Schutzbund," *AZ*, 28 November 1925, in WB, TA Schutzbund; W. Nowack, "Deutschösterreich," *DR*, 1 July 1926, 100–101; "Aufmarsch der proletarischen Wehrorganisation," *AZ*, 11 July 1926, 1–2; "Der erste Reichsordnertag," *AZ*, 11 July 1926, 7; "Reichsbanner und Schutzbund," *Der Abend*, 4 November 1926, in WB, L121260, Bd. 5, Fasz. IV, Untermappe 13, 4.

118. "Reichsbanner und Schutzbund," *DR*, 1 November 1926, 161. Also see W. Nowack, "Deutschösterreich," *DR*, 1 July 1926, 100–101; "Strich durch die Rechnung," *DR*, 1 August 1926, 111; "Die Tage in Wien," *DR*, 1 December 1926, 182.

119. Karl Heinz, "Die Lage Deutsch-Oesterreichs," *DR*, 5 October 1929, 325–326; Karl Renner, "Meilensteine auf dem Marsche," *DR*, 7 June 1930 (1. Beilage), 181.

120. Reprinted in "Hörsings Eigenmächtigkeit," *Germania* (Abendausgabe), 22 July 1927, o.S.

prompt a break between the Center Party and the Reichsbanner. Chancellor Wilhelm Marx, the most prominent Center Party affiliate of the republican veterans' association, resigned his membership. For Marx, Hörsing's actions amounted to "an unjustified interference in the political relations of friendly Austria and a grave debasement and insult of the federal government."[121] And, once again, Center members of the Reichsbanner expressed their frustration with the intrusion of party politics into the organization. This time, however, they threatened that the Center Party would have to disassociate from the republican group altogether if such violations of party neutrality continued.[122] While giving such a warning to the Reichsbanner, the Center members of the association did not follow Marx's lead. *Germania*, for instance, was confident that this problem would be solved. It supported a call by the *Badische Zentrums-Korrespondenz* that urged Reichsbanner members from Center backgrounds to remain in the organization.[123]

This asymmetrical relationship between the multiparty Reichsbanner and the socialist Schutzbund undoubtedly generated problems between the two groups; however, much of the tension between them was actually due to the interference of the political right. Even before this incident, conservatives and right-wing radicals in both countries repeatedly sought to drive wedges between the Reichsbanner and the Schutzbund on the one hand and the Center Party and the Reichsbanner on the other. The political right in the Reich labeled the Schutzbund as bolshevist and Jewish in an effort to dissuade the Reichsbanner from collaborating with the Austrian socialists. In an article on the 1925 Reichsbanner anniversary in Magdeburg, for example, the *Miesbacher Anzeiger* was upset that Austrian socialists not only had come to Germany, but had also claimed that an Anschluss would occur only on republican grounds. Yet it was not the political orientation of the Austrians alone that troubled the publication. Particularly upsetting, according to the newspaper, was that the "Hungarian Jewish descendant" and "scoundrel" Julius Deutsch opened his "treasonous yap among us in the Reich."[124] The conservative *Schlesische Zeitung* also went on the attack when reporting on a soccer match that the Schutzbund had hosted for Soviet workers in 1926. At

---

121. "Reichskanzler Marx ausgetreten," *Germania* (Abendausgabe), 25 July 1927, o.S. The other consequence of this incident was that Hörsing resigned his position as president of Saxony.

122. "Reichsbanner und Preußenpolitik," *Kreuz-Zeitung* (Morgenausgabe), 23 July 1927, o.S.; "Die Reichsbanner-Krisis," *Kreuz-Zeitung* (Abendausgabe), 30 July 1927, o.S.

123. "Zentrum und Reichsbanner," *Germania* (Abendausgabe), 27 July 1927, o.S.; "Zentrum und Reichsbanner," *Germania* (Abendausgabe), 28 July 1927, o.S.; "Kein Bruch mit dem Reichsbanner," *Germania* (Morgenausgabe), 29 July 1927, o.S.

124. "Der Magdeburger Festredner der Barmattruppen," *Miesbacher Anzeiger*, 28 February 1925, reprinted in Abschrift, J.Nr.451, enclosed in Letter from the Reichsbanner Schwarz-Rot-Gold (Der Bundesvorstand) to Julius Deutsch, Magdeburg, 5 March 1925, in VGA, Parteiarchiv vor 1934, Mappe 35.

this event, Deutsch apparently proclaimed that the two groups were involved in a common "fight against the hated bourgeoisie." Such radical statements, the paper hoped, would "help the blind men in the Center and among the Democrats see."[125] Given the allegedly radical nature of the Schutzbund, the conservative, Prussian *Kreuz-Zeitung* concluded that republican *großdeutsch* nationalism and support for an Anschluss were "not simply not national, but rather antinational." Instead of a display of the "consciousness of the national community [*Volksgemeinschaft*]," the Schutzbund's participation in Reichsbanner events was a demonstration of "the shared party spirit."[126] Because of the relationship between the Reichsbanner and the Schutzbund, the Reich German organization maintained only "the mask of neutrality."[127] The political right in Germany thus hoped to weaken the organization by fraying the bonds holding the Reichsbanner together.

At the forefront of this endeavor to break up the cross-border republican coalition was the right wing of the Christian Social Party and its allies. Alarmed that Catholics in Germany were collaborating with their biggest foe at home, Seipel's circle and the Heimwehr waged a concerted campaign to destroy this republican partnership.[128] They aimed to persuade Reich Catholics to end their participation in the Reichsbanner. Moreover, they hoped that by destabilizing the Reichsbanner, they could halt the organization's support for the Schutzbund. In particular, their efforts gained momentum following the 1926 Workers' Gymnastics and Sport Festival in Vienna. They gave public speeches, wrote newspaper articles, and entered into direct correspondence with Center Party members, arguing that the "Republikanischer Schutzbund has not the slightest to do with the protection of the republican form of government and likewise with the government interests of the Republic of Austria."[129] Instead, as Heinrich Mataja, a leading Christian Social aligned with Seipel, argued in a speech given weeks after the festival, the Schutzbund was a "Social Democratic Party army" that assaulted Catholics and aspired to create a "dictatorship and class rule of the proletariat." Claiming that he did not want to interfere in the Reichsbanner's internal matters, he stated that the festival had left him no other option. "For us Austrian Christian Socials, it is

125. "Reichsbanner und Schutzbund," *Schlesische Zeitung*, 23 October 1926, in Letter from the Redaktion "Das Reichsbanner" to Deutsch, Magdeburg, 30 October 1926, in VGA, Parteiarchiv vor 1934, Mappe 35.

126. hl., "Der Vefassungstag," *Kreuz-Zeitung* (Abendausgabe), 11 August 1925, o.S.

127. "Warnende Flammenzeichen," *Kreuz-Zeitung* (Abendausgabe), 16 July 1927, o.S.

128. Letter from the Deutsches Konsulat to Herr Ministerialdirektor, Innsbruck, 14 September 1926, in PAAA, R73298, IIOe1634.

129. Quote is from a letter sent by leading CSP circles to *Germania*, which reprinted it. "Der rote Sonntag in Wien," *Germania* (Morgenausgabe), 6 August 1926, o.S. Also see "Was sagt das Reichsbanner dazu?," *Wiener Stimmen*, 19 October 1926, in WB, TA, Schutzbund.

unbearable," he continued, "that the Center takes part in an organization that has anything in common with the Republikanischer Schutzbund."[130] The right wing of the CSP continued throughout the First Republic to make such accusations against the Schutzbund, calling its members "red fascists," in an effort to cause divisions between the Austrian socialists and the Reichsbanner, as well as between the Center Party and the Reichsbanner.[131]

Wilhelm Marx's resignation from the Reichsbanner should be seen in this light. His resignation was not simply due to the simmering tensions within the Reichsbanner over the relationship with the Schutzbund. Agitation from the political right over the July riots was instrumental in his decision. In fact, the right wing of the Center Party had been against his joining the Reichsbanner from the start because it felt that cooperation with the Social Democrats would hinder efforts to reunite the Center Party and the BVP.[132] Additionally, following the formation of a conservative coalition government consisting of the Center, the BVP, the DVP, and the DNVP in January 1927, Marx's membership had become increasingly untenable. These parties, especially the BVP and DNVP, were against Marx's cooperation with the socialists in the Reichsbanner. Marx's situation was not helped by the fact that the Reichsbanner was attacking his cabinet's reactionary policies.[133]

Thus, the political right seized on the July Revolt as a way to lend urgency and legitimacy to its ongoing attacks on the partnership between the Reichsbanner and Schutzbund. According to articles in such conservative papers as the *Kreuz-Zeitung*, the Austrian socialists provoked the riots in an attempt to create a dictatorship of the proletariat. The Prussian conservatives hoped that Hörsing's support for the Schutzbund had finally demonstrated the radical socialist nature of the republican leadership and that it had "made a conflict ripe within the Reichsbanner."[134] The "repeated participation of the Reichsbanner in downright Social Democratic events in Austria, as well as countless lapses in the Reich itself," provided "sustained proof for the incompatibility of the present situation with the independent and powerful continuation of the Center's politics."[135]

---

130. Heinrich Mataja, "Die bewaffneten Parteigarden," *Neues Wiener Journal*, 11 July 1926, in WB, TA, Schutzbund.

131. "Das Ausland wird gegen Oesterreich scharf gemacht," *RP*, 11 August 1929, and "Der 'Freundschafts'-Gruß aus Berlin," *RP*, undated [August 1929], both in WB, L121260, Bd. 19.

132. "Reichskanzler Marx ausgetreten," *DR*, 1 August 1927, 113.

133. "Marx und Hörsing," *DR*, 11 August 1927, 123–124; "Kamerad Hörsing," *DR*, 7 October 1928, 275. Also see Knapp, "German Center Party and the Reichsbanner," 171.

134. "Reichsbanner und Preußenpolitik," *Kreuz-Zeitung* (Morgenausgabe), 23 July 1927, o.S.

135. "Die Reichsbanner-Krisis," *Kreuz-Zeitung* (Abendausgabe), 30 July 1927, o.S.; "Reichsbanner und republikanischer Schutzbund Oesterreichs," *Deutsche* [*Zeitung*], 20 July 1927, in BAB, R72/1959.

Republicans were unwilling to let these attacks pass without a response. Following the uproar over the Workers' Gymnastics and Sport Festival in 1926, the *Arbeiter-Zeitung* and later Deutsch in a letter to the Reichsbanner leadership responded by attacking Mataja and the Christian Social circle around Seipel as "an enemy of the Anschluss, in general an enemy of the German Reich."[136] Concurring with this assessment, the Reichsbanner's journal stated that only a "black-yellow Anschluss opponent" and friend of fascism like Mataja would be upset by such a powerful Anschluss demonstration at the festival in Vienna. The Center Party, according to this article, would be outraged that Mataja abused the Catholic religion to create "a new national rupture and the perpetuation of the national fracturing of the German Volk."[137] Similar claims surfaced again after the 1927 July riots, with Hörsing defending his initial criticism of the federal government by stating that the CSP had "monarchist and fascist tendencies."[138] Even the *Kölnische Zeitung*, a pro-republican Center newspaper, agreed that Seipel and Mataja were hostile to an Anschluss and friendly to fascists. That article did, however, take a more nuanced view of the CSP, arguing that other wings of the party in the provinces were sincere democrats.[139] Republicans thus responded to Mataja's denunciations of the Schutzbund's bolshevism with denunciations of Mataja's betrayal of the German cause. The political right likewise answered these further rebukes, and a vicious circle of recriminations continued as long as both republics existed.[140]

Beyond the usual name-calling, which failed to break up the cross-border republican alliance, conservatives and the radical right also resorted to inventing tales of impending attempts by the Reichsbanner and the Schutzbund to

---

136. "Mataja möchte das Zentrum hofmeistern," *AZ*, 29 July 1926, in WB, L121260, Bd. 5, Fasz. 4, Untermappe 13, 2; Deutsch's letter is reprinted in "Reichsbanner und Schutzbund," *DR*, 1 November 1926, 161.

137. "Strich durch die Rechnung," *DR*, 1 August 1926, 111.

138. "Hörsing zurückgetreten," *Germania* (Abendausgabe), 25 July 1927, o.S.; "Reichskonferenz in Magdeburg," *DR*, 1 August 1927, 113–114, here 114.

139. "Christlichsoziale, Republik und Anschluß," *Kölnische Zeitung*, 28 November 1926, in WB, L121260, Bd. 5, Fasz. IV, Untermappe 13, 13.

140. See the Christian Social response to Deutsch's letter in "Das Zentrum und der rote Faschismus in Oesterreich," *RP*, 7 November 1926, and "Hörsing—Dr. Deutsch' Komplice?," *Wiener Stimmen*, 10 November 1926, both in WB, TA, Schutzbund. This met with further condemnation from the socialist press in "Reichsbanner, Schutzbund und Mataja," *AZ*, 10 November 1926, in WB, TA, Schutzbund; "Reichsbanner und Schutzbund," *Der Abend*, 4 November 1926, in WB, L121260, Bd. 5, Fasz. IV, Untermappe 13, 4. The *Reichspost* and Mataja replied to these socialist articles in Dr. Mataja, "Die Auslandspropaganda der österreichischen Rotfaschisten," *RP*, 11 November 1926, and "Dr. Mataja und Oberpräsident Hörsing," *RP*, 16 November 1926, both in WB, TA, Schutzbund. Also see flurry of articles that appeared during the July riots, including: "Deutschnationaler Volksverrat," *DR*, 1 August 1927, 119; "Der 'Dolchstoß,'" *Kreuz-Zeitung* (Abendausgabe), 23 July 1927, o.S.

overthrow the Christian Social–led government in Austria. Such rumors first surfaced in 1927. Before the Nationalrat elections that year, the nationalist Berlin newspaper *Der Tag* and the right-wing *Wiener Neueste Nachrichten* wrote that the two groups possessed "red putsch plans in Austria," a claim vigorously denied by the republican organizations.[141] That fall, the Heimwehr leader Waldemar Pabst, a German exile living in Austria because of his role in the Kapp Putsch, started a more subtle version of this rumor, reporting that Joseph Wirth, the *enfant terrible* of the Center Party, was going to attempt to form an Austrian Reichsbanner that would bring together the left wing of the CSP with the SDAP. The aim of such an alliance was to topple Seipel's government. According to a German consular official in Innsbruck, no such plans existed for an Austrian Reichsbanner; the Heimwehr had started this lie in order to prevent such a partnership from forming.[142]

Rumors of another putsch attempt by the two republican organizations in 1929 gained the most traction on the political right. That summer, Hörsing had vowed at a Reichsbanner rally in Munich that "100,000 Reichsbanner fists" were ready to aid the Schutzbund in its growing struggle with the Austrofascist Heimwehr.[143] Calling attention to this statement, reactionary forces once again tried to discredit both organizations. In doing so, they hoped to drive the Schutzbund and Reichsbanner apart, as well as the Center Party out of the Reichsbanner once and for all. Moreover, Anschluss opponents within the Heimwehr hoped to lessen the appeal of a political union by highlighting the dangers of the cross-border republican connections. In particular, Heimwehr leaders like Pabst and Richard Steidle argued that the only threat to "the republic and democracy" was the Schutzbund and its ally, the Reichsbanner. Demanding that the Reichsbanner keep its "hands off Austria," they declared that if the Reichsbanner proceeded to "meddle in the inner affairs of a foreign state," the Heimwehr would just as "gladly take on" the German republicans in addition to the Schutzbund.[144] Spread by the conservative and right-wing press, their message gathered momentum.[145]

---

141. "Ein Lügenmanöver der Einheitsliste für das Ausland," *AZ*, 24 April 1927, in WB, TA, Schutzbund.

142. Copy of a letter from the Deutsches Konsulat Innsbruck to the Auswärtige Amt Berlin, Innsbruck, 10 September 1927, in PAAA, R73300, IIOe1397; "Gründung eines österreichischen Reichsbanners," *Der Tag*, 10 September 1927, in BAB, R72/1959.

143. "Das Bündnisfall des Reichsbanners," *Deutsche Zeitung*, 22 October 1929, in BAB, R72/1959.

144. "Die Heimatwehranwort an Hörsing," *RP*, 6 June 1929, in WB, TA, Schutzbund.

145. For additional examples see "Eine verdiente Abfuhr für Hörsing," *Deutsche Zeitung*, 4 June 1929, in BAB, R72/1959; "Reichsbanner und Schutzbund zum Bürgerkrieg bereit," *BBZ*, 20 August 1929, in BAB, R72/1959; A.R., "Die Heimwehr am Scheidewege," *Völkischer Beobachter*, 24 August 1929, in BAB, R72/1959; "Höltermanns Bekenntnisse," *BBZ*, 21 October 1929, in BAB, R72/1959; "Gegen fremde Einmischungsversuche, *RP*, 22 October 1929, in WB, TA, Schutzbund; "Oesterreichs Protest gegen das 'Reichsbanner,'" *BBZ*, 24 October 1929, in BAB, R72/1959; "Reichsbanner finanziert

This round of fabricated stories was given credence following additional speeches by Reichsbanner leaders pledging support for the Schutzbund, as well as a bloody conflict between the Heimwehr and the Schutzbund outside Vienna in August. The *Völkischer Beobachter*, the flagship Nazi newspaper in the Reich, even reported that Heimwehr leader Ernst Rüdiger Starhemberg had evidence that the Reichsbanner had promised the Schutzbund ten thousand automatic rifles, of which three thousand had already been delivered. Once again, republicans hotly contested these trumped-up charges, arguing that the Reichsbanner only lent the Schutzbund moral support.[146]

Although the political right's agitation did play a role in Marx's leaving the Reichsbanner, it failed in its endeavor to separate Center Party members from the Reichsbanner or the Reichsbanner from the Schutzbund. Interested in preserving unity within each organization and between them, leaders stressed once again that the reason the Reichsbanner maintained a relationship with an Austrian socialist organization was the lack of other republican parties in Austria. Such refrains appeared in speeches at Reichsbanner rallies and in the pages of *Das Reichsbanner* in an attempt to justify the association with a purely socialist group. "It is argued in Germany that it would be better if the Reichsbanner belonged only to the socialists," elaborated Deutsch in a 1929 speech to the Reichsbanner chapter in Leipzig that was later reprinted in *Das Reichsbanner*. "We in Austria would gladly be ready to work together with Democrats and Center people in the Schutzbund. Among us, the only convinced republicans are in the Social Democratic camp. All other parties are antirepublicans. That's why the republican-democratic bourgeoisie, as you call it, is not represented in the Schutzbund."[147] It was not that the

---

österreichischen Bürgerkrieg," *BBZ*, 31 October 1929, in BAB, R72/1959; "Das Reichsbanner soll in Oesterreich einmarschieren," *Extrablatt*, 10 October [sic] 1929, in WB, TA, Schutzbund; "Reichsbanner Aufmarsch für Bürgerkrieg in Oesterreich," *Berlin Lokalanzeiger*, 10 November 1929, in BAB, R72/1959; "Was Hörsing dementiert—und was er nicht dementiert!," *BBZ*, 17 November 1929, in BAB, R72/1959.

146. "10000 Gewehre des Reichsbanners," *Völkischer Beobachter*, in BAB, R72/1959; "Die Heimwehren gegen den Anschluß," *AZ*, 7 June 1929, in WB, L121260, Bd. 19. A couple of local Reichsbanner chapters did send small amounts of money to the Schutzbund of their own accord, but there was no supply of weapons or coordinated financial support.

147. "Kamerad Dr. Deutsch (Wien) im Gau Leipzig," *DR*, 6 July 1929 (Beilage Jungbanner), 216. Also see "Die Reichskonferenz des Republikanischen Schutzbundes," *Der Abend*, 13 November 1925, in WB, TA, Schutzbund; "Das einige Reichsbanner," *Germania* (Abendausgabe), 10 August 1927, o.S.; "Eine Kundgebung des Reichsbanners Schwarzrotgold," *AZ*, 24 April 1930, in WB, TA, Reichsbanner; "Für ein überparteiliches Reichsbanner," *DR*, 17 May 1930, 155. Deutsch seemed genuine about this, for in a letter to Hörsing he encouraged the SPD to enter into a coalition government with bourgeois parties following the 1928 Reichstag elections. Deutsch explained that he had learned from the Austrian scenario that "remaining in opposition is also not without its dangers" because it allowed "the state apparatus and above all portions of the army to slide into the reactionary camp." Letter from [Deutsch] to Otto Hörsing, 5 June 1928, in VGA, Parteiarchiv vor 1934, Mappe 35.

Austrian socialists hated the bourgeoisie in general; it was simply that none of the Austrian middle classes shared a love for the republic, according to the socialists. By educating Reichsbanner members about the distinctions between Austrian and German political cultures, the Social Democratic leaders of both organizations hoped to reassure the nonsocialist Reichsbanner members that there was nothing untoward about the cross-border relationship.

Such reassurances worked, and with the exception of Marx, no other prominent Center Party activists left the organization.[148] Even after Marx's resignation in 1927, the leading figures of the Center Party in the Reichsbanner met and unanimously decided that there would be "no break with the Reichsbanner."[149] As Ludwig Kaas, the priest who chaired the Center Party from 1928 until 1933, explained to a meeting of party delegates in Trier shortly thereafter, "Partisanship that harms the republican organizations and aids the antirepublican associations is out of the question for the Center, which is dutifully bound to the idea of inner peace but at the same time serves the cause of the protection and safety of the constitution."[150] And despite the numerous putsch rumors spread by the political right in 1929, the Reichsbanner members from the Center Party still "heartily took part in the welcome of the Republikanischer Schutzbund" at the 1930 Reichsbanner Bundesfest.[151] Ironically, while the DDP's relationship with the Reichsbanner was much less fraught than that of the Center Party, it was the German State Party (Deutsche Staatspartei), the more conservative successor of the collapsed German Democratic Party, that ultimately decided against working with the Reichsbanner in late 1930.[152]

Moreover, the ties between the Reichsbanner and the Schutzbund remained intact. Time and again, the leaders of the two organizations swore their loyalty to one another. "All attempts from Austria to thwart the connection between the Reichsbanner and the Schutzbund are condemned to failure," exclaimed Höltermann to a Schutzbund conference in May 1927.[153] Attending another

---

148. One Center Party man in the Reichsbanner commented that the "Center republicans" were grateful for Deutsch's comments, which reassured them that the Reichsbanner would be able to maintain its nonpartisan stance. "Trotz alledem!," *DR*, 17 May 1930, 155. Also see Rohe, *Das Reichsbanner*, 293–303.

149. "Kein Bruch mit dem Reichsbanner," *Germania* (Morgenausgabe), 29 July 1927, o.S.

150. "Zentrum und Reichsbanner," *Germania* (Morgenausgabe), 2 August 1927, o.S. Also see "Zentrum und Reichsbanner," *Volksstimme*, 27 July 1927, in BAB, R72/1954, Bl. 65; "Das einige Reichsbanner," *Germania* (Abendausgabe), 10 August 1927, o.S.

151. "Schutzbund und Reichsbanner Schwarz-Rot-Gold," *AZ*, 11 June 1930, in WB, TA, Reichsbanner.

152. "Staatspartei und Reichsbanner," *DR*, 22 November 1930, 374.

153. "Die Reichskonferenz des Republikanischen Schutzbundes," *AZ*, 22 May 1927, in WB, TA, Schutzbund.

Schutzbund conference that fall, after the July riots, he once again proclaimed that the "friendship between the Reichsbanner and the Schutzbund . . . remains unchanged."[154] And, in the midst of the 1929 rumor campaign by the political right, he told a gathering of the Schutzbund that the Reichsbanner "stands side by side with you!"[155] It was, as we saw in the previous section, a combination of factors—limited funds, political crisis, and the failure of a customs union—that ultimately weakened this cross-border coalition after 1930.

The fact that the political right felt the need to break up the relationship between German and Austrian republicans, and the fact that many republicans forged ahead with the partnership despite disagreements, attest to the importance of this transborder alliance in the battles over political and national legitimacy in interwar Central Europe. For republicans, the *großdeutsch* idea was central to their endeavor to create their own form of nationalism that could fend off attacks by the political right and popularize the postwar form of government. Both prominent figures and rank-and-file members consequently exerted a great deal of effort in creating and maintaining cross-border links. As the next two chapters demonstrate, republicans did not simply limit their interactions to like-minded individuals in the promotion of their cause; they also joined their political opponents in celebrating German cultural heroes and in lobbying for an Anschluss. In doing so, they found additional platforms to publicize and prove their national convictions.

---

154. "Fünfte Reichskonferenz des Republikanischen Schutzbundes," *AZ*, 16 October 1927, in WB, TA, Schutzbund.

155. "Reichsbanner und Schutzbund," *Vorwärts*, 20 October 1929, in BAB, R72/1959.

5

COMPOSING THE VOLK

Cultural Commemorations with Political Implications

The French minister of foreign affairs, Aristide Briand, fumed. Twice during the summer of 1928 prominent politicians in the Reich had loudly proclaimed their desire for an Anschluss. Paul Löbe gave a pro-Anschluss speech at a commemoration in Vienna for the one-hundredth anniversary of Schubert's death, while Gustav Radbruch had called for an Austro-German union in his keynote address during the Constitution Day festivities. Adding to Briand's dismay were recent remarks made by the German foreign minister, Gustav Stresemann, regarding the existence of an Austro-German cultural community. Trying to calm Briand down, Stresemann pointed out that he had not once mentioned an Anschluss during his five years in the position. Plus, he added, the peace settlement did not completely rule out the possibility of an Anschluss in the future. Stresemann went on to imply that Briand was being unreasonable on the matter, for "this cultural community is indeed self-evident." In an earlier conversation with the French prime minister, Raymond Poincaré, Stresemann had already clarified that "certain emotional attitudes in Germany and Austria would always break through at shared celebrations and events. One cannot make a distinction between German and Austrian poets and composers, and one celebrates Schiller and Goethe in Vienna just as one in Germany views Schubert and Beethoven as German composers."[1]

---

1. Untitled transcript of conversation between Briand and Stresemann, enclosed in a telegram from Stresemann, Lugano, 10 December 1928, in PAAA, R73303, IIOe2003/28. While Stresemann supported the idea of an Austro-German cultural community, an Anschluss was not a foreign policy

This chapter examines a string of historic death anniversaries for German-speaking cultural luminaries that took place in the late 1920s and early 1930s: the one-hundredth anniversaries of Ludwig van Beethoven's, Franz Schubert's, and Johann Wolfgang von Goethe's deaths, in 1927, 1928, and 1932 respectively, along with the supposed seven-hundredth anniversary, in 1930, of Walther von der Vogelweide's death. Each of these anniversaries prompted a flurry of activity on the parts of governments, political parties, cultural associations, and enthusiastic individuals. These commemorations, however, were not simply designed to celebrate these men's lives and work. As Stresemann's remarks suggest, cultural figures were central to the attempt to forge a German national community that stretched across legal state boundaries. Additionally, Germans and Austrians hoped that a focus on culture would help them to avoid and even overcome the political and social divisions plaguing both societies. Such an endeavor was not specific to the interwar period. Since the nineteenth century, music and literature served as a way to create the idea of a *Kulturnation* (a nation based on a shared culture) in a German-speaking Central Europe populated by numerous duchies, free cities, and kingdoms.[2] Music, in particular, was believed to have "community-building powers" that could "hea[l] the wounds of a fractured society and promot[e] feelings of camaraderie."[3] For many organizers and participants alike, these festivities served as opportunities to address and overcome the sociopolitical hardships of the interwar period.

Nevertheless, the focus on culture did not allow for the avoidance of politics. As the histories of reception demonstrate, cultural products and their creators were often interpreted and used in ways that promoted specific political and social agendas.[4] Political disagreements therefore emerged about the meaning

---

priority for him. Moreover, he was frequently exasperated by Löbe's travels to Austria and demands for an Anschluss, since it led to protests from France and others, which could hinder his own attempts to revise the Treaty of Versailles. Suval, *Anschluss Question*, 92–95.

2. Helmut Loos, "Franz Schubert im Repertoire der deutschen Männergesangvereine. Ein Beitrag zur Rezeptionsgeschichte," *Archiv für Musikwissenschaft* 57, no. 2 (2000): 113–129; Friedhelm Brusniak, "Der Deutsche Sängerbund und das 'deutsche Lied,'" in *Nationale Musik im 20. Jahrhundert: Kompositorische und soziokulturelle Aspekte der Musikgeschichte zwischen Ost- und Westeuropa*, ed. Helmut Loos and Stefan Keym (Leipzig: Gudrun Schröder Verlag, 2004), 409–21; Celia Applegate and Pamela Potter, "Germans as the 'People of Music': Genealogy of an Identity," in *Music and German National Identity*, ed. Applegate and Potter (Chicago: University of Chicago Press, 2002), 1–35; Rainer Noltenius, "Schiller als Führer und Heiland: Das Schillerfest 1859 als nationaler Traum von der Geburt des zweiten deutschen Kaiserreichs," in *Öffentliche Festkultur: Politische Feste in Deutschland von der Aufklärung bis zum Ersten Weltkrieg*, ed. Dieter Düding, Peter Friedemann, and Paul Münch (Hamburg: Rowohlt Taschenbuch Verlag, 1988), 237–256.

3. Applegate and Potter, "Germans as the 'People of Music,'" 21.

4. David Dennis, *Beethoven in German Politics, 1870–1989* (New Haven, CT: Yale University Press, 1996); Steinberg, *Austria as Theater and Ideology*; Loos, "Franz Schubert"; Brusniak, "Der Deutsche

of these men and the commemorations for them. Each political group hoped to lay claim to these national heroes in order to legitimize its partisan views. In demonstrating the competing efforts to monopolize the meaning of a German cultural legacy, this chapter once again highlights that transborder nationalism did not simply stem from the political right.

Theaters for *Großdeutschtum*

During the commemorations for the medieval minnesinger Walther von der Vogelweide, famed composers Beethoven and Schubert, and the literary giant Goethe, Reich Germans and Austrians alike made it clear that they were not simply paying tribute to the so-called genius of these men. Discussing the Beethoven, Schubert, and Walther festivities, Reichskunstwart Edwin Redslob explained that such events highlighted "the intellectual togetherness of all Germans, but in particular point[ed] to the commonality between Germany and Austria."[5] Reich Germans and Austrians thus used these occasions to discuss and fashion a transborder community despite the prohibition on a political union between the two countries. And unlike the political commemorations explored in the previous chapters, the focus on culture during these anniversary celebrations brought together not only Germans and Austrians, but also people from across the political spectrum. Given the diversity of participants, these cultural commemorations provide a window into the heterogeneous ways that Reich Germans and Austrians understood a national community that extended beyond the boundaries of the state, and hence a purely civic conception of nationhood.

In seeking to elucidate the bonds between Reich Germans and Austrians at these ceremonies, participants advanced a number of different arguments. Unsurprisingly, speakers at the various events made reference to the increasingly popular biological—ethnic and racial—ideas to explain the existence of a transborder nation. Invoking an ethnocultural definition of an Austro–Reich German community, Ludwig Landmann, the mayor of Frankfurt am Main and a member of the German Democratic Party, explained that "the bond of blood, history, and culture" had brought about a "harmony of feelings" between Reich Germans and Austrians at the Tenth German Singers' League Festival (Deutsches

Sängerbund"; Noltenius, "Schiller als Führer und Heiland"; Applegate and Potter, *Music and German National Identity*.

5. Edwin Redslob quoted in draft, Käthe Miethe, "Tradition und Zukunftswille. Ein Gespräch mit Reichskunstwart Dr. Redslob," 1930, in BAB, R32/258, here Bl. 93.

Sängerbundesfest), which was held in honor of Schubert in the summer of 1928.[6] It is interesting to note, however, that the language of blood did not surface frequently at the public commemorations. And when it did, the concept did not necessarily entail exclusionary ways of thinking, as we saw in chapter 1. After all, Landmann was born into the Jewish community. It was only during the Reich's official 1932 Goethe celebration in Weimar that public ceremonies became filled with exclusionary rhetoric. By this point, the Nazis occupied key positions in the provincial government of Thuringia and used the occasion to give voice to their racist conception of a German nation.[7] Instead of *völkisch* definitions of nationhood, the speakers at the different celebrations focused on the existence of a shared language and culture as important factors that bound Reich Germans and Austrians together. "One language, one mind, one heart unites us into a lasting community of fate [*Schicksalsgemeinschaft*]," the president of the Würzburg Provincial Finance Ministry proclaimed at a Walther von der Vogelweide celebration in the town during the spring of 1930.[8]

In addition to such refrains, participants at the Beethoven and Walther commemorations promoted the idea of a cross-border German community by pointing to the fact that the two men had resided in places now found in both the Reich and the Austrian Republic. Because Beethoven had lived in both Bonn and Vienna, it did not take much finessing for the mayor of Bonn to pronounce that the Beethoven festivities there had "strengthened the cultural bond between the two brother peoples [*Brudervölkern*]." After all, the mayor emphasized, Beethoven was "the greatest musical hero, who belongs equally to Germany and Austria."[9] Similarly, Walther was reported to have lived in numerous areas that, according to the map of Central Europe after the First World War, included Austria, Germany, Czechoslovakia, and Italy. Hence, in a radio address to educate listeners about the importance of Walther, Redslob explained: "But also as a wanderer between the Danube and the Main, he has seen one thing for all times: the togetherness of Germany and Austria. We do not know with certainty whether his cradle stood somewhere between Bozen (Bolzano, Italy) and Meran

---

6. "Die Feststadt Wien und der Anschlußgedanke. Aeußerungen der Oberbürgermeister von Nürnberg und Frankfurt," *NFP*, 23 July 1928, 6, in ÖStA, AdR, PrK 5149/1928.

7. For instance see Albrecht v. Heinemann, "Der Abschluß der Weimarer Tage," *Deutsche Zeitung* (Abendausgabe), Berlin, 30 March 1932, in BAB, R32/284, Bl. 87; "Wie die Juden das Goethe-Jahr einleiten!," *Der Nationalsozialist*, 16 January 1932, in BAB, R32/284, Bl. 107.

8. Prugger, "Willkommen in Würzburg!," *OeD*, May 1930, in BAB, R32/545, here Rs. of Bl. 113.

9. Letter from the mayor of Bonn (Johannes Falk) to the Austrian president (Michael Hainisch), Bonn, 9 June 1927, ÖStA, AdR, PrK 4204/1927. Also see speeches by Austrian president Hainisch and the Austrian ambassador to Germany, Felix Frank, reprinted in *Deutsches Beethovenfest zu Bonn 1927 anläßlich des 100. Todestages Ludwigs van Beethoven* (Sonderabdruck aus dem Städtischen Verwaltungsbericht, 1927).

(Merano, Italy) or in Franconia; but we do know one thing: his being, his heart belong as much to Tyrol as to Franconia, belong as much to Germany as to Austria, belong to the single German fatherland."[10] Whereas today's claims by Germans and Austrians to such figures lead to disagreements between citizens of these two countries, *großdeutsch* enthusiasts before 1945 highlighted the multiple homes of historical persons to further support their claims for the strong and historical links between Reich Germans and Austrians.[11]

Even in the ceremonies for Schubert, who had resided only in the area around Vienna, and for Goethe, who had lived only in places within the current borders of Germany, participants emphasized a common German culture. For many contemporaries it was self-evident that commemorations for Schubert and Goethe were just as suitable as those for Beethoven and Walther in celebrating the idea of a national community spanning the border between Austria and Germany. "Everything that the German spirit [*Geist*] created is the shared cultural treasure of all Germans regardless of citizenship," Felix Frank, the Austrian ambassador to Germany and a member of the GDVP, explained.[12] Although he made this statement on the occasion of the Bonn Beethoven festival, it nicely sums up a particular view of the relationship between cultural achievements and the idea of a transborder German nation.

Such an interpretation of these figures was not new. Dating back to the late eighteenth century, the rise of a literary culture among members of the middle classes helped to spawn a German national consciousness in the absence of a single German political or territorial entity. This development of a national consciousness among educated elites was due not only to the work of intellectuals in uncovering an alleged essence of the German Volk, but also to the expanding print culture that enabled educated German speakers throughout Central Europe to engage in an exchange of ideas.[13] Throughout the nineteenth century, writers such as Goethe and Schiller became well-known and symbolic figures among the German-vernacular writing and reading publics. The Schiller celebrations held in November 1859 exemplified both how widespread territorially a

---

10. "Rundfunkvortrag," in BAB, R32/545, Bl. 5.

11. For example, the Austrian press decried the inclusion of Mozart, Bach, Haydn, and Freud in a German television station's program in 2003 on the one hundred greatest Germans. See Norbert Mayer, "Größte Deutschen aller Zeiten," *Die Presse*, http://diepresse.com/home/meinung/feuilleton/210618/index.do; "Österreich und Deutschland streiten um Mozart," *Netzeitung*, http://www.netzeitung.de/entertainment/people/250180.html; "Österreicher empört über ZDF," *Spiegel Online*, http://www.spiegel.de/kultur/gesellschaft/0,1518,260307,00.html.

12. *Deutsches Beethovenfest zu Bonn 1927*, 13–14, here 13.

13. Sheehan, *German History*, esp. 3–7, 160–174, 371–388; David Luft, "Das Intellektuelle Leben Österreichs in seiner Beziehung zur deutschen Sprache und der Modernen Kultur," *Center for Austrian Studies Working Papers in Austrian History* 07–1 (February 2007).

German literary culture had become and how far a German cultural canon had developed by the middle of the nineteenth century. Within German-speaking areas of Central Europe, celebrations were held in over four hundred cities.[14] The three-day Schiller commemoration also demonstrated the importance of cultural festivals in providing a forum for numerous sectors of society to participate in discussions about nationhood and politics. Celebrants saw Schiller as a symbolic figure for a variety of different causes, ranging from liberal demands for more political freedom to calls for German national unity based on either the *kleindeutsch* or *großdeutsch* ideas.[15]

Given the destruction of the Bismarckian *kleindeutsch* solution and the subsequent possibility of redrawing Germany's borders, commentators on the Beethoven, Schubert, Walther, and Goethe celebrations during the Weimar era overwhelmingly viewed these figures, and even the 1859 Schiller festival, through a *großdeutsch* lens. In doing so, they sought to connect their current celebrations and demands for an Anschluss with a longer tradition of a German *Kulturnation*. On the occasion of the Walther celebrations in 1930, Redslob thus remarked that "the earlier celebrations honoring the intellectual leaders of our Volk, particularly up to the Schiller festival in 1859, as well as those since the recent festivities for Beethoven and Schubert, are influenced time and again by the *großdeutsch* idea."[16] And Wilhelm Miklas, a member of the Christian Social Party and the president of Austria from 1928 until 1938, used the 1932 Goethe commemoration in Vienna to call attention to the fact that Vienna had "the oldest German Goethe community," which was founded in 1878.[17] Celebrants could thus point to a shared language and literary canon in their efforts to transcend the legal boundary between the two states.

Alongside literary culture, music played an important role in the formation and definition of a German national consciousness. In fact, historian Celia Applegate contends that music was "quite possibly of more importance than German literature" in "the spread of German national feeling in the nineteenth century."[18]

---

14. Noltenius, "Schiller als Führer und Heiland," 239.

15. Noltenius, "Schiller als Führer und Heiland"; Sheehan, *German History*, 868; Bruce Duncan, "Remembering Schiller: The Centenary of 1859," *Seminar: A Journal of Germanic Studies* 35, no. 1 (1999): 1–22. Pieter Judson argues that liberal political aims trumped nationalism in these festivals. Judson, *Exclusive Revolutionaries*, 85.

16. "Notiz für [illegible] des Rundfunks. durchgesagt 19.5.1930," in BAB, R32/545, Bl. 2. Also see the text of "Wir feiern Walther von der Vogelweide," where he also draws connections to the 1828 Dürer celebrations in Nuremberg and the Goethe festivities of 1850 (in BAB, R32/545, Bl. 6–19, here Bl. 7–10).

17. Hand-corrected version of "Aussprache des Herrn Bundespräsidenten anl. Goethefeier am 22. März 1932 (Musikvereinsgebäude)," in ÖStA, AdR, PrK, 2754/1932.

18. Celia Applegate, "What Is German Music? Reflections on the Role of Art in the Creation of the Nation," *German Studies Review* 15 (Winter 1992): 25.

During this period, music scholars, critics, and singers' associations increasingly interpreted both classical music and folk songs from a nationalist point of view. They developed the idea of "German music" and "the German song," the notion that music produced by German speakers originated from a specific German national character and therefore amounted to an expression of the German soul.[19] Such ideas continued to inform the views of festivalgoers during the Weimar era. As the Reich president, Paul von Hindenburg, an honorary patron for the Tenth German Singers' League Festival in Vienna, wrote for the first issue of the event's commemorative newsletter, "The German song [Lied] is the most beautiful and deepest expression of the German mind and the German essence."[20]

Moreover, music and the Lied were seen as possessing a transcendental quality that could unite German speakers across Central Europe. Once again, contemporaries in the interwar period relied on a tradition dating to the nineteenth century, when German speakers assembled a German musical canon that extended beyond the many political boundaries in Central Europe, even those established in 1866 and 1871 that excluded Austria from Germany. Hence, in the 1920s, citizens of Germany and Austria easily drew on an already established German musical canon that could disregard the political boundaries set by the Treaties of Versailles and Saint-Germain. Continuing a nineteenth-century practice, German speakers on both sides of the Austro-German border referred to the Viennese-born-and-bred Schubert as the "creator of the German song,"[21] the "grandmaster of the German song,"[22] "the singer of the Heimat, of the Germans,"[23] and "the song prince of the German Volk."[24] As an Austrian, Schubert had become the crucial figure during the nineteenth century who enabled national activists to construct

---

19. Dietmar Klenke, Der singende "Deutsche Mann": Gesangvereine und deutsches Nationalbewusstsein von Napoleon bis Hitler (Münster: Waxmann Verlag, 1998); Brusniak, "Der Deutsche Sängerbund."

20. PrK 3379/1927, Amtsveranlassung, Zehntes Deutsches Sängerbundesfest in Wien 1928; Beitrag des H.B.(Herrn Bundes)Präsidenten für die erste Nummer der Festzeitung, in ÖStA, AdR, PrK 5149/1928.

21. "Im Zeichen Schuberts," Das Neue Badener Blatt, 3 November 1928, 1, in WB, C 276954, Bd. 1. Also see the reference to "Schöpfer unseres deutsche Liedes" in Dr. Franz Strauß, "Zu der Errichtung der Linzer Schubert-Gedenktafel," Oberösterreichische Tageszeitung (Linz), 15 November 1928, in WB, C 276954, Bd. 1.

22. Rich. Oehmichen, "Franz Schubert als Liederkomponist," Signale für die musikalische Welt (Berlin), 14 November 1928, in WB, C 276954, Bd. 1.

23. Dr. Hertha Vogl, "Franz Schubert zum hundersten Todestag," Werkszeitung der Oesterreichisch-Alpinen Montangesellschaft, 16 November 1928, 467, in WB, C 276954, Bd. 1. This article also makes a reference to Schubert as "Schöpfer des deutschen Liedes" (467).

24. Ivo v. Werdandl, "Armer Franz Schubert: Ein zeitgemäßes Märchen mit Abklang von Wirklichkeit," Deutschösterreichische Tages-Zeitung (DöTZ), 18 November 1928, 14, in WB, C 276954, Bd. 3.

a German musical canon that reflected a *großdeutsch* vision of the nation.[25] This special position occupied by Schubert helps to explain the fervor of the celebrations for him—both the singers' festival and the November commemorations on the anniversary of his death. In an era when many citizens of the Reich and Austria desired a revision of the Treaties of Versailles and Saint-Germain, Schubert served as a rallying figure.

This persistent talk of unity, however, was due to the fragmentation of cultural, religious, political, economic, and social life in German-speaking Central Europe.[26] During the interwar period, individuals seeking to create a Greater Germany had to contend with a host of historical divisions that persisted after the First World War. Regional differences—which stemmed from the existence of numerous (sometimes opposed) political entities and divisions between the Catholic south and Protestant north—created particular difficulties for the formation of a Germany that included Austria. On pragmatic and symbolic levels, the staging of the cultural commemorations provided a forum to demonstrate that the division between northern and southern German speakers could be overcome. The practical side of the staging involved bringing together participants from both sides of the Austro–Reich German border, and beyond. In particular, the Schubert celebration of the Tenth German Singers' League Festival in the summer of 1928 brought over one hundred thousand German speakers from around the world to Vienna. This gathering of German speakers from various regions at the official festival events, as well as in pubs and landmarks around Vienna, encouraged them to interact and learn about one another. In response to a question posed by a *Reichspost* reporter, "How are you doing in Vienna?" one singer from Wannweil, Germany, commented with tears in his eyes: "How should we be doing? This geniality, this love of the Viennese for us, allows us to overlook any inconveniences. However, everything is just so, that it could not be better. Until now, we have not known the Austrians; we had no idea that such a Volk lives here. We could not have greeted ourselves more sincerely. We really feel ourselves as brothers among brothers."[27] As this singer's emotional response demonstrates, contact between Reich Germans and Austrians served an educational purpose; it revealed that they were part of the same Volk by fostering a feeling of familial togetherness.

Both the coordination of events and spontaneous exchanges between citizens of Germany and Austria prompted observers to declare that the historical antagonism between northern and southern German speakers had been overstated.

---

25. Loos, "Franz Schubert," 122.
26. James Sheehan, "What Is German History?"; Sheehan, *German History*.
27. Hans Pittioni, "'Wie geht es Ihnen in Wien? Eine Rundfrage an Sängergäste," *RP*, 21 July 1928, 1.

FIGURE 4. "The parade before the parliament. The university and Burgtheater in the background," *Offizielles Erinnerungsalbum an das 10. Deutsche Sänger-bundesfest* (Vienna: R. Lechner, o.D.), 29. Courtesy of the Wienbibliothek im Rathaus.

Reporting on the crowning event of the Singers' League Festival, a nine-hour parade with over two hundred thousand marchers and seven hundred thousand spectators, the *Neues Wiener Tagblatt* rhetorically asked, "Are Vienna and Berlin really antagonistic cities as one generally assumes?" The paper's answer was no because "almost no German city received greater jubilation than Berlin."[28] Also commenting on this enthusiastic reception of the Berlin singers by the (mainly Viennese) spectators, the Austrian *Neue Freie Presse* provided a more flowery explanation of this occurrence: "As though the crowd had instinctively felt it, we must provide evidence that all the legends about any antithesis between the characters of these two cities are libel. We must demonstrate that the capital of the German Reich is equally as dear and precious to us as the other great centers of the German character."[29] It should not be entirely surprising that this festival provided fertile ground to show what another Viennese paper called the "avowal of brotherhood [*Verbrüderung*] between the German north and the

28. "Der Festzug der deutschen Sänger: Der Beginn des Zuges: Die Sänger aus dem Reiche," *NWT*, 23 July 1928, 3, in ÖStA, AdR, PrK 5149/1928.

29. "Der Ehrentag für Wien," *NFP*, 23 July 1928, in ÖStA, AdR, PrK 5149/1928.

German south."[30] After all, the founding principle of the German Singers' League (Deutscher Sängerbund) from 1862 stated that it would use the German *Lied* to unite the German *Stämme* (tribes).[31]

According to the press coverage of the 1928 festival, this goal of unity appeared to be realized, as there were numerous reports of "scenes of fraternization [*Verbrüderungsszenen*]" happening over the course of the four-day event.[32] Even the most minor and seemingly unimportant occurrences were viewed as evidence of a coming together of Austrians and Reich Germans. For instance, the *Neues Wiener Tagblatt* included an anecdote about a singer from Ulm, Germany, who asked a Viennese girl watching the parade to retie his shoes. Upon her doing so, the singer leaned down and kissed the blushing girl on the lips. This impromptu action on the part of the singer became for the newspaper "the most beautiful kiss representing the avowal of brotherhood [*Verbrüderungskuß*] during the entire Tenth German Singers' League Festival."[33] Moreover, between organized events, this reconciliation continued in cafés and pubs. As the Austrian socialist *Arbeiter-Zeitung* remarked, "The tables unite the tribal groups [*Stammesgruppen*]."[34] Celebrants regarded the commemorative activities that brought large numbers of Reich German and Austrian citizens together as opportunities to dispel stereotypes that German speakers had about the other country.

Although perceptions about one another shifted at these commemorations, there still existed the difficulty of communication experienced by German speakers from different regions. Some newspaper accounts of the July festival poked fun at the various dialects and the fact that not all German speakers could actually understand one another.[35] As the saying (which can be found today on postcards in Austria) goes: A common language differentiates the Germans from the Austrians. Other articles emphasized that even this obstacle could be overcome. The *Neue Freie Presse* reported that the native population was quickly able to teach Reich Germans the Viennese dialect, so much so that the visitors from Hanover or Danzig could eventually understand the ways that people in the districts

---

30. "Der Riesenaufmarsch der deutschen Sänger," *Wiener Sonn- und Montagszeitung*, 23 July 1928, 1.

31. Friedrich List (Vorsitzender des Deutschen Sängerbundes), "Dem Feste zum Geleit," *Festblätter für das 10. Deutsche Sängerbundesfest Wien 1928*, Folge 1, June 1927, 5; Brusniak, "Der Deutsche Sängerbund," 415.

32. "Rund um die Sängerhalle: Bilder vom Sängerfest," *AZ*, 21 July 1928, 5; "10. Deutsches Sängerbundesfest Wien 1928," *WNN*, 20 July 1928, 4.

33. "Aus dem Publikum," *NWT*, 23 July 1928, 4, in ÖStA, AdR, PrK 5149/1928.

34. "Das Sängerfest: Zweihunderttausend und zwei Millionen," *AZ*, 22 July 1928, 6.

35. "Was ein deutscher Sänger in Wien erleben kann," *Das Kleine Blatt*, 22 July 1928, 1; "Das Sängerfest," *AZ*, 20 July 1928, 7.

of Hernals and Ottakring spoke. With the Viennese also quickly picking up other German dialects, the paper concluded that "one soon gratifyingly realizes that we already understand each other very well."[36]

While most of the events scheduled for the Beethoven, Schubert, Walther, and Goethe commemorations did not involve such large numbers of Germans and Austrians interacting, the organizers of these celebrations found other ways to demonstrate Austro-German unity. One strategy pursued by planners was the involvement of both Austrian and Reich German high-profile figures. The Bonn Beethoven celebrations and the Tenth German Singers' League Festival were both held under the patronage of the Reich's President Hindenburg and Austria's President Hainisch.[37] Moreover, politicians, ambassadors, and academics from the Reich attended ceremonies in Austria, and vice versa. One of the most notable examples occurred during the November celebrations for Schubert when the municipal government of Vienna invited mayors from the Reich's major cities—Berlin, Hamburg, Munich, Dresden, Leipzig, Frankfurt am Main, Nuremberg, Stuttgart, Chemnitz, Magdeburg, Königsberg, Mannheim, and Essen—to attend commemorative events and learn about the city's public housing and works projects. This trip, according to organizers, participants, and the press, "should document in new, especially striking ways the intellectual and cultural togetherness of Germany and Austria."[38] To loud applause, the Viennese mayor, Karl Seitz of the SDAP, thus concluded his speech at the welcoming ceremony: "As Viennese, we wholeheartedly thank you for coming. We Viennese generally like to see foreigners and they are always welcome. But when Germans from the Reich come to us, then—excuse me if I become almost sentimental—our hearts burst and we are doubly happy. Wherever you stroll through the city, you will

---

36. "Heitere Episoden vom Festzug," *NFP*, 23 July 1928, 5, in ÖStA, AdR, PrK 5149/1928.

37. On the Bonn Beethoven festival see PrK 1792/1927, Uebernahme des Ehrenprotektorates über die Deutsche Beethovenfeier durch den H.B.Präsidenten gemeinsam mit Reichspräsidenten Hindenburg, ÖStA, AdR, PrK 1792/1927. For the Sängerbundesfest see Letter from the Hauptausschuss des 10. Deutschen Sängerbundesfestes Wien 1928 to the Bundesministerium für Unterricht, Ansuchen um eine Subvention für die Durchführung des 10. Deutschen Sängerbundesfest Wien 1928, Vienna, May 1927, in ÖStA, AVA, U.Allg. 3258, 16058/1927. Also consult the following sets of documents, all enclosed in ÖStA, AdR, PrK 5149/1928: PrK 7107/1926, Einbringer: BKA, Gegenstand: Zehntes Deutsches Sängerbundesfest in Wien 1928; Ehrenschutz durch den H.B.Präs.; PrK 6007/1926, Einbringer: BKA, Gegenstand: Uebernahme des Ehrenschutzes durch den H.B.Präs. über das 10. deutsche Sängerbundesfest in Wien im Jahre 1928; PrK 5567/1926, Einbringer: Ostmärkischer Sängerbund, Gegenstand: Ansuchen um Uebernahme des Ehrenschutzes über das 10. Deutsche Sängerbundesfest in Wien im Jahre 1928. Also see the first issue of *Festblätter für das 10. Deutsche Sängerbundesfest Wien 1928*, June 1927, 2–4; and Loos, "Franz Schubert," 119–120.

38. "Wien feiert Schubert," *Hamburger Nachrichten*, 10 November 1928, in WB, C 276954, Bd. 1.

always be heartily welcomed. You will see the joy on account of this manifestation of our unity, our tribal brotherhood [*Stammesbrüderschaft*], our love of art,
our reverence for the great common treasure of German culture."[39] The German
mayors responded in kind. "I bring the greetings of millions of Germans, who
in this minute feel one with their brothers in Austria," Gustav Böß, the mayor
of Berlin and a member of the DDP, proclaimed at a ceremony by the Schubert
monument in the Stadtpark.[40]

Likewise, the Walther ceremonies held in Würzburg left little doubt that the
purpose of the commemoration was to demonstrate the strength of an Austro–
Reich German community. Officials from Germany and Austria attended the
city's celebrations.[41] Reich German and Austrian children gathered as well for
a youth weekend held in honor of Walther on Pentecost.[42] Additionally, the
Österreichisch-Deutscher Volksbund decided to hold its annual meeting in
Würzburg to coincide with the city's celebration, because, as Redslob put it,
"Walther von der Vogelweide belongs jointly to Germany and Austria; he heralds
the idea of togetherness through his figure and his work."[43]

Even in times when the staging of a transborder German community did
not seem prudent, the idea of Austro–Reich German unity continued to be performed, but in a more subtle fashion. After the German Foreign Office sent
out feelers to the Austrian government to see if it would be interested in having representation on the honorary committee for the 1932 Goethe celebrations in Weimar, Austrian officials decided against participation because of
their need to negotiate new loans from the West and the fact that Austria would
hold its own celebrations.[44] Moreover, the Austrian president, Wilhelm Miklas,
ruled out attending the Reich's official Goethe ceremonies for fear of reper-
cussions in the realms of domestic and international politics. For the German
ambassador to Austria, these setbacks would not completely rule out depicting a *großdeutsch* community. Although disappointed by Miklas's decision, the
ambassador remarked, "One has endeavored to grant Austria a particularly

39. Quoted in "Schubert-Zentenarfeier der Stadt Wien," *NFP*, 16 November 1928, in WB,
C 276954, Bd. 1.

40. Quoted in "Der Schubert-Tag in Wien," *Deutsche Allgemeine Zeitung*, 18 November 1928, in
WB, C 276954, Bd. 3.

41. "Wir feiern Walther von der Vogelweide," in BAB, R32/545, Bl. 12; Program for the Öffentliche Feier auf dem Residenzplatz zu Würzburg, in BAB, R32/545, Rs. of Bl. 63.

42. Letter from the mayor of Würzburg Dr. Löffler to Reichskunstwart Redslob, Würzburg,
9 October 1929, in BAB, R32/545, Bl. 219; Stadtrat Würzburg, Merkblatt Nr. 1, betreffend Deutsch-
Österreichisches Jugendtreffen an Pfingsten 1930, 21 March 1930, in BAB, R32/545, Bl. 211–215.

43. "Wir feiern Walther von der Vogelweide," in BAB, R32/545, Bl. 13.

44. See correspondence in ÖStA, AdR, BKA, AA, NPA, Kt. 164, Liasse Deutschland 33/13,
Goethe-Feier.

preferential position at this celebration."[45] Rather than being included later in the program with the "foreign academics," Professor Hans Eibl from Vienna gave his address alongside Walter von Molo from Berlin and Erwin Kolbenheyer from Munich during an event titled "Hour of the German National Community [*Volksgemeinschaft*]." Furthermore, the Viennese Burgtheater was the only theater company outside the Reich to give a performance as part of the Weimar festivities.[46] And the Austrian government sent its education minister as an official representative, despite worries about the economic means to do so.[47] Thus, whether it was a trip made by mayors from the Reich to Austria or the official representation of Austria at the Weimar Goethe ceremonies, the presence of leading personalities from the other country served as a way to surmount the imposed Austro-German border.

There were other concerted and well-planned efforts to transcend the legal boundary as well. To honor Schubert and literally place him in the company of other great German speakers, the Bavarian government installed a bust of Schubert in Walhalla, a shrine built by King Ludwig I in the mid-nineteenth century to memorialize great "Germans." The official representative of the Austrian government at the ceremony, Justice Minister Franz Slama of the GDVP, proclaimed "that for us it is a gratifying and uplifting certainty that across the border, which exists only on the map but not in our consciousness, a friend and brother lives."[48] Making the idea of "two states, one Volk" even more tangible, Germany and Austria issued commemorative marks and schillings with the same illustration of Walther von der Vogelweide in 1930.[49] Additionally, the planners of the Austrian commemoration for Goethe emphasized that they would broadcast the celebration in Weimar on the Austrian radio station (RAVAG) immediately before the Viennese ceremony in order to establish a direct link between the German and Austrian events.[50]

---

45. PrK 1481/1932, Einbringer: BKA, AA, Gegenstand: Goethe-Feier in Weimar, 20 February 1932, in ÖStA, AdR, PrK 1481/1932.

46. Program is in "Goethe-Gedächtnis-Woche, Weimar 20.–28. März 1932," in ÖStA, AdR, PrK 1481/1932.

47. BKA, AA Z. 20478-13, Antrag an den Ministerrat, 1 February 1932, in ÖStA, AdR, BKA, AA, NPA, Kt. 164, Liasse Deutschland 33/13 Goethe-Feier.

48. Gedanken zu einer Rede für Dr. Slama, 22 November 1928, in ÖStA, AdR, BKA, AA, NPA, Kt. 340, Liasse Österreich 33/34 Schubertfeier.

49. The quoted phrase comes from Ottfried Neubecker (Berlin), "Gedenkmünzen für Walther von der Vogelweide," *OeD*, January 1931, in BAB, R32/545, Rs. of Bl. 356. The original suggestions and support for the joint coin and a joint stamp came from the writer G. E. Brand, as well as Redslob and the mayor of Würzburg Löffler. Löbe and the Austrian chancellor Schober also approved the idea of a joint coin. See correspondence in BAB, R32/545, Bl. 84, 222, 224, 309 Rs., 310, 316–317, 415, 456, 470.

50. Geschäftszeichen 50, Grundzahl 1962-Pr/32, in ÖStA, AdR, BKA, Präs. 1932, Kt. 374.

Other ideas for depicting an Austro–Reich German community were aspired to but not realized. Redslob, for instance, had hoped to coordinate Walther celebrations to occur simultaneously in Berlin, Vienna, Innsbruck, Würzburg, Dux (Duchcov, Czechoslovakia), and Eisenach. At the end of these ceremonies, he wanted to orchestrate a release of doves so that "not only the capitals and the sites devoted to Walther von der Vogelweide's memory would commemorate him, but also that countless others, who see the flight of the doves and are advised of its meaning through the stories of teachers and the announcements in the press and on the radio, would participate in this celebration, which would simultaneously embody the cultural connection between Germany and Austria." He thereby expected to "develop the fantasy not only of the onlooker, but also of the entire Volk."[51] Owing to the increasingly desperate financial and political situations in both countries, however, these plans could not be carried out.[52] Although commemorative events in Berlin and Vienna could not be arranged, celebrations did occur in Würzburg, Innsbruck, Eisenach, Mödling, Marienbad (Mariánské Lázně, Czechoslovakia), and Dux / Duchcov, which still demonstrated the expanse of a German nation.

Individuals, associations, and municipalities also came up with their own initiatives in order to join in the commemorations. Writing from Marienbad / Mariánské Lázně, Czechoslovakia, a retired general of the Austro-Hungarian army, Rudolf Krauss, enthusiastically devoted himself to the cause of strengthening a transborder German community through a Walther celebration. His recommendations for ways to depict a German nation that transcended state boundaries included the following: ensuring that a book about Walther was in every home; creating Walther national parks in all communities; naming streets, plazas, and forests after Walther; planting Walther linden; dressing people in folk costumes from Walther's time at wreath-laying ceremonies; making a film of the ceremony; and, bordering on the absurd, naming all German boys born in 1930 Walther von der Vogelweide.[53]

Some of these initiatives were in fact implemented, and appeared to be especially important to German-speaking communities outside the Reich as a way to prove their Germanness. A commemorative plaque was unveiled in Mödling, Austria, for the "greatest German minstrel."[54] The municipal government of

---

51. Letter from the Reichskunstwart to the Reichsminister des Innern, Berlin, 30 November 1929, in BAB, R32/545, Bl. 328.

52. Letter from Reichskunstwart Dr. Redslob to the Austrian ambassador Dr. Frank, 4 March 1930, in BAB, R32/545, Rs. of Bl. 309.

53. Copy of General Rud. Krauss, "Anregungen für die 700jahr-Feier für 'Walther v.d. Vogelweide' 1230–1930," Marienbad, 2 August 1929, in BAB, R32/545, Bl. 333–335.

54. Text für die zwei auf der Burg Mödling anzubringenden Gedenktafeln, in ÖStA, AVA, U.Allg. V2 3096, 28508-I/6a/1930.

Salzburg named a street *Vogelweiderstrasse* "after this German."[55] In Marienbad / Mariánské Lázně, the local chapter of the League of Germans in Bohemia (Bund der Deutschen in Böhmen), various German associations, and Krauss led efforts to create a commemorative plaque for Walther. At the unveiling ceremony, a city councilor gave the monument over to the care of the city, remarking "that it may always be a reminder for the German population of Marienbad of their national loyalty." Moreover, according to the *Marienbader Zeitung*, "Through the erection of a monument, Marienbad, alongside the population of Dux, is the only one of the German areas of the Sudetenland to have found the most dignified and impressive form that will also show future generations that the Germans of our *Heimat* have upheld their national consciousness and the veneration of their intellectual greatness even in the most difficult of times."[56] By honoring figures considered to be German heroes and creating monuments for them, German speakers outside Germany could become active members of the German nation and claim contested territory for their own national cause.[57]

For all these attempts to bring German speakers together, especially Reich Germans and Austrians, such festivities did not present the idea of a homogeneous German community. In the ongoing debate about whether a German nation should be characterized by the sameness or diversity of its members,[58] the commemoration organizers, speakers, and many observers often emphasized and praised the latter of the two options. The frequent reference to *Stamm* and *Heimat* on the part of Reich Germans and Austrians at these celebrations demonstrates that they did not aim to erase differences for the sake of national unity. Visually, the parade at the singers' festival provided the most striking representation of this idea. It did not seek "cultural totality and the resistance to fragmentation and ambiguity," which historian Michael Steinberg identifies as the fundamental and problematic characteristics of such events as the Salzburg

---

55. Protokoll aufgenommen in der öffentlichen Sitzung des Gemeinderates der Landeshauptstadt Salzburg am 7. Juli 1930, in Archiv der Stadt Salzburg, Haus der Geschichte, Gemeindesitzungsprotokolle 1930, 215.

56. "Enthüllung der Gedenktafel für Walther von der Vogelweide," *Marienbader Zeitung*, 30 June 1930, enclosed in a letter from General a.D. Krauss to Reichskunstwart Redslob, Marienbad, 12 July 1930, in BAB, R32/545, here Bl. 420.

57. On the importance of monuments in the battle between nationalists in the Bohemian lands see Wingfield, *Flag Wars and Stone Saints*.

58. For discussions of the nineteenth- and twentieth-century parameters of this debate see Celia Applegate, "The Mediated Nation: Regions, Readers, and the German Past," in *Saxony in German History: Culture, Society, and Politics, 1830–1933*, ed. James Retallack (Ann Arbor: University of Michigan Press, 2000), 33–50; Applegate, *Nation of Provincials*; Sheehan, "What Is German History?"; van Rahden, "Germans of the Jewish *Stamm*."

Festival and the 1934 Nazi Nuremberg Rally.[59] Marching according to region, the singers used signs, floats, symbols of their hometowns, and folk costumes to demonstrate both their pride in their regional specificities and their attachment to an overall German national community.[60] As Seitz remarked, "We see before us the parade, a wonderful picture of the solidarity of all Germans. We see in the parade the variety of German work, German art, German intellect, and bec[ome] strengthened anew in the vigor and in the self-assurance of our Volk."[61] According to this point of view, it was precisely the heterogeneity of the German Volk that contributed to its dynamism.

Not everyone was happy with how this diversity was represented at the parade. Although Seitz, the Social Democratic mayor of Vienna, spoke only words of praise for the events at the festival, Austrian socialist papers in particular were critical of the use of imperial uniforms and songs, as well as folk costumes and scenes. "Heralds, accoutrements of knighthood, medieval times, Old Vienna," commented *Das Kleine Blatt*, "a bit too much from back then, too little from today, and nothing at all that points to the future."[62] Yet the festival and other commemorative events were not simply backward looking. Alongside such traditional floats as those for Old Vienna and an Upper Austrian farmers' wedding, singers from Zwickau portrayed a coal-mining scene, and Dessau was represented with a small airplane.[63] More nuanced reports observed the blend between the past and present found during the festival. As a writer for the *Neues Wiener Tagblatt* noted: "The space of the [Singers'] Hall—the aesthetics of engineering, the beauty of the purpose, the director on a tower, the gigantic deployment of the troops of singers, the transmitting station—[is] not just work, but modern work, work from 1928, which scarcely a year earlier could have been achieved properly. Modern and yet with ties to the past, to the traditional culture, which

59. Steinberg, *Austria as Theater and Ideology*, 225.

60. This parade has many interesting similarities and differences when compared with the *Kaiser-Huldigungs-Festzug* held in 1908 in Vienna. Like the 1908 parade, the 1928 procession was organized around the symbols and traditional dress of various regions in an attempt to display both diversity and unity. However, whereas the 1908 celebration was to demonstrate that the various nationalities of the Habsburg Empire supported Franz Joseph and thereby Austrian patriotism, the 1928 festivities aimed to demonstrate the unity of the German nation regardless of state boundaries. This shift highlights how radical the geopolitical transformations after the First World War were for Austrians. On the 1908 celebrations see Unowsky, *Pomp and Politics*, conclusion.

61. "Der Empfang der Sänger im Rathaus," *NFP*, 23 July 1928, 5, in ÖStA, AdR, PrK 5149/1928.

62. "Das Sängerfestzug auf der Ringstraße," *Das Kleine Blatt*, 23 July 1928, 2. Also see "Der Festzug der deutschen Sänger," *AZ*, 23 July 1928, 3.

63. For a detailed report see "Der Sängerfestzug," *NFP*, 23 July 1928, 3–4, in ÖStA, AdR, PrK 5149/1928; Anton Weiß, "Der Festzug," *Festblätter für das 10. Deutsche Sängerbundesfest Wien 1928*, Folge 11, October 1928, 297–303.

one loves about Vienna and which one searches for in Vienna."[64] The endeavors to build a transborder German community, therefore, did not advocate a flight from modernity. Rather, the festivities used modern technologies, as well as a mixture of older and modern symbols, to showcase the diversity and strength of a transborder community.

Although many commemorations aimed to demonstrate that regional variations and state boundaries could not prevent a show of cultural unity between Reich Germans and Austrians, organizers and participants still had to address postwar political divisions. State holidays, especially in Austria, often became flashpoints in the struggles between different political parties. That this was not the case for the cultural festivities can be quickly gleaned from a comparison of the number of violent, political incidents that occurred on the Ringstrasse for the state holiday on November 12 and at the singers' festival. Whereas many fights were registered between followers of the SDAP and supporters of conservative or right-wing organizations during November 12 celebrations, only one minor skirmish reportedly occurred during the festival.[65] Indeed, for many of the cultural festivities, organizers tried to avoid association with a particular political party or ideology, for they hoped that the focus on a shared literary and musical culture would enable them to transcend the increasing political polarization. In a request for the Austrian president to be an honorary chairman of the Singers' League Festival, the leaders of the Ostmärkischer Sängerbund (Eastern March Singers' League) and the steering committee of the festival stated that they rejected any political affiliation.[66] It was on these grounds that the Austrian army decided to participate in the festival, even though regulations stated that the military could not take part in private events.[67] Additionally, in the suggestions for celebrating Walther, Krauss stressed "*everything unpolitical*," and another letter writer

---

64. Helene Tuschak, "Die Kraftprobe," *NWT*, 23 July 1928, 3, in ÖStA, AdR, PrK 5149/1928. The hall referred to in the article is the Singers' Hall constructed in the Prater to hold the main performances and as many as one hundred thousand people.

65. According to police reports, some communists and streetcar workers encircled a group of singers and tried to pull them from their cars and beat them up. Although the singers retreated, a crowd remained and was divided between those who were for and against the singers. The police were called and eventually broke up the crowd. Bundes-Polizeidirektion in Wien, Pr.Zl.IV-1406/30/28, 10. Deutsches Sängerbundesfest, 26 July 1928, in ÖStA, AdR, BKA, Berichte der Wiener Polizeidirektion, Kt. 12.

66. Letter from the Leitung des Ostmärkischen Sängerbundes and the Hauptausschuss für das 10. Deutsche Sängerbundesfest to the Austrian President, [o.D.], enclosed in PrK 5567/1926, in ÖStA, AdR, PrK 5149/1928.

67. BMfHW, Zl. 55115-Präs./1927, Vortrag für den Ministerrat, "10. Deutsches Sängerbundesfest Wien 1928—Förderung durch das Heeresressort," 29 November 1927, in ÖStA, AdR, BMfHW, A, 1927, 23½, 54087/Präs.

to the Reichskunstwart emphasized that the festivities must be "nonpartisan."[68] Because cultural figures were at the center of the celebrations, participants and observers deemed that such lofty aspirations were possible. The admiration for personalities such as Beethoven, Schubert, Walther, and Goethe extended across party lines, with everyone from communists to Nazis showing an appreciation for these men and their works.

Although there was agreement on the importance of recognizing these cultural accomplishments, consensus on how these cultural figures should be interpreted for the present day remained elusive.[69] Organizations with a certain political agenda arranged their own celebrations, which interpreted the cultural figures and the commemoration of them according to the association's ideology. For instance, the Christian Social Workers' Association combined the thirty-sixth anniversary of its founding with a celebration of Schubert. The speaker at the event decried the modern-day situation while looking back fondly at the time of Schubert, and described Schubert as the "creator of authentic German and—as we must see for ourselves particularly in the German Mass—authentic Christian feeling."[70] Members of the association therefore saw Schubert as the embodiment of their particular understanding of German nationhood.

Newspapers that supported a particular political platform also reported on the large celebrations according to their worldview. It was in the pages of the press that the battle between political viewpoints during the commemorations primarily took place. During the singers' festival and the November Schubert celebrations, recriminations broke out between Austrian socialist-leaning newspapers, on the one hand, and the range of nonsocialist publications on the other. Many of the socialist papers came to ambivalent conclusions about the meaning of the singers' festival: they criticized the "lower-middle-class" (*kleinbürgerlich*) motives and motifs of the German Singers' League but took pride in showing off the achievements of "Red Vienna" to the many visitors and reveled in the depictions of *Großdeutschtum*.[71] The left liberal *Neue Freie Presse* accused the *Arbeiter-Zeitung* in particular of "perversity" for bringing in party politics, claiming the cause of *Großdeutschtum* for the workers alone and

---

68. Copy of General Rud. Krauss, "Anregungen für die 700jahr-Feier für 'Walther v.d. Vogelweide' 1230–1930," Marienbad, 2 August 1929, in BAB, R32/545, Bl. 333. Emphasis in original. Letter from G. E. Brand to the Reichskunstwart, The Hague, 20 July 1929, in BAB, R32/545, Bl. 454.

69. Examining the reception of Beethoven in the nineteenth and twentieth centuries, David Dennis argues that various political parties interpreted Beethoven according to their ideologies and used him to promote their political agendas. Dennis, *Beethoven in German Politics*.

70. "Schubertfeier der christlichen Arbeiterschaft: Das 36. Gründungsfest des christlichsozialen Arbeitervereines," *RP*, 6 November 1928, in WB, C 276954, Bd. 1.

71. For example see "Sängerfeste," *AZ*, 20 July 1928, 1.

disdaining the lower middle class.[72] Again, during the November commemorations, a similar dispute took place when it came to light that a socialist member of the advisory board of RAVAG had criticized the radio station's Schubert programming for having too much religious music and declared that Schubert was a proletarian.[73]

Ideological interpretations of the cultural figures and the contemporary commemorations were almost exclusively confined to the press and associational gatherings. They were rarely voiced during the larger ceremonies. The plans for the general festivities were politically neutral, as were the speeches. Moreover, for many of the celebrations, participants hailed from across the political spectrum. For example, although the German Singers' League was a movement of the middle classes, Social Democratic leaders—Reich minister of the interior Carl Severing, Reichstag president Löbe, and Viennese mayor Seitz—enthusiastically participated in the Singers' League Festival. The German mayors that traveled to Vienna for the November Schubert commemorations and the Austrian mayors that visited Würzburg to celebrate Walther represented various political parties. And during the ceremony in Würzburg, both middle-class and working-class singers' associations performed.[74] This divergence between how the press covered the commemorations and what happened at the celebrations is due in part to the different audiences being addressed. Whereas the newspapers were writing for a like-minded readership, the large commemorative ceremonies had to appeal to people from various social and political backgrounds.

Also crucial to understanding the ability of such commemorations to draw together a wide range of social and political actors was the fact that many of the festivities were celebrating the idea of a *großdeutsch* nation. "In any case, the entire city was out and about," the German ambassador to Austria stated in his report on the parade at the Singers' League Festival; "great enthusiasm dominated, the decisive source being the common German [*gemeindeutsch*] feeling."[75] That such a politically and socially divided city as Vienna could be brought together in this instance was possible because the imagining of a transborder German

72. "Klassenkampf bis in das Sängerbundesfest: Eine seltsame Begrüßung der Gäste durch das sozialdemokratische Organ," *NFP* (Morgenblatt), 21 July 1928, 1–2.

73. For the nonsocialist interpretations of this incident see the following articles in WB, C 276954, Bd. 1: "'RAVAG'-Programm und Politik: 'Schubert der Prolet,'" *NFP*, 7 November 1928; "Schubert der Austromarxist: Merkwürdige sozialdemokratische Kritik an der Ravag," *Neues Wiener Journal*, 7 November 1928; "Franz Schubert—der Prolet," *Weltblatt*, 8 November 1928; "(Parteipolitik auf Aetherwellen)," *NFP*, 8 November 1928.

74. "Öffentliche Feier zum Gedächtnis Walthers v.d. Vogelweide auf dem Residenzplatz zu Würzburg," in BAB, R32/545, Bl. 207–208, here 208.

75. Letter from the Deutsche Gesandtschaft Wien (Lerchenfeld) to the Auswärtige Amt Berlin, A. 345, Vienna, 24 July 1928, in PAAA, R73302, IIOe1280.

community was not exclusive to the extreme political right during the Weimar era. Individuals from across the political spectrum participated in the commemoration of this Greater German cultural nation.

Rehearsals for Anschluss

For many supporters of *Großdeutschtum*, there still existed a tangible division that prevented the full realization of unity between Reich Germans and Austrians: the Entente-enforced boundary between their two states. The community that various organizers and participants sought to embody at the celebrations was not simply that of a *Kulturnation* united by language, culture, history, and in some cases blood. Whether explicitly stated or not, they hoped to overcome the disjunction between imaginings of a German cultural nation and the political realities of two separate states. Even after the victorious powers outlawed an Anschluss between the two countries, support for it remained strong on both sides of the border. Whereas some Anschluss advocates lobbied and prepared for a political union with detailed treatises on the coordination of the two states' legal and economic systems, others saw a shared culture, history, and experience as the principal building blocks for a future Anschluss. Thus, on the occasion of the Walther celebrations in Würzburg, an unnamed writer explained that economic and political unity would follow from the "will of the heart."[76] Or, as Karl Hosius, rector of the University of Würzburg, commented, "If peoples of the same language, same culture, and centuries-long solidarity live next to each other, then the will to a unitary state [*Einheitsstaat*] is a matter of course."[77] As a consequence of this type of thinking, these cultural commemorations provided fertile ground for Anschluss demonstrations.

Not content simply to say that the Austro–Reich German border did not exist in people's consciousness, as Franz Slama did at the Walhalla ceremony, organizers and participants at these commemorations boldly declared that they wanted the legal boundary to be eliminated. In welcoming the Österreichisch-Deutscher Volksbund to Würzburg, Mayor Hans Löffler stated that "Walther's spirit . . . makes clear that the border markers between the Germans in the east and the west must be loosened and lifted up as soon as possible."[78] Furthermore, at this commemoration, Löbe, Redslob, the mayors from Graz, Linz, and Salzburg, and the deputy mayor from Innsbruck all declared themselves in favor

---

76. Dr. Kl, "Zur Anschlußkundgebung in Würzburg," *OeD*, May 1930, in BAB, R32/545, Rs. of Bl. 113.

77. Karl Hosius, "Willkommen in Würzburg!," *OeD*, May 1930, in BAB, R32/545, Rs. of Bl. 113.

78. Hans Löffler, "Willkommen in Würzburg!," *OeD*, May 1930, in BAB, R32/545, Bl. 113.

of an Anschluss. The former chancellor of Austria, Ernst Streeruwitz, a Christian Social, closed his speech with the words: "One Volk, one Reich."[79] The Tenth German Singers' League Festival in 1928 was even more spectacular in its promotion of these ideas. Because of the festival's large scale, its broadcast to millions of radio listeners in Austria and the Reich, and the uproar it prompted at the international level, the remainder of this section focuses on this event.

From the early planning stages of the festival, the organization's leaders saw an Anschluss as a central component of the celebrations and made no secret of it. Already a year in advance of the festivities, the chairman of the German Singers' League wrote in the first issue of the commemorative newsletter, "Both main performances are dedicated to the German song and the German fatherland. Never before was this great aim so obviously embodied as in the honoring of the German song prince Franz Schubert and in the rally for the Anschluss idea." The parade, he continued, would fulfill the organization's "task of the mental preparation of the entire German Volk for the coming union [*Zusammenschluss*]."[80] The organizing committee even went so far as to title the third main performance "Anschluss-Rally." And, as one might infer from the festival's success in bolstering a sense of unity among German speakers, the planners' expectations to stage an Anschluss demonstration were not disappointed.

For those who witnessed it, almost every detail of the festival pointed to the desire for and potential success of a future Anschluss. "Deutschland, Deutschland über alles" permeated the air during the festival at the main events, as well as open-air concerts held by the various regional singers' associations. Reporting on the "Anschluss-Rally" performance, the *Wiener Neueste Nachrichten* stated that whoever "heard the 'Deutschlandlied,' sung from one hundred thousand people . . . had the impression that *Großdeutschland* has actually already been created and everything in the future is only the work concerning implementation."[81] Toward the beginning of the parade, flag swingers offered viewers a performance involving black-red-gold flags and red-white-red flags. If there were any doubts of the political implications of this staging, one only had to look at a design by Secession artist Franz Wacik for the official commemorative ribbons: a young man was standing on a platform with the insignia of the German Singers' League and holding up the two countries' flags. A streamer

---

79. "'Ein Volk, ein Reich," *VZ*, 13 May 1930, in BAB, R32/545, Bl. 73.

80. Friedrich List, "Dem Feste zum Geleit," *Festblätter für das 10. Deutsche Sängerbundesfest, Wien 1928*, Folge 1, June 1927, 5.

81. "Deutschland über alles: Eine mächtige Anschlußkundgebung in der Sängerhalle," *WNN*, 22 July 1928, 1.

coming from one of the flags proclaimed "Anschluss!"[82] The attendance of political leaders from the Reich and Austria at the events also provided a striking visual of a special relationship between the two states. One report by the Austrian president's office pointed out how he, his wife, the Austrian chancellor, the Reich minister of the interior, and the Viennese mayor were all seated together at the opening event. It added that "naturally," the German ambassador sat in the president's box and not in the diplomats' section.[83]

In the eyes of many participants, the visual pageantry of the weekend exceeded the organizers' goal of staging an Anschluss rally. In a speech at the city hall, Löbe declared, "After the great experience of the festival and particularly after the nine-hour viewing of the parade, it is for me a certainty that this day has become the greatest rally for Anschluss and the unity of Germans that the world has ever seen."[84] The size and success of the festival events provided observers with proof that the political union of the two states could occur successfully. "The hundreds of thousands, who came together this week in Vienna, have proved that *Großdeutschland* is no longer just a dream, a desire, but it has become firmly rooted in the consciousness of the Reich German and Austrian peoples as a living idea," a Berlin-based illustrated weekly wrote.[85]

If there remained those who were wary of an Anschluss, prominent political figures tried to put their doubts to rest. The Nuremberg mayor, Hermann Luppe, a member of the DDP, attempted to allay the fears of both Reich German and Austrian skeptics. He assured Reich Germans, who worried that Austria could be a political or economic "burden," that "on the contrary, we [democratic politicians] consider the Austrian Volk as a very valuable acquisition if one surveys the diversity of the German tribes [*deutschen Stämme*]." Valuing this diversity, he cited the example of the parade to assure unconvinced Austrians that "that which concerns the particularity of its [Austrian] culture, will also be preserved in the great German Reich."[86] During a visit to Eisenstadt after the singers' festival, Löbe proclaimed that the events in Vienna, as well as the follow-up Anschluss rallies in Eisenstadt and Graz, proved that the Anschluss movement was not simply

---

82. For this design, as well as four others, see "5 offizielle Erinnerungsbänder," *Festblätter für das 10. Deutsche Sängerbundesfest Wien 1928*, Folge 10, July 1928, 277.

83. PrK 5149/1928, Einbringer: Amtsveranlassung, Gegenstand: 10. Deutsches Sängerbundesfest in Wien 1928, Teilnahme des Herrn Bundespräsidenten an den Veranstaltungen, 23 July 1928, in ÖStA, AdR, PrK 5149/1928.

84. "'Die größte Kundgebung für die deutsche Einheit.' Eine Rede des Präsidenten Loebe im Rathaus," *NFP*, 23 July 1928, in ÖStA, AdR, PrK 5149/1928.

85. "Das Wiener Sängerfest," *Hackebeils Illustrierte: Aktuelle Wochenschrift*, 2 August 1928, in ÖStA, AdR, PrK 5149/1928.

86. Quoted in "Die Feststadt Wien und der Anschlußgedanke. Aeußerungen der Oberbürgermeister von Nürnberg und Frankfurt," *NFP*, 23 July 1928, 6, in ÖStA, AdR, PrK 5149/1928.

"a north German doing." Rather, Reich Germans and Austrians pursued a shared goal of political union.[87]

Festivals were not confined to the realm of culture when it came to the national question; they moved firmly into the realm of politics just as the nineteenth-century commemorations had. In both cases, the honoring of cultural figures turned into calls for national unity. Unlike the events of the previous century, however, the commemorations of the late 1920s and early 1930s were not directed against the participants' governments. Rather, organizers and participants held these rallies in opposition to the Paris Peace Settlement and the foreign governments that supported these treaties. They called for the revision of the Treaties of Versailles and Saint-Germain on the grounds that the German right to self-determination had been violated. "We want to be a united German Volk!" Löbe exclaimed in his speech at the Viennese city hall during the festival. "Should today not also be for all foreigners a sign? Can one permanently deny a people of seventy million what every other people is guaranteed? No one is capable of this; little could have been done to prevent the Italian unification and the independence of the Slavic people." He continued to stormy applause: "Still even less will one be able to prevent the German Volk from achieving its right to self-determination."[88] Although not all attendees of the festival made such demands—prime examples being Seipel and his circle—the greater part of festivalgoers challenged the postwar territorial settlement in no uncertain terms.

Besides opposing the forbiddance of an Anschluss, participants protested the awarding of South Tyrol to Italy and the French occupation of the Rhineland, Ruhr, and Saar. According to newspaper and police accounts, throughout the weekend and especially at the parade, one heard the frequent singing of "Wacht am Rhein" and the "Andreas-Hofer Lied," a song from 1831 commemorating the deeds of a Tyrolean patriot who had led battles against Napoleonic forces. Singers from these regions at the parade also provided visuals to make their political desires clear. A group from the Saar dressed in black and carried a sign that read "Saarland, back to the fatherland." To symbolize the loss of South Tyrol (and perhaps owing to the inability of the South Tyroleans to travel to the festival), a mere three men in Tyrolean folk costume were followed by a large gap where the South Tyroleans should have been marching. Additionally, floats from Tyrol were decorated with black flags, as well as the coats of arms of South Tyrolean

---

87. "Das Burgenland will heim ins Reich!," *WNN*, 26 July 1928, enclosed in a letter from the Deutsche Gesandtschaft Wien to the Auswärtige Amt Berlin, A 364, Vienna, 31 July 1928, in PAAA, R73302, IIOe1327.

88. "'Die größte Kundgebung für die deutsche Einheit,'" *NFP*, 23 July 1928, in ÖStA, AdR, PrK 5149/1928.

cities.[89] The representation of these areas in the open-air concerts and the parade reportedly elicited a supportive and emotional response from the hundreds of thousands of spectators. Singers from the occupied territories were greeted with particular enthusiasm and sympathy, as well as calls of "Hail the free song and the free Rhine!"[90] When the lone representatives of South Tyrol marched by, the onlookers spontaneously rose from their seats and stood in momentary silence. The crowd greeted the Tyrolean references to South Tyrol with "Hail South Tyrol," as well as a few individuals calling out "Boo Italy" and "Back to the fatherland."[91]

Just as singers' associations during the nineteenth century used opposition to foreign enemies as a "new legitimative and integrative principle" to bolster their calls for national unity among different social and political groups,[92] so too did participants in the singers' festival of 1928. In other words, alongside the more abstract idea of *Großdeutschtum*, calls for the revision of the peace treaties created a common cause for people from various political and social milieus. Although contemptuous of the middle-class origins of the singers, the *Arbeiter-Zeitung* granted that sociopolitical divisions could be overcome through the common goal of an Anschluss. "Other political, other cultural ideals preoccupy us than those of the lower-middle-class singers, who gather in Red Vienna," the newspaper stated; "but one idea, one will unites us with them, the idea of a great republic of the entire German Volk."[93] The Bavarian press, on both the right and the left of the political spectrum, also enthusiastically endorsed the Anschluss displays, according to a report by the Reich's representative to the province.[94]

Furthermore, the Anschluss rallies physically brought together members of political parties who would under other circumstances not choose to associate with one another. A reporter for the Berlin-based left liberal *Vossische Zeitung* pointed out that parliamentary representatives from the Christian Social, Greater German, and Rural Federation Parties attended the "Anschluss-Rally"

---

89. Regarding the "Andreas-Hofer-Lied" see Bundes-Polizeidirektion in Wien, Pr.Zl.IV-1406/28, 10. Deutsches Sängerbundesfest, 21 July 1928, in ÖStA, AdR, BKA, Berichte der Wiener Polizei-direktion, Kt. 12. For relevant descriptions of the parade see Bundes-Polizeidirektion in Wien, Pr.Z.IV-1406/28, 10. Deutsches Sängerbundesfest, 22 July 1928, in ÖStA, AdR, BKA, Berichte der Wiener Polizeidirektion, Kt. 12; "'Das Volk hat gesprochen,'" VZ, 24 July 1928, and "Der Sängerfest-zug. Wiens größtes und schönstes Volksschauspiel," NFP, 23 July 1928, 2, both in ÖStA, AdR, PrK 5149/1928; "Der Festzug der deutschen Sänger," AZ, 23 July 1928, 3.

90. "Der Festzug der deutschen Sänger," NWT, 23 July 1928, 4, in ÖStA, AdR, PrK 5149/1928.

91. Bundes-Polizeidirektion in Wien, Pr.Z.IV-1406/28, 10. Deutsches Sängerbundesfest, 22 July 1928, in ÖStA, AdR, BKA, Berichte der Wiener Polizeidirektion, Kt. 12.

92. Klenke, *Der Singende "Deutsche Mann,"* 96.

93. "Der Festzug der deutschen Sänger," AZ, 23 July 1928, 3.

94. Letter from the Vertretung der Reichsregierung München to the Reichskanzlei Berlin, A. Nr. 273, Munich, 25 July 1928, in PAAA, R73302, IIOe1299.

alongside the socialists Seitz, Löbe, and Severing.[95] And when members of the Schwabian Singers' League passed through Tyrol on their way home from the festival in Vienna, a representative from the Württemberg Landtag pointed out that a prior Anschluss gathering in the Burgenland had shown how desire for a Greater Germany prevailed over party politics. "Next to the German National People's Party member with the Stahlhelm emblem stood the Social Democrat with the Reichsbanner emblem and spoke about the great, German unified Reich [*Einheitsreich*]," Walter Hölscher of the DNVP announced. "There, for perhaps the first time, the idea of the Reich publicly bridged the separating divide of the parties."[96] Hölscher's statement highlights the ability of cultural celebrations, which were connected with Anschluss demonstrations, to bring together members of openly hostile political organizations that in the context of Constitution Day would not appear with one another.

Although participants viewed the Singers' League Festival as an opportunity to transcend political divisions, we saw in the previous section how politics pervaded such events. Thus, despite the festival being a middle-class affair, republicans—socialists and liberals alike—seized the chance once again to emphasize the connection between an Anschluss and democracy.[97] Whereas those further right on the political spectrum stressed that an Anschluss would lead to a greater Reich or state, republicans underlined that the desired political union would be between two republics. For example, at the end of his speech in which he challenged the Allies to recognize the German people's right to self-determination, Löbe "finally raised his glass to the lively calls hailing the *großdeutsch* republic of the future."[98] An Austrian socialist newspaper, which displayed ambivalence about the fact that the singers were from the middle classes, still enthusiastically saw the festival as "an impressive rally for Austria's Anschluss with the great, German republic."[99] The cultural commemorations became another way for republicans to publicize and prove their claim to an audience beyond their party bases that the *großdeutsch* idea and democracy were intertwined. Luppe, the DDP mayor of Nuremberg, expressed such a view in hoping that the widespread

95. Karl Lahm, "Sang und Anschluß: Eine Riesenkundgebung, Seipels Abwesenheit, Löbe und Severing, Der Jubel in Wien," *VZ*, 22 July 1928, 2.

96. "Ein schwäbisch-tirolisches Verbrüderungsfest," *Innsbrucker Nachrichten*, 27 July 1928, enclosed in a letter from the Deutsches Konsulat Innsbruck to the Auswärtige Amt Berlin, No. 569, Innsbruck, 27 July 1928, in PAAA, R73302, IIOe1300.

97. Eric Bryden addresses republicans' use of cultural commemorations but overlooks the *großdeutsch* aspect of the celebrations addressed here. Bryden, "In Search of Founding Fathers," chap. 2.

98. "Empfang im Rathause," *NWT*, 23 July 1928, 5, in ÖStA, AdR, PrK 5149/1928.

99. "Das Sängerbundesfest in Wien," *Volksbote: Sozialdemokratisches Wochenblatt für das Viertel unter dem Manhartsberg*, 28 July 1928, 4.

display of the Weimar Republic's contested colors of black-red-gold during the singers' festival would lead to "the attitude toward the new Germany
experienc[ing] a fundamental intensification" among Reich Germans.[100] Republicans hoped that their support of an Anschluss would aid them in demonstrating their sincere national convictions at a time when the nation had become a
primary source of identification for many Europeans.[101] In return, they hoped
that they would be able to fend off claims by the political right that democracy
was antinational.

The participation of numerous Social Democratic leaders in these festivals
underlines the fact that the nationalism of many Austrian and German socialists was not simply a result of their viewing Germany as the birthplace of the
Social Democratic movement. Their pronouncements at the commemorations
for the musical and literary figures also point to their belief in a German nation
predicated on a cultural and ethnic community.[102] Whether socialist or liberal,
the proponents of republican *großdeutsch* nationalism demonstrated that the political right was not the sole voice of German nationalism after the First World
War. For the Weimar era, it would be more accurate to speak of German nationalisms, for, as this book shows, there were numerous definitions of Germanness.
Until the National Socialist and the Austrofascist usurpations of power in 1933
and 1934 respectively, no one political or social group controlled the textual and
visual discourses related to German nationalism. Individuals from the left to the
right of the political spectrum participated in the definition and redefinition of
what it meant to be German, as well as Austrian. Through the idea of a shared
culture, the cultural commemorations provided an opportunity different from
that of political commemorations: individuals from varied and opposing viewpoints could voice their particular ideas about a German nation while still rallying around a common cause, whether it was the honoring of cultural heroes or
the desire for an Anschluss. The next chapter looks more closely at the politics
of the Anschluss movement, which once again brought conflicting sociopolitical
groups together. However, just as disagreements arose over the cultural commemorations, so too did debates arise within the Anschluss movement about
the best way to achieve a political union of the two countries and the final form
a Greater Germany should take.

---

100. "Die Feststadt Wien und der Anschlußgedanke," *NFP*, 23 July 1928, 6, in ÖStA, AdR, PrK
5149/1928.

101. Suval, *Anschluss Question*; Heß, "*Das ganze Deutschland.*"

102. Steinberg makes such an argument with regard to Renner and Bauer. Steinberg, *Austria as
Theater and Ideology*, 120.

6

ANSCHLUSS BEFORE HITLER

The Politics of the Österreichisch-Deutscher Volksbund

"The scene was strange enough," wrote a reporter for *Der Tag*. "Students in fraternity caps stood next to members of the Republikanischer Schutzbund, dignified professors with full beards next to the unemployed, greeting one another with '*Heil!*' [the nationalist salutation] and '*Freundschaft!*' [the socialist salutation]."[1] This diverse crowd had gathered for the founding of a Viennese branch of the Österreichisch-Deutscher Volksbund (Austro-German People's League) in June 1925. Drawn together by a shared desire for an Anschluss, the audience listened to speeches from the Christian Social Hans Eibl, Rudolf Birbaumer of the GDVP, General Theodor Körner and Paul Speiser of the SDAP, Landbund member Anton Gasselich, the partyless Hermann Neubacher, and the liberal economist Gustav Stolper, who was also of Jewish heritage.[2] Additionally, speakers read aloud congratulatory telegrams from the Reichsbanner, the republican veterans' association in Germany, and the president of the German side of the Volksbund, SPD member Paul Löbe.[3] So many Anschluss enthusiasts turned out for the rally

---

1. "Die Anschlußversammlung vor dem Rathause," *Der Tag*, 24 June 1925, in WB, L121260, Bd. 1, Fasz. I, Untermappe IVa, 12.

2. "Die Anschlußkundgebung des Oesterreichisch-Deutschen Volksbundes," *NWT*, 24 June 1925, and "Eine Anschlußkundgebung," *Neues Wiener Journal*, 24 June 1925, both in WB, L121260, Bd. 1, Fasz. I, Untermappe IVa, 6 and 7 respectively. The articles note that the GDVP representative was a Bierbaumer, who served in the Bundesrat. However, the only GDVP delegate who has a name close to this is Rudolf Birbaumer.

3. "Die Anschlußkundgebung," *Österreichische Volkszeitung*, 24 June 1925, and "Die Anschlußkundgebung des Oesterreichisch-Deutschen Volksbundes," *NWT*, 24 June 1925, both in WB, L121260, Bd. 1, Fasz. I, Untermappe IVa, 9 and 6 respectively.

that the room inside the city hall reserved for the event was too small. Consequently, organizers staged a second rally in front of the Viennese landmark. For a society as divided as interwar Austria, this peaceful gathering of the different sociopolitical camps was indeed "strange," but it was also one of the stated goals of the Volksbund. As a resolution drafted by the lawyer Arthur Seyss-Inquart and unanimously passed by the two rallies declared, "The numerous assembled women and men, regardless of party affiliation, profess anew their desire to aid in the fulfillment of the natural ambition of the German-Austrian Volk to be united with the Reich."[4]

Founded in Germany in the aftermath of the First World War, the Österreichisch-Deutscher Volksbund became the most prominent organization in the Weimar era devoted to the realization of an Anschluss. To achieve this goal, its members produced propaganda, staged mass rallies, fought for Austrians living in the Reich to be treated as citizens, lobbied for legislation that would pave the way for an eventual political union, and educated the public about the plight of German minorities.

As the anecdote above illustrates, the association was an anomaly in an era of increasing political fragmentation and violence. It included the supporters and opponents of democracy, Jews and anti-Semites, Catholics and Protestants, workers and the bourgeoisie. The countervailing forces involved in the association were typified by two of the figures serving in the Volksbund leadership: the chairman of the Berlin branch of the association was the Social Democrat and Reichstag president Löbe, while an important individual in the Viennese branch, Seyss-Inquart, would later gain notoriety as one of the defendants at the Nuremberg trials executed for his role in perpetrating Nazi crimes.[5] This chapter will explore the curious politics of the association. It will consider not only the ways in which these disparate sectors of society could momentarily collaborate, but also the political battles about the association and the Anschluss idea. Although the Volksbund's diverse members had the shared goal of an Austro-German union, political clashes arose because of their fundamentally different ideas about where the boundaries of a Greater Germany should lie, what political system the future state should have, and who could be members of a *großdeutsch* nation.

Indeed, one had to look no further than the June 1925 rally in Vienna to see how fragile any compromise would be. While the speakers, who were normally

---

4. "Die Anschlußkundgebung des Oesterreichisch-Deutschen Volksbundes," *AZ*, 24 June 1925, in WB, L121260, Bd. 1, Fasz. I, Untermappe IVa, 10.

5. On Seyss-Inquart's involvement in the Volksbund and his desire to use the organization as a way to enhance his political profile and connections see Wolfgang Rosar, *Deutsche Gemeinschaft: Seyss-Inquart und der Anschluß* (Vienna: Europa Verlag, 1971), 45–53.

bitter enemies, underlined the nonpartisan nature of the Volksbund, the political battles that emerged both within and about the association were immediately apparent. *Der Tag*, the liberal, pro-republican Viennese newspaper, reported that Nazis shamefully interrupted Körner's speech, shouting, "Jews out!" and "National traitors!" The right-wing *Deutschösterreichische Tages-Zeitung* contended that it was not its Nazi readers who had disturbed the rally; rather, it was a small group of communists, who had sung the French revolutionary anthem, "La Marseillaise." The *Reichspost*, the main paper associated with Ignaz Seipel's circle of the Christian Socials, indignantly claimed it had been socialist youths who had sung "La Marseillaise," "after a national rally!" The socialist *Arbeiter-Zeitung* advanced its own interpretation of events, concluding that Körner received "the strongest applause" of all the speakers.[6] Any unity demonstrated by the various supporters of these parties at the rally was thus momentary and superficial.

In highlighting the diversity of the members involved in the Anschluss movement, this chapter presents further evidence of the depth of republicans' commitment to national causes. As we will see, both prominent politicians and rank-and-file republicans were enthusiastic participants in Volksbund activities. Republicans, like some politicians on the political right, were willing to work alongside their political foes to support and achieve an Anschluss. Yet even in collaborating with their opponents, republicans used the Volksbund as another platform to promote their more open understanding of nationhood and to demonstrate that democracy and German nationalism were compatible. Republicans' investment of time and resources in the Volksbund illustrates that support for transborder German nationalism in the Weimar era was not simply a precursor to a Nazi-occupied Europe. As the final section of this chapter shows, it was only after Hitler's appointment to chancellor in January 1933 that the Anschluss movement, and German nationalism more generally, became dominated by the Nazis.

Aims, Activities, and Organization

The origins of the Volksbund dated back to the chaotic days of the revolution of 1918. As the Habsburg Empire broke up toward the end of the war and

---

6. "Die Anschlußversammlung vor dem Rathause," *Der Tag*, 24 June 1925, in WB, L121260, Bd. 1, Fasz. I, Untermappe IVa, 12; "Eine Anschlußkundgebung," *DöTZ*, 24 June 1925, in WB, L121260, Bd. 1, Fasz. I, Untermappe IVa, 11; "Eine Anschlußkundgebung," *RP*, 24 June 1925, in WB, L121260, Bd. 1, Fasz. I, Untermappe, IVa, 8; "Die Anschlußkundgebung des Oesterreichisch-Deutschen Volksbundes," *AZ*, 24 June 1925, in WB, L121260, Bd. 1, Fasz. I, Untermappe IVa, 10.

it became clear to observers that only a small, overwhelmingly German piece of Austria would remain, Austrians' desire for a political union with Germany grew. The idea to organize this impulse into a movement first came from Felix Stössinger, an Austrian living in Berlin and a member of the left-wing Independent Social Democratic Party of Germany. In a conversation with Stefan Großmann, a fellow Austrian with socialist sympathies and the later founder of *Das Tage-Buch*, Stössinger suggested that one of them should seize the initiative and convene an assembly in Berlin of both Reich Germans and Austrians. Although Stössinger realized that such a movement would have to be "nonpartisan" (*überparteilich*), he was unwilling to work with the bourgeoisie because of his political convictions. Großmann consequently took the initiative and began to meet with Austrians and Reich Germans and formed the Österreichisch-Deutscher Arbeitsausschuss (Austro-German Working Committee).[7] On November 17, within days of both Germany and Austria becoming republics, the Arbeitsausschuss held its first public rally in the Hochschule für Musik. Thousands of people from "all strata and ranks" gathered to hear the likes of Großmann, Hermann Kienzl (an Austrian writer and theater critic), Konrad Haenisch (a Reich German socialist and Prussian minister of cultural affairs and education), Werner Sombart (a Reich German sociologist), and Hermann Ullmann (a Bohemian activist for the Verein für das Deutschtum im Ausland [the Association for Germandom Abroad]) speak about their desire for an Anschluss and social justice.[8]

Over the course of the next year, in light of the hesitation of the population and government regarding an Anschluss and ultimately the peace treaties' prevention of one, it became clear that an Austro-German union would not be possible in the near future. The organizers of the working committee therefore decided to reconstitute the association in order to engage in the long-term work needed to realize a Greater Germany.[9] On 19 January 1920, the Österreichisch-Deutscher Volksbund für Berlin und nordöstliche Deutschland (Austro-German People's League for Berlin and Northeastern Germany) came into being at a public rally in the Philharmonie. To a crowd of "burghers and workers, women and men," the head of the organization, the Austrian Hermann Kienzl, explained, "The watchword

---

7. Stefan Großmann, "Die Anfänge der Anschlußbewegung," *OeD*, November 1928, 4–6.

8. "Die Grundsteinlegung des Österreichisch-Deutschen Volksbundes," *OeD*, November 1926, 1–9; Großmann, "Die Anfänge der Anschlußbewegung," 4–6.

9. Großmann, "Die Anfänge der Anschlußbewegung," 4–6. Also see Alfred Werre, typed manuscript of "Der Oesterreichisch-Deutsche Volksbund," enclosed in a letter from Werre to Legationsrat Lindner, Berlin, 3 August 1925, in PAAA, R73314, IIOe1425.

of the Volksbund is to begin with the anchoring of *Großdeutschland* in the hearts and minds of all Germans in order to help its realization."[10]

As Kienzl's statement suggests, the Volksbund recognized that it needed to win over the "hearts and minds" of all Germans, especially those with Reich citizenship, to the Anschluss idea. Although the idea of a Greater Germany cropped up frequently in the manifold attempts of Reich Germans to reimagine the boundaries of their country after the First World War, numerous Reich Germans were misinformed about their German-speaking neighbors. The attempts to create a *kleindeutsch Staatsnation*, a nation based on the idea of a Prussian-led smaller German state, after 1871 had in a number of ways seemingly succeeded. Writing in October 1920, the Austrian consulate in Dortmund explained that the city's residents were "completely uninterested in the question of Austria's Anschluss with Germany." The vice-consul blamed this situation on "the political immaturity of the local population" and the "faulty German schooling" that left Reich citizens with an "absolute confusion about Austrian relations." This lack of knowledge was so great that the consular official reported that Reich Germans asked him, "Is it not true that Austrian is spoken in Austria?"[11] Such grievances continued throughout the 1920s.[12]

Complaints also abounded about the legal status of Austrian citizens living in the Reich. Volksbund supporters were indignant that Austrians in Germany had the same standing as foreigners. Like all other noncitizens, Austrians in Germany could not vote, had to obtain permits to work (*Arbeiterlegitimationskarte*) in Prussia or were required to pay for certificates that would exempt them from needing the work permit (*Befreiungsscheine*), and underwent the same difficult process to attain Reich citizenship. It was intolerable, Volksbund members declared, that authorities levied a fee of 1.50 Reichsmarks for Austrians to renew their work permits or that the district presidents of Arnsberg, Münster, and Düsseldorf denied 90 percent of Austrians' citizenship applications as late as 1928.[13] In times of crisis—particularly the hyperinflation of 1923, the occupation of the Rhine and Ruhr, and the Great Depression—the problems facing Austrians became more

---

10. "Der Volksbund für zehn Jahre," *OeD*, January 1930, 20; "Für den Anschluss—trotz alledem," *VZ* (Morgenausgabe), 21 January 1920, 3.

11. Report from the Oesterreichisches Konsulat Dortmund sent to the Staatsamt für Aeusseres, Dortmund, 16 October 1920, in ÖStA, AdR, NPA, BKA, AA, Kt. 110, Liasse Deutschland 2/3, 1920–1921, Zl. 4652/13.XI.1920.

12. Fritz Machatschek, "Angleichung im Geographie-Unterricht," *OeD*, June 1929, 5.

13. "Arbeiterlegitimation 1926," *OeD*, January 1926, 16; "Gautag Rheinland-Westfalen am 7. Juli in Hamborn," *OeD*, August 1928, 20. Further complaints are littered throughout the Mitteilungen and St. Bürokratis sections of *Oesterreich-Deutschland*, which ran from 1924 until 1933.

acute as foreigners were the first to be dismissed from jobs. "Under the influence of economic distress," explained a 1932 article in *Oesterreich-Deutschland*, the monthly journal of the Berlin Volksbund, "an unfavorable attitude toward foreigners asserts itself and increasingly takes hold. A difference between random foreigners and 'German foreigners' is in many cases unknown. Understandably all Germans from foreign countries, as far as they are not naturalized in the German Reich, are foreigners in the eyes of the law." Because of the perseverance of this legalistic definition of Germanness, the Volksbund strove to ensure that "the public, authorities, and schools are made to understand that in effect such 'foreigners' are Germans by their nationality."[14] The Volksbund thus hoped its work would increase consciousness that "national comrades" (*Volksgenossen*) and "state comrades" (*Staatsgenossen*) were not the same. In the changed postwar circumstances, national comradery should take precedent, according to the organization.[15]

While the failings of the bureaucracy were mainly due to a lack of knowledge about Austrians, along with a *kleindeutsch* outlook, there were also outright opponents and skeptics of an Anschluss. Volksbund members sought to counter arguments that Austria's financial weaknesses made an Anschluss undesirable. Responding to a 1922 *8-Uhr-Abendblatt* article that contended Austrian economic instability would only add to Germany's turmoil should a political union come to pass, Löbe wrote, "We are convinced that a problem that is so tightly connected to the honor and existence of the nation should not be viewed from a purely economic [standpoint] like a trade agreement."[16] In addition to nationally shaming economic foes of a political union, Anschluss proponents pointed out that Austria's trade routes to the east would be a boon for the Reich, an argument that won many heavy industrialists over to the cause.[17] Volksbund supporters also tried to assuage Protestants and conservatives who had concerns about increasing the number of Catholics and socialists in Germany.[18]

Consequently, one of the main aims of the Volksbund was to produce propaganda that would educate Reich Germans about Austria, thereby increasing the visibility of the Anschluss question and the desire to solve it. To accomplish this goal, the executive committee and local chapters pursued a wide range of activities. They published a monthly journal, organized tours of Austria with

---

14. Oskar Reitzner, "Die Rechtslosigkeit der Auslandsdeutschen," *OeD*, July 1932, 11.

15. Werner Stephan, "Das Reichstagswahlrecht der Deutsch-Oesterreicher," *OeD*, December 1928, 1.

16. "Oesterreich und das Deutsche Reich," *Heim ins Reich (HiR)*, May 1922, 2.

17. "Neue Ortsgruppen," *OeD*, August 1927, 21–22.

18. Rudolf Laun, "Konfessionelle Aengste," *OeD*, June 1925, 11–12.

discounted tickets, petitioned officials to change street names that were reminders of Prussia's 1866 victory over Austria, helped to organize exhibitions on subjects such as Austrian art and the sights of Vienna, staged mass rallies, invited speakers, arranged lectures and radio broadcasts on topics ranging from "The Austrian Landscape and the Song of the Niebelungs" to "Locarno and the Anschluss Question," and held slide shows underlining Austria's natural beauty and the plight of German national minorities elsewhere.[19] Following a radio address on Germandom in Austria, the head of the chapter in Breslau expressed his hope "that ever so many Reich Germans have heard this lecture" so that they would "overcom[e] the erroneous views about Austria and its successor states that still exist today in the Reich."[20] By demolishing misconceptions about Austria through its myriad programs, the Volksbund aimed to reorient national thinking in Germany. "We must get ourselves used to thinking more *großdeutsch* and less *kleindeutsch*," argued Ludwig Haas in response to the Reich postmaster general's issuing of Hohenzollern stamps.[21] Whereas national activists had endeavored before the Great War to force people to identify with a national group,[22] national activists after 1918 encouraged Reich Germans to reimagine their *kleindeutsch* understandings of nationhood.

To maintain and garner further support, local chapters also organized social events. Wine harvest festivals, costume balls with Austrian themes, goulash and dumpling dinners, field trips to the countryside, and Christmas celebrations were popular ways for the branches of the Volksbund to make Austrians feel at home while raising awareness of Austrian traditions among Reich Germans. Although a few provincial Volksbund leaders grumbled that some members seemed to care only about socializing,[23] many extolled the virtues of such activities. Reporting on its 1927 wine festival, the Frankfurt chapter argued against the notion that "such amusements all too easily become trivial . . . and profane the Anschluss idea." Rather, the wine festival "proved that it was indeed possible to combine a lighthearted, lively celebration with the *großdeutsch* character." In its coverage of the event, the left liberal *Frankfurter Zeitung* affirmed the chapter's assessment: "Through [a] popular festival [*Volksfest*] one captures new circles, which perhaps come out of other motives, but nevertheless can be acquainted with and recruited

---

19. Good descriptions of these activities can be found in the Mitteilungen sections of *OeD*.
20. "Ortsgruppe Breslau," *OeD*, February 1926, 26.
21. "Die Friedericus-Marke und Oesterreich," *OeD*, December 1926, 16.
22. Cohen, *Politics of Ethnic Survival*; King, *Budweisers*; Judson, *Guardians of the Nation*; Zahra, *Kidnapped Souls*.
23. Franz Rohs, "Mitteilungen aus dem Gau Hessen u. Hessen-Nassau," *HiR*, August 1923, 5; "Ortsgruppe Uebach-Palenberg," *OeD*, April 1929, 21.

for the Anschluss idea." As the paper pointed out, the event drew six times the number of members of the Frankfurt chapter.[24]

Although the Volksbund became best known for its propaganda campaigns and rallies, it also addressed technical issues that would lay the groundwork for a future Anschluss. Rallies were useful for whipping up support for the cause, but, as Paul Nathan, the Social Democratic founder of the Hilfsverein der deutschen Juden (Aid Association of German Jews), and Richart Mischler pointed out, they could not in and of themselves accomplish a political union.[25] The organization therefore formed committees to investigate the harmonization of German and Austrian policies in the following areas: administration, education, the press, culture, and commerce. By promoting reforms that would bring German and Austrian laws in line with one another, such committee work would facilitate an Anschluss when the League of Nations finally permitted it. The importance of such activities for the Volksbund leadership became apparent following the founding of the Deutsch-Österreichische Arbeitsgemeinschaft (German-Austrian Working Committee) in the summer of 1925. Created as a smaller and more politically conservative association of experts, the Arbeitsgemeinschaft became known by contemporaries as the Anschluss organization that in "close circles" undertook "quiet, factual work." In contrast, the Volksbund earned the characterization as the Anschluss organization concerned with "propagandistic" activities that involved "the broad masses of the Volk."[26] Taking issue with this distinction, the Volksbund asserted that such a new organization was unnecessary because of its own established activities in this area.[27]

In addition to preparing the way for an Anschluss, Volksbund members worked to alleviate the current situation of Austrian citizens in Germany. Given that a political union was not immediately possible, one of the Volksbund's central campaigns was to fight for Austrians to achieve "legal equality with German citizens of the Reich."[28] Both the main executive committee and local chapters invested a great deal of time into petitioning government officials to ease the process for Austrians to achieve Reich citizenship, to grant voting rights to Austrians in Germany, to abolish time-consuming applications and fees required for

---

24. "Ortsgruppe Frankfurt a.M.," *OeD*, November 1927, 23–24.

25. Paul Nathan, "Von politischer Gesinnung zur politischer Tat," *OeD*, March 1924, 6–7; Richart Mischler, "Bilanz," *OeD*, June 1927, 1.

26. Letter from the Deutsche Gesandtschaft Wien to the Auswärtige Amt, 5 June 1925, Vienna, in PAAA, R73314, IIOe877.

27. "Ortsgruppe Berlin," *OeD*, March 1926, 18; Paul Löbe, "Unser Bundestag," *OeD*, June 1926, 1–2; Paul Löbe, "Der Stand der Anschlußfrage," *OeD*, July 1926, 1–4, here 4.

28. "Auszug aus den Satzungen," Rs. of Oesterreichisch-Deutscher Volksbund, Vereinsjahr 1925, in PAAA, R73314.

work permits, and to prevent Austrians from being dismissed from jobs during the periods of great economic turmoil.

The Volksbund was never able to accomplish the goal of full legal equality for Austrians in the Reich, but it was able to effect smaller changes on policies concerning Austrians. In the spring of 1925, the Volksbund achieved the ability to issue certificates of German descent (*Deutschstämmigkeit*) for citizenship applications in Prussia, an act it hoped would better Austrians' chances.[29] The following year, Mischler announced at a meeting of the Gau Silesia II that the Volksbund had aided 825 members with their citizenship applications.[30] Other regions also noted that the organization was helping Austrians to gain citizenship, even in areas where numerous applications had previously been rejected by the authorities.[31] The association's activists also persuaded local officials across Germany to repeal fees charged to Austrians as foreigners.[32] And, during the Great Depression, the Volksbund prevented Austrian workers in the Gau Rhineland-Westphalia from being sent home and denied welfare benefits.[33]

Beginning in 1925, the Volksbund in Austria joined its associates in the Reich in the struggle for a political union. Like its counterpart, the Austrian side of the organization invited political and cultural figures from Germany to give speeches, held large public rallies, and organized lectures on the Anschluss question. While much of the activities and aims of the two sides overlapped, there were nuanced differences in their chief tasks. Whereas the German half of the Volksbund saw one of its main responsibilities as reorienting Reich Germans' *kleindeutsch* understanding of nationhood, the Austrian activists specifically endeavored to combat Anschluss skeptics at home. As stated in the first issue of the Austrian Volksbund's journal, *Der Anschluss*, there were two main goals: fighting both domestic and foreign opponents of an Anschluss. Of the two, the article identified the "enemy in [our] own country" as "more dangerous." Although an estimated 90 percent of the Austrian population supported an Anschluss, the foes at home—particularly the Christian Socials in control of the federal government—weakened other Austrians' attempts to persuade foreign powers

---

29. "Gutachten über Deutschstämmigkeit ehem. Oesterreicher," *OeD*, April 1925, 20; "Ortsgruppe Berlin," *OeD*, April 1925, 21–22, here 22.

30. "Gau Schlesien II," *OeD*, November 1926, 31.

31. "Die Delegierten-Sitzung," *OeD*, May 1927, 17; "Gau Rheinland-Westfalen," *OeD*, July 1929, 18–20.

32. "Ortsgruppe Osterfeld," *OeD*, March 1927, 24; "Erhöhte Kosten für Befreiungsscheine?," *OeD*, April 1927, 19.

33. "Gau Rheinland-Westfalen," *OeD*, June 1930, 20–22, here 21; "Wohlfahrtsunterstützung für arbeitslose Oesterreicher in Berlin," *OeD*, December 1931, 5–7; "Mitteilungen," *OeD*, January 1932, 14–18; "Mitteilungen," *OeD*, December 1932, 14–19.

to permit an Anschluss. The Volksbund headquartered in Vienna thus wanted to "direct a fight internally against [the enemy] with writings and speeches, words of encouragement and conviction."[34]

In addition to orchestrating activities to attract members, both halves of the Volksbund aimed to win over the maximum number of supporters by emphasizing their inclusiveness. As the charter of both the German and Austrian sides of the association stated, "Every German who avows him/herself to the *großdeutsch* idea regardless of citizenship, party affiliation, and religion can become a member."[35] The organization did in fact draw a diverse group of individuals to join its ranks, and this strange amalgamation of people became one of its hallmarks. The ability of the Volksbund to span the divisions in German and Austrian societies became a constant refrain in its publications and the speeches given at its events.

With regard to citizenship, Volksbund members included not only Reich Germans and Austrian citizens but also German minorities who found themselves belonging to new nation-states like Czechoslovakia and Yugoslavia; yet Austrians dominated both the German and Austrian branches of the organization. Such a development was to be expected in Austria. In Germany, there were two main reasons that Austrians composed a large portion of the membership. First, one of the chief ways that the association spread beyond Berlin was through incorporating specifically Austrian organizations that decided to become part of the Volksbund. For example, the Reichsbund der Deutschen aus dem früheren Österreich-Ungarn (Reich League of Germans from the former Austria-Hungary), founded in 1919 in Rhineland-Westphalia, joined the Volksbund in 1921, becoming the Gau Rhineland-Westphalia.[36] Second, an Anschluss was a more pressing matter for Austrians. Between believing their home state to be unviable and being treated as foreigners in the Reich, Austrians had more incentive to join the Volksbund. Indeed, a few complaints arose among local leaders that some members had joined only out of self-interest in order to get help with citizenship applications (*Interessenmitglieder*); but Volksbund activists

---

34. "Unser Ziel!," *Der Anschluss*, 15 January 1927, 1.

35. "Auszug aus den Satzungen," Rs. of Oesterreichisch-Deutscher Volksbund, Vereinsjahr 1925, in PAAA, R73314; "Satzungen des Oesterreichisch-Deutschen Volksbundes, Ortsgruppe Wien," VGA, Parteiarchiv vor 1934, Mappe 132, 4.

36. "Gau Rheinland-Westfalen," *OeD*, October 1924, 17. Other Austrian associations that became Volksbund chapters were the Bund der Deutschösterreicher in Mitteldeutschland, the Deutsch-österreichische Verein in Erckenschwieck, the Verein Österreichischer Landsleute in Buer-Hassel, and the Verein der Deutschen aus dem ehemaligen Österreich-Ungarn in Halle am Saale. "Landesverband Hessen und Hessen-Nassau," *OeD*, April 1929, 20; "Ortsgruppe Erckenschwieck," *OeD*, May 1926, 19; "Neue Ortsgruppe," *OeD*, June 1926, 27; "Kreis Mitteldeutschland," *OeD*, July 1929, 18.

insisted that more often than not, committed members (*Gesinnungsmitglieder*) filled their ranks.[37]

As one of the main goals of the Volksbund was to win support for the Anschluss idea in the Weimar Republic, the organization made a concerted effort to bring in Reich German members. The Volksbund's chief success was in attracting prominent politicians and public figures to serve on the executive committee. The assumption of Paul Löbe to the chairmanship of the Volksbund in March 1921 was the most notable achievement in this regard.[38] Furthermore, local chapters, including those that had started as exclusively Austrian associations, reached out to German citizens. In 1924, for example, one of the leaders of the Gau Rhineland-Westphalia encouraged fellow members to substitute the term "fellow countryman" (*Landsmann*) with "league brother" (*Bundesbruder*). Continued use of *Landsmann* as a form of address "must make it appear to outsiders as though the Österreichisch-Deutscher Volksbund were a purely Austrian association for fellow countrymen, when in fact the Volksbund is thought of as a *großdeutsch* organization [built] on the broadest political, social, and all-German [*gesamtdeutsch*] basis."[39] Over the course of the Volksbund's existence, the Gau Rhineland-Westphalia and a number of chapters recorded an increase in Reich German participants.[40] Reich Germans even made up the majority of members in Gleiwitz (now Gliwice, Poland), while Sudeten Germans dominated the membership rolls in Gau Rhineland II.[41]

The defining feature of the Volksbund, however, was its ability to draw followers from across the political spectrum. Its members frequently promoted and extolled this point, advertising it as "the Anschluss organization above party politics [*überparteiliche*]."[42] At a time when political feuds proliferated, the Volksbund managed to bring together individuals who under other circumstances were staunch opponents. Indeed, members of almost every major party in Germany and Austria joined the organization. In Germany, participants hailed

---

37. "Gau Rheinland-Westfalen," *OeD*, June 1932, 14.

38. Hermann Kienzl, "Unser Erster Vorsitzender," *OeD*, January 1926, 1–2.

39. "Gau Rheinland-Westfalen: Vom Gau Vertreter in Berlin," *OeD*, July 1924, 25.

40. "Gau Rheinland-Westphalen [*sic*]," *OeD*, October 1924, 17–19, here 18; "Ortsgruppe Vorbeck," *OeD*, September 1925, 22; "Ortsgruppe Gelsenkirchen," *OeD*, May 1926, 22; "Ortsgruppe Marl," *OeD*, August 1926, 27; "Ortsgruppe Dörnberg," *OeD*, January 1929, 22; "Neue Ortsgruppe bei Wölfersheim bei Friedberg," *OeD*, December 1929, 19; "Ortsgruppe Ravensburg," *OeD*, July 1930, 24; "Neue Ortsgruppe Beuthen," *OeD*, September 1931, 15.

41. "Ortsgruppe Gleiwitz," *OeD*, March 1929, 23; "Mitteilungen," *OeD*, June 1930, 16.

42. Backside of Oesterreichisch-Deutscher Volksbund E.V., Berlin, November 1926, announcement of a talk titled "Paneuropa und Großdeutschland" by Viktor Mittermann, in PAAA, R73314. Also see Löbe and Dr.ing. Neubacher, *Die Oesterreichisch-Deutsche Anschlussbewegung* (Wurzen/Leipzig: Unikum Verlag, [1926]), 8.

from the SPD, the DDP, the Center Party, the DVP, and the DNVP (see appendix 1). Only the communists and, before 1933, the Nazis remained absent from the Volksbund's roster. Consequently, as late as July 1932, when political street fighting had become customary, the chairman of the chapter in Groß-Duisburg continued to press this issue, underlining "the necessity to cultivate the idea of the nonpartisanship [*Überparteilichkeit*] of the league and the Anschluss even now in a period ripped apart by party politics."[43]

Across the border, the Austrian side of the association also managed to unite people across the highly fractured political landscape. Individuals from the SDAP, the CSP, the GDVP, and the Landbund participated in the Volksbund (see appendix 2).[44] "For the first time," wrote the *Darmstädter Tagblatt* in 1925 about the founding of the Volksbund and Arbeitsgemeinschaft, "the three big Austrian parties—the Christian Socials, the Greater Germans, and the Social Democrats—have joined themselves together in a unified whole despite all the extraordinary antagonisms that exist among them in order to help fulfill the unanimous wish of their Volk."[45] Even as politics became more violent in Austria, the organization attempted to remain above party politics. In a 1930 advertisement for a talk by the socialist Karl Renner titled "The *Großdeutsch* Idea in the History of the German Nation," the local chapter in Graz stressed that the Volksbund was "a completely nonpartisan movement, which exclusively serves the Anschluss idea." While inviting all "friends of the Anschluss" to attend, the group tellingly felt the need to ask individuals "to appear without [party] emblems and in civilian clothes since the lecture is dedicated to the Anschluss idea and serves the common ambition of all German-Austrians regardless of party."[46] The fleeting ability of the Austrian Volksbund to include such a diverse group of people was due not only to the widespread support for an Anschluss in the rump state, but also to the fact that its leader, Hermann Neubacher, moved fluidly between the different sociopolitical camps. A man with German nationalist leanings, he maintained good contacts with socialists in the Viennese government because

---

43. "Ortsgruppe Groß-Duisburg," *OeD*, July 1932, 18.

44. The list of corporate members also illustrated the diverse viewpoints represented in the Austrian Volksbund, including groups that ranged from the Christlichsoziale Volksverband to the Republikanischer Schutzbund for Upper Austria to the German-Völkisch Gymnastics Association in Kleinmünchen. "Verzeichnis der dem Österreichisch-Deutschen Volksbund als Mitglieder angehörenden Körperschaften vom 1. Jaenner 1930 (Stand v. 1.I.1931)" in BKA, Zl. 20746 pn–9.II.1931, in ÖStA, AdR, BKA, AA, NPA, Kt. 289, Liasse Österreich 19/48, Bl. 219–230.

45. "Aus der Presse," *OeD*, September 1925, 11.

46. "Vom Oesterreichisch-Deutscher Volksbund," *Grazer Tagespost*, 20 June 1930, in WB, L121260, Bd. 26. See a similar ad in "Der 'Oesterreichisch-Deutscher Volksbund,' Landesgruppe Graz," *Arbeiterwille*, 20 November 1931, in WB, L121260, Bd. 31.

of his job with the Gemeinschaftliche Siedlungs- und Bauanstalt (Community Housing and Building Institute) until he became a Nazi activist in 1933.[47]

One consequence of the Volksbund's political diversity was that various social classes also became involved in the movement. In promoting its nonpartisan nature, the Volksbund publicized its social inclusiveness as well. The flyer announcing the creation of the Viennese Volksbund, for example, stated that it would "unite men and women of the most varied occupations regardless of party."[48] Although the Gau Rhineland-Westphalia was predominantly workers,[49] even its leadership included people from widely varied backgrounds. A government official, a member of the city theater, a painter, two salesmen, a master plumber, a master tailor, and four miners were among the members of the Gau's executive committee.[50] Likewise, events drew a cross-section of society. A general assembly in Berlin in March 1924 included "followers of many political party tendencies, members and friends of the Volksbund, men and women, Reich Germans and Austrians, intellectuals and individuals performing practical jobs, officials and workers," as did a host of other events in both countries.[51]

Just as the Volksbund spanned political and social divisions, so too did it draw members from different religious backgrounds. In Germany, where the Catholic minority had been labeled "enemies of the Reich" by Bismarck, Volksbund members stressed that anyone committed to the *großdeutsch* idea was welcome regardless of confession. "One is not first a Catholic or Protestant, but a German," Theodor Heuß, a member of the DDP and future president of West Germany, declared at a 1925 Volksbund rally in Vienna.[52] Even those without religious beliefs were admitted, as a homemade dirigible at a 1926 wine harvest festival in Buer-Hassel made clear. The five hundred attendees laid eyes upon a "zeppelin" that carried the following message: "Whether democrat, whether socialist,

47. Harry Ritter, "Hermann Neubacher and the Austrian *Anschluss* Movement, 1918–1940," *Central European History* 8, no. 4 (1975): 348–369.

48. "Abschrift! Oesterreichisch-Deutscher Volksbund, Kundgebung für den Anschluss an Deutschland," enclosed in Polizeidirektion in Wien, Pr.Zl.IV-2286/25 [stamped 14016 pn 20.VI.1925], Vienna, 19 June 1925, in ÖStA, AdR, BKA, AA, NPA, Kt. 84, Liasse Deutschland I/1, Bl. 754–755, here 755.

49. "Gau Rheinland-Westfalen," *OeD*, January 1924, 25; "Die Delegierten-Sitzung," *OeD*, June 1927, 17.

50. "Gau Rheinland-Westfalen," *OeD*, July 1925, 21–22.

51. "Oeffentliche Versammlung im Herrenhaus," *OeD*, April 1924, 19; "Ortsgruppe Breslau," *OeD*, July 1924, 25; "Ortsgruppe Gelsenkirchen," *OeD*, August 1924, 22; "Konstituierung der Ortsgruppe Linz des Oesterreichisch-Deutschen Volksbundes," untitled paper, 23 May 1926, in WB, L121260, Bd. 4, Fasz. III, Untermappe 6, 37; "Ortsgruppe Frankfurt a.M.," *OeD*, November 1927, 23–24; Report from the Deutsches Konsulat Innsbruck to the Auswärtige Amt, "Tirol für deutschoesterr. Zollunion," Innsbruck, 24 March 1930, Oe510, in PAAA, R73305; "Ortsgruppe Gleiwitz," *OeD*, November 1930, 23.

52. "Heims in Reich!," *BT*, 31 August 1925, in PAAA, R73310.

whether non-believer, whether Christian, join the Österreichisch-Deutscher Volksbund! The border posts between Vienna and Berlin must disappear!"[53]

More surprising was the fact that individuals with Jewish backgrounds were accepted into the ranks of the Volksbund. Given that many associations devoted to national causes included "Aryan paragraphs," the Volksbund was striking for its inclusiveness before 1933. The organization publicly listed Jews or people of Jewish heritage in its executive committee and corporate lists. They included Felix Behrend (a member of the DDP and a leader of the German Philologists' League), Georg Bernhard (a member of the DDP and the chief editor of the *Vossische Zeitung*), Richard Bernstein (the Austrian-born editor of the SPD's main newspaper, *Vorwärts*), Walther Bloch (an employee of the Berlin police presidium), Julius Deutsch (the head of the Republikanischer Schutzbund), Emil Faktor (the Prague-born chief editor of the *Berliner Börsen-Courier*), Stefan Großmann, Ludwig Haas (a member of the DDP and a leading figure in the Central Association of German Citizens of Jewish Faith), Rudolf Hilferding (an Austrian-born Reichstag delegate for the SPD and a Reich minister of finance), Leopold Jessner (the director of the Berlin State Theater), Alfred Klaar (a writer), Paul Nathan, Walter Prerauer (a director of the Deutsche Verkehrs-Kredit-Bank), Hugo Preuss (author of the Weimar Constitution and a member of the DDP), Adele Schreiber-Krieger (an Austrian-born Reichstag representative for the SPD), Friedrich Stampfer (a Moravian-born editor of *Vorwärts* and Reichstag representative from the SPD), Hedwig Wachenheim (an SPD delegate in the Prussian Landtag), Theodor Wolff (chief editor of the left liberal *Berliner Tageblatt*), and the Jewish Community of Salzburg (Israelitische Kultusgemeinde Salzburg).[54] The ability of these Jews to have a prominent profile in the association was due to the influence of republican politicians. As we have seen, republicans embraced an understanding of nationhood—even one extending beyond state borders—that was inclusive.

By opening its door to all members of society, the Volksbund succeeded in becoming a mass organization in Austria. As of 1931, the Austrian side of the association claimed to have 1.8 million members, nearly one-third of the country's total population.[55] Its journal, *Der Anschluss*, had a circulation of eight

---

53. "OG Buer-Hassel," *OeD*, November 1926, 30.

54. The names are found on executive committee lists (see appendices). The Jewish Community of Salzburg is listed in "Verzeichnis der dem Österreichisch-Deutschen Volksbund als Mitglieder angehörenden Körperschaften vom 1. Jaenner 1930 (Stand v. 1.I.1931)," in BKA, Zl. 20746 pn–9.II.1931, in ÖStA, AdR, BKA, AA, NPA, Kt. 289, Liasse Österreich 19/48, Bl. 213–231, here 223.

55. Ibid., 213–231. The Austrian half of the organization included corporate membership in its numbers, thereby inflating them.

thousand.[56] The German half of the Volksbund never rivaled the Austrians in attracting such widespread support, with historian Stanley Suval estimating a peak membership of 21,600.[57] Regardless of its numbers, the German organization was significant in that it not only attracted powerful public figures from an array of political and social backgrounds who served in its leadership ranks, but also drew large crowds to its rallies. On the surface, the Volksbund did appear to be an organization that could bridge sociopolitical divisions.

A Nation Divided

Although the Volksbund included Germans and Austrians from rival factions, it could not paper over the political, social, and cultural divisions plaguing both countries. Volksbund members praised their organization for its nonpartisanship while simultaneously bringing their own political views to their work within it. Moreover, observers of the movement interpreted the activities of the Volksbund according to their divergent political beliefs, as the opening vignette demonstrated. Indeed, the founding of the Volksbund in Vienna in June 1925 was not the sole instance of political feuds arising during an Anschluss event. A Volksbund rally a few months later in Vienna, this one including Reich German members, once again pointed to the tensions within and about the association. Occurring during a period of relative stability in both states, this second public rally in the Austrian capital serves to highlight further the uneasy relationship between a nonpartisan organization and its politically inclined members.

In late August 1925, only two months after the creation of the Viennese branch, between three and four hundred members of the German side of the Volksbund traveled to Austria for the first time to hold an Anschluss rally. A few weeks before the German contingent set off on its journey, a piece in *Oesterreich-Deutschland* explained that members of every major German party and social class would be among the participants. Given the diversity of the travelers, as well as the mission statement of the organization, the journal reminded its readers that emblems of a political nature—such as flags and uniforms—would not be allowed on the trip and that coarse behavior to other participants would lead to immediate expulsion without a refund.[58]

---

56. Report from the Deutsche Gesandtschaft to the Auswärtige Amt, "Österreichisch-Deutsche Arbeitsgemeinschaft und Österreichisch-Deutscher Volksbund," Vienna, 30 March 1931, in PAAA, R73315.

57. Suval, *Anschluss Question*, 30.

58. "Die Volksbund-Reise nach Wien," *OeD*, August 1925, 22.

Most of the German delegation first met in Passau, a German town on the border with Austria. To loud cheers, Löbe and Neubacher gave speeches declaring their wish that the legal boundary would soon disappear. The group next proceeded by train to Linz, where a jubilant crowd greeted the arrivals and listened to another round of speeches by Franz Langoth (a member of the GDVP), Josef Dametz (the socialist mayor of Linz), Löbe, and Rudolf Schetter (a Center Party delegate in the Reichstag). The rally ended with the singing of the "Deutsch-landlied," whereupon the German contingent boarded a ship decorated with black-red-gold flags to sail down the Danube to Vienna. Although heavy flooding prevented the ship from making prearranged stops along the way, crowds gathered along the shore to show their support. They cheered, waved handkerchiefs, and a few towns organized gun salutes to honor the passing vessel and consequently the Anschluss idea. Such a response demonstrated, according to the *Neue Freie Presse*, "how deep this idea is already anchored in the consciousness of the Volk."[59] Thousands gathered along bridges and the pier to welcome the ship when it arrived in Vienna. As the passengers disembarked, a band from the Republikanischer Schutzbund played and onlookers called out, "Cheers to Germany!" Both Löbe and Paul Speiser, a socialist city councilor in Vienna, spoke, once again underlining their desire for Austro-German unity.[60]

The main Anschluss rally took place the following day at the Viennese city hall, which was flying black-red-gold flags. Politicians from almost every major party in Germany and Austria proclaimed their support for an Anschluss. A number of them also used the opportunity to highlight the Anschluss movement's ability to bridge the fault lines running through German and Austrian societies. "Whether they stand on the right or left, they are all filled by the great thought that we all have to serve the *großdeutsch* idea," declared Viktor Mittermann, who at the time was a member of the GDVP. So many Anschluss enthusiasts turned out to hear Neubacher, Löbe, Mittermann, Schetter, Karl Leuthner (SDAP), Heinrich Engberding (DVP), Rudorff (DNVP), Heuß (DDP), Gasselich (Landbund), and Stolper that the room inside the city hall reserved for the event was too small. Despite heavy rain, thousands gathered before the Viennese landmark to listen to another round of speeches by prominent politicians, including Gasselich, Löbe, Körner, Schetter, Hoffmann, Mischler, Neubacher, and Speiser, as well as Georg

---

59. "Die Anschlußfahrt des Oesterreichisch-Deutschen Volksbundes," *NFP*, 30 August 1925, in WB, L121260, Bd. I, Fasz. I, Untermappe IVa, 32. For additional reports see "Der Besuch des Oesterreichisch-Deutschen Volksbundes," *NWT*, 30 August 1925, in WB, L121260, Bd. I, Fasz. I, Untermappe IVa, 34; "Der Empfang in Linz," *Tagblatt*, 1 September 1925, in WB, L121260, Fasz. I, Untermappe IVa, 86; "Die Reise nach Wien," *OeD*, October 1925, 2–5.

60. "Die Kundgebungen für den Anschluß an Deutschland," *AZ*, 30 August 1925, in WB, L121260, Bd. I, Fasz. I, Untermappe IVa, 39.

FIGURE 5. Scene in front of the Viennese city hall during the visit from the Reich members of the Volksbund in August 1925. "The mass gathering before the Viennese Rathaus," *OeD*, October 1925, 5. Courtesy of the Wienbibliothek im Rathaus.

Sparrer (DDP), Otto Nuschke (DDP), Heinz Strakele (Jungdemokraten), Josef Schober (SDAP), and Friedrich Austerlitz (SDAP). Once again, a cross-section of Austrian society was visible by their clothes: socialists stood next to right-wing fraternity members and workers stood alongside members of the middle classes. Both the rallies in front of and inside the city hall ended with the singing of "Deutschland, Deutschland über alles."[61]

At first glance, the Reich Germans' visit to Austria seemed to embody the lofty goals of the association. The Volksbund did facilitate cross-party collaboration; however, it could not overcome existing political rivalries or erase the enormous differences of opinion about the basis of a future *Großdeutschland*. Even before the rally was under way, the GDVP asked one of its representatives in the Volksbund to see if the events could be pushed back until a later date. The Greater German People's Party desired the delay because it was planning to hold a joint

---

61. "Große Kundgebung für den Anschluss in Deutschland," *NFP*, 31 August 1925, in WB, L121260, Bd. I, Fasz. I, Untermappe IVa, 54. Also see "Für den Anschluß," *Der Morgen*, 31 August 1925, in WB, L121260, Bd. I, Fasz. I, Untermappe IVa, 51. For film of the event see "Die Österreichische Anschlußbewegung," 1925, in WStLA, Filmarchiv der Media Wien, 016, http://mediawien-film.at/film/302/.

rally with the DNVP in Vienna during the fall. It did not want the Volksbund rally to preempt its own Anschluss event because it viewed the leaders of the Berlin Volksbund as its opponents. If the Volksbund rally were held in August, many members of the GDVP would be away on summer holiday, meaning that socialists and the "quite egregious Jews" at the head of the Berlin Volksbund would dominate the event.[62] Neither Jews nor socialists fit within the party's definition of the national community, and it wanted to ensure that these allegedly un-German groups did not claim the mantle of the Anschluss movement.

And, as with the founding rally a few months earlier, newspapers interpreted the event in line with their particular worldview. According to the conservative and right-wing press, the socialists and communists had tried to hijack the event. The *Reichspost* expressed disgust that the socialists disrupted the "Deutschland-lied" by singing "The Internationale," "La Marseillaise," and "We Swear by the Flag Pure Pure Red." Showing the usual tendency on the part of the political right to conflate the socialists and communists even though the leftist parties hated one another, the paper concluded that "the few non-Marxists left indignantly, having realized that it had less to do with an Anschluss rally for Germany than a rally for Soviet Russia."[63] The right-wing newspaper *Deutschösterreichische Tages-Zeitung* made similar claims, decrying the appearance of red carnations and symbols of the Reichsbanner, as well as some participants' use of party-specific slogans, such as "Cheers to German Social Democracy!" "Cheers to Red Vienna!" "Cheers to the International!" It also reported that the socialists were not alone in interrupting the singing of "Deutschland, Deutschland über alles." According to the publication, communists sang "The Internationale" and "La Marseillaise," while the socialists sang the "Lied der Arbeit," the anthem of the SDAP.[64] Police observers affirmed this description of events, adding that socialists sang the "Lied der Arbeit," and a smaller group of nationalists sang the "Stahlhelm Song" in response to the communists' rendition of "The Internationale."[65]

Newspapers affiliated with the Christian Social Party also objected to the attacks made on two of its most important figures, the priest Ignaz Seipel, who served as

---

62. Unsigned letter [sent from Piaristengasse 2] to Hubert Partisch, Vienna, 13 June 1925, in ÖStA, AdR, Parteiarchive, GDVP Allgemein, Kt. 41, RI-33a.

63. "An Deutschland oder Sowjetrußland?," *RP*, 31 August 1925, in WB, L121260, Bd. I, Fasz. I, Untermappe IVa, 58. Also see "Berliner Gäste in Wien," *RP*, 30 August 1925, and "Auseinanderführer," *RP*, 31 August 1925, both in WB, L121260, Bd. I, Fasz. I, Untermappe IVa, 35 and 57 respectively.

64. "Eine Anschlußkundgebung," *DöTZ*, 31 August 1925, in WB, L121260, Bd. I, Fasz. I, Untermappe IVa, 62; "Innere Politik: Ein Urteil über die Anschlußkundgebung des Volksbundes," *DöTZ*, in WB, L121260, Bd. I, Fasz. I, Untermappe IVa, 74.

65. Polizeidirektion Wien to the BKA-Abt. 13, Pr.Z.IV-3384/25, 30 August 1925, ÖStA, AdR, BKA, AA, NPA, Kt. 154, Liasse Deutschland 19/1, Bl. 30–32.

chancellor for much of the First Austrian Republic, and Heinrich Mataja, who was foreign minister at the time. There was no disagreement among the various political parties about whether the socialists had criticized the CSP. At least three socialist speakers, and one left liberal, used the rallies to condemn recent anti-Anschluss statements made by Seipel, as well as Mataja's foreign policy, which sought to draw Austria closer to Italy and other foreign opponents of an Anschluss. Much of the crowd was apparently socialist, as calls of "Boo Seipel" rang out in agreement.[66] For the Christian Socials, as well as others on the political right, these denunciations were simply more evidence that the socialists misused the Anschluss movement for their own party purposes. In the eyes of the political right, the Social Democrats were solely to blame for the politicization of the Volksbund.[67]

The socialists and left liberals bridled at these accusations. For one, they argued, the criticisms of the Christian Socials were accurate: Seipel had made anti-Anschluss statements at a recent gathering of Catholics in Düsseldorf, and Mataja was pursuing a foreign policy hostile to an Anschluss. And, they added, if any further evidence were needed to support their attacks, one had only to look at the number of Christian Social speakers at the rallies in Vienna. As the socialist and liberal press emphasized, Christian Socials, while members of the Volksbund, were conspicuously absent from the roster of speakers.[68] It was therefore not the political left that was hostile to the Anschluss idea, but the Christian Socials themselves. Pointing to the large crowd of ordinary workers in attendance at the rallies, the *Arbeiter-Zeitung* insisted, "Yesterday has proven more insistently than before that above all the working people of Vienna want the Anschluss. Only intentional lies are capable of still denying what announced itself so strikingly and so spontaneously."[69] These leftist newspapers also made no mention of socialists singing party songs; in their reports, the communists alone had caused disturbances.[70] Each of the political groupings therefore accused the other of politicizing the Anschluss movement in an attempt to undermine its opponents' legitimacy. Despite the endeavors of Volksbund members to put aside their differences, party politics pervaded the organization.

---

66. "Heim ins Reich," *BT*, 31 August 1925, in PAAA, R73310; "Vor dem Rathaus," *Wiener Sonn-und Montags-Zeitung*, 31 August 1925, in WB, L121260, Bd. I, Fasz. I, Untermappe IVa, 49.

67. "Auseinanderführer," *RP*, 31 August 1925, and "'Anschluß' und sozialdemokratische Parteiagitation," *Neuigkeits-Weltblatt*, 1 September 1925, both in WB, L121260, Bd. I, Fasz. I, Untermappe IVa, 57 and 70 respectively.

68. "Kampf für den Anschluss," *AZ*, 30 August 1925, and "Immer wieder Anschluß," *Der Abend*, 31 August 1925, both in WB, L121260, Bd. I, Fasz. I, Untermappe IVa, 38 and 64 respectively.

69. "Die Kundgebungen für den Anschluss an Deutschland," *AZ*, 30 August 1925, in WB, L121260, Bd. I, Fasz. I, Untermappe IVa, 39.

70. "Für den Anschluß," *Der Tag*, 31 August 1925, in WB, L121260, Bd. I, Fasz. I, Untermappe IVa, 60.

As the two rallies held in Vienna in 1925 demonstrate, political tensions developed within and about the Volksbund because of the fact that its members hailed from opposing political parties. When the question arose of whether it was possible to have an *überparteilich* organization whose participants had party affiliations, Volksbund leaders answered in the affirmative. "Nobody abandons one's party post with membership in the Volksbund," explained Löbe at a meeting of the executive committee in Berlin in November 1930. "Thereby one has been given the power, actually a particular duty, also to be active in one's own party for the purposes of the Anschluss."[71] According to the Volksbund's leadership, the inclusion of members from various parties was one way to spread the Anschluss idea to as many different sectors of society as possible. The problem for the Volksbund, however, was that information did not simply flow one way. While politicians brought the Anschluss idea to their constituencies, they also brought their political views and suspicions into the Volksbund.

Various political figures participated in (or protested) the Volksbund not only as a way to demonstrate a genuine commitment to the Anschluss idea, but also as a means to advance their own particular vision of what a Greater Germany should look like. When it came to the questions of the political basis of a future *Großdeutschland* and qualifications for membership in a transborder national community, the various political groups came up with radically divergent answers. Thus, the participants in the Volksbund all spoke about Anschluss, *Großdeutschland*, and the Volk, but they filled these ideas with different meanings. Once those involved in the Anschluss movement went beyond vague calls for "*ein Volk, ein Reich*" and tried to define what the Volk and Reich should look like, any sense that they had the same goals rapidly vanished.

From the beginning, individuals with republican sympathies were predominant in the Volksbund, especially in the Reich, and utilized it as a platform to impart their views of nation and state. Löbe served as president from 1921 until 1933. His fellow socialist Richart Mischler was the business director and later editor of *Oesterreich-Deutschland*. Preceding Mischler in the position of editor was Hermann Kienzl, who also served as a vice chairman and the first president of the organization. An Austrian-born theater critic and brother of the composer Wilhelm, Kienzl was not a card-carrying member of any party. His contemporaries, however, characterized him as "a German republican and upstanding democrat."[72] As the overseers of the journal's content, Mischler and Kienzl exerted a great deal of control over the German Volksbund's message. Rounding

---

71. "Ortsgruppe Berlin," *OeD*, January 1931, 19.
72. "Auf Seipels Befehl?," *AZ*, 9 August 1927, in WB, L121260, Bd. 10, Fasz. IV, Untermappe 12, 8.

out the high-ranking republican members of the Volksbund was Wilhelm Heile of the DDP, who also performed the duties of a vice chairman.

In addition to the outsize role played by republicans in the leadership of the Reich Volksbund, republican organizations were conspicuous participants in Volksbund activities. The Reichsbanner took part in a number of Volksbund events, ranging from the 1925 annual conference in Dortmund to a wine harvest festival for the chapter in Bottrop-Boy in 1929.[73] The Reichsbanner chose to participate in Volksbund activities because it provided the republican association with another forum to express its *großdeutsch* sentiments and because the Volksbund in Germany had republican leanings. This stance contrasted with the Reichsbanner's rejection of collaboration with the Verein für das Deutschtum im Ausland (VDA). "The VDA turns the ideas of the *großdeutsch* cultural community, which the Reichsbanner has taken into its care as the democratic-republican inheritance, into black-white-red, nationalistic, and pan-German [*alldeutsch*] ones," explained an article in the Reichsbanner's journal.[74] Although committed to the idea that a German national community did not end at the borders of the Reich, republicans were once again careful to distinguish their *großdeutsch* nationalism from their opponents' *alldeutsch* nationalism. Dominated by conservative and right-wing individuals, the VDA preached a form of transborder nationalism unacceptable to the Reichsbanner.

The Volksbund in Berlin also organized events alongside the Reichsbanner. In 1926, for example, the two groups held a joint *großdeutsch* rally, with Philipp

---

73. Other events included a 1925 rally in Gelsenkirchen, the 1926 Bundestag in Frankfurt, a 1927 rally orchestrated by the chapter in Hamborn, a 1927 exceptional meeting of the chapter in Gladbeck, a rally organized by the Gau Rhineland-Westphalia in 1927, the founding festival of the chapter in Osterfeld i.W., a lecture organized by the chapter in Meerbeck-Moers in 1928, the 1928 district day in Hamborn, a Volksbund celebration for the tenth anniversary of the declaration of the Austrian Republic in Meerbeck-Moers, flag dedication ceremonies of the chapters in Homberg-Hochheide and Rheinhausen in 1929, the tenth anniversary festival in Bottrop-Boy, an Anschluss rally held by the Gau Rhineland-Westphalia in Meerbeck-Moers, and a Walther von der Vogelweide commemoration in Würzburg in 1930. "Bundestag 1925 in Dortmund," *OeD*, June 1925, 22–23; "Ortsgruppe Gelsenkirchen," *OeD*, December 1925, 21; "Bundestagung des Oesterreich-Deutschen Volksbundes," *Gross-Frankfurter Volksstimme*, 15 June 1926, in WB, L121260, Bd. 4, Fasz. III, Untermappe 8, 31; "Ortsgruppe Hamborn," *OeD*, April 1927, 23; "Ortsgruppe Gladbeck," *OeD*, January 1927, 25–26; "Ortsgruppe Gladbeck," *OeD*, April 1927, 23; "Anschlußkundgebung in Gelsenkirchen," *OeD*, July 1927, 21–22; "Ortsgruppe Meerebeck-Mörs," *OeD*, June 1928, 17; "Anschlußkundgebung des Volksbundes in Hamborn," *OeD*, August 1928, 21; "Ortsgruppe Bottrop-Boy," *OeD*, August 1929, 23; "Ortsgruppe Homberg-Hochheide," *OeD*, October 1929, 18; "Ortsgruppe Bottrop-Boy," *OeD*, December 1929, 21; "Gau Rheinland-Westfalen," *OeD*, June 1930, 21; "Die Tagung des Oesterreichisch-Deutschen Volksbundes," *Neue Bayerische Landeszeitung*, 12 May 1930, in WB, L121260, Bd. 28.

74. "Mißbrauch des Auslandsdeutschtums," *DR*, 15 June 1926, 92. Also see "Verein für das Deutschtum im Ausland: Wie soll sich das Reichsbanner zum VDA stellen?," *DR*, 24 October 1931, 342.

Scheidemann speaking for the Reichsbanner, Wilhelm Heile for the Volksbund, and the socialist Paul Mielitz for the city of Berlin. Unsurprisingly, the rally was far from politically neutral. Following a march of the Reichsbanner, the event opened with a reading of the poem "Cheers to the Republic," and Mielitz remarked that "the majority of Berlin's citizenry is liberal- and republican-minded and actively takes part in the Anschluss movement."[75] That same year, on the occasion of a visit from the Viennese Freie Typographia, the working-class choral association for book printers, the two organizations greeted the Austrians, and various speakers called for a *großdeutsch* republic.[76]

The reverse was also true. Volksbund members took part in republican celebrations, such as a *großdeutsch* rally held by the Reichsbanner and the Cartel of Republican Students in Breslau in 1925, Anschluss rallies organized by the Reichsbanner in Hamborn and Bottrop-Boy in 1927, and the 1928 district celebration of the Reichsbanner in Herten.[77] When members of the Volksbund chapter in Ottmachau protested the Breslau group's attendance at the 1925 Reichsbanner rally on the grounds that it was a "danger to the party-political neutrality" of the Volksbund, the leaders of the district Silesia I disagreed. They argued that the Volksbund should take part in all *großdeutsch* rallies "regardless of which side organizes them" in order to spread Anschluss propaganda far and wide.[78] Although those in charge of this district stated their support for participation in the Anschluss rallies of any political organization, the leadership of the Reich Volksbund was less magnanimous in practice. In 1924, just a year before the defense of the Breslau chapter's participation in a Reichsbanner celebration, it concluded that the Volksbund could no longer associate with the Deutscher Schutzbund (German Protection League) because of the "preponderance of the political right" in that organization. Contact with such a group would harm the Volksbund's nonpartisan nature and make it difficult to uphold the belief that "*Großdeutschland* is a national cause, not a party cause," according to *Oesterreich-Deutschland*.[79] Acting from a favorable position within the German half of the Volksbund, republicans could afford to decide which political alliances to forge.

---

75. "Aus den Ortsvereinen: Berlin," *DR* (Gaubeilage Berlin-Brandenburg), 15 June 1926, o.S.

76. "Die Ankuft der Typographia in Berlin," *AZ*, 24 July 1926, and "Eine Anschlußkundgebung in Berlin," *Neue Zeitung*, 25 July 1926, both in WB, L121260, Bd. 4, Fasz. III, Untermappe 8, 37 and 39 respectively.

77. "Ortsgruppe Breslau," *OeD*, August 1925, 25–26, here 26; "Ortsgruppe Hamborn" and "Ortsgruppe Bottrop-Boy," *OeD*, June 1927, 23; "Ortsgruppe Herten," *OeD*, July 1928, 22–23.

78. "Ortsgruppe Breslau," *OeD*, August 1925, 25–26.

79. "Die Schutzbund-Tagung in Graz," *OeD*, July 1924, 9–10, here 9.

Fahnengruppe des Reichs-
banners und des öster-
reichisch-deutschen Volksbundes in Meerbeck
(Kreis Moers).

FIGURE 6. "Banner groups of the Reichsbanner and the Österreichisch-Deutscher Volksbund in Meerbeck (District Moers)," *Illustrierte Reichsbanner-Zeitung*, February 12, 1927, 100. Reproduced with permission of Verlag J. H. W. Dietz Nachf.

This is not to say that only republican organizations took part in the German side of the Volksbund. A number of patriotic associations and choral groups attended Volksbund events, ranging from the Sudetendeutscher Heimatbund (Sudeten German Homeland League) to the VDA to the Hindenburgbund (Hindenburg League).[80] It is also clear that not every chapter had a close relationship

---

80. For example, the Sudetendeutscher Heimatbund attended the 1925 Bundestag, the VDA joined in a flag consecration ceremony in Homberg-Hochheide in 1929, the Volksbund chapter in Wiesdorf elected to join the VDA, and the chapter in Dortmund worked closely with the youth wing of the Hindenburgbund and the VDA in 1932. "Bundestag 1925 in Dortmund," *OeD*, June 1925,

with republicans; on more than one occasion, local groups held activities on August 11, meaning that they did not celebrate Constitution Day.[81] Although republicans were not necessarily predominant in every part of the German side of the Volksbund, they were involved to a higher degree than the political right. Politicians from the right participated (see appendix 1), but their organizations tended to keep their distance. In contrast to the Reichsbanner and its numerous appearances at Volksbund activities, groups like the Stahlhelm were noticeably absent.

Joining the Reich republicans in their involvement in the Volksbund were the Austrian socialists. Although individuals with affinities for the political right occupied a number of the top positions in the Austrian half of the organization, Austrian socialists and their attendant associations were highly visible. Over thirty-five hundred Schutzbund men went to welcome the arrival of the Volksbund members from the Reich for the August 1925 rally in Vienna.[82] The band of the Schutzbund and the Freie Typographia performed at the departure of the German delegation from the Austrian capital.[83] Socialist groups were found alongside bourgeois ones in the corporate membership register for the Austrian Volksbund.[84] Moreover, the socialist-led Viennese municipal government donated 10,000 schillings a year to the organization.[85]

Owing to the preponderance of republicans in the Volksbund, republican ideas became pervasive at Volksbund rallies and in Volksbund publications. On multiple occasions, republican speakers left no doubt about their preferred political basis for a future *Großdeutschland*. At a 1925 rally in Dortmund, Austrian socialist Theodor Körner elicited an enthusiastic response when he ended his speech with "Cheers to the German republic," indicating that individuals with republican sympathies made up a sizable portion of the audience.[86] That same year, during the visit of Reich Volksbund members to Vienna, Paul Speiser of the SDAP talked about his desire to see "the entire free German Volk in a free

22–23; "Ortsgruppe Homberg-Hochheide," *OeD*, October 1929, 18; "Ortsgruppe Wiesdorf a.Rh.," *OeD*, December 1929, 21; "Ortsgruppe Dortmund-Stadt," *OeD*, December 1932, 16.

81. "Ortsgruppe Ravensburg" and "Ortsgruppe Gleiwitz," *OeD*, September 1929, 23–24; "Ortsgruppe Iserlohn," *OeD*, December 1929, 20.

82. "Die Volksbündler in Wien," *Volkszeitung*, 30 August 1925, in WB, L121260, Bd. I, Fasz. I, Untermappe IVa, 36.

83. "Der Abschiedsabend," *OeD*, October 1925, 16.

84. "Verzeichnis der dem Österreichisch-Deutsch Volksbund als Mitglieder angehörenden Körperschaften vom 1. Jaenner 1930 (Stand v. 1.I.1931)," in BKA, Zl. 20746 pn–9.II.1931, in ÖStA, AdR, BKA, AA, NPA, Kt. 289, Liasse Österreich 19/48, Bl. 213–231.

85. Ritter, "Hermann Neubacher," 354.

86. "Die Anschlußkundgebung in Dortmund," *BT*, o.D., in PAAA, R73310.

republic." Löbe echoed this sentiment by greeting the prospect of a "free great German republic of the future."[87]

The rally stages of the Volksbund and the pages of its publications also provided republicans another opportunity to advance their argument that only democracy could pave the way for an Anschluss. Löbe used the platform provided by the August 1925 rally in Vienna to proclaim, "This will to unification, to the centralization in a unified body politic, it is the fulfillment of the dream that the best of our Volk dreamed of one hundred years ago; it is the fulfillment of the wish that motivated the Frankfurt Parliament in 1848. It has been delayed by the particularist interests of the different German dynasties, but it cannot be delayed permanently where democracy rules, where the will of the Volk rules."[88] Or as Fritz Fay, the general secretary of the Deutscher Republikansicher Reichsbund (German Republican Reich Federation), explained at a 1927 lecture delivered to the Frankfurt chapter of the Volksbund, "The Weimar Constitution is the necessary prerequisite that we need for the creation of *Großdeutschland*."[89] Given this point of view, republicans within the Volksbund insisted that the association and its members must support the Weimar Constitution. At the yearly meeting of the Berlin chapter in 1925, Kienzl stated that the Volksbund was "a nonpartisan organization, but one that naturally stands on the legal basis of the constitution."[90] Notable, too, was the fact that Kienzl said this as he mourned the recently deceased Friedrich Ebert. This stance on the constitution and the fact that he spoke with reverence about the socialist Ebert were hardly politically neutral positions at the time. After all, as the debates about a national holiday in Germany demonstrated, the parties on the right found no cause for celebration in the Weimar Constitution. Moreover, in the months preceding his death, Ebert had been at the center of a libel trial in which a nationalist journalist accused him of treason for participating in munitions strikes during the First World War. For the political right, Ebert was no German patriot; rather, he was a contributor to the alleged stab-in-the-back of the German army, a claim opposed by Kienzl.

To further stress the close links between a democratic form of government and an Anschluss, republican members of the Volksbund launched attacks on their political opponents. According to republican logic, if democracy were the best political system to achieve an Anschluss, then those seeking to challenge it were undermining the possibilities for an Austro-German political union. Just as we

---

87. "Die Reise nach Wien," *OeD*, October 1925, 2–5.
88. "Massenversammlung und Anschlußkundgebung," *OeD*, October 1925, 5–7, here 6.
89. "Ortsgruppe Frankfurt a.M.," September 1927, *OeD*, 20.
90. "Ortsgruppe Berlin," *OeD*, April 1925, 21.

saw with the case of the Reichsbanner and the Schutzbund in chapter 4, Seipel and Mataja in particular aroused the ire of republicans in the Volksbund. At Volksbund events and in the pages of *Oesterreich-Deutschland*, prominent republican sympathizers condemned the anti-Anschluss stance of the two men and their allies.[91] On occasion, these criticisms were tempered by the acknowledgment that the CSP in the provinces took a position different from that of the federal leaders of the party. As Richard Bernstein recognized in an obituary for the Upper Austrian governor Johann Hauser printed in *Oesterreich-Deutschland*, "Hauser came into conflict with the party leader Prelate Seipel because of his open commitment to the republic and to the Anschluss with Germany."[92] Nonetheless, such praise for some Christian Socials was always offset with attacks on Seipel's circle.

The German political right was not entirely immune from republicans' condemnation, although criticisms in this regard were fewer. Following the election of Hindenburg to the Weimar presidency in 1925, for example, *Oesterreich-Deutschland* ran articles that said Wilhelm Marx, a leader of the Center Party and the republican candidate, would have been a better choice to accomplish an Austro-German union. Marx was more eager for an Anschluss than were Hindenburg and his fellow conservatives, one piece read. Another article, by Stefan Großmann, argued that Marx had a better chance than the Prussian Junker and general of achieving reconciliation with France, an act that would clear the way for the creation of a Greater Germany.[93] Articles in *Oesterreich-Deutschland* were also quick to condemn anti-Anschluss statements by conservatives. When the *Deutsche Allgemeine Zeitung*, the *Acht-Uhr-Abendblatt*, the *Reichspost*, the *Düsseldorfer Nachrichten*, the *Kreuz-Zeitung*, and Freikorps leader Hermann Ehrhardt spoke out against an Anschluss at various times, the Volksbund journal

---

91. "Politische Rundschau: Oesterreich," *OeD*, May 1925, 11; Hermann Kienzl, "Die Abberufung des Gesandten Riedl," *OeD*, June 1925, 7; "Die Bedeutung unseres Dortmunder Bundestages," *OeD*, June 1925, 1–4; "Bundestag 1925 in Dortmund," *OeD*, June 1925, 22–23; Hermann Kienzl, "Die Anschlußbewegung in Österreich," *OeD*, July 1925, 1–2; Gustav Stolper, "Herr Mataja und der 'Temps,'" *OeD*, September 1925, 4–5; Richart Mischler, "Die großdeutschen Tage von Wien," *OeD*, October 1925, 1–2; "Heim ins Reich," *BT*, 31 August 1925, in PAAA, R73310; "Intrigen des Seipel-Blattes," *OeD*, October 1925, 26; Richart Mischler, "Seipel in Berlin," *OeD*, March 1926, 1–2; Paul Löbe, "Der Stand der Anschlußfrage," *OeD*, July 1926, 1–4; Karl Heinz, "Hetze gegen Demokratie und Anschluß," *OeD*, December 1926, 13–14; "Dr. Deutsch gegen Dr. Seipel," *Morgen*, 14 June 1926, in WB, L121260, Bd. 4, Fasz. III, Untermappe 8, 7; "Ins Merkbuch," *OeD*, November 1927, 10. The socialist mayor of Graz, Vinzenz Muchitsch, even got thunderous applause for statements against the "Christian Social Heimatschutz movement." "Anschluß-Kundgebung," *OeD*, June 1930, 17.

92. Richard Bernstein, "Landeshauptmann Hauser," *OeD*, March 1927, 8. For more on the democratic views of the CSP in Upper Austria, see Bukey, *Hitler's Hometown*, chaps. 2–4.

93. Richart Mischler, "Die Reichspräsidenten-Wahl" and Stefan Großmann, "Frankreich und der Anschluß," *OeD*, May 1925, 4–7.

argued that they did not "understand the primitive demands of the German national feeling."[94]

Contrasting themselves with the hesitancy of conservatives, republican speakers at Volksbund events emphasized their fervent support for an Anschluss. Republicans within the Volksbund saw their involvement as a way to disprove the arguments made by the political right that they were un-German. In case their participation in the Volksbund was not evidence enough, republicans explained their deep national convictions in speeches and publications for the association. Noting that it "has often been made very difficult for workers and republicans to still feel German," Georg Schöpflin of the SPD used the 1926 Volksbund annual meeting to underline that, along with the Reichsbanner, "the working class holds fast to this idea [that people of the same language and culture belong together] and fosters confidence that Austria and Germany will become one."[95] Republicans thus used the Volksbund as another forum to brandish their national credentials, question the national commitment of their opponents, and defend democracy.

The preponderance of republican participants in the Volksbund and their openly political tracts prompted many on the political right to question how nonpartisan the organization really was. Among conservatives and the radical right, there was a widespread perception that the association was really a front for leftist politics. In a tempered fashion, the *Neues Grazer Tagblatt* explained that the Volksbund included all parties, but "it should not be denied that the Volksbund here and in the Reich have a certain leftist streak in common."[96] Consequently, conservatives and right-wing radicals grumbled that the socialists were guilty of politicizing the organization. Pointing to the appearance of the Reichsbanner and a "party speech" by the Austrian Social Democrat Paul Speiser at a Volksbund rally held during the 1930 Walther commemorations in Würzburg, the *Neue Bayerische Landeszeitung,* an anti-Semitic and agrarian newspaper, declared, "It is sad that here in Germany events can no longer proceed without a political coloring." It was, according to the paper, "crudity" to invite the residents of Würzburg

---

94. Quote from "Der Nationalist Ehrhardt," *OeD*, December 1927, 11. Also see Hans Erich Wolff, "Nach den Reichstagswahlen," *OeD*, December 1924, 8–10; "Intrigen des Seipel-Blattes," *OeD*, October 1925, 26; Hermann Kienzl, "Sauerwein und Kreuzzeitung," *OeD*, August 1927, 5–6.

95. "In der Paulskirche," *OeD*, July 1926, 22–23, here 23.

96. "Der 'Oesterreichisch-Deutsche Volksbund,'" *Neues Grazer Tagblatt*, 26 June 1925, in WB, L121260, Bd. 1, Fasz. I, Untermappe IV, 8. For other examples see statements by Heimwehr leader General Hülgerth and Vice Chancellor Johannes Schober. Report from Deutsches Konsulat Klagenfurt to the Deutsche Gesandtschaft Wien, "Tagung des Oesterreichisch-Deutsches Volksbundes u.a.," 23 June 1930, PAAA, R73315, IIOe1145/30; BKA, 20746 pn-9.II.1931, "Oesterr.-deutscher Volksbund-Beitritt d.H. Vizekanzlers Dr. Schober," in ÖStA, AdR, BKA, AA, NPA, Kt. 289, Liasse Oesterreich 19/48, Bl. 213.

to a "rally of the Volk" that was in reality a party rally.[97] Likewise, following the publication of an article in *Oesterreich-Deutschland* that claimed the SDAP was the only party supporting an Anschluss in Austria, the *Wiener Neueste Nachrichten* reprimanded the "Social Democratic–oriented employees of the journal" and reminded them of the "nonpartisanship of the Volksbund."[98]

Furthermore, there was the fact that the association's most prominent activist was the socialist Paul Löbe. Following his assumption of the Volksbund presidency, individuals on the political right told the Austrian ambassador in Berlin that "one would have rather seen a neutral personality instead of a Social Democrat represented at the head of the Volksbund."[99] The Austrian Nazis were far less diplomatic in their appraisal of Löbe. "It must fill every *völkisch* person with worry to see that the 'Österreichisch-Deutscher Volksbund' under the leadership of its chairman, the Social Democratic Reichstag president Paul Löbe, continually emerges as the leading advocate of the Anschluss idea in the Reich," wrote the *Deutschösterreichische Tages-Zeitung*.[100] Whereas Löbe did go on to earn the respect of many on the political right, the Nazi-affiliated publication labeled Löbe "an active leader in the stab in the back" who "smells of treason."[101] By associating Löbe with the "stab in the back" myth, the radical right insisted that the socialists, and by proxy the Volksbund, could not be leaders of a national movement.

In line with this assessment, many on the political right kept their distance from the Volksbund. Noting that most attendees at a 1921 summer festival in Berlin were workers, merchants, and members of the SPD or the DDP, the chargé d'affaires at the Austrian embassy in Berlin wrote that the "better circles" of the Austrian colony in the city stayed away.[102] Similarly, a German diplomat explained that "many supporters of the Anschluss from the political right kept their distance" from the August 1925 rally in Vienna "because the entire event appears to occur too obviously under the Social Democratic flag."[103] Viewing

---

97. "Die Tagung des Deutsch-Oesterr. Volksbundes," *Neue Bayerische Landeszeitung*, 12 May 1930, in WB, L121260, Bd. 28.

98. "Kritik vom Tage," *WNN*, 6 May 1927, in WB, L121260, Bd. 10, Fasz. 4, Untermappe 12, 21.

99. Report sent to the Bundesministerium fuer Äusseres Politische Sektion in Wien in 1921, "Generalversammlung des österreichisch-deutschen Volksbundes," Berlin, 6 April 1921, in ÖStA, AdR, BKA, AA, NPA, Kt. 107, Liasse Deutschland I/1, Anschlussfrage, 1145 pn-11.IV.1921, Bl. 101–105, here 102.

100. Reprinted in Dr. K.P., "Ortsgruppe Wien," *OeD*, October 1926, 23–25, here 25.

101. "Ein 'deutscher Führer,'" *DöTZ*, 29 January 1926, in WB, L121260, Bd. 4, Fasz. III, Untermappe 6, 1.

102. Report from the Geschäftsträger to the Bundesministerium für Äusseres Wien, Berlin, 27 June 1921, in ÖStA, AdR, BKA, AA, NPA, Kt. 84, Liasse Deutschland I/1, Anschlusskundgebungen 1921, Bl. 152–155.

103. Report from the Deutsche Gesandtschaft Wien to the Auswärtige Amt Berlin, "Der Besuch des Österreichisch-Deutschen Volksbundes," 31 August 1925, in PAAA, R73314, IIOe1356.

the Volksbund in Cologne as "much too much left-oriented in its makeup and also in its work," politicians from the DVP in that city elected to join the Arbeitsgemeinschaft following its creation of a local chapter in 1926.[104] The Christian Social circle around Seipel refused to attend the Rhine-Danube rally held in Vienna in May 1926 because of the Volksbund's close association with their political opponents, although the official excuse given by the government for its absence was its desire to adhere to the Treaty of Saint-Germain.[105] Even the Greater German People's Party in Styria was reluctant to dispatch a speaker to a 1928 Volksbund rally in Graz after it learned that only speakers from the SPD, the Center Party, and the DDP had been confirmed. The regional branch insisted that the Volksbund send members of the DNVP and the DVP so that it could avoid "a most embarrassing situation."[106]

At times, conservatives and the radical right instructed their followers to forgo Volksbund events altogether. The *Deutschösterreichische Tages-Zeitung* told its readers to avoid the Rhine-Danube rally because of the likelihood that the "poisonous Marxists" would try to cause trouble.[107] Causing a greater stir was the decision by Mataja to instruct members of the CSP to decline the invitation to a Volksbund-organized talk by fellow Catholic Richard Kuenzer, a member of the Center Party and editor of *Germania*. This action occurred during Mataja's 1926 campaign to drive a wedge between the Center Party and the Reichsbanner because of the Reichsbanner's association with the Schutzbund. In addition to seeing the Volksbund as aligned with his archenemies, Mataja was upset that Karl Lahm, a key figure in the Austrian Volksbund and the Viennese correspondent for the *Vossische Zeitung*, had written a scathing piece on financial corruption among CSP leaders involved in regional banks.[108] In the end, only Karl Gottfried Hugelmann and Karl Drexel, neither of whom was in Seipel's circle, attended the talk.

---

104. Report from the Österreichisches General Konsulat Köln, "Oesterr.-Deutscher Volksbund und Oesterr.-Deutsche Arbeitsgemeinschaft," 14 April 1926, in ÖStA, AdR, BKA, AA, NPA, Kt. 154, Liasse Deutschland I/1, 11.961/13–1926, Bl. 39–43. Because individuals from the BVP and DNVP had founded the Arbeitsgemeinschaft in Bavaria, it had more appeal for the political right than a leftist organization run out of Berlin. Winfried Garscha, *Die Deutsch-Oesterreichische Arbeitsgemeinschaft: Kontinuität und Wandel deutscher Anschlusspropaganda und Angleichungsbemühungen vor und nach der nationalsozialistischen "Machtergreifung"* (Wien: Geyer Edition, 1984), 104.

105. BKA, 13.147–13/1926, "Die 'Rhein-Donau'-Veranstaltung des Oesterreichisch-deutschen Volksbundes in Wien," in ÖStA, AdR, BKA, AA, NPA, Kt. 289, Liasse Österreich 19/48, Bl. 179–193.

106. Letter from the GDVP für die Steiermark to the Reichsparteiletung der GDVP, Graz, 16 July [1928], in ÖStA, AdR, Parteiarchive, GDVP Allgemein, Kt. 41, RI 33-a-34.

107. Quoted in "Eine imposante Anschlußkundgebung," *Der Montag mit dem Sport-Montag*, 17 May 1926, in WB, L121260, Bd. 4, Fasz. III, Untermappe 7, 14.

108. Report from the Deutsche Gesandtschaft Wien to the Auswärtige Amt Berlin, "Der Volksbund und die christlich-soziale Partei," 10 November 1926, in PAAA, R73314, IIOe1946.

As Hugelmann and Drexel's participation demonstrates, not all those on the right of the political spectrum eschewed the organization. Yet they tended to be outsiders in their parties. And even they expressed reservations about the political makeup of the Volksbund. For instance, in 1926, Richart Mischler wrote to Julius Deutsch that a schism had opened between the Berlin and Vienna branches of the Volksbund. In hopes of strengthening the political right's influence in the German half of the association, Hermann Neubacher made it known that he wanted Mischler removed from his position. The reason was Mischler's supposed switch from the "national camp" to the Social Democrats and the Reichsbanner, although, as Mischler noted, he had belonged to no party before joining the SPD.[109] Neubacher lent further credence to the criticisms of the Volksbund from the political right when he sought to distance the Austrian half of the organization from the Berlin one following an article in *Oesterreich-Deutschland* that accused the Austrian federal police of firing first during the July riots in 1927 and criticized Seipel's policies.[110] In a letter to the *Reichspost*, which had taken offense at the article, Neubacher claimed that he had no control over the Berlin publication and that the Austrian Volksbund had its own separate journal.[111]

The friction besetting the association stemmed from the fact that the daily political battles fought over the republics were also being waged about the shape a Greater Germany should take. Whereas republicans in the organization were quick to proclaim their desire for a *Großdeutschland* to be based on the Weimar Constitution, the conservative and nationalist members of the Volksbund were mostly silent about the political foundations of a Greater Germany. Only on rare occasions did Volksbund participants from the political right bring up the matter, and even then their statements tended to be vague. During a visit to a Volksbund gathering in Berlin in 1924, Hermann Kandl of the GDVP exclaimed, "We say: Happiness or misfortune—my fatherland! Republic or monarchy—my fatherland! North or south—everything, everything is my fatherland!"[112] Three years later at a general Volksbund meeting in Cologne, Hans Arthur von Kemnitz of the DNVP came to a similar conclusion. Stating that the "constitutional question would not be touched in this struggle [for an Anschluss]," he went on to explain that he "can imagine as an outcome a republic, but can also imagine that the Emperor's Bell [*Kaiserglocke*] in Cologne would sound one day for a

---

109. Reprinted in a letter from Karl Renner to Julius Deutsch, Vienna, 8 December 1926, in VGA, Parteiarchiv vor 1934, Mappe 35.

110. "Ein Vorstoß des Oesterreichisch-deutschen Volksbundes," *RP*, 5 August 1927, 2.

111. Neubacher's letter reprinted in "Ein Vorstoß des Oesterreichisch-deutschen Volksbundes," *RP*, 7 August 1927, in WB, L121260, Bd. 10, Fasz. IV, Untermappe 12, 7.

112. Hermann Kandl, "Oesterreich und die Anschlußbewegung," *OeD*, April 1924, 4–7, here 7.

großdeutsch emperor." Displeased with the mention of a monarchy, the apparently republican audience booed the latter part of this statement.[113] Even more unusual for the pre-1933 Volksbund was a pro-Nazi comment made by his fellow party man, Walter Hölscher. At a Volksbund rally in Klagenfurt in 1930, he declared that the "present time of corruption and conflict" would be replaced by "the Third German Reich . . . for which we live, for which we fight, and for which, if it should be necessary, we will die."[114] This reticence to speak about the future form of government for a united Germany was most likely due to the inability of the political right to agree on how to restructure Central Europe politically once the democratic republics were destroyed.

Beyond the divisions regarding the political basis of a Greater Germany, the criteria for membership in a *großdeutsch* nation became another lightning rod in the Volksbund. Jews and those of Jewish heritage were prominent members of the association, as the previous section demonstrated. Their ability to participate was due to republicans' dominance in the organization and expansive definition of a German Volk.[115] As other organizations, such as the Alpenverein (Alpine Club) and the Deutsche Studentenschaft (German Student Union), introduced so-called Aryan paragraphs to their statutes, the Reich German leaders of the Volksbund explicitly rejected the adoption of anti-Semitic principles. Allowing that some of its members were anti-Semites and that chapters with "Aryan paragraphs" might be permitted to join, Kienzl made clear that "an attempt to bring about anti-Semitic divisions in [the Volksbund's] ranks is never undertaken and would be nipped in the bud at a moment's notice."[116]

Just as republicans used the Volksbund to advance their claims about democracy, they also viewed the Volksbund as a way to construct a more inclusive Greater German national community. In championing Austrians' rights in Germany, republicans made it clear that they did not simply believe in a civic form of nationhood. "National belonging" (*Volkszugehörigkeit*) mattered more to them than "state belonging" (*Staatszugehörigkeit*).[117] At times, such a

---

113. "Eine Anschlußkundgebung in Köln," *Kölnische Zeitung*, 24 October 1927, in WB, L121260, Bd. 10, Fasz. IV, Untermappe 12, 54. The *Kaiserglocke*, which hung in the Cologne Cathedral, was a large bell created from French canons seized during the Franco-Prussian War of 1870–1871. Due to the material exigencies of the First World War, it was melted down in 1918.

114. "Oesterreichisch-deutsche Volksbundtagung in Klagenfurt," *Freie Stimmen*, 24 June 1930, in PAAA, R73315, IIOe1145/1930.

115. Also of note here is the fact that Stefan Großmann, one of the founders of the organization, was of Jewish heritage.

116. Hermann Kienzl, "Antisemitische Studenten und Großdeutschland," *OeD*, February 1927, 1–2, here 2. Also see "Sektion 'Donauland,'" *OeD*, August 1924, 15.

117. Richart Mischler, "Bilanz," *OeD*, June 1927, 1; Werner Stephan, "Das Reichstagswahlrecht der Deutsch-Oesterreicher," *OeD*, December 1928, 1.

belief led them to make racist statements, such as the objection by Carl Falck of the DDP to Austrians being treated like "the Australian outback Negroes [*Buschneger*], the Poles, the French, the Turks, the Chinese, and the Japanese."[118] Much of the time, however, republicans were quick to stress the openness of the concept of *Volkszugehörigkeit*. "If today no all-German [*gesamtdeutsch*] state community is yet possible, a great German national community [*grosse deutsche Volksgemeinschaft*] still is," wrote the German socialist Konrad Haenisch in an article reprinted in *Heim ins Reich*, the Volksbund journal preceding *Oesterreich-Deutschland*. "National community, most certainly not in the sense of a narrow-minded and bigoted racial fanaticism or a wild nationalist arrogance, but rather in the sense of a powerful union of all Germans through the great cultural community of everyone who feels German and thinks German that grows out of the cultivated soil of a common language."[119] Nor was he alone in expressing such a sentiment within the Volksbund, as other members also rejected a "racial political interpretation of the concept of 'German descent' [*Deutschstämmigkeit*]."[120] Once again, republicans used the idea of *Stamm* to create a national community that could be inclusive of Jews and immigrants, thereby mounting a direct challenge to the political right's notions about Germanness.[121]

Because of this embrace of Jews as Germans, the radical right maligned the Volksbund by labeling it Jewish. To underline its distaste for the Volksbund, the *Deutschösterreichische Tages-Zeitung* argued that party speeches by socialists and the appearance of the Schutzbund at the August 1925 rally in Vienna demonstrated "that a 'national cause' is not to be carried out together with the Jewish Marxist leaders."[122] Again, in February 1933, the same paper printed a letter to the editor that warned its Nazi readers against joining the Volksbund given its inclusion of Jews.[123] Volksbund members hailing from parties with anti-Semitic platforms were silent in public on this issue. However, as the letter from the GDVP regarding the rally in August 1925 shows, at least some members expressed their unease in private about appearing with Jews at Anschluss events.

---

118. C. Falck, "Doppelte Staatsangehörigkeit für Deutschösterreicher und Reichsdeutsche," *OeD*, January 1928, 1–2, here 1.

119. Konrad Haenisch, "Deutsche Volksgemeinschaft," *HiR*, 1 May 1922, 1–2, here 2.

120. "Ortsgruppe Berlin," *OeD*, April 1925, 21–22, here 22.

121. "Politische Gedanken eines Unpolitischen," *OeD*, July 1924, 4–8; "Ludo Hartmann," *OeD*, December 1924, 1–5; "Auch ein Anschlußredner," *OeD*, December 1925, 11; Richart Mischler, "Das Reichs- und Staatsangehörigkeitsgesetz," *OeD*, November 1926, 10–11.

122. "Eine Anschlußkundgebung," *DöTZ*, 31 August 1925, in WB, L121260, Bd. I, Fasz. I, Untermappe IVa, 62.

123. "Was man uns schreibt," *DöTZ*, 10 February 1933, in WB, L121260, Bd. 58.

Thus, while Mischler proclaimed at a 1926 gathering in Essen that Volksbund supporters were "first a German and then a party member," the organization was unable fully to overcome the divisions running through the two republics.[124] Avowing oneself to be a German before being a party member did not solve the intractable differences among the Anschluss supporters. After all, each of the political factions involved in the Volksbund understood in opposing ways what it meant to be German.

The Decline and Dissolution of the Volksbund

Political differences were not the only problems facing the Volksbund. A number of events colluded to hamper the organization in its work and to decrease the appeal of an Anschluss. During the early postwar years, the Volksbund had to contend with the consequences of the hyperinflation and the Belgian and French occupation of Germany's western border. The effects of the hyperinflation were immediately apparent. In the Gau Rhineland-Westphalia, for example, dues were raised to 1,500 marks in July 1923, 7,500 marks in August 1923, and 1.5 million marks in September 1923.[125] Needless to say, the destabilization of the currency caused a number of members to leave the association and created difficulties in producing and distributing *Heim ins Reich*.[126] Compounding the economic problems was the occupation of the Rhineland and Ruhr in 1923, during which the occupation authorities forbade the Volksbund from producing propaganda and even arrested twenty members of the chapter in Gladbeck.[127] The inability to organize events there until the departure of French and Belgian troops resulted in suppressed membership numbers. Once these crises subsided, the leaders of these local groups and the national organization were, as we have seen, able to reenergize the movement.

While the Volksbund weathered these early challenges, the turmoil beginning at the close of the decade greatly diminished the appeal of the group's main goal. The troubles began in Austria, where the economy remained unstable and the prospects of a civil war began to loom following the July riots in 1927. The German

---

124. "Heims in Reich!," *Sport-Anzeiger*, 31 May 1926, in WB, L121260, Bd. 4, Fasz. III, Unter-mappe 8, 1.

125. "Mitteilungen der Gauleitung des Gaues Rheinland-Westfalen," *HiR*, 1 July 1923, 8; Sellner, "An unsere Mitglieder!," *HiR*, 1 August 1923, 3; "Aus den Ortsgruppen: Bottrop-Eigen," *HiR*, 1 October 1923, 8.

126. "An unsere Mitglieder!," *HiR*, 1 February 1923, 3; "Mitteilung aus dem Gau Rheinl.-Westfalen," *HiR*, 1 April 1923, 3; "Gau Hessen und Hessen-Nassau," *HiR*, 1 October 1923, 6.

127. "Mitteilung aus dem Gau Rheinl.-Westfalen," *HiR*, 1 October 1923, 4.

consul in Klagenfurt, for example, reported that the founding of a chapter there in May 1929 had "run all too perfunctorily" and lacked popular enthusiasm. In part, he attributed this reaction to the "Carinthian Volk character," which was not easily excitable. Yet, in his view, the main cause was that "the inner party fights, the playing with fascist ideas, the economic hardships, etc. by far absorb the interests of the population."[128] Growing economic and political problems in Austria in turn caused Germans to worry that "the warring fronts would be spread from Austria over to Germany."[129] Austria's mounting difficulties prompted Reich citizens to question the idea of amalgamating the two countries.

Austria, of course, was not the only state suffering economically by 1930. Just as the hyperinflation of 1923 had prompted members to leave the organization, so too did the economic turmoil of the early 1930s. Despite the challenge of the Great Depression, some leaders of the Volksbund endeavored to remain optimistic. As late as the fall of 1932, the head of the Gau Rhineland-Westphalia insisted that "there are local chapters in which three-fourths of the members are unemployed. They nonetheless save up their pennies for the great Anschluss cause, which has become their belief and their promise."[130] The section of *Oesterreich-Deutschland* that contained reports from the local chapters painted a bleaker picture. While some groups continued staging activities, numerous others had to cancel events.[131] Adding to the Volksbund's problems with maintaining an active profile was a cut in government subsidies. The Reich Ministry of the Interior, which had been contributing 12,000 marks a year to the Volksbund, reduced its funding to 5,000 marks per year because of the economic crisis.[132]

The Great Depression also informed the foreign policies of the Austrian and German governments, which had the result of making an Anschluss seem even more distant. One of the biggest setbacks for the Anschluss movement was the decision by the International Court in The Hague to forbid an Austro-German customs union in 1931. With the Volksbund, and especially the republicans within it, hoping to accomplish an Anschluss by winning Western countries' approval, a peaceful path to Austro-German unity seemed closed off. At the October 1931 meeting of the executive committee in the Reich, Mischler explained that the "unhappy end of the Customs Union has made many members

128. Deutsches Konsulat Klagenfurt to the Auswärtige Amt Berlin, "Anschlusskundgebung in Klagenfurt," 27 May 1929, in PAAA, R73314, IIOe879.

129. "Kundgebung im Plenarsaal am 10. November," *OeD*, December 1929, 16–17, here 16.

130. "Bundestag 1932," *OeD*, December 1932, 14.

131. See the Mitteilungen sections in *OeD*.

132. Abschrift eines Schreibens des Pressattachés Dr. Erwin Wasserbäck, Berlin, vom 31. Oktober d.J., Zl. 5336, an Gesandten Ludwig, enclosed in BKA, Zl. 26322–13/pol., in ÖStA, BKA, AA, NPA, Kt. 154, Liasse Deutschland 19/1, Bl. 180.

waver."[133] In fact, a number of chapters—including those in Hamburg, Kiel, and Königsberg—folded.[134] This disillusionment with the Anschluss idea was only heightened following the Austrian government's acceptance of Western loans in the Lausanne Agreement of 1932. According to the deal, Austria would receive money in exchange for forsaking an Austro-German political union until 1952. In his annual report, Mischler noted that the Lausanne Agreement led to "the resignation of members, communities, and groups that have lost faith in the Anschluss cause."[135] The Volksbund was thus experiencing a dramatic decline as the possibilities for an Anschluss became more remote in the early 1930s.

It was in this climate that the Nazis entered the halls of power in January 1933, an event that radically transformed the politics of the Volksbund and hastened its end in Germany. Worried about declining membership and widespread pessimism about the possibilities of realizing an Anschluss, the organization quickly became a champion of the new Nazi government. By March 1933, a change in tone was noticeable. While maintaining that the organization was nonpartisan, speakers at Volksbund events began to praise Hitler and the so-called national revolution. At a general assembly held that month, the audience gave its spirited approval to the "hope that the new Reich government is able to use the far-reaching powers of the Enabling Act in order to advance our way to the *großdeutsch* state of the future and to prepare decisively for the merger of both German states."[136] Many members welcomed Hitler's dictatorial powers, for they hoped that the new regime, unlike the Weimar governments, would act with determination on the Anschluss issue. There was an additional reason that Volksbund activists thought that the change in Reich politics would reenergize their movement. As Ernst Bollmann, a cofounder of the Nazi Party in Duisburg, explained to the Meerbeck-Mörs chapter in April 1933, "The Führer of today's youthful Germany, Reich Chancellor Adolf Hitler, a born Austrian, fought in 1914 as a German soldier for Germany's honor and greatness. This fact justifies the hope that if the German Volk gets together in a great community, the day can no longer be far in which one sees a *großdeutsch* Reich."[137] After the disappointments accompanying the customs union project and the Lausanne Agreement, there was hope

---

133. "Sitzung des Hauptvorstandes am Freitag, den 30. Oktober, im Reichstag," *OeD*, November 1931, 15.

134. Abschrift eines Schreibens des Presseattachés Sektionsrates Dr. Erwin Wasserbäck to Gesandten Ludwig, Berlin, vom 31. October 1931, enclosed in BKA, 26322–13/pol., in ÖStA, AdR, BKA, AA, NPA, Kt. 154, Liasse Deutschland 19/1, Bl. 179.

135. "Bundestag 1932," *OeD*, December 1932, 14.

136. "Ortsgruppe Berlin," *OeD*, April 1933, 16; Erich Stückrath, "Neue Wege zum alten Ziel," *OeD*, April 1933, 1–3.

137. "Ortsgruppe Meerbeck-Mörs," *OeD*, May 1933, 18.

that Hitler could accomplish an Anschluss because of his Austrian roots, strong leadership, and rabid nationalism.

Bollmann's speech was noteworthy for another reason. Absent before 1933, Nazis suddenly began making frequent appearances at Volksbund events. As we have seen, the Nazis had previously rejected the group because of its inclusiveness. Following the appointment of Hitler, however, there was a noticeable change in Volksbund participants. Not only did Nazi Party members and ideas become fixtures of the Volksbund, but the republican members of the organization reduced their profile or quit the group altogether. The rightward slide of the Volksbund prompted its most prominent representative, Paul Löbe, to resign as chairman. Despite his obvious commitment to the German national cause, the Nazis increased their attacks on him. In particular, they took a statement made by Löbe out of context to cause him trouble. To fend off Nazi attacks on him as a "traitor" and "November criminal" and to point out that Nazi references to Austrians as "Galicians" (and not Germans) was insulting, Löbe referred to Hitler as "Adolf the Slovenian." The Nazis claimed this comment was further proof that Löbe was un-German. On the defensive, Löbe wrote a letter, reprinted in *Oesterreich-Deutschland*, explaining that he would never denigrate Austrians. After all, he had even supported granting Hitler German citizenship because of the Austrian's service in the German army.[138] Although *Oesterreich-Deutschland* stood by Löbe in its March 1933 issue, he gave up his leadership role in the Volksbund that same month. About a week before Hitler passed the Enabling Act—the moment historians label as the Nazi seizure of power—Löbe stated that he could no longer work with the various wings of the association, given the tense political relations. He did, however, retain his membership in the organization, an act decried by the editors at the *Arbeiter-Zeitung*. "In contrast to comrade Löbe, we are of the opinion that no Social Democrat can willingly remain in any organization with members of the other 'wing,' i.e. the Nazis," the Austrian socialists objected.[139] Their protest was unnecessary; by the April 1933 issue of *Oesterreich-Deutschland*, Löbe's name no longer even appeared on the executive committee list, although the names of a few other republicans and even a couple of individuals from Jewish backgrounds still did.[140]

With its leading socialist gone, the Volksbund pursued further avenues to align itself with the new political situation. To replace Löbe, the executive board voted Hans Arthur von Kemnitz of the DNVP as its new chairman. It also chose to demonstrate its "respect for today's government" by changing its flag and

---

138. "Löbe und Hitler," *OeD*, March 1933, 2–3.
139. "Löbe nicht mehr Volksbundvorsitzender," *AZ*, 18 March 1933, in WB, L121260, Bd. 59.
140. "Vorstandsliste des Österreichisch-Deutschen Volksbundes," *OeD*, April 1933, 17–18.

emblem. Originally containing the colors black-red-gold and red-white-red to reflect the flags of both the Weimar Republic and the Austrian republic, the Volksbund took away Germany's republican colors. In their stead, it substituted black-white-red, the old imperial colors that Reich President Hindenburg had begun to use again for official occasions. Explaining this decision to a meeting of the leadership of the Gau Rhineland-Westphalia, Mischler reminded members to "hold fast to nonpartisanship." The attendees agreed, but simultaneously undermined this position, for they also passed a resolution welcoming the new Nazi government.[141] As the changes in the Volksbund reveal, both individuals and voluntary associations were actively participating in the Nazi *Gleichschaltung*, a process whereby the new regime used a mixture of legislation, coercion, rewards, and terror to bring state and society under its control. In supporting the removal of black-red-gold from the Volksbund's symbols, Mischler, who had served as the chairman of the Reichsbanner Schwarz-Rot-Gold chapter in Potsdam, had decided fundamentally to alter his politics to go along with the Nazis.

Increasingly, Volksbund meetings included the phrase "Heil Hitler" and the singing of the "Horst-Wessel-Lied," the Nazi anthem for one of its members murdered by a communist in 1930. The most striking evidence of the Volksbund's shifting politics was the decision made in early September 1933 to modify the statutes of the organization.[142] "Every German of Aryan descent who avows himself to the *großdeutsch* idea can become a member regardless of citizenship," the revised membership clause read.[143] For an association that had once welcomed Jews in its ranks, the Volksbund had undertaken a complete transformation and now fully adopted Nazi beliefs about nationhood. Just as membership in the national community was contingent on "Aryan" blood for the Nazis, so too was membership in the Volksbund in September 1933.

However, before the new Nazified statutes could be introduced, four-fifths of the Volksbund executives voted to dissolve the association. Like so many other organizations at the time, the Volksbund leadership decided that different times called for different measures. In clarifying this decision, von Kemnitz stated that because of the disappearance of political parties—by July 1933, Germany was a one-party state—a politically neutral organization was no longer necessary. "The entire Volk has become for all intents and purposes a single party," he wrote in the final issue of *Oesterreich-Deutschland*, "and because of this, formations standing above party politics have lost their meaning." He then proceeded to criticize the former leftist leadership of the group for not fully

---

141. "Gau Rheinland-Westfalen," *OeD*, April 1933, 18.
142. On this shift see Mitteilungen sections in *OeD*, April–October 1933.
143. "Ortsgruppe Berlin," *OeD*, October 1933, 15.

avoiding party politics. Although the Volksbund's members felt sadness over the end of their organization, von Kemnitz told them to feel proud for accomplishing one of their goals. While no Anschluss had yet been accomplished, they could be gratified that the government would now actively pursue the issue of Austrian self-determination. "Long live the German Volk and the *großdeutsch* Third Reich," he enthusiastically concluded.[144] Yet this positive interpretation of the Volksbund's end in Germany did not tell the whole story. Despite the change in leadership and support for Hitler, the new regime refused to help the organization. Both Hitler and Hermann Goering declined to serve in honorary positions in the Volksbund, and the Reich Ministry of the Interior decided to no longer grant subsidies to the group given the organization's previous "Social Democratic" orientation and an alleged reticence toward *Gleichschaltung*.[145] Eight months after Hitler's appointment to chancellor, the fifteen-year-old organization ceased to exist, both because of pressure from the Nazi regime and the desire of the remaining Volksbund members to ingratiate themselves with Germany's new leaders.

Nonetheless, the association did continue its work in Austria, although its actions in the Austrofascist regime remain somewhat murky. Just as had happened in Germany, the organization fell into the hands of Nazi sympathizers in 1933. With Hitler's seizure of power in the Reich, the dynamics of the Anschluss movement completely changed in Austria as well. No longer was a political union going to occur with a democratic Germany, or even one that was increasingly authoritarian in the early 1930s. Rather, an Anschluss would entail joining a full-fledged dictatorship inspired by Nazi values.

For Austrian socialists, the shift in power in Germany was too much to bear. They had been willing to support an Anschluss even after Hindenburg, a symbol of Prussian militarism and the aristocracy, assumed the Weimar presidency in 1925. However, following the Nazi seizure of power, they qualified their position. While they maintained that "the Anschluss with a free and peaceful Germany remains our aim," they dropped the demand for an Anschluss from their party program in October 1933.[146] As a result of this action, they also resigned their membership in the Volksbund.[147] Just four months later, these onetime

---

144. Hans Arthur von Kemnitz, "Selbstauflösung des Österreichisch-Deutschen Volksbundes," *OeD*, October 1933, 1.

145. "Empfang beim Reichskanzler," *OeD*, May 1933, 18; Letter from the Preußische Minister des Innern to the Auswärtige Amt Berlin, Berlin, 2 June 1933, in PAAA, R73315, IIOe745.

146. "Oesterreichs staatliche Zukunft und die Sozialdemokratie," *AZ*, 13 May 1933, in VGA, Sacharchiv, Lade 1, Mappe 41, A.

147. "Austritt aus dem Oesterreichisch-Deutschen Volksbund," *Innsbrucker Volkszeitung*, 18 October 1933, in WB, L121260, Bd. 118.

champions of an Anschluss ceased to exist altogether, when the Austrofascists crushed and disbanded the socialist movement during the brief civil war of February 1934.

Even before the Austrofascists defeated the socialists, the regime had begun to crack down on the Nazis. Seeing the Nazi movement on their own territory as a threat to Austrian independence and consequently their own power, the Austrofascists declared the Nazi Party illegal in June 1933. The Austrofascists were thus openly hostile to an Austro-German union. Despite this changed political situation, the Volksbund in Austria continued to exist. Even with the dissolution of the socialists and the opposition of the Austrofascist regime to an Anschluss, the organization insisted that it remained "above party politics," despite having only one party supporting its goal. It also initially dispelled rumors that its leader, Hermann Neubacher, was a Nazi.[148] However, such murmurings were not untrue. Although he had been unaffiliated with any party in the 1920s, Neubacher expressed Nazi sentiments by the spring of 1932 and became involved informally with the Nazi movement a year later.[149] Given the Austrofascists' rejection of both an Anschluss and the Nazis, the Volksbund no longer held mass rallies. However, it did organize lectures by the likes of Neubacher and Seyss-Inquart, another Nazi sympathizer.[150] And while the Volksbund journal, *Der Anschluss*, stopped publication in August 1933, the organization helped to produce the Arbeitsgemeinschaft's *Deutsche Einheit* until Austrofascist authorities banned it in May 1935.[151]

---

148. "Zu den Mitteilungen des Ministers Dr. Schuschnigg," *NWT*, 7 July 1933, and "Eine Aktuelle Aufklärung," *RP*, 16 January 1935, both in WB, L121260, Bd. 118.

149. Although some press reports described Neubacher as a Nazi Party member, Harry Ritter contends that Neubacher was involved in the Nazi movement beginning in 1933 but was not a member until 1938. Ritter, "Hermann Neubacher." In April 1933, for example, Neubacher turned down an appointment by Dollfuss because of Dollfuss's oppression of the "national opposition," to which Neubacher declared loyalty despite having no official Nazi membership. "Großdeutschland lehnt Dollfuß ab," *Der Panther*, 29 April 1933, in WB, L121260, Bd. 118. According to another piece, Neubacher had gone over to the Nazis by May 1933. "Herr Neubacher belehrt den Bundeskanzler," *Die Stunde*, 4 May 1933, in WB, L121260, Bd. 118. Neubacher was also named as an NSDAP member in "Schuschnigg enthuellt," *Wiener Mittags-Zeitung*, 6 July 1933, and "Der Selbstmörder- und Mörderklub der Nazi," *Oesterreichisches Abendblatt*, 6 July 1933, both in WB, L121260, Bd. 118.

150. See the following articles in WB, L121260, Bd. 118: "Vortrag Professor Dr. Hassingers im Oesterreichisch-Deutschen Volksbund," *NFP*, 13 December 1933; "Vortrag Professor Eibls," *NFP*, 24 January 1934; "Das deutsche Volk in der Weltpolitik von heute," *NFP*, 28 February 1934; "Bardolff-Vortrag verboten," *WNN*, 6 June 1934; "Rechtsgrundlage der Friedensverträge," *WNN*, 25 October 1934; "Die Grundlagen der Rechtsentwicklung im deutschen Raum," *WNN*, 30 March 1935; "Vortrag Dr. Neubacher neuerlich verschoben," *WNN*, 1 May 1935; "Randbemerkungen," *Der Wiener Tag*, June 1937.

151. "Arische Zeitschriften," *Mitteilungen der Ortsgruppe "Jung Wien,"* 17 April 1935, and "Neubacher beruft," *Das Echo*, 31 May 1935, both in WB, L121260, Bd. 118.

Outed as a leading figure within the illegal Nazi movement in 1935, Neubacher was arrested and imprisoned in June, forcing him to renounce his leadership of the Volksbund.[152] The organization appeared to halt its activities following Neubacher's arrest. Surprisingly, the regime did not ban the Volksbund, despite the organization's goal of a union with Nazi Germany and widespread suspicion among Austrofascists that the organization was part of the Nazi underground.[153] Following a period of inactivity, the Volksbund issued new statutes in December 1936 that did not call directly for an Anschluss. Rather, the stated goal of the association was the "deepening of the cultural and economic connections between Austria and the German Reich." The toned-down language earned the approval of the Austrian authorities.[154] A plenary meeting held by the Volksbund in the summer of 1937 suggested new life in the organization.[155] Seyss-Inquart, who had recently been appointed to represent the "national opposition" (that is, the Nazis) in the Austrian cabinet, was now head of the association. He explained that membership was growing. With the founding of a new journal, *Die Warte*, and lectures, the leadership pledged to spread the organization's message.[156] The rebirth of the association was likely due to the July 1936 agreement between Hitler and Kurt Schuschnigg, the Austrofascist chancellor following the Austrian Nazis' murder of his predecessor, Engelbert Dollfuss. This agreement worked in Hitler's favor: Nazi political prisoners, Neubacher among them, would be amnestied, a select number of German newspapers would be allowed to circulate in Austria following an earlier ban, and Nazi symbols would be permitted again on certain occasions. Schuschnigg, on the other hand, gained little, aside from assurances that Austrian sovereignty would be respected. Following this agreement, the Volksbund at least nominally pledged its loyalty to the Austrian chancellor.[157]

While the Volksbund members assured Schuschnigg of their trustworthiness, those devoted to Austrofascism expressed their skepticism. The Volksbund was, according to the *Neuigkeits-Welt-Blatt*, a "thoroughly un-Austrian union . . . involved in all grudges and intrigues that were developed against true Austrians." It was a front for the Nazi movement, the newspaper argued. Any pledge of

---

152. Ritter, "Hermann Neubacher," 364–365.

153. "Politische Schattierungen," *Ö.Z. am Abend*, 22 June 1935, in WB, L121260, Bd. 118.

154. *Österreichisch-Deutscher Volksbund: Satzungen* (Vienna: Österreichisch-Deutscher Volksbund, [1936]), in WB, 115800A.

155. "Wieder 'Oesterreichisch-deutscher Volksbund,'" *Prager Presse*, 29 June 1937, in WB, L121260, Bd. 118.

156. "Oesterreichisch-Deutscher Volksbund," *Volkszeitung*, 27 June 1937, and "Vollversammlung des Oesterreichisch-Deutschen Volksbundes," *WNN*, 27 June 1937, both in WB, L121260, Bd. 118.

157. "Oesterreichisch-Deutscher Volksbund," *Volkszeitung*, 27 June 1937, in WB, L121260, Bd. 118.

loyalty was therefore suspect.[158] Others concurred, pointing out that the Volksbund had been revived to replace the newly disbanded Deutschsozialer Volksbund (German Social People's League), another organization that operated in
place of the illegal Nazi Party. One glance at the Volksbund's executive committee members affirmed this view. A number of known Nazi activists, including
Seyss-Inquart, Neubacher, Heinrich von Srbik, Ferdinand Kernmaier, and Ed-
mund Glaise-Horstenau, were in control of the association.[159] A "propaganda
trip" organized by the Volksbund to Munich in September 1937 to view the De-
generate Art and South German Folk Art exhibitions provided further proof. Although the Volksbund insisted that the excursion was apolitical, observers argued
that additional stops in Braunau am Inn, Hitler's birthplace, and Berchtesgaden,
Hitler's retreat, suggested otherwise.[160]

These skeptics were correct in their assessment of the Volksbund. After all,
the Volksbund's leader, Seyss-Inquart, was spearheading the Nazi attempts at a
"peaceful penetration" of the Austrian government.[161] In doing so, Seyss-Inquart
and other Austrian Nazis hoped to imitate Hitler's strategy of *Gleichschaltung*
from 1933. And, just six months following the Volksbund trip to Munich, the
Nazis did manage to seize power in Austria. Leading figures within the recon-
stituted Volksbund helped to orchestrate the takeover. Seyss-Inquart delivered
Hitler's ultimatum to Schuschnigg on March 11, 1938. Following Schuschnigg's
resignation and President Wilhelm Miklas's capitulation, Seyss-Inquart served as
the Nazi chancellor of Austria before its incorporation into the Reich a couple of
days later. Hermann Neubacher became the new Nazi mayor of Vienna. A number of other Volksbund participants became representatives in the *Großdeutscher*
and Nazi Reichstag. With its goal achieved, the leadership of the Volksbund dissolved the organization in a celebration held in May 1938.[162]

The Volksbund had undergone a dramatic transformation in its twenty-year
existence. From an organization once dominated by republicans, who sought to
achieve an Anschluss on the basis of the Weimar Constitution and welcomed Jews
as fellow Germans, the Volksbund had become a wholehearted supporter of Nazi

---

158. "'Wir lassen uns nicht hineinlegen!,'" *Neuigkeits-Welt-Blatt*, 29 June 1937, in WB, L121260,
Bd. 118.

159. "Oesterreichisch-Deutscher Volksbund," *Volkszeitung*, 27 June 1937, in WB, L121260,
Bd. 118.

160. "Wohin rollst du, Aepfelchen?," *Telegraf am Mittag*, 25 August 1937, and "Münchener Fahrt
des Österreichisch-Deutschen Volksbundes," *Innviertler Nachrichten*, 25 September 1937, both in
WB, L121260, Bd. 118.

161. Pauley, *Hitler and the Forgotten Nazis*, chaps. 11 and 12.

162. "Die letzte Vollversammlung des Oesterreichisch-Deutschen Volksbundes," *Die Warte*, August 1938, 12–14.

politics in 1933. That year marked a rupture in the association and demonstrated that there was no straight line from 1918 to 1938 with regard to the Anschluss movement or German nationalism more generally. It is true that some individuals involved in the Volksbund became adherents of Hitler. They included not only those already harboring radical nationalist beliefs, but even men like Mischler, who had apparently forsaken his earlier republican views. However, there were also a number of Volksbund members who opposed the Nazis' chauvinistic nationalism and dictatorial rule. In the wake of the Nazi seizure of power in Germany, republican members of the Volksbund not only retreated from public life, but also had to go into exile or suffer imprisonment in concentration camps because of their political beliefs or their Jewish heritage. Some of these former members of the Volksbund, including Richard Bernstein and Rudolf Hilferding, were even murdered by the regime.[163] In his speech to the final meeting of the Volksbund, Neubacher acknowledged the break in the organization's politics that had occurred with the Nazi seizure of power in 1933. Following the "turn" (*Wende*) in 1933, "the struggle of the Volksbund on a nonpartisan basis belongs henceforth to the honorable past," Neubacher told his audience. From that point forward "the German *völkisch*-minded seed of the Österreichisch-Deutscher Volksbund" understood that "there can only be one group that had the right to fight . . . : Adolf Hitler's National Socialist Party."[164] Although it was politically expedient for Neubacher to claim that the *Wende* in German political life also resulted in a *Wende* in the Volksbund, he was not incorrect in his observation. It was only after 1933 that the Nazis co-opted the Anschluss movement. Before that point, republicans were leading the fight to create a Greater Germany—one, however, that looked vastly different from the Greater Germany established in 1938.

---

163. Emil Faktor and Theodor Wolff also lost their lives at the hands of the regime. Carl Falck, Peter Graßmann, Benedikt Kautsky, Heinrich Krone, Paul Löbe, and Otto Nuschke were imprisoned in concentration camps. Wilhelm Abegg, Felix Behrend, Georg Bernhard, Walther Bloch, Robert Breuer, Julius Deutsch, Wilhelm Ellenbogen, Stefan Großmann, Leopold Jessner, Marie Juchacz, Adele Schreiber-Krieger, Friedrich Stampfer, Gustav Stolper, Hedwig Wachenheim, and Joseph Wirth fled the Third Reich. Hermann Dietrich, Anton Erkelenz, and Theodor Heuß fared better; they left public life although opposed the Nazis in various ways (despite the fact that Dietrich and Heuß voted in favor of the Enabling Act in 1933). On the complicated views of left liberals after 1933 see Eric Kurlander, *Living with Hitler: Liberal Democrats in the Third Reich* (New Haven, CT: Yale University Press, 2009), chaps. 4 and 5. As Kurlander points out, a number of left liberals, such as Heuß, were not necessarily against all Nazi foreign policy goals that aligned with their own aims from the Weimar period. Even then, many left liberals drew a distinction between a nationalism compatible with democratic principles and the aggressive, antidemocratic, and exclusionary nationalism of the Nazis. Others like Erkelenz, who had switched party affiliation to the SPD in 1930, remained resolutely opposed to Nazism, and a few former members of the DDP, such as Werner Stephan, worked for the regime.

164. "Die Ansprache des Obmannes Bürgermeister Dr.-Ing. Neubacher," *Die Warte*, August 1938, 12–14, here 14.

Conclusion

"No," lamented Otto Bauer from his Parisian exile in April 1938, "this is not the Anschluss for which the Austrian Volk fought in the years 1918 and 1919, not the voluntary integration of a German *Stamm* into the German Reich on the basis of freedom and free self-government; rather, it is the violent annexation of the Austrian country and Volk through the armed violence of the Third Reich!"[1] Of course, Bauer was not entirely accurate in how the Anschluss in March 1938 came to pass. The Nazis only had to use the threat of force to get the Austrofascist leaders to capitulate. Once the German army crossed over the Austrian border, not a shot was needed to accomplish the "reunification" of the two states. There was no outbreak of hostilities; instead, Austrians joyously greeted the news of the dissolution of the Austrofascist government. Across the country, Nazi flags quickly appeared on houses and government buildings, local police donned swastika armbands, the "Horst-Wessel-Lied" and the "Deutschlandlied" resounded, and torchlight parades spontaneously occurred throughout the night.[2] The most striking of these demonstrations was Hitler's appearance at the Heldenplatz in Vienna a few days later. Hundreds of thousands of Austrians gathered to catch a glimpse of the Führer. They let out a deafening roar when he proclaimed, "As

---

1. Heinrich Weber [Otto Bauer], "Oesterreichs Ende," *Der Kampf*, April 1938, in WB, TA, Anschluss March–December 1938.

2. For examples see "Der Einmarsch deutscher Truppen in Tirol," *Neueste Zeitung*, 12 March 1938, and "Freudenkundgebungen in den Bundesländern," *WNN*, 12 March 1938, both in WB, TA, Anschluss bis 15 March 1938.

the Führer and chancellor of the German nation and the Reich, I now announce before history the entry of my homeland into the German Reich."[3]

While Bauer ignored Austrians' enthusiastic reception of the representatives of the Third Reich, he was correct in his assessment that the long-desired Anschluss occurred in a way far different from what many people, especially republicans, had imagined in the Weimar era. The fact that Bauer, as a socialist and particularly as a Jew, would have faced immediate terror had he still been in Austria was a testament to these competing visions of Anschluss. In 1938, an Anschluss was the first step in the expansion of the Nazi dictatorship beyond the borders of the Reich. Immediately, Austria became a bastion of Nazi ideology and anti-Semitism. Austrians quickly turned on their Jewish neighbors, ransacking their homes and businesses, assaulting them, and taunting them while forcing them to scrub the streets. "The plight of the Jews in Austria is much worse than that of the Jews in Germany at the worst period there, for the fate of the latter came to them only over a period of years," concluded the *New York Times* correspondent stationed in the former rump state. "In Austria, overnight, Vienna's 290,000 Jews were made free game for mobs, despoiled of their property, deprived of police protection, ejected from employment and barred from sources of relief."[4]

Such scenes stood in direct opposition to the republicans' understanding of an Anschluss and ideas of nationhood in general. As we have seen, the republicans' Anschluss idea grew out of their endeavor to create their own form of nationalism that could be used to fend off the attacks made by the political right on the democratic republics and their supporters. To accomplish this feat, republicans posited a distinction between a nationalism based on the *großdeutsch* ideal and nationalisms rooted in the *alldeutsch* and *kleindeutsch* principles. *Alldeutsch* nationalism, in their eyes, was predicated on imperialism, militarism, and a narrow understanding of membership in the national community, the very ideas that triumphed in 1938. The supporters of a "Smaller Germany," as well as of Habsburg traditions, were particularists who prevented German unity both in the nineteenth century and the present, according to republicans. In contrast to these allegedly inferior forms of nationalism, *großdeutsch*

3. "Bollwerk der Nation," *Das Kleine Blatt*, 16 March 1938, 2. Also see film clip "One People, One Nation, One Leader!," 1938, in United States Holocaust Museum and Memorial, Ephemeral Films Project: National Socialism in Austria, EF-NS_031_OeFM, http://efilms.ushmm.org/film_player?movieID=31&movieSig=EF-NS_031_OeFM&movieSpeed=24.

4. G. E. R. Gedye, "Nazis' Terrorism in Austria Bared," *New York Times*, 3 April 1938, 1 and 36, here 36. For summaries of the 1938 Anschluss see Bukey, *Hitler's Austria*, chap. 2; Dieter Wagner and Gerhard Tomkowitz, *"Ein Volk, Ein Reich, Ein Führer!" Der Anschluß Österreichs 1938* (Munich, Piper & Co. Verlag, 1968).

nationalism was seen as the most authentic expression of the German Volk. The *großdeutsch* idea enabled republicans to fit themselves and their belief in democracy squarely into the history of the German national movement, as their narratives about the Frankfurt Parliament in 1848–1849 demonstrated. And whereas both the *alldeutsch* and *kleindeutsch* nationalisms excluded potential members of a German national community, republicans included not only Austrians, but also the very groups that the political right labeled as un-German: Jews, socialists, and democrats. Republicans hoped that their *großdeutsch* nationalism would enable them to prove their national credentials and legitimize the democratic republics that emerged after the First World War. Their vision of German unity thus diverged significantly from the national visions of the political right.

In spite of these disparate understandings of nationalism, the Nazis did manage to co-opt the support of individual republicans. Karl Renner, the other towering figure of the SDAP alongside Bauer, infamously came out in support of the Nazi-orchestrated Anschluss. On the eve of a referendum in April 1938 to affirm the already legalized union of the two countries, Renner told a reporter that he would vote in favor of "the reunification [*Wiedervereinigung*] of Austria with the German Reich," as well as Hitler's list of candidates for the new *Großdeutscher* Reichstag.[5] "Although not with those methods which I believe in," Renner explained, "the Anschluss is nonetheless accomplished," which brought the "sad interlude of half a century from 1866 to 1918" to a happy end.[6] Yet it would be a mistake to take such examples as proof of a direct line between the republican Anschluss movement during the Weimar period and Hitler's foreign policy. As historians Winson Chu, Jesse Kauffman, and Michael Meng have powerfully argued with regard to German intervention in Poland from the outbreak of World War I until the end of World War II, scholars need to avoid "creating a new type of *Sonderweg* [special path] that ascribes a kind of pathological expansionism or 'eliminationist anti-Slavism' to German culture." If they do not, then scholars run the risk of "obscur[ing] the more ambivalent, heterogeneous and complex history of German relations in and perceptions of eastern Europe."[7] The same could be said of the Anschluss movement after World War I, for as this book has illustrated, there were significant qualitative differences between republican and Nazi ideas about an Anschluss and nationalism.

---

5. These were the two items that people either voted yes or no for on the ballot. "Volksabstimmung 10. April 1938," in VGA, Sacharchiv, Lade 1, Mappe 88, C.

6. "Der frühere österreichische Staatskanzler Dr. Renner stimmt am 10. April mit 'Ja,'" *Kleiner Volks-Zeitung*, 3 April 1938, in WB, TA, Volksabstimmung 1938.

7. Chu, Kauffman, and Meng, "A *Sonderweg* through Eastern Europe?," 343.

Republican nationalism and involvement in the Anschluss movement were not simply the antecedents of Nazi expansionist and racial policies. For republicans, an Anschluss was not simply a first step in building "Hitler's Empire."[8] As participants in pacifist and pan-European movements, they asserted that a political union between Germany and Austria would foster not only peace, but also a united states of Europe. Moreover, they thought that it would strengthen the cause of democracy in German-speaking Central Europe. Bauer was therefore not the only republican dismayed by the turn of events in 1938. Reports from the socialist underground movement in Nazi Germany talked of "rancor" among workers and other segments of the population because "the same Western powers, which denied the [Weimar] republic a unification with Austria, have now once again given way before brutal violence."[9] And, as we saw in chapter 6, republicans involved in the Anschluss movement were persecuted by the Nazi regime. Drawing a direct connection between the republican and Nazi Anschluss ideas also ignores the fact that a political union between Germany and Austria did not rank highly on Hitler's list of foreign policy goals,[10] another distinction between the Third Reich and the Weimar-era republicans.

Furthermore, republicans' use of nationalism to legitimize democracy was not a symptom of a German "special path" that led to the Nazi seizure of power. That republicans would attempt to link nationalism and democracy should not be surprising in an era when "the right to national self-determination" became a watchword around the world.[11] Indeed, in their efforts to support the new republics, republicans argued that a democratic form of government was best suited to realizing the national principle. "Nationalism and democracy belong together; they herald the great idea of the united Volk that governs itself," explained Gerhard Anschütz, the rector of the University of Heidelberg and renowned legal scholar, in a defense of the republican constitution.[12] Republicans insisted that

---

8. For a reading of the history that views *großdeutsch* nationalism as a precursor to Nazi expansionism see Mazower, *Hitler's Empire*, esp. chap. 1.

9. *Deutschland-Berichte der Sozialdemokratischen Partei Deutschlands (SOPADE) 1934–1940: Fünfter Jahrgang 1938* (Frankfurt: Verlag Petra Nettelbeck and Zweitausendeins, 1980), 256. Also see pp. 262, 269, 280, 284.

10. Gerhard Weinberg, *Germany, Hitler and World War II* (Cambridge: Cambridge University Press, 1996), chap. 7. Weinberg points out that Hitler's main concerns revolved around rearmament, and he turned his attention to Austria only when he felt that the German army had been sufficiently rebuilt and the international situation was favorable. This chimes with the claim by Chu, Kauffman, and Meng that pragmatic concerns often took precedence over *völkisch* visions in Nazi Germany. Chu, Kauffman, and Meng, "*Sonderweg* through Eastern Europe?," 331–344.

11. Manela, *Wilsonian Moment*.

12. "Der Wert der Verfassung von Professor Dr. Gerhard Anschütz, Rektor der Universität Heidelberg," *VZ*, 14 August 1923, in BAB, R1501/116871, Bl. 138.

unlike the monarchies, which placed their own dynastic interests over the cause of German unity in the nineteenth century, a democratic republic could best create national unity because it was derived from the Volk (understood in both a national and civic sense). Nor were republicans in Germany and Austria the only supporters of democracy who understood their chosen form of government in national terms. Historians of interwar Czechoslovakia have likewise revealed that liberal politicians in that country, seen as the paragon of democracy in East Central Europe between the world wars, also viewed democracy through a national lens.[13] German and Austrian republicans were therefore not unique in connecting nationalism and democracy.

Similarly, we should not view republican *großdeutsch* nationalism as a manifestation of *völkisch* sentiment. Alongside the criteria of culture and choice, republicans did appeal to the concepts of *Stamm* (tribe) and blood when discussing their "brothers" in the neighboring country. However, these concepts did not necessarily herald an exclusionary and racist way of thinking; their meanings were flexible and ambiguous. Not only did republicans welcome Jews and foreign-language immigrants into this transborder national community, but Jews themselves also used such terminology when extolling the virtues of a *großdeutsch* nation. Given the complexities of national thinking during the Weimar era, this book has illustrated that it is impossible to develop a neat distinction between supposedly good civic nationalism and bad ethnic nationalism.

As we have seen, the guardians of the Weimar and First Austrian Republics were significantly able to use *großdeutsch* nationalism to mount a transnational defense of democracy and to mobilize supporters. Historians have thus far underestimated the significance of the *großdeutsch* idea to republican nationalism. However, the flag and anthem debates, the cross-border journeys of the Reichsbanner and Schutzbund, and republican participation in both the cultural commemorations and the activities of the Volksbund demonstrate that republicans spent a great deal of time and effort to bring the ideas of a *großdeutsch* nation and republic to life. Their endeavors achieved a measure of success as numerous ordinary individuals enthusiastically participated in these debates, rallies, and celebrations. Republican *großdeutsch* nationalism had an emotional resonance for socialists and liberals, the working class and the bourgeoisie, as well as Protestants, Catholics, and Jews alike. In allowing these diverse groups to participate in a national community that was compatible with a democratic and pluralistic society, *großdeutsch* nationalism was a critical aspect in republicans' energetic

13. Wingfield, *Flag Wars and Stone Saints*, chaps. 5–7; Zahra, *Kidnapped Souls*, chaps. 4 and 5; Orzoff, *Battle for the Castle*.

attempts to legitimize the embattled republics. It is true that republicans on both sides of the Austro-German border were never able to convince the political right that they were loyal Germans or that parliamentary democracy was a German form of government. However, their inability to do so does not mean that we should dismiss their attempts to create a democratic and peaceful *großdeutsch* nationalism. After all, the political right's refusal to accept republicans' national claims was due to fundamentally opposing visions of a German nation and state. The political right could never recognize the republicans' *großdeutsch* nationalism because it was based on democratic principles and practices, a broader understanding of membership in a German national community, and internationalism. By investigating republicans' intense commitment to craft their own form of nationalism, we can appreciate the depth of support for the democratic republics in both states after the First World War. Likewise, in recognizing the importance of the exchange of ideas and people across the Austro-German border to the republican defense of democracy, we can better grasp the complexities of German nationalism between the world wars. The triumph of Nazi ideas about politics and nationhood was, as the republican *großdeutsch* project shows, far from inevitable.

POLITICAL AFFILIATIONS OF EXECUTIVE BOARD MEMBERS OF THE VOLKSBUND IN GERMANY

Social Democratic Party of Germany and Its Sympathizers

Richard Bernstein (the Austrian-border editor of *Vorwärts*); Eduard David (a Reichstag representative and briefly Reich interior minister in 1919); Albert Falkenberg (a member of the Reichstag and chairman of the General Association of German Civil Servants [Allgemeiner Deutscher Beamtenbund]); Peter Graß-mann (a chairman of the General Federation of German Trade Unions [Allge-meiner Deutscher Gewerkschaftsbund]); Stefan Großmann (Austrian-born editor of *Das Tage-Buch*); Konrad Haenisch (Prussian minister of cultural affairs from 1919 to 1921); Rudolf Hilferding (an Austrian-born Reichstag delegate and Reich minister of finance in 1923 and from 1928 to 1929); Leopold Jessner (the director of the Berlin State Theater); Marie Juchacz (a member of the Reichstag); Alexander Knoll (a leader of the Allgemeiner Deutscher Gewerkschaftsbund); Paul Löbe (president of the Reichstag from 1920 to 1924 and 1925 to 1932); Rich-art Mischler (chairman of the Potsdam branch of the Reichsbanner); Hermann Müller (Reich chancellor in 1920 and from 1928 to 1930 and a Reichstag repre-sentative); Paul Nathan (founder of the Aid Association of German Jews [Hilfs-verein der deutschen Juden]); Gustav Radbruch (Reich minister of justice from 1921 to 1922 and 1923 and a Reichstag delegate); Johannes Sassenbach (a leader of the Allgemeiner Deutscher Gewerkschaftsbund); Wilhelm Schluchtmann (a delegate in the Prussian Landtag); Adele Schreiber-Krieger (an Austrian-born Reichstag representative); Carl Severing (a Reich minister of the interior from 1928 to 1930 and a Reichstag member); Hans Simons (a government councilor);

Friedrich Stampfer (Moravian-born editor of *Vorwärts* and a Reichstag representative); Hedwig Wachenheim (representative in the Prussian Landtag); and Hildegard Wegscheider (a representative in the Prussian Landtag)

German Democratic Party

Wilhelm Abegg (a state secretary in Prussia); Gertrud Bäumer (a Reichstag delegate); Felix Behrend (a leader of the German Philologists' League [Deutscher Philologenbund]); Georg Bernhard (chief editor of the *Vossische Zeitung*); Hermann Dietrich (a Reichstag delegate who also served in a number of ministerial roles in Baden and the Reich); Anton Erkelenz (a Reichstag representative who switched to SPD affiliation in 1930); Carl Falck (a director in the Reich Ministry of the Interior); Friedrich Fick (a factory owner and a Reichstag delegate); Günther Grzimek (a Prussian Landtag representative); Ludwig Haas (a Reichstag delegate); Konrad Hausmann (a Reichstag member); Wilhelm Heile (a Reichstag delegate); Theodor Heuß (a Reichstag member and leader of the Hochschule für Politik); Rosa Kempf (a representative in the Provisional National Assembly and the Bavarian Landtag); Werner Mahrholz (an editor at the *Vossische Zeitung*); Maximilian Müller-Jabusch (a writer for the *Berliner Tageblatt* and the *Vossische Zeitung*); Otto Nuschke (a member of the Prussian Landtag and editor of the *Berliner Volkszeitung*); Hugo Preuß (a Reich minister of the interior in 1919, a Reichstag delegate, and the author of the Weimar Constitution); and Theodor Wolff (chief editor of the *Berliner Tageblatt*)

Center Party

Constantin Fehrenbach (Reich chancellor from 1920 to 1921 and a Reichstag delegate); Heinrich Krone (a Reichstag member and leader of the Windhorstbund); Maximilian Pfeiffer (a Reichstag representative and ambassador to Austria); Felix Porsch (a vice president of the Prussian Landtag); Georg Schreiber (a member of the Reichstag); Christine Teusch (a Reichstag delegate); and Joseph Wirth (Reich chancellor from 1921 to 1922 and a Reichstag representative)

Partyless Republicans

Victor Hahn (editor of the *8-Uhr-Abendblatt*); Heinrich Herkner (a cofounder of the German Society for Sociology); Martin Hobohm (a professor and Reichsbanner member); Hermann Kienzl (Austrian-born writer and theater critic); Walther Nernst (a Nobel Prize winner in chemistry); and Edwin Redslob (the Reichskunstwart)

German People's Party

Theodor Bickes (a Reichstag delegate and leading figure in the Red Cross); Carl Cremer (a Reichstag member); Rudolf Heinze (Reich vice-chancellor from 1920 to 1921, Reich minister of justice from 1920 to 1923, and a Reichstag delegate); Fritz Klein (chief editor of the *Deutsche Allgemeine Zeitung*); Clara Mende (a Reichstag representative); Fritz Mittelmann (a Reichstag delegate); Heinrich Rippler (a Reichstag representative and the chief editor of the *Tägliche Rundschau*); and Georg Streiter (a Reichstag member and union leader)

German National People's Party

Hermann Dietrich (a Reichstag delegate); Otto Hötzsch (a Reichstag delegate and expert on Russia); Hans Arthur von Kemnitz (a Reichstag member who was in the DVP until 1924); and Hans-Erdmann von Lindeiner-Wildau (a Reichstag and Prussian Landtag member)

Partyless Conservatives

Richard Bahr (an editor at the *Berliner Neueste Nachrichten* and the *Tägliche Rundschau*); Friedrich Hupfeld (director of the German Togo Society); Ludwig Klitzsch (film magnate); and Bernhard Kumsteller (a cartographer)

Sources

"Vorstandsmitglieder des österreichisch-deutschen Volksbundes Vereinsjahr 1921," in ÖStA, AdR, BKA, AA, NPA, Kt. 107, Liasse Deutschland I/1, Bl. 105; "Aus dem Bunde," *HiR*, May 1922, 7; "Berliner Hauptvorstand," *OeD*, January 1924, 23; "Ortsgruppe Berlin," *OeD*, April 1924, 18–19; "Ortsgruppe Berlin," *OeD*, September 1925, 20–21; Österreichisch-Deutscher Volksbund "Vereinsjahr 1925 Hauptvorstand" and two different sheets titled "Hauptvorstand," all in PAAA, R73314; "Ortsgruppe Berlin," *OeD*, October 1926, 23; "Ortsgruppe Berlin," *OeD*, April 1927, 21–22; "Mitgliederversammlung," *OeD*, May 1928, 21–22; "Hauptvorstand," *OeD*, November 1928, 17–18; "Berichte der Gau- und Ortsgruppen," *OeD*, November 1931, 15; "Hauptvorstand des Österreichisch-Deutschen Volksbundes, E.V.," *OeD*, December 1932, 15–16

POLITICAL AFFILIATIONS OF EXECUTIVE BOARD MEMBERS OF THE VOLKSBUND IN AUSTRIA

Social Democratic Party of Austria

Julius Deutsch (state secretary of defense from 1919 to 1920, founder of the Republikanischer Schutzbund, and a Nationalrat representative); Wilhelm Ellenbogen (a member of the Nationalrat); Karl Heinz (general secretary of the Schutzbund and a member of the Nationalrat); Benedikt Kautsky (secretary of the Chamber for Workers and Employees); Ludwig Leser (provincial governor of Burgenland from 1922 to 1934); Robert Mehr (mayor of Linz from 1927 to 1929); Vinzenz Muchitsch (mayor of Graz from 1919 to 1934); Josef Pichler (a vice-mayor of Klagenfurt); Robert Preußler (a representative in the Salzburg Landtag); Josef Schober (a district representative in Vienna); Hugo Schulz (an editor of the *Arbeiter-Zeitung*); and Paul Speiser (a representative in the Bundesrat and Vienna city council)

German Nationalist Circles

Max Albegger (a delegate on the Graz city council); Wilhelm Bauer (a professor); Heinrich Bercht (mayor of Klagenfurt from 1926 to 1931); Hermann Neubacher (employee of the Community Housing and Building Institute [Gemeinschaftliche Siedlungs- und Bauanstalt]); Max Ott (mayor of Salzburg from 1912 to 1919 and 1927 to 1935); Hubert Partisch (a secondary-school director); Walter Pembaur (first vice-mayor of Innsbruck); Arthur Seyss-Inquart (a lawyer); and Alfred Walheim (a professor)

Landbund

Hubert Dewaty (a delegate in the Nationalrat); Anton Gasselich (a member of the Lower Austrian Landtag who was affiliated with the GDVP before 1923)

Christian Social Party

Hans Eibl (a professor); Christian Fischer (an editor in Graz); and Josef Preis (mayor of Salzburg from 1919 to 1927)

Partyless Left Liberals

Karl Brockhausen (a professor); Karl Lahm (the Vienna correspondent for the *Vossische Zeitung*); and Gustav Stolper (the editor of the *Österreichische Volkswirt*)

Sources

"Die Kundgebung der Ortsgruppe Wien," *OeD*, July 1925, 3–6, here 5–6; *Warum fordern wir den Anschluß?* (Vienna: Verlag Hölder/Pichler/Tempsky AG, 1926), 16 in PAAA, R73314, IIOe345; "Wiener Hauptvorstand," on a sheet by the Österreichisch-Deutscher Volksbund Berlin, "Hauptvorstand," in PAAA, R73314; Form letter from the Österreichisch-Deutscher Volksbund to Euer Hochwohlgeboren, Vienna, enclosed in BKA, Zl. 20746 pn-9.11.31, in ÖStA, AdR, BKA, AA, NPA, Kt. 289, Liasse Österreich 19/48, Rs. of Bl. 214; Letter from the Österreichisch-Deutscher Volksbund to the Vizekanzler und Bundesminister für auswärtigen Angelegenheiten, Bundeskanzler a.D. Johannes Schober, Vienna, 9 January 1931, in BKA, Zl. 20746 pn–9.II.1931, in ÖStA, AdR, BKA, AA, NPA, Kt. 289, Liasse Österreich 19/48, Bl. 216–218; "Was will der Österreichisch-Deutsche Volksbund," in VGA, Sacharchiv, Lade 1, Mappe 41

Bibliography

ARCHIVAL SOURCES

Germany

Archiv der Sozialdemokratie der Friedrich-Ebert-Stiftung, Bonn
  Nachlass Adolf Köster
  Nachlass Carl Severing
  Nachlass Franz Osterroth
  Nachlass Hermann Müller Franken
  Nachlass Willy Müller
  Reichsbanner Schwarz-Rot-Gold

Bundesarchiv Berlin
  R32   Reichskunstwart
  R43I/II   Neue Reichskanzlei
  R72   Stahlhelm Bund der Frontsoldaten
  R707   Vertretung der Reichsregierung in München
  R1501   Reichsministerium des Innern
  R8011   Deutsch-Österreichische Arbeitsgemeinschaft
  R8048   Alldeutscher Verband

Politisches Archiv des Auswärtigen Amts, Berlin
  R9005–R9013   Beziehungen Österreichs zu Deutschland, 1918–1920
  R9133–R9135   Die allgemeine österreichische Politik, 1918–1919
  R73285–R73309   Politische Beziehungen Österreichs zu Deutschland
                    (einschliesslich Anschlußfrage), 1920–1936
  R73310–R73311   Presseäußerungen zur Anschlußfrage, 1925–1933
  R73314–R73315   Deutsch-oesterreichischer Volksbund in Berlin und der
                    oesterreichisch-deutsche Volksbund in Wien
  R73372–R73384   Innere Politik in Österreich, 1920–1934
  R98311–R98326   Deutsche Flaggen, Nationalfeiertag, Nationalhymne

Austria

Archiv des Karl von Vogelsang-Instituts, Vienna
  Christlichsoziale Partei, Parlamentsklub, Anschluss

Archiv der Stadt Salzburg, Haus der Geschichte
  Gemeindesitzungsprotokolle

Österreichisches Staatsarchiv, Archiv der Republik, Vienna
  Bundeskanzleramt, Berichte der Wiener Polizeidirektion
  Bundeskanzleramt, Kabinettsratsprotokolle
  Bundeskanzleramt, Ministerratsprotokolle

Bundeskanzleramt, Staatsratsprotokolle
Bundesministerium für Heereswesen
Neues Politisches Archiv, Auswärtige Angelegenheiten
Neues Politisches Archiv, Präsidium
Parteiarchive, Großdeutsche Volkspartei
Präsidentschaftskanzlei

Österreichisches Staatsarchiv, Allgemeines Verwaltungsarchiv, Vienna
    Bundesministerium für Unterricht, Allgemein

Salzburger Landesarchiv
    Rehrl-Brief
    Rehrl-Politica

Steiermärkisches Landesarchiv, Graz
    Zeitgeschichtliche Versammlung
    L. Reg. 384 R 21/1928

Verein für die Geschichte der Arbeiterbewegung, Vienna
    Nachlass Theodor Körner
    Parteiarchiv vor 1934
    Parteistellen
    Sacharchiv

Wienbibliothek im Rathaus, Tagblattarchiv
    Anschluß
    Deutschland: Reichsbanner
    Nationalfeiertag (12. November)
    Nationalhymne 342.228
    Republikanischer Schutzbund
    Volksabstimmung 1938

Wienbibliothek im Rathaus
    C 276954   Zeitungsausschnitte zum Schubertgedenkjahr
    L121260   Österreichisch-Deutscher Volksbund in Wien, Anschlußpolitik
                  1925–1938, Zeitungsausschnittesammlung

Wiener Stadt und Landesarchiv
    Stenographisches Bericht über die öffentlichen Sitzung des Gemeinderates der
        Bundeshauptstadt Wien

NEWSPAPERS AND PERIODICALS

6-Uhr-Blatt des Grazer Volksblattes
Der Anschluss
Arbeiterwille
Arbeiter-Zeitung
Central-Verein-Zeitung
Festblätter für das 10. Deutsche Sängerbundesfest Wien 1928
Grazer Volksblatt
Heim ins Reich

Illustrierte Reichsbanner-Zeitung/Illustrierte Republikanische Zeitung
Das Kleine Blatt
Kreuz-Zeitung
Neue Freie Presse
New York Times
Der Notschrei
Oesterreich-Deutschland (Heim ins Reich)
Das Reichsbanner
Reichspost
Salzburger Chronik
Salzburger Volksblatt
Salzburger Wacht
Völkischer Beobachter
Vorwärts
Vossische Zeitung
Die Wahrheit
Wiener Neueste Nachrichten

PUBLISHED PRIMARY SOURCES

"Anschlusskundgebung im Ebert-Hof." 1929. StadtFilmWien. http://stadtfilm-wien.at/
    film/133/.
Bernstein, Eduard. *The Preconditions of Socialism.* Translated by Henry Tudor.
    Cambridge: Cambridge University Press, 1993. First published in 1899 as
    Voraussetzungen des Sozialismus und die Aufgaben der Sozialdemokratie.
Deutsche Einheit, Deutsche Freiheit: Gedenkbuch der Reichsregierung zum 10.
    Verfassungstag, 11. August 1929. Berlin: Zentralverlag, 1929.
Deutsches Beethovenfest zu Bonn 1927 anläßlich des 100. Todestages Ludwigs van
    Beethoven. Sonderabdruck aus dem Städtischen Verwaltungsbericht, 1927.
Deutschland-Berichte der Sozialdemokratischen Partei Deutschlands (SOPADE)
    1934–1940: Fünfter Jahrgang 1938. Frankfurt: Verlag Petra Nettelbeck and
    Zweitausendeins, 1980.
Deutschnationale Volkspartei. "Gegen den Marxismus und seine Schleppenträger!:
    Schwarz-weiß-rot gegen schwarz-rot-gelb!" [1924].
Exekutivkomitee der Feier. *Festbericht: Beethoven-Zentenarfeier, Wien 26. bis 31. März 1927,*
    Veranstaltet von Bund und Stadt, unter dem Ehrenschutz des Herrn Bundespräsidenten
    Dr. Michael Hainisch. Vienna: Otto Maass' Söhne, 1927.
German People's Party (DVP). "Program 1931." In *The Weimar Republic Sourcebook,*
    edited by Anton Kaes, Martin Jay, and Edward Dimendberg, 115–116. Berkeley:
    University of California Press, 1994.
Hitler, Adolf. *Mein Kampf.* Translated by Ralph Manheim. Boston: Houghton
    Mifflin, 1971.
Isherwood, Christopher. *Goodbye to Berlin.* London: Triad/Panther Books, 1977. First
    published in 1939 by Hogarth Press.
Jäger, Ernst. *Schwarz-Rot-Gold in der deutschen Geschichte: Kulturhistorischer Beitrag*
    zur Flaggenfrage. Berlin: Druck- und Verlagsgesellschaft Sawage and Co.
    [1925].
Löbe, Paul. "Österreichs Recht und die Weimarer Nationalversammlung." In
    Deutsche Einheit, Deutsche Freiheit: Gedenkbuch der Reichsregierung zum 10.
    Verfassungstag, 11. August 1929, 197–200. Berlin: Zentralverlag, 1929.

——. *Der Weg war lang: Erinnerungen.* 1949. Reprint, Berlin: arani-Verlag, 1990.

Löbe, Paul, and Hermann Neubacher. *Die Oesterreichisch-Deutsche Anschlussbewegung.* Wurzen: Unikum Verlag, undated.

"One People, One Nation, One Leader!" 1938. In United States Holocaust Museum and Memorial, Ephemeral Films Project: National Socialism in Austria, EF-NS_031_OeFM. http://efilms.ushmm.org/ film_player?movieID=31&movieSig=EF-NS_031_OeFM&movieSpeed=24.

"Die Österreichische Anschlußbewegung." 1925. In WStLA, Filmarchiv der Media Wien, 016. http://mediawien-film.at/film/302/.

Österreichisch-Deutscher Volksbund: Satzungen (Vienna: Österreichisch-Deutscher Volksbund, [1936]).

Preuss, Hugo. *Staat, Recht und Freiheit: Aus 40 Jahren deutscher Politik und Geschichte.* Tübingen: Verlag von J. C. B. Mohr, 1926.

Stenographische Protokolle über die Sitzungen der Konstituierenden Nationalversammlung der Republik Österreich. Vol. 1. Vienna: Österreichische Staatsdruckerei, 1919.

Stenographische Protokolle über die Sitzungen der Provisorischen Nationalversammlung für Deutschösterreich. Vol. 1. Vienna: Deutschösterreichische Staatsdruckerei, 1919.

Staatsgesetzblatt für den Staat Deutschösterreich. Jahrgang 1918. Vienna: Deutschösterreichischen Staatsdruckerei, 1918.

Treue, Wolfgang, ed. *Deutsche Parteiprogramme seit 1861.* Göttingen: Musterschmidt Verlag, 1954.

Valentin, Veit, and Ottfried Neubecker. *Die deutschen Farben.* Leipzig: Verlag von Quelle & Meyer, 1928.

SECONDARY SOURCES

Achilles, Manuela. "Re-forming the Reich: Symbolics of the Republican Nation in Weimar Germany." PhD diss., University of Michigan, 2005.

——. "With a Passion for Reason: Celebrating the Constitution in Weimar Germany." *Central European History* 43, no. 4 (2010): 666–689.

Ackerl, Isabella. "Thesen zu Demokratieverständnis, parlamentarischer Haltung und nationaler Frage bei der Großdeutschen Volkspartei." In *Das Parteienwesen Österreichs und Ungarns in der Zwischenkriegszeit*, edited by Anna Drabek, Richard Plaschka, and Helmut Rumpler, 147–156. Vienna: Verlag der Österreichischen Akadamie der Wissenschaften, 1990.

Anderson, Benedict. *Imagined Communities: Reflections on the Origin and Spread of Nationalism.* Rev. ed. London: Verso, 1991.

Anderson, Margaret Lavinia. *Practicing Democracy: Elections and Political Culture in Imperial Germany.* Princeton, NJ: Princeton University Press, 2000.

Andics, Hellmut. *Der Staat den keiner wollte: Österreich 1918–1938.* Vienna: Verlag Herder, 1962.

Applegate, Celia. "The Mediated Nation: Regions, Readers, and the German Past." In *Saxony in German History: Culture, Society, and Politics, 1830–1933*, edited by James Retallack, 33–50. Ann Arbor: University of Michigan Press, 2000.

——. *A Nation of Provincials: The German Idea of Heimat.* Berkeley: University of California Press, 1990.

——. "What Is German Music? Reflections on the Role of Art in the Creation of the Nation." *German Studies Review* 15 (Winter 1992): 21–32.

Applegate, Celia, and Pamela Potter. "Germans as the 'People of Music': Genealogy of an Identity." In *Music and German National Identity*, edited by Celia Applegate and Pamela Potter, 1–35. Chicago: University of Chicago Press, 2002.

Baumgartner, Gerhard. "Der nationale Differenzierungsprozess in den ländlichen Gemeinden des südlichen Burgenlandes." In *Vom Ethnos zur Nationalität: Der nationale Differenzierungsprozess am Beispiel ausgewählter Orte in Kärnten und im Burgenland*, edited by Andreas Moritsch, 93–155. Vienna: Verlag für Geschichte und Politik, 1991.

Behrenbeck, Sabine, and Alexander Nützenadel, eds. *Inszenierungen des Nationalstaats: Politische Feiern in Italien und Deutschland seit 1860/71*. Cologne: SH-Verlag, 2000.

Beller, Steven. "Kraus's Firework: State Consciousness Raising in the 1908 Jubilee Parade in Vienna and the Problem of Austrian Identity." In *Staging the Past: The Politics of Commemoration in Habsburg Central Europe, 1848 to the Present*, edited by Maria Bucur and Nancy Wingfield, 46–71. West Lafayette, IN: Purdue University Press, 2001.

——. *Vienna and the Jews, 1867–1938: A Cultural History*. Cambridge: Cambridge University Press, 1989.

Beneš, Jakub. "Socialist Popular Literature and the Czech-German Split in Austrian Social Democracy, 1890–1914." *Slavic Review* 72, no. 2 (2013): 327–351.

Bergen, Doris. "The Nazi Concept of 'Volksdeutsche' and the Exacerbation of Anti-Semitism in Eastern Europe, 1939–45." *Journal of Contemporary History* 29, no. 4 (1994): 569–582.

Bessel, Richard. "The Formation and Dissolution of a German National Electorate from Kaiserreich to Third Reich." In *Elections, Mass Politics, and Social Change in Modern Germany: New Perspectives*, edited by Larry Eugene Jones and James Retallack, 399–418. Cambridge: Cambridge University Press, 1992.

——. *Germany after the First World War*. Oxford: Clarendon Press, 1993.

Blackbourn, David. *History of Germany, 1780–1918: The Long Nineteenth Century*. 2nd ed. Oxford: Blackwell, 2003.

Boemeke, Manfred, Gerald Feldman, and Elisabeth Glaser, eds. *The Treaty of Versailles: A Reassessment after 75 Years*. Cambridge: Cambridge University Press, 1998.

Boyer, John. *Culture and Political Crisis in Vienna: Christian Socialism in Power, 1897–1918*. Chicago: University of Chicago Press, 1995.

——. *Karl Lueger (1844–1910): Christlichsoziale Politik als Beruf*. Wien: Böhlau Verlag, 2010.

——. "Silent War and Bitter Peace: The Revolution of 1918 in Austria." *Austrian History Yearbook* 34 (2003): 1–56.

——. "Some Reflections on the Problem of Austria, Germany, and Mitteleuropa." *Central European History* 22, no. 3/4 (1989): 301–315.

Brechenmacher, Thomas. "'Österreich steht außer Deutschland, aber es gehört zu Deutschland': Aspekte der Bewertung des Faktors Österreich in der deutschen Historiographie." In *Ungleiche Partner? Österreich und Deutschland in ihrer gegenseitigen Wahrnehmung: Historische Analysen und Vergleiche aus dem 19. und 20. Jahrhundert*, edited by Michael Gehler et al., 31–53. Stuttgart: Franz Steiner Verlag, 1996.

Brenner, Michael, and Derek Penslar, eds. *In Search of Jewish Community: Jewish Identities in Germany and Austria, 1918–1933*. Bloomington: Indiana University Press, 1998.

Breuilly, John. *Austria, Prussia and Germany, 1806–1871*. London: Longman, 2002.

Brix, Emil, and Hannes Stekl, eds. *Der Kampf um das Gedächtnis: Öffentliche Gedenktage in Mitteleuropa*. Vienna: Böhlau Verlag, 1997.

Brubaker, Rogers. *Citizenship and Nationhood in France and Germany*. Cambridge, MA: Harvard University Press, 1992.

——. *Ethnicity without Groups*. Cambridge, MA: Harvard University Press, 2004.

——. "In the Name of the Nation: Reflections on Nationalism and Patriotism." *Citizenship Studies* 8, no. 2 (2004): 115–127.

——. *Nationalism Reframed: Nationhood and the National Question in the New Europe*. Cambridge: Cambridge University Press, 1996.

Bruckmüller, Ernst. *The Austrian Nation: Cultural Consciousness and Socio-Political Processes*. Translated by Lowell Bangerter. Riverside, CA: Ariadne, 2003.

——. "Die Entwicklung des Österreichbewusstseins." In *Österreichische Nationalgeschichte nach 1945: Die Spiegel der Erinnerung: Die Sicht von innen*, edited by Robert Kriechbaumer, Vol. 1: 369–396. Vienna: Böhlau, 1998.

Bruendel, Steffen. *Volksgemeinschaft oder Volksstaat: Die "Ideen von 1914" und die Neuordnung Deutschlands im Ersten Weltkrieg*. Berlin: Akademie Verlag, 2003.

Brusniak, Friedhelm. "Der Deutsche Sängerbund und das 'deutsche Lied.'" In *Nationale Musik im 20. Jahrhundert: Kompositorische und soziokulturelle Akspekte der Musikgeschichte zwischen Ost- und Westeuropa*, edited by Helmut Loos and Stefan Keym, 409–421. Leipzig: Gudrun Schröder Verlag, 2004.

Bryden, Eric. "Heroes and Martyrs of the Republic: Reichsbanner Geschichtspolitik in Weimar Germany." *Central European History* 43, no. 4 (2010): 639–665.

——. "In Search of Founding Fathers: Republican Historical Narratives in Weimar Germany, 1918–1933." PhD diss., University of California–Davis, 2008.

Buchner, Bernd. *Um nationale und republikanische Identität: Die deutsche Sozialdemokratie und der Kampf um die politischen Symbole in der Weimarer Republik*. Bonn: Verlag J. H. W. Dietz Nachf., 2001.

Bucur, Maria, and Nancy Wingfield, eds. *Staging the Past: The Politics of Commemoration in Habsburg Central Europe, 1848 to the Present*. West Lafayette, IN: Purdue University Press, 2001.

Bukey, Evan Burr. *Hitler's Austria: Popular Sentiment in the Nazi Era, 1938–1945*. Chapel Hill: University of North Carolina Press, 2002.

——. *Hitler's Hometown: Linz, Austria 1908–1945*. Bloomington: Indiana University Press, 1986.

Bussenius, Daniel. "Eine ungeliebte Tradition: Die Weimarer Linke und die 48er Revolution 1918–1925." In *Der Griff nach der Deutungsmacht: Zur Geschichte der Geschichtspolitik in Deutschland*, edited by Heinrich August Winkler, 90–114. Göttingen: Wallstein, 2004.

Canning, Kathleen. "Class vs. Citizenship: Keywords in German History." *Central European History* 37, no. 2 (2004): 225–244.

Canning, Kathleen, Kerstin Barndt, and Kristin McGuire, eds. *Weimar Publics / Weimar Subjects: Rethinking the Political Culture of Germany in the 1920s*. New York: Berghahn Books, 2010.

Carsten, Francis. *Revolution in Central Europe, 1918–1919*. London: Temple Smith, 1972.

Chickering, Roger. *Imperial Germany and the Great War, 1914–1918*. Cambridge: Cambridge University Press, 1998.

——. *We Men Who Feel Most German: A Cultural Study of the Pan-German League, 1886–1914*. Boston: George Allen & Unwin, 1984.

Chu, Winson. *The German Minority in Interwar Poland*. Cambridge: Cambridge University Press, 2012.

Chu, Winson, Jesse Kauffman, and Michael Meng. "A *Sonderweg* through Eastern Europe? The Varieties of German Rule in Poland during the Two World Wars." *German History* 31, no. 3 (2013): 318–344.

Cohen, Gary. *The Politics of Ethnic Survival: Germans in Prague, 1861–1914.* 2nd ed. West Lafayette, IN: Purdue University Press, 2006.

——. "Reinventing Austrian and Central European History." *German Studies Association Newsletter* 33, no. 2 (2008–2009): 28–38.

Cole, Laurence. "Patriotic Celebrations in Late-Nineteenth- and Early-Twentieth-Century Tirol." In *Staging the Past: The Politics of Commemoration in Habsburg Central Europe, 1848 to the Present,* edited by Maria Bucur and Nancy Wingfield, 75–111. West Lafayette, IN: Purdue University Press, 2001.

Confino, Alon. *The Nation as a Local Metaphor: Württemberg, Imperial Germany, and National Memory, 1871–1918.* Chapel Hill: University of North Carolina Press, 1997.

Conrad, Sebastian. *Globalization and the Nation in Imperial Germany.* Translated by Sorcha O'Hagan. Cambridge: Cambridge University Press, 2010.

"Culture of Politics—Politics of Culture: New Perspectives on the Weimar Republic," Special Issue of *Central European History* 43, no. 4 (2010): 567–689.

Davis, Belinda. *Home Fires Burning: Food, Politics, and Everyday Life in World War I Berlin.* Chapel Hill: University of North Carolina Press, 2000.

Deak, John. "Ignaz Seipel (1876–1932): Founding Father of the Austrian Republic." In *Austrian Lives,* edited by Günter Bischof, Fritz Plasser, and Eva Maltschnig, 32–55. New Orleans: University of New Orleans Press, 2012.

Dennis, David. *Beethoven in German Politics, 1870–1989.* New Haven, CT: Yale University Press, 1996.

Diamant, Alfred. "Austrian Catholics and the First Republic, 1918–1934: A Study in Anti-Democratic Thought." *Western Political Quarterly* 10, no. 3 (1957): 603–633.

——. *Austrian Catholics and the First Republic: Democracy, Capitalism, and the Social Order, 1918–1934.* Princeton, NJ: Princeton University Press, 1960.

Düding, Dieter, Peter Friedemann, and Paul Münch, eds. *Öffentliche Festkultur: Politische Feste in Deutschland von der Aufklärung bis zum Ersten Weltkrieg.* Reinbeck: Rowohlt, 1988.

Duncan, Bruce. "Remembering Schiller: The Centenary of 1859." *Seminar: A Journal of Germanic Studies* 35, no. 1 (1999): 1–22.

Edmondson, C. Earl. *The Heimwehr and Austrian Politics, 1918–1936.* Athens: University of Georgia Press, 1978.

Eley, Geoff. *Forging Democracy: The History of the Left in Europe, 1850–2000.* Oxford: Oxford University Press, 2002.

——. *From Unification to Nazism: Reinterpreting the German Past.* Boston: George Allen & Unwin, 1986.

——. "Making a Place in the Nation: Meanings of 'Citizenship' in Wilhelmine Germany." In *Wilhelminism and Its Legacies: German Modernities, Imperialism, and the Meanings of Reform, 1890–1930,* edited by Geoff Eley and James Retallack, 16–33. New York: Berghahn Books, 2003.

Eley, Geoff, and Jan Palmowski, eds. *Citizenship and National Identity in Twentieth-Century Germany.* Stanford, CA: Stanford University Press, 2008.

Erdmann, Karl Dietrich. *Die Spur Österreichs in der deutschen Geschichte: Drei Staaten, zwei Nationen, ein Volk?* Zurich: Manesse–Verlag, 1989.

Evans, Ellen Lovell. *The German Center Party: A Study in Political Catholicism, 1870–1933.* Carbondale: Southern Illinois University Press, 1981.

Evans, Robert, Tara Zahra, Nancy Wingfield, and Mark Cornwall. "Forum: Habsburg History." *German History* 31, no. 2 (2013): 225–238.

Fellner, Fritz. "Die Historiographie zur österreichisch-deutschen Problematik als Spiegel der nationalpolitischen Diskussion." In *Österreich und die deutsche Frage im 19. und 20. Jahrhundert: Probleme der politisch-staatlichen und soziokulturellen Differenzierung im deutschen Mitteleuropa*, edited by Heinrich Lutz and Helmut Rumpler, 33–59. Munich: R. Oldenbourg Verlag, 1982.

——. "The Problem of the Austrian Nation after 1945." *Journal of Modern History* 60, no. 2 (1988): 264–289.

Föllmer, Moritz. "The Problem of National Solidarity in Interwar Germany." *German History* 23, no. 2 (2005): 202–231.

Föllmer, Moritz, Rüdiger Graf, and Per Leo. "Einleitung: Die Kultur der Krise in der Weimarer Republik." In *Die "Krise" der Weimarer Republik: Zur Kritik eines Deutungsmusters*, edited by Moritz Föllmer, Rüdiger Graf, and Per Leo, 9–41. Frankfurt am Main: Campus Verlag, 2005.

Friedel, Alois. *Deutsche Staatssymbole: Herkunft und Bedeutung der politischen Symbolik in Deutschland*. Frankfurt am Main: Anthenäum Verlag, 1968.

Friedländer, Saul. *Nazi Germany and the Jews: The Years of Persecution, 1933–1939*. New York: HarperCollins, 1997.

Friedrich, Karin, ed. *Festive Culture in Germany and Europe from the Sixteenth to the Twentieth Century*. Lewiston, NY: Edwin Mellen, 2000.

Fritz, Stephen. "The Search for Volksgemeinschaft: Gustav Stresemann and the Baden DVP, 1926–1930." *German Studies Review* 7, no. 2 (1984): 249–280.

Fritzsche, Peter. "Did Weimar Fail?" *Journal of Modern History* 68, no. 3 (1996): 629–656.

——. *Germans into Nazis*. Cambridge, MA: Harvard University Press, 1998.

Früh, Eckart. "Gott erhalte? Gott bewahre! Zur Geschichte der österreichischen Hymnen und des Nationalbewußtseins zwischen 1918 und 1938." *Österreich in Geschichte und Literatur mit Geographie* 32, no. 5 (1988): 280–315.

Gay, Peter. *Weimar Culture: The Outsider as Insider*. New York: Harper Torchbooks, 1968.

Gerwarth, Robert. "The Past in Weimar History." *Contemporary European History* 15, no. 1 (2006): 1–22.

Gillis, John, ed. *Commemorations: The Politics of National Identity*. Princeton, NJ: Princeton University Press, 1994.

Gosewinkel, Dieter. *Einbürgern und Ausschließen: Die Nationalisierung der Staatsangehörigkeit vom Deutschen Bund bis zur Bundesrepublik Deutschland*. Göttingen: Vandenhoeck and Ruprecht, 2001.

Graf, Rüdiger. *Die Zukunft der Weimarer Republik: Krisen und Zukunftsaneignungen in Deutschland, 1918–1933*. Munich: R. Oldenbourg Verlag, 2008.

Grandner, Margarete, Gernot Heiss, and Oliver Rathkolb. "Österreich und seine deutsche Identität. Bemerkungen zu Harry Ritters Aufsatz 'Austria and the Struggle for German Identity.'" *German Studies Review* 16, no. 3 1993: 515–520.

Grasberger, Franz. *Die Hymnen Österreichs*. Tutzing: H. Schneider, 1968.

Green, Abigail. *Fatherlands: State-Building and Nationhood in Nineteenth-Century Germany*. Cambridge: Cambridge University Press, 2001.

Greenfeld, Liah. *Nationalism: Five Roads to Modernity*. Cambridge, MA: Harvard University Press, 1992.

Groh, Dieter, and Peter Brandt. *"Vaterlandslose Gesellen": Sozialdemokratie, 1860–1990*. Munich: Verlag C. H. Beck, 1992.

Guettel, Jens-Uwe. "The Myth of the Pro-Colonialist SPD: German Social Democracy and Imperialism before World War I." *Central European History* 45, no. 3 (2012): 452–484.

Haas, Hanns. "Otto Bauer und der Anschluß 1918/1919." In *Sozialdemokratie und "Anschluß": Historische Wurzeln, Anschluß 1918 und 1938, Nachwirkungen*, edited by Helmut Konrad, 36–44. Vienna: Europaverlag, 1978.

——. "Staats- und Landesbewußtsein in der Ersten Republik." In *Handbuch des politischen Systems Österreichs: Erste Republik, 1918–1933*, edited by Emmerich Tálos et al., 472–487. Vienna: Manz Verlag, 1995.

Hanisch, Ernst. "Das Fest in der fragmentierten politischen Kultur: Der österreichische Staatsfeiertag während der Ersten Republik." In *Politische Teilkulturen zwischen Integration und Polarisierung: zur politischen Kultur in der Weimarer Republik*, edited by Detlef Lehnert and Klaus Megerle, 43–60. Opladen: Westdeutscher Verlag, 1990.

——. *Der Grosse Illusionist: Otto Bauer, 1881–1938*. Vienna: Böhlau Verlag, 2011.

——. *Der lange Schatten des Staates: Österreichische Gesellschaftsgeschichte im 20. Jahrhundert*. Österreichische Geschichte. Edited by Herwig Wolfram. Vienna: Verlag Carl Ueberreuter, 1994.

——. "Politische Symbole und Gedächtnisorte." In *Handbuch des politischen Systems Österreichs: Erste Republik, 1918–1933*, edited by Emmerich Tálos et al., 421–430. Vienna: Manz Verlag, 1995.

Harsch, Donna. *German Social Democracy and the Rise of Nazism*. Chapel Hill: University of North Carolina Press, 1993.

Haslinger, Peter. "Building a Regional Identity: The Burgenland, 1921–1938." *Austrian History Yearbook* 32 (2001): 105–123.

Healy, Maureen. "Becoming Austrian: Women, the State, and Citizenship in World War I." *Central European History* 35, no. 1 (2002): 1–35.

——. *Vienna and the Fall of the Habsburg Empire: Total War and Everyday Life in World War I*. Cambridge: Cambridge University Press, 2004.

Heffen, Annegret. *Der Reichskunstwart, Kunstpolitik in den Jahren 1920–1933: Zu den Bemühungen um eine offizielle Reichskunstpolitik in der Weimarer Republik*. Essen: Verlag Die Blaue Eule, 1986.

Heß, Jürgen. *"Das ganze Deutschland soll es sein": Demokratischer Nationalismus in der Weimarer Republik am Beispiel der Deutschen Demokratischen Partei*. Kieler Historische Studien. Stuttgart: Klett-Cotta, 1978.

Hobsbawm, Eric. *Nations and Nationalism since 1780: Programme, Myth, Reality*. Cambridge: Cambridge University Press, 1983.

Hobsbawm, Eric, and Terence Ranger, eds. *The Invention of Tradition*. Cambridge: Cambridge University Press, Canto Edition, 1992.

Hochman, Erin. "Staging the Nation, Staging Democracy: The Politics of Commemoration in Germany and Austria, 1918–1933/34." PhD diss. University of Toronto, 2010.

Holzer, Andreas, ed. Katalog und Regestenheft zur Ausstellung "Österreich-Ideologie in der Musik." http://www.musikgeschichte.at/regesten/Regesten-1995-s.pdf.

Jarausch, Konrad, and Michael Geyer. *Shattered Past: Reconstructing German Histories*. Princeton, NJ: Princeton University Press, 2003.

Jenkins, Jennifer. *Provincial Modernity: Local Culture and Liberal Politics in Fin-de-Siècle Hamburg*. Ithaca, NY: Cornell University Press, 2003.

Jones, Larry Eugene. *German Liberalism and the Dissolution of the Weimar Party System, 1918–1933*. Chapel Hill: University of North Carolina Press, 1988.

——. "Hindenburg and the Conservative Dilemma in the 1932 Presidential Elections." *German Studies Review* 20, no. 2 (1997): 235–259.

——. "Nationalists, Nazis, and the Assault against Weimar: Revisiting the Harzburg Rally of October 1931." *German Studies Review* 29, no. 3 (2006): 483–494.

Judson, Pieter. *Exclusive Revolutionaries: Liberal Politics, Social Experience, and National Identity in the Austrian Empire, 1848–1914*. Ann Arbor: University of Michigan Press, 1996.

——. *Guardians of the Nation: Activists on the Language Frontiers of Imperial Austria*. Cambridge, MA: Harvard University Press, 2006.

Judson, Pieter, and Marsha Rozenblit, eds. *Constructing Nationalities in East Central Europe*. New York: Berghahn Books, 2005.

Kann, Robert, and Friedrich E. Prinz, eds. *Deutschland und Österreich: Ein bilaterales Geschichtsbuch*. Vienna: Jugend und Volk Verlagsgesellschaft, 1980.

Katzenstein, Peter. *Disjoined Partners: Austria and Germany since 1815*. Berkeley: University of California Press, 1976.

Kershaw, Ian, ed. *Weimar: Why Did German Democracy Fail?* New York: St. Martin's Press, 1990.

Kertzer, David. *Ritual, Politics, and Power*. New Haven, CT: Yale University Press, 1988.

King, Jeremy. *Budweisers into Czechs and Germans: A Local History of Bohemian Politics, 1848–1948*. Princeton, NJ: Princeton University Press, 2002.

Kitchen, Martin. *The Coming of Austrian Fascism*. Montreal: McGill–Queen's University Press, 1980.

Klemm, Claudia. *Erinnert—umstritten—gefeiert: Die Revolution von 1848/49 in der deutschen Gedenkkultur*. Göttingen: V&R unipress, 2007.

Klenke, Dietmar. *Der singende "Deutsche Mann": Gesangvereine und deutsches Nationalbewusstsein von Napoleon bis Hitler*. Münster: Waxmann Verlag, 1998.

Knapp, Thomas. "The German Center Party and the Reichsbanner: A Case Study in Political and Social Consensus in the Weimar Republic." *International Review of Social History* 14, no. 2 (1969): 159–179.

Kocka, Jürgen. "Asymmetrical Historical Comparison: The Case of the German *Sonderweg*." *History and Theory* 38, no. 1 (1999): 40–50.

——. "Comparison and Beyond." *History and Theory* 42, no. 1 (2003): 39–44.

Kohn, Hans. *The Idea of Nationalism: A Study in Its Origins and Background*. 1944; reprint, New Brunswick, NJ: Transaction, 2005.

Königseder, Angelika. "Antisemitismus 1933–1938." In *Austrofaschismus: Politik—Ökonomie—Kultur, 1933–1938*, edited by Emmerich Tálos and Wolfgang Neugebauer, 54–65. Vienna: LIT Verlag, 2005.

Konrad, Helmut. "Demokratieverständnis, Parlamentarische Haltung und Nationale Frage bei den Österreichischen Sozialdemokraten." In *Das Parteienwesen Österreichs und Ungarns in der Zwischenkriegszeit*, edited by Anna Drabek, Richard Plaschka, and Helmut Rumpler, 107–126. Vienna: Verlag der Österreichischen Akadamie der Wissenschaften, 1990.

——. "Wurzeln deutschnationalen Denkens in der österreichischen Arbeiterbewegung." In *Sozialdemokratie und "Anschluß": Historische Wurzeln, Anschluß 1918 und 1938, Nachwirkungen*, edited by Helmut Konrad, 19–30. Vienna: Europaverlag, 1978.

Kurlander, Eric. *Living with Hitler: Liberal Democrats in the Third Reich*. New Haven, CT: Yale University Press, 2009.

——. *The Price of Exclusion: Ethnicity, National Identity, and the Decline of German Liberalism, 1898–1933*. New York: Berghahn Books, 2006.

Langewiesche, Dieter. *Liberalism in Germany*. Translated by Christiane Banerji. London: Macmillan, 2000.

Lehnert, Detlef, and Klaus Megerle, eds. *Politische Identität und nationale Gedenktage: Zur politischen Kultur in der Weimarer Republik*. Opladen: Westdeutscher Verlag, 1989.

——. "Problems of Identity and Consensus in a Fragmented Society: The Weimar Republic." In *Political Culture in Germany*, edited by Dirk Berg-Schlosser and Ralf Rytlewski, 43–59. Houndmills, Basingstoke, UK: Macmillan, 1993.

Lehnert, Detlef, and Christoph Mueller. "Perspectives and Problems of a Rediscovery of Hugo Preuss." Hugo-Preuss-Gesellschaft e.V.: http://www2.hu-berlin.de/Hugo-Preuss-Gesellschaft/intro_e.pdf.

Leser, Norbert. "Austria between the Wars: An Essay." *Austrian History Yearbook* 17 (1981): 127–142.

——. "Austro-Marxism: A Reappraisal." *Journal of Contemporary History* 11, no. 2/3 (1976): 133–148.

Lidtke, Vernon. *The Alternative Culture: Socialist Labor in Imperial Germany*. New York: Oxford University Press, 1985.

Loewenberg, Peter. "Otto Bauer as an Ambivalent Party Leader." In *The Austrian Socialist Experiment: Social Democracy and Austromarxism, 1918–1934*, edited by Anson Rabinbach, 71–79. Boulder, CO: Westview Press, 1985.

Loos, Helmut. "Franz Schubert im Repertoire der deutschen Männergesangvereine. Ein Beitrag zur Rezeptionsgeschichte." *Archiv für Musikwissenschaft* 57, no. 2 (2000): 113–129.

Low, Alfred. *The Anschluss Movement and the Paris Peace Conference, 1918–1919*. Philadelphia: American Philosophical Society, 1974.

——. *The Anschluss Movement, 1931–1938, and the Great Powers*. Boulder, CO: East European Monographs, 1985.

Luft, David. "Austria as a Region of German Culture: 1900–1938." *Austrian History Yearbook* 23 (1992): 135–148.

——. "Das Intellektuelle Leben Österreichs in seiner Beziehung zur deutschen Sprache und der Modernen Kultur." *Center for Austrian Studies Working Papers in Austrian History* 07–1 (February 2007).

Luža, Radomír. *Austro-German Relations in the Anschluss Era*. Princeton, NJ: Princeton University Press, 1975.

MacMillan, Margaret. *Paris 1919: Six Months That Changed the World*. New York: Random House, 2002.

Manela, Erez. *The Wilsonian Moment: Self-Determination and the International Origins of Anticolonial Nationalism*. Oxford: Oxford University Press, 2007.

Mazower, Mark. *Dark Continent: Europe's Twentieth Century*. London: Penguin, 1998.

——. *Nazi Empire: How the Nazis Ruled Europe*. New York: Penguin, 2008.

McElligott, Anthony. *Rethinking the Weimar Republic: Authority and Authoritarianism, 1916–1936*. London: Bloomsbury, 2014.

Mergel, Thomas. *Parlamentarische Kultur in der Weimarer Republik: Politische Kommunikation, symbolische Politik und Öffentlichkeit im Reichstag*. Düsseldorf: Droste Verlag, 2002.

Mommsen, Hans. *The Rise and Fall of Weimar Democracy*. Translated by Elborg Forster and Larry Eugene Jones. Chapel Hill: University of North Carolina Press, 1996.

Mosse, George. *The Nationalization of the Masses: Political Symbolism and Mass Movements in Germany from the Napoleonic Wars through the Third Reich*. New York: H. Fertig, 1975.

Murdock, Caitlin. *Changing Places: Society, Culture, and Territory in the Saxon-Bohemian Borderlands, 1870–1946.* Ann Arbor: University of Michigan Press, 2010.

Myers Feinstein, Margarete. *State Symbols: The Quest for Legitimacy in the Federal Republic of Germany and the German Democratic Republic, 1949–1959.* Boston: Brill Academic, 2001.

Niewyk, Donald. "Jews and the Courts in Weimar Germany." *Jewish Social Studies* 37, no. 2 (1975): 99–113.

——. *The Jews in Weimar Germany.* 2nd ed. New Brunswick, NJ: Transaction, 2001.

——. *Socialist, Anti-Semite, and Jew: German Social Democracy Confronts the Problem of Anti-Semitism, 1918–1933.* Baton Rouge: Louisiana State University Press, 1971.

Noltenius, Rainer. "Schiller als Führer und Heiland: Das Schillerfest 1859 als nationaler Traum von der Geburt des zweiten deutschen Kaiserreichs." In *Öffentliche Festkultur: Politische Feste in Deutschland von der Aufklärung bis zum Ersten Weltkrieg,* edited by Dieter Düding, Peter Friedemann, and Paul Münch, 237–258. Hamburg: Rowohlt Taschenbuch Verlag, 1988.

O'Donnell, Krista, Renate Bridenthal, and Nancy Reagin, eds. *The Heimat Abroad: The Boundaries of Germanness.* Ann Arbor: University of Michigan Press, 2005.

Orzoff, Andrea. *Battle for the Castle: The Myth of Czechoslovakia in Europe, 1914–1948.* New York: Oxford University Press, 2009.

Pauley, Bruce. "A Case Study in Fascism: The Styrian Heimatschutz and Austrian National Socialism." *Austrian History Yearbook* 12/13 (1976–1977): 251–273.

——. *From Prejudice to Persecution: A History of Austrian Anti-Semitism.* Chapel Hill: University of North Carolina Press, 1992.

——. *Hitler and the Forgotten Nazis: A History of Austrian National Socialism.* Chapel Hill: University of North Carolina Press, 1981.

Pelinka, Anton. "Christliche Arbeiterbewegung und Austrofaschismus." In *Austrofaschismus: Politik—Ökonomie—Kultur, 1933–1938,* edited by Emmerich Tálos and Wolfgang Neugebauer, 88–97. Vienna: LIT Verlag, 2005.

Peukert, Detlev. *The Weimar Republic: The Crisis of Classical Modernity.* Translated by Richard Deveson. New York: Hill & Wang, 1989.

Poscher, Ralf. "Verfassungsfeier in verfassungsfeindlicher Zeit." In *Der Verfassungstag: Reden deutscher Gelehrter zur Feier der Weimarer Verfassung,* edited by Ralf Poscher, 11–50. Baden-Baden: Nomos Verlagsgesellschaft, 1999.

Pulzer, Peter. *Jews and the German State: The Political History of a Minority, 1848–1933.* Detroit: Wayne State University Press, 2003.

——. "The Tradition of Austrian Antisemitism in the Nineteenth and Twentieth Centuries." *Patterns of Prejudice* 27, no. 1 (1993): 31–46.

Rabinbach, Anson, ed. *The Austrian Socialist Experiment: Social Democracy and Austromarxism, 1918–1934.* Boulder, CO: Westview Press, 1985.

——. *The Crisis of Austrian Socialism: From Red Vienna to Civil War, 1927–1934.* Chicago: University of Chicago Press, 1983.

Rath, R. John. "The Deterioration of Democracy in Austria, 1927–1932." *Austrian History Yearbook* 27 (1996): 213–259.

Reifowitz, Ian. "Otto Bauer and Karl Renner on Nationalism, Ethnicity and Jews." *Journal of Jewish Identities* 2, no. 2 (2009): 1–19.

Ritter, Harry. "Austria and the Struggle for German Identity." *German Studies Review* (Winter 1992): 111–129.

——. "Hermann Neubacher and the Austrian *Anschluss* Movement, 1918–1940." *Central European History* 8, no. 4 (1975): 348–369.

———. "On Austria's German Identity: A Reply to Margarete Grandner, Gernot Heiss, and Oliver Rathkolb." *German Studies Review* 16, no. 3 (1993): 521–523.

Rohe, Karl. *Das Reichsbanner Schwarz Rot Gold: Ein Beitrag zur Geschichte und Struktur der politischen Kampfverbände zur Zeit der Weimarer Republik.* Düsseldorf: Droste Verlag, 1966.

Rosar, Wolfgang. *Deutsche Gemeinschaft: Seyss-Inquart und der Anschluß.* Vienna: Europa Verlag, 1971.

Rossol, Nadine. "Flaggenkrieg am Badestrand: Lokale Möglichkeiten repräsentativer Mitgestaltung in der Weimarer Republik." *Zeitschrift für Geschichtswissenschaft* 7/8 (2008): 617–637.

———. *Performing the Nation in Interwar Germany: Sport, Spectacle and Political Symbolism, 1926–1936.* Basingstoke: Palgrave Macmillan, 2010.

Rozenblit, Marsha. "Jewish Ethnicity in a New Nation-State: The Crisis of Identity in the Austrian Republic." In *In Search of Jewish Community: Jewish Identities in Germany and Austria, 1918–1933,* edited by Michael Brenner and Derek Penslar, 134–153. Bloomington: Indiana University Press, 1998.

———. "Sustaining Austrian 'National' Identity in Crisis: The Dilemma of the Jews in Habsburg Austria, 1914–1919." In *Constructing Nationalities in East Central Europe,* edited by Pieter Judson and Marsha Rozenblit, 178–191. New York: Berghahn Books, 2005.

Rumpler, Helmut. "Parlamentarismus und Demokratieverständnis in Österreich, 1918–1933." In *Das Parteienwesen Österreichs und Ungarns in der Zwischenkriegszeit,* edited by Anna Drabek, Richard Plaschka, and Helmut Rumpler, 1–17. Vienna: Verlag der Österreichischen Akadamie der Wissenschaften, 1990.

Sammartino, Annemarie. *The Impossible Border: Germany and the East, 1914–1922.* Ithaca, NY: Cornell University Press, 2010.

Schellack, Fritz. *Nationalfeiertage in Deutschland von 1871 bis 1945.* Frankfurt am Main: Peter Lang, 1990.

Schönwälder, Karen. "The Constitutional Protection of Minorities in Germany: Weimar Revisited." *Slavonic and East European Review* 74, no. 1 (1996): 38–65.

Schorske, Carl. *Fin-de-Siècle Vienna: Politics and Culture.* New York: Vintage, 1981 [1961].

Schubart, Friederike. "Zehn Jahre Weimar—Eine Republik blickt zurück." In *Der Griff nach der Deutungsmacht: Zur Geschichte der Geschichtspolitik in Deutschland,* edited by Heinrich August Winkler, 134–159. Göttingen: Wallstein, 2004.

Schumann, Dirk. *Political Violence in the Weimar Republic, 1918–1933: Fight for the Streets and Fear of Civil War.* Translated by Thomas Dunlap. New York: Berghahn Books, 2009.

Sharp, Alan. *The Versailles Settlement: Peacemaking in Paris, 1919.* London: Macmillan, 1991.

Sheehan, James. *German History, 1770–1866.* Oxford: Oxford University Press, 1989.

———. "What Is German History? Reflections on the Role of the Nation in German History and Historiography." *Journal of Modern History* 53, no. 1 (1981): 1–23.

Smith, Helmut Walser. *German Nationalism and Religious Conflict: Culture, Ideology, Politics, 1870–1914.* Princeton, NJ: Princeton University Press, 1995.

———, ed. *Protestants, Catholics and Jews in Germany, 1800–1914.* Oxford: Berg, 2001.

Spann, Gustav. "Fahne, Staatswappen und Bundeshymne der Republik Österreich." http://www.demokratiezentrum.org/media/data/staatswappen.pdf.

———. "Der österreichische Nationalfeiertag." In *Der Kampf um das Gedächtnis: Öffentliche Gedenktage in Mitteleuropa*, edited by Emil Brix and Hannes Stekl, 145–170. Vienna: Böhlau Verlag, 1997.

———. "Zur Geschichte von Flagge and Wappen der Republik Österreich." In *Österreichs Politische Symbole: Historisch, ästhetisch und ideologiekritisch beleuchtet*, edited by Norbert Leser and Manfred Wagner, 37–64. Vienna: Böhlau Verlag, 1994.

Stadler, Karl. "Austrian Social Democracy: The Image and the Facts." In *The Austrian Socialist Experiment: Social Democracy and Austromarxism, 1918–1934*, edited by Anson Rabinbach, 81–87. Boulder, CO: Westview Press, 1985.

Staudinger, Anton. "Austrofaschistische 'Österreich-Ideologie.'" In *Austrofaschismus: Politik—Ökonomie—Kultur, 1933–1938*, edited by Emmerich Tálos and Wolfgang Neugebauer, 28–52. Vienna: LIT Verlag, 2005.

Steinbauer, Johannes. *Land der Hymnen: Eine Geschichte der Bundeshymnen Österreichs*. Vienna: Sonderzahl, 1997.

Steinberg, Michael. *Austria as Theater and Ideology: The Meaning of the Salzburg Festival*. Ithaca, NY: Cornell University Press, 2000.

Steiner, Guenther. *Wahre Demokratie? Transformation und Demokratieverständnis in der Ersten Republik Österreich und im Ständestaat Österreich, 1918–1938*. Frankfurt am Main: Peter Lang, 2004.

Steinhart, Eric. "Policing the Boundaries of 'Germandom' in the East: SS Ethnic German Policy and Odessa's 'Volksdeutsche,' 1941–1944." *Central European History* 43, no. 1 (2010): 85–116.

Stern, Fritz. *The Politics of Cultural Despair: A Study in the Rise of the Germanic Ideology*. Berkeley: University of California Press, 1961.

Stiftung Haus der Geschichte der Bundesrepublik. *Verfreundete Nachbarn: Deutschland-Österreich: Begleitbuch zur Ausstellung im Haus der Geschichte der Bundesrepublik Deutschland, Bonn, 19. Mai bis 23. Oktober 2005, im Zeitgeschichtlichen Forum Leipzig, 2. Juni bis 9. Oktober 2005, in Wien 2006*. Bielefeld: Kerber Verlag, 2005.

Sully, Melanie. "Social Democracy and the Political Culture of the First Republic." In *The Austrian Socialist Experiment: Social Democracy and Austromarxism, 1918–1934*, edited by Anson Rabinbach, 57–70. Boulder, CO: Westview Press, 1985.

Suval, Stanley. *The Anschluss Question in the Weimar Era: A Study of Nationalism in Germany and Austria, 1918–1932*. Baltimore: Johns Hopkins University Press, 1974.

Sweet, Paul. "Seipel's Views on Anschluss in 1928: An Unpublished Exchange of Letters." *Journal of Modern History* 19, no. 4 (1947): 320–323.

Swett, Pamela. "Celebrating the Republic without Republicans: The Reichsverfassungstag in Berlin, 1929–1932." In *Festive Culture in Germany and Europe from the Sixteenth to the Twentieth Century*, edited by Karin Friedrich, 281–302. Lewiston, NY: Edwin Mellen, 2000.

Tálos, Emmerich, and Wolfgang Neugebauer, eds. *Austrofaschismus: Politik—Ökonomie—Kultur, 1933–1938*. Vienna: LIT Verlag, 2005.

Tálos, Emmerich, Herbert Dachs, Ernst Hanisch, and Anton Staudinger, eds. *Handbuch des Politischen Systems Österreichs: Erste Republik, 1918–1933*. Vienna: Manz Verlag, 1995.

Thaler, Peter. *The Ambivalence of Identity: The Austrian Experience of Nation-Building in a Modern Society*. West Lafayette, IN: Purdue University Press, 2001.

Ther, Philipp. "Beyond the Nation: The Relational Basis of a Comparative History of Germany and Europe." *Central European History* 36, no. 1 (2003): 45–73.

Thorpe, Julie. *Pan-Germanism and the Austrofascist State, 1933–1938*. Manchester: Manchester University Press, 2011.

Unowsky, Daniel. *The Pomp and Politics of Patriotism: Imperial Celebrations in Habsburg Austria, 1848–1916*. West Lafayette, IN: Purdue University Press, 2005.

van Rahden, Till. "Germans of the Jewish *Stamm*: Visions of Community between Nationalism and Particularism, 1850 to 1933." In *German History from the Margins*, edited by Neil Gregor, Nils Roemer, and Mark Roseman, 27–48. Bloomington: Indiana University Press, 2006.

Vick, Brian. *Defining Germany: The 1848 Frankfurt Parliamentarians and National Identity*. Cambridge, MA: Harvard University Press, 2002.

Vogt, Stefan. "Strange Encounters: Social Democracy and Radical Nationalism in Weimar Germany." *Journal of Contemporary History* 45, no. 2 (2010): 253–281.

von Klemperer, Klemens. *Ignaz Seipel: Christian Statesman in a Time of Crisis*. Princeton, NJ: Princeton University Press, 1972.

von Saldern, Adelheid. "Volk and Heimat Culture in Radio Broadcasting during the Period of Transition from Weimar to Nazi Germany." *Journal of Modern History* 76, no. 2 (2004): 312–346.

Wagner, Dieter, and Gerhard Tomkowitz. *"Ein Volk, Ein Reich, Ein Führer!" Der Anschluß Österreichs 1938*. Munich: Piper & Co. Verlag, 1968.

Wandruszka, Adam. "Österreichs politische Struktur: Die Entwicklung der Parteien und der politischen Bewegungen." In *Geschichte der Republik Österreich*, edited by Heinrich Benedikt, 289–485. Vienna: Verlag für Geschichte und Politik, 1954.

Wasserman, Janek. *Black Vienna: The Radical Right in the Red City, 1918–1938*. Ithaca, NY: Cornell University Press, 2014.

Watson, Alexander. *Ring of Steel: Germany and Austria-Hungary in World War I*. New York: Basic Books, 2014.

Wehler, Hans-Ulrich. *The German Empire, 1871–1918*. Translated by Kim Traynor. Oxford: Berg, 1985.

Weinberg, Gerhard. *Germany, Hitler and World War II*. Cambridge: Cambridge University Press, 1996.

Weitz, Eric. *Weimar Germany: Promise and Tragedy*. Princeton, NJ: Princeton University Press, 2007.

West, Franklin. *A Crisis of the Weimar Republic: A Study of the Referendum of 20 June 1926*. Philadelphia: American Philosophical Society, 1985.

Whiteside, Andrew. *The Socialism of Fools: Georg Ritter von Schönerer and Austrian Pan-Germanism*. Berkeley: University of California Press, 1975.

Wingfield, Nancy. *Flag Wars and Stone Saints: How the Bohemian Lands Became Czech*. Cambridge, MA: Harvard University Press, 2007.

Zahra, Tara. *Kidnapped Souls: National Indifference and the Battle for Children in the Bohemian Lands, 1900–1948*. Ithaca, NY: Cornell University Press, 2008.

Ziemann, Benjamin. *Contested Commemorations: Republican War Veterans and Weimar Political Culture*. Cambridge: Cambridge University Press, 2013.

Index

CPSIA information can be obtained at www.ICGtesting.com
Printed in the USA
BVOW08*1221120816

458824BV00003B/4/P